You Need This Book

Like a Fish Needs a Bicycle

OTHER BOOKS BY JIM TOOMEY

Sherman's Lagoon: Ate That, What's Next?

Poodle: The Other White Meat

An Illustrated Guide to Shark Etiquette

Another Day in Paradise

Greetings from Sherman's Lagoon

Surf's Up!

The Shark Diaries

Catch of the Day

A Day at the Beach

Surfer Safari

Planet of the Hairless Beach Apes

Yarns and Shanties (and Other Nautical Baloney)

Sharks Just Wanna Have Fun

Confessions of a Swinging Single Sea Turtle

Discover Your Inner Hermit Crab

Never Bite Anything That Bites Back

Think Like a Shark

Here We Go Again

Lunch Wore a Speedo

Tales From the Deep: That Are Completely Fabricated

Happy as a Clam

Onward and Downward

The Adventures of Superfish and His Superfishal Friends

If You Can't Beat 'Em, Eat 'Em

Evolution Is Hard Work!

Adventures in Aquaculture

TREASURIES

Sherman's Lagoon 1991 to 2001: Greatest Hits and Near Misses

In Shark Years I'm Dead: Sherman's Lagoon Turns Fifteen

You Need This Book
Like a Fish Needs a Bicycle

The Twenty-Seventh *Sherman's Lagoon* Collection
JIM TOOMEY

Andrews McMeel
PUBLISHING®

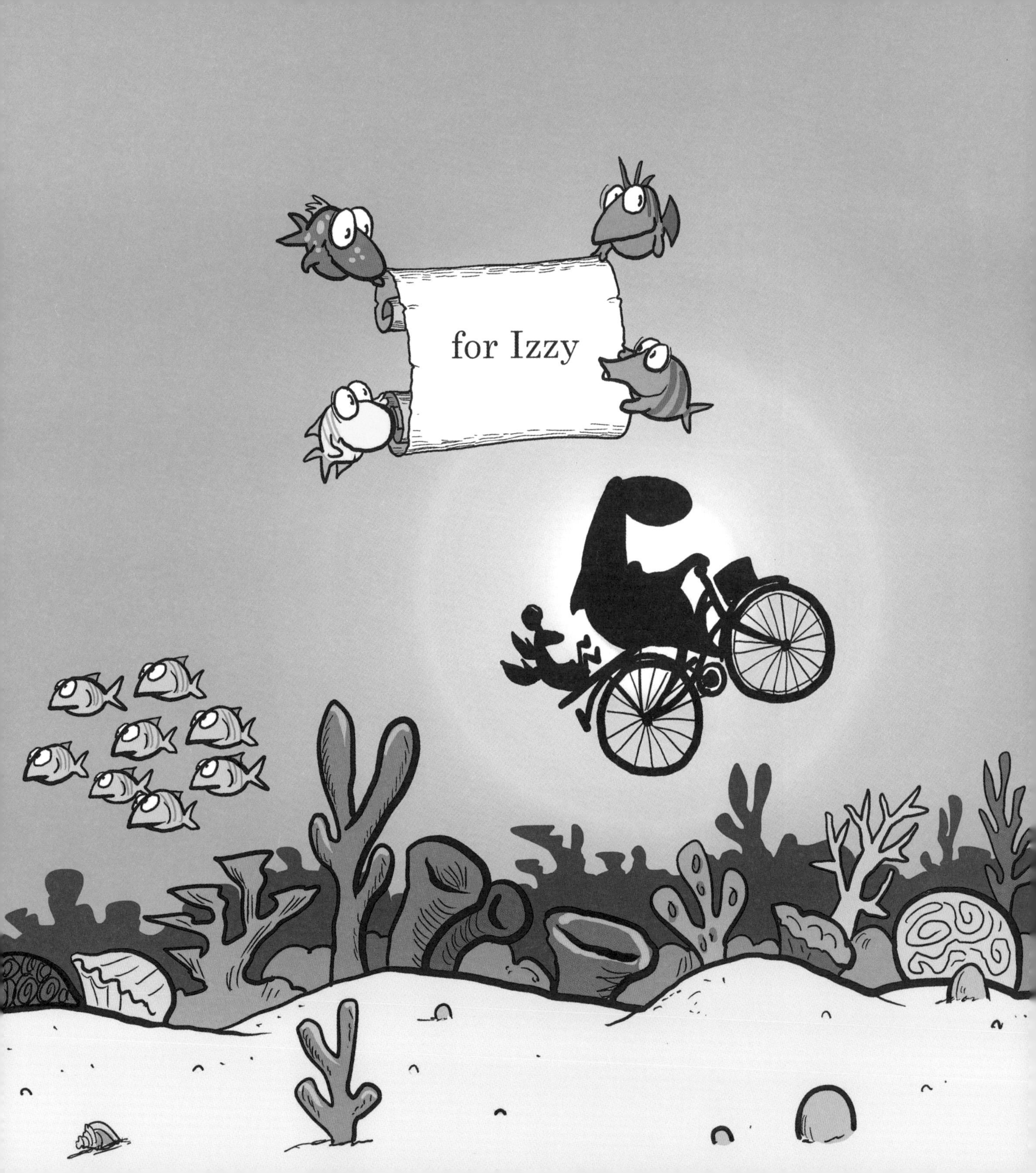
for Izzy

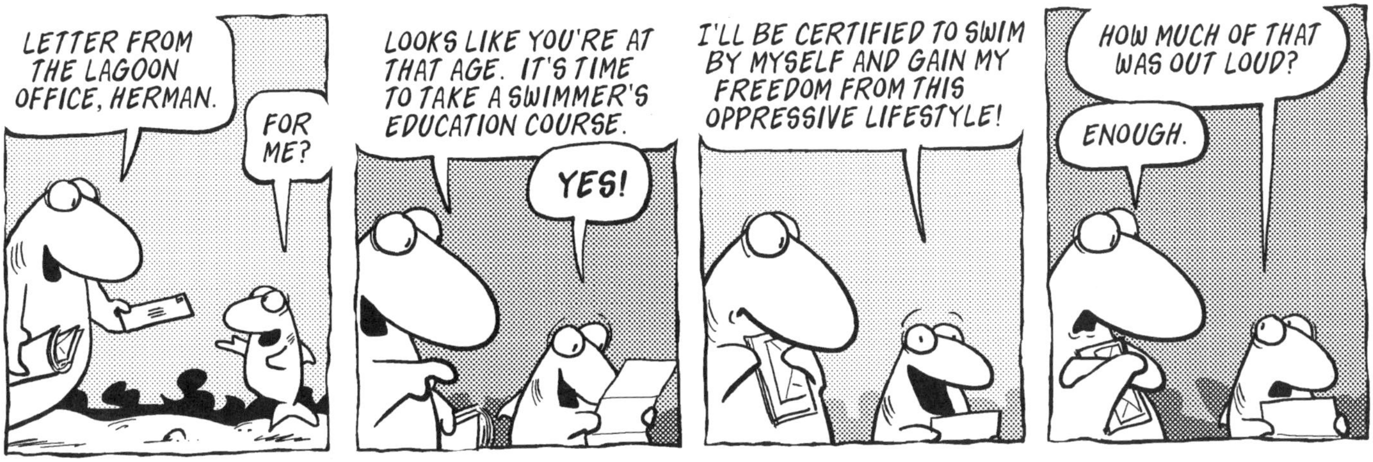
LETTER FROM THE LAGOON OFFICE, HERMAN.
FOR ME?
LOOKS LIKE YOU'RE AT THAT AGE. IT'S TIME TO TAKE A SWIMMER'S EDUCATION COURSE.
YES!
I'LL BE CERTIFIED TO SWIM BY MYSELF AND GAIN MY FREEDOM FROM THIS OPPRESSIVE LIFESTYLE!
HOW MUCH OF THAT WAS OUT LOUD?
ENOUGH.

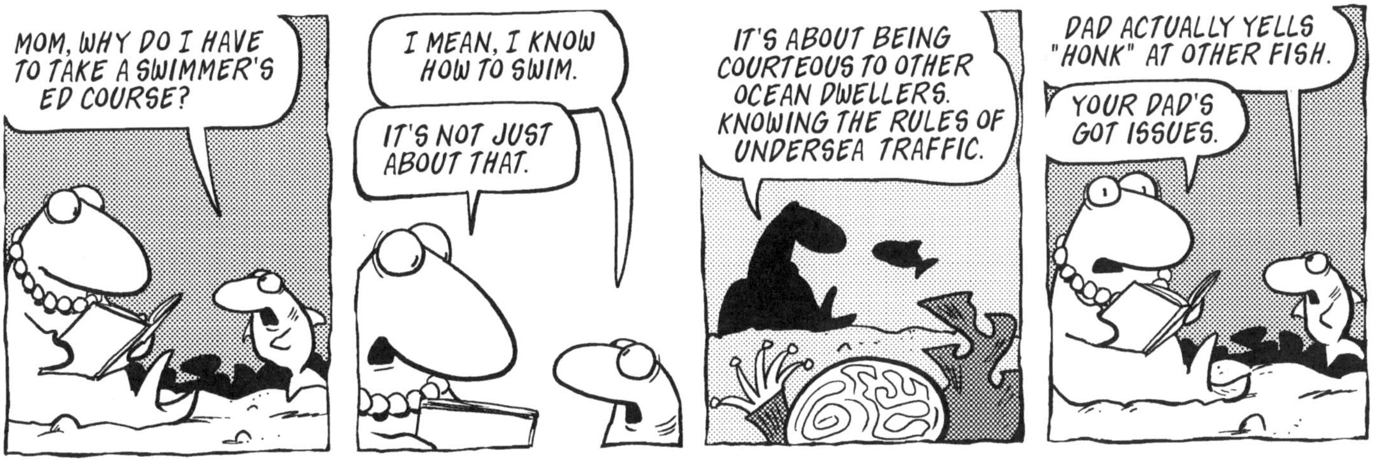
MOM, WHY DO I HAVE TO TAKE A SWIMMER'S ED COURSE?
I MEAN, I KNOW HOW TO SWIM.
IT'S NOT JUST ABOUT THAT.
IT'S ABOUT BEING COURTEOUS TO OTHER OCEAN DWELLERS. KNOWING THE RULES OF UNDERSEA TRAFFIC.
DAD ACTUALLY YELLS "HONK" AT OTHER FISH.
YOUR DAD'S GOT ISSUES.

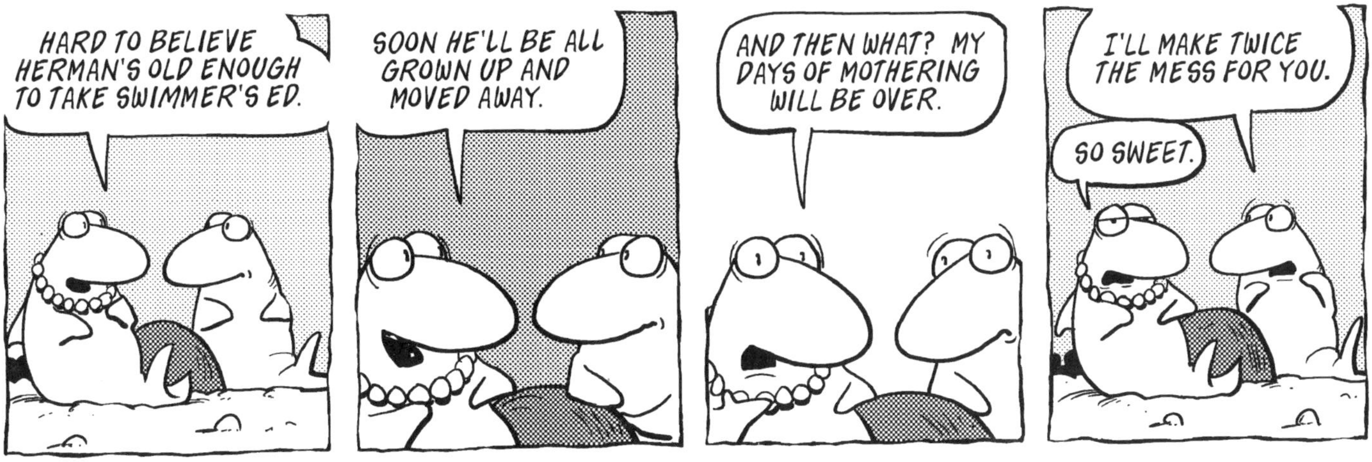
HARD TO BELIEVE HERMAN'S OLD ENOUGH TO TAKE SWIMMER'S ED.
SOON HE'LL BE ALL GROWN UP AND MOVED AWAY.
AND THEN WHAT? MY DAYS OF MOTHERING WILL BE OVER.
I'LL MAKE TWICE THE MESS FOR YOU.
SO SWEET.

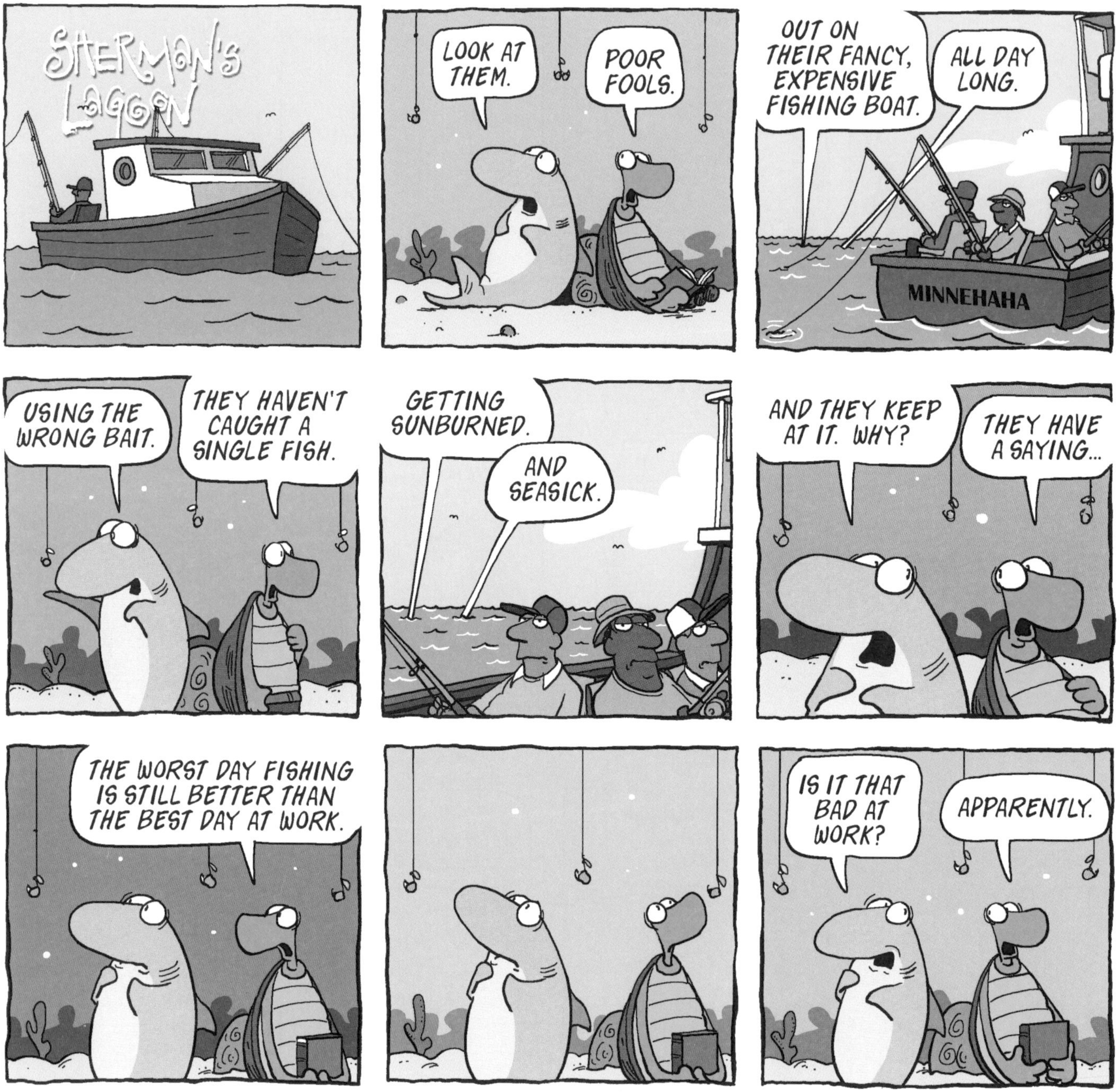
SHERMAN'S LAGOON
LOOK AT THEM.
POOR FOOLS.
OUT ON THEIR FANCY, EXPENSIVE FISHING BOAT.
ALL DAY LONG.
MINNEHAHA
USING THE WRONG BAIT.
THEY HAVEN'T CAUGHT A SINGLE FISH.
GETTING SUNBURNED.
AND SEASICK.
AND THEY KEEP AT IT. WHY?
THEY HAVE A SAYING...
THE WORST DAY FISHING IS STILL BETTER THAN THE BEST DAY AT WORK.
IS IT THAT BAD AT WORK?
APPARENTLY.

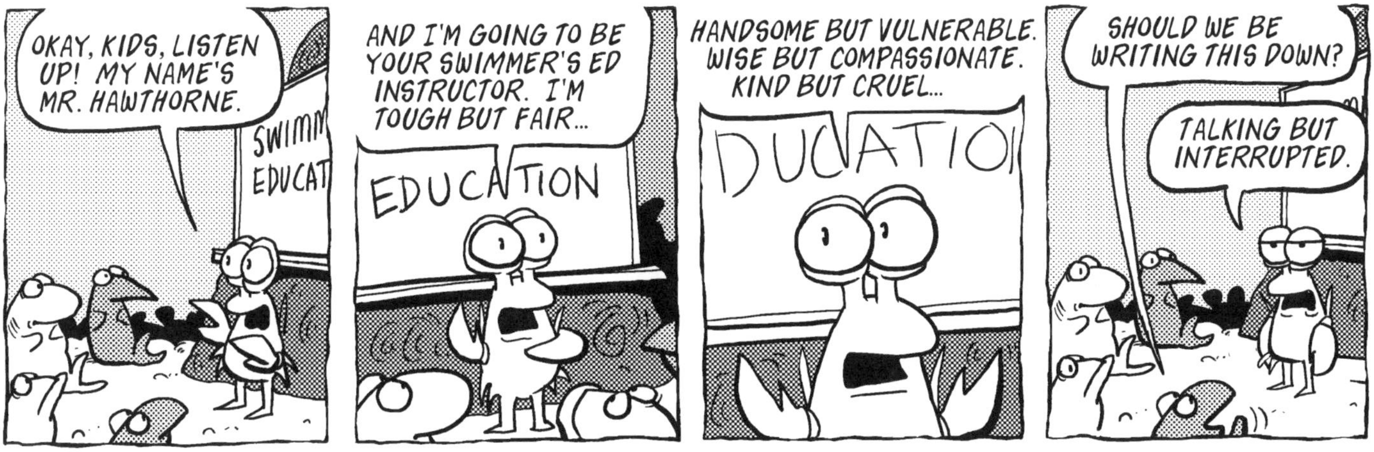
OKAY, KIDS, LISTEN UP! MY NAME'S MR. HAWTHORNE.
SWIMM
EDUCAT
AND I'M GOING TO BE YOUR SWIMMER'S ED INSTRUCTOR. I'M TOUGH BUT FAIR...
EDUCATION
HANDSOME BUT VULNERABLE. WISE BUT COMPASSIONATE. KIND BUT CRUEL...
DUCATIO
SHOULD WE BE WRITING THIS DOWN?
TALKING BUT INTERRUPTED.

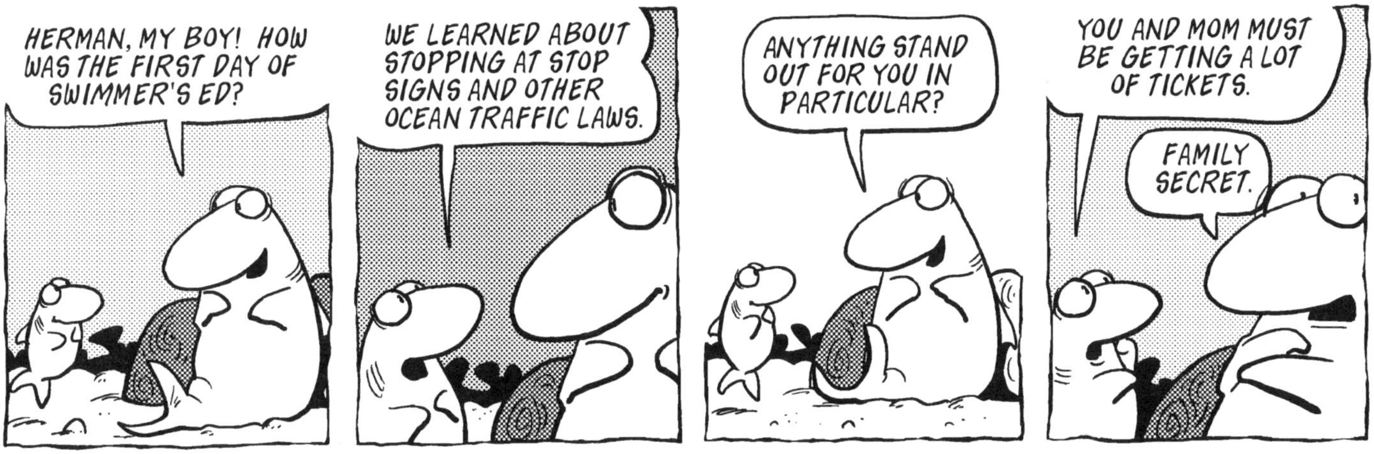
HERMAN, MY BOY! HOW WAS THE FIRST DAY OF SWIMMER'S ED?
WE LEARNED ABOUT STOPPING AT STOP SIGNS AND OTHER OCEAN TRAFFIC LAWS.
ANYTHING STAND OUT FOR YOU IN PARTICULAR?
YOU AND MOM MUST BE GETTING A LOT OF TICKETS.
FAMILY SECRET.

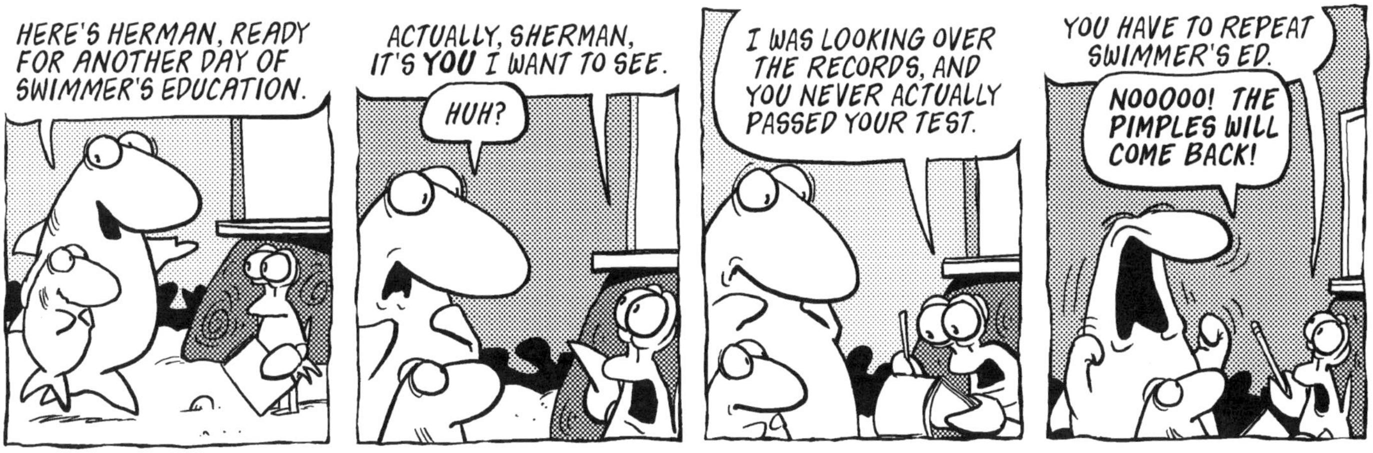
HERE'S HERMAN, READY FOR ANOTHER DAY OF SWIMMER'S EDUCATION.
ACTUALLY, SHERMAN, IT'S **YOU** I WANT TO SEE.
HUH?
I WAS LOOKING OVER THE RECORDS, AND YOU NEVER ACTUALLY PASSED YOUR TEST.
YOU HAVE TO REPEAT SWIMMER'S ED.
NOOOOO! THE PIMPLES WILL COME BACK!

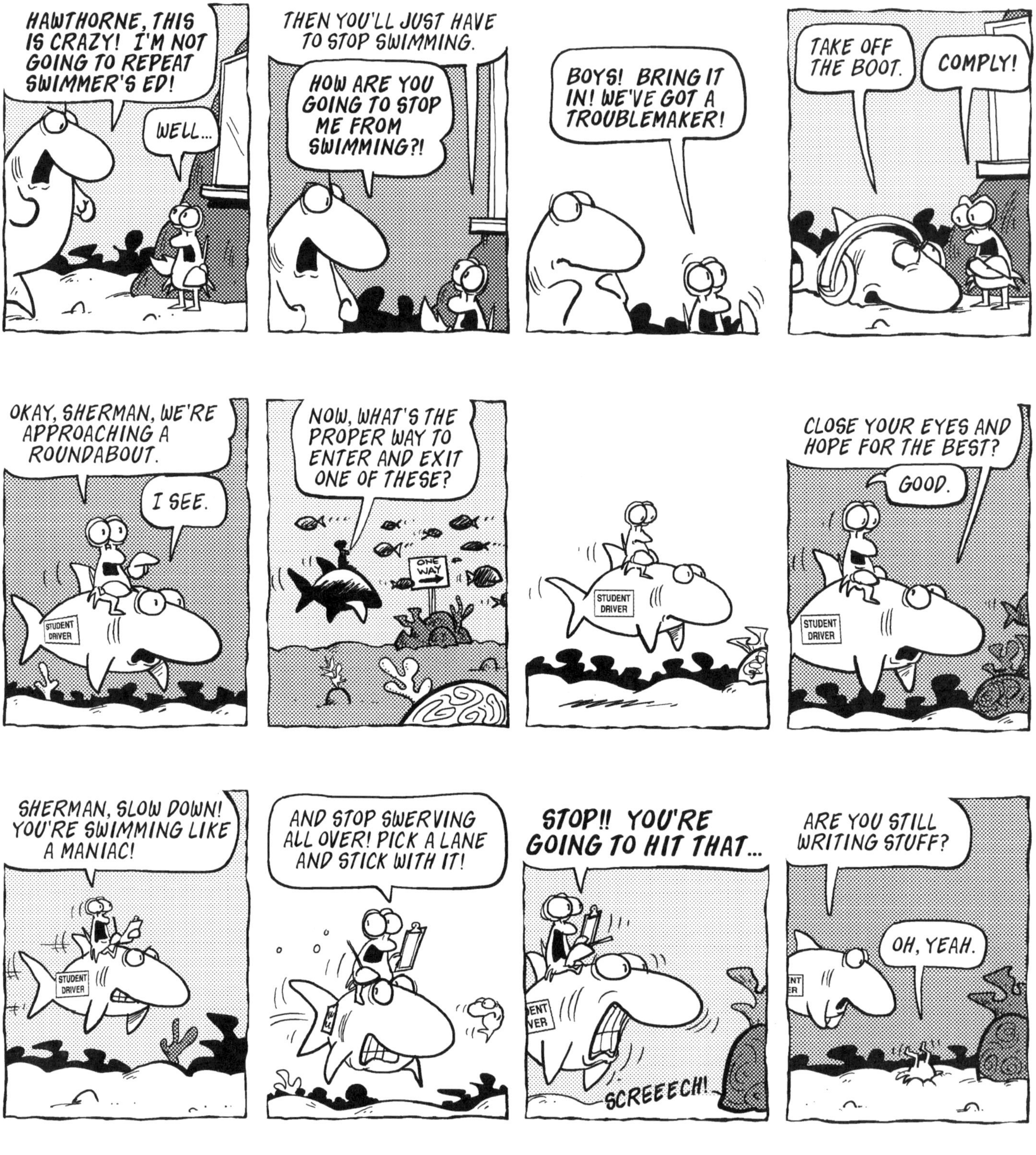
HAWTHORNE, THIS IS CRAZY! I'M NOT GOING TO REPEAT SWIMMER'S ED!
WELL...
THEN YOU'LL JUST HAVE TO STOP SWIMMING.
HOW ARE YOU GOING TO STOP ME FROM SWIMMING?!
BOYS! BRING IT IN! WE'VE GOT A TROUBLEMAKER!
TAKE OFF THE BOOT.
COMPLY!
OKAY, SHERMAN, WE'RE APPROACHING A ROUNDABOUT.
I SEE.
STUDENT DRIVER
NOW, WHAT'S THE PROPER WAY TO ENTER AND EXIT ONE OF THESE?
ONE WAY
STUDENT DRIVER
CLOSE YOUR EYES AND HOPE FOR THE BEST?
GOOD.
STUDENT DRIVER
SHERMAN, SLOW DOWN! YOU'RE SWIMMING LIKE A MANIAC!
STUDENT DRIVER
AND STOP SWERVING ALL OVER! PICK A LANE AND STICK WITH IT!
STOP!! YOU'RE GOING TO HIT THAT...
SCREEECH!
ARE YOU STILL WRITING STUFF?
OH, YEAH.

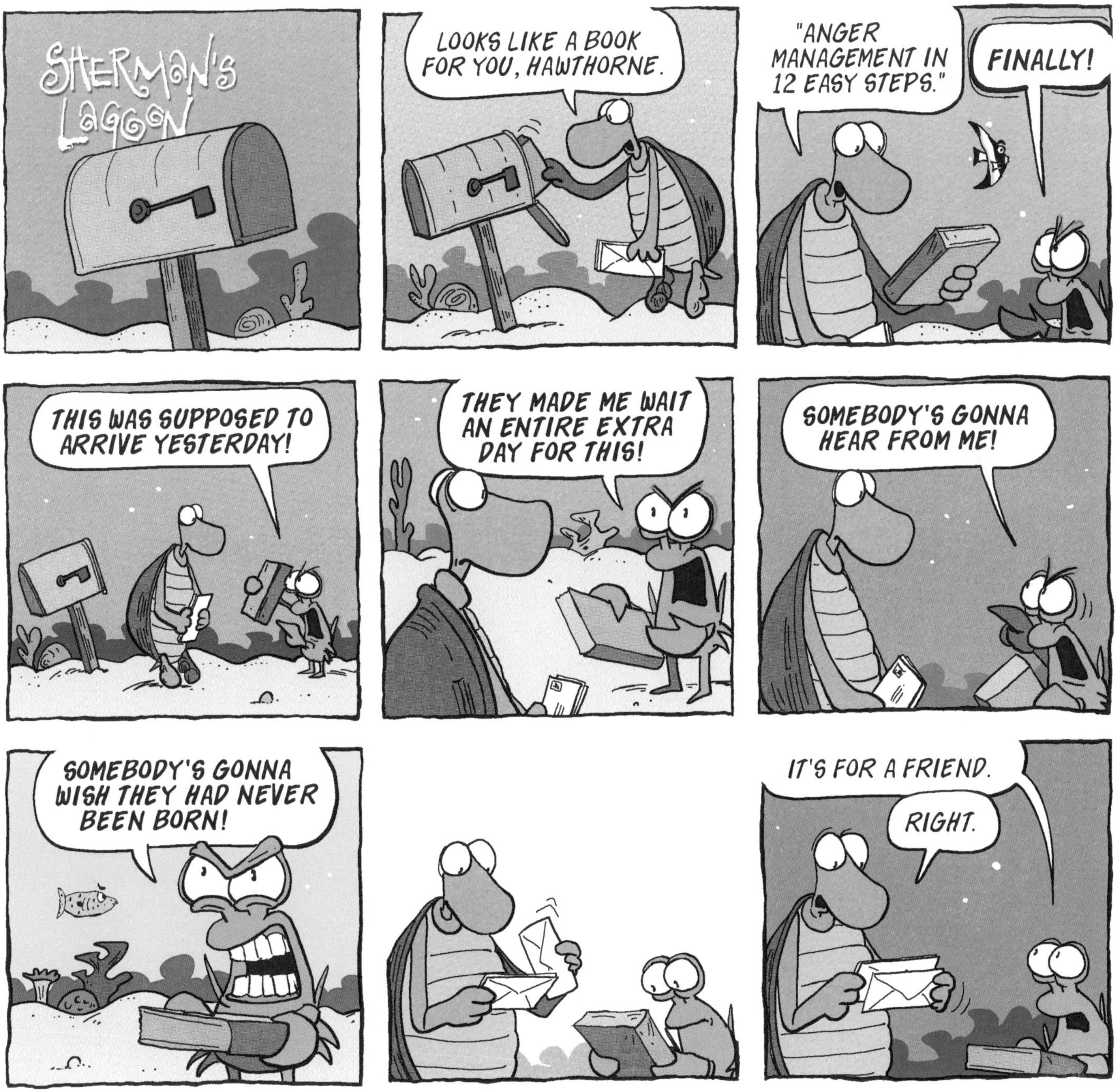
SHERMAN'S LAGOON
LOOKS LIKE A BOOK FOR YOU, HAWTHORNE.
"ANGER MANAGEMENT IN 12 EASY STEPS."
FINALLY!
THIS WAS SUPPOSED TO ARRIVE YESTERDAY!
THEY MADE ME WAIT AN ENTIRE EXTRA DAY FOR THIS!
SOMEBODY'S GONNA HEAR FROM ME!
SOMEBODY'S GONNA WISH THEY HAD NEVER BEEN BORN!
IT'S FOR A FRIEND.
RIGHT.

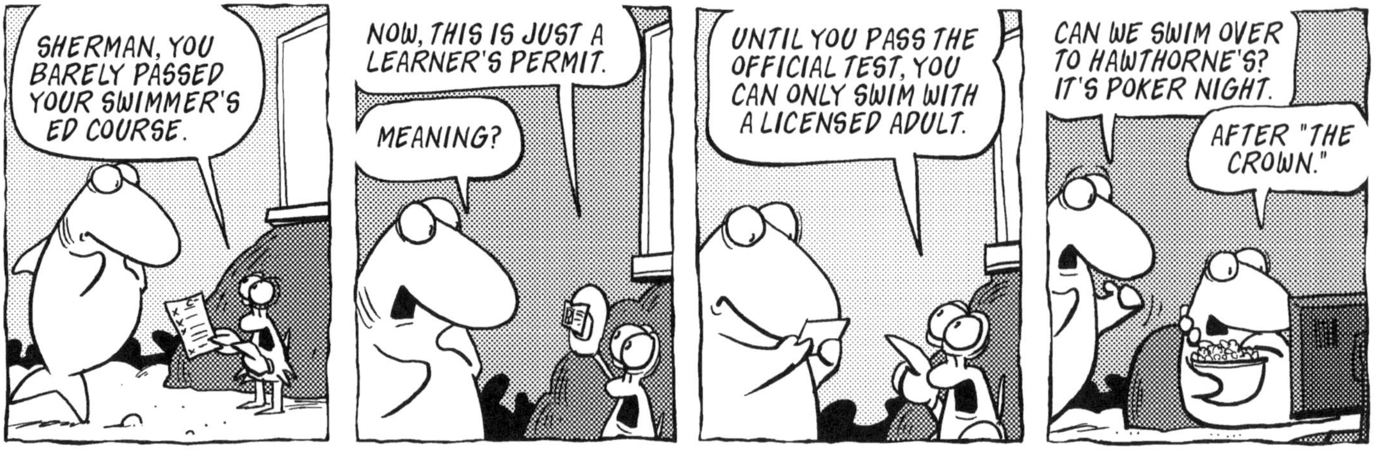
SHERMAN, YOU BARELY PASSED YOUR SWIMMER'S ED COURSE.
NOW, THIS IS JUST A LEARNER'S PERMIT.
MEANING?
UNTIL YOU PASS THE OFFICIAL TEST, YOU CAN ONLY SWIM WITH A LICENSED ADULT.
CAN WE SWIM OVER TO HAWTHORNE'S? IT'S POKER NIGHT.
AFTER "THE CROWN."

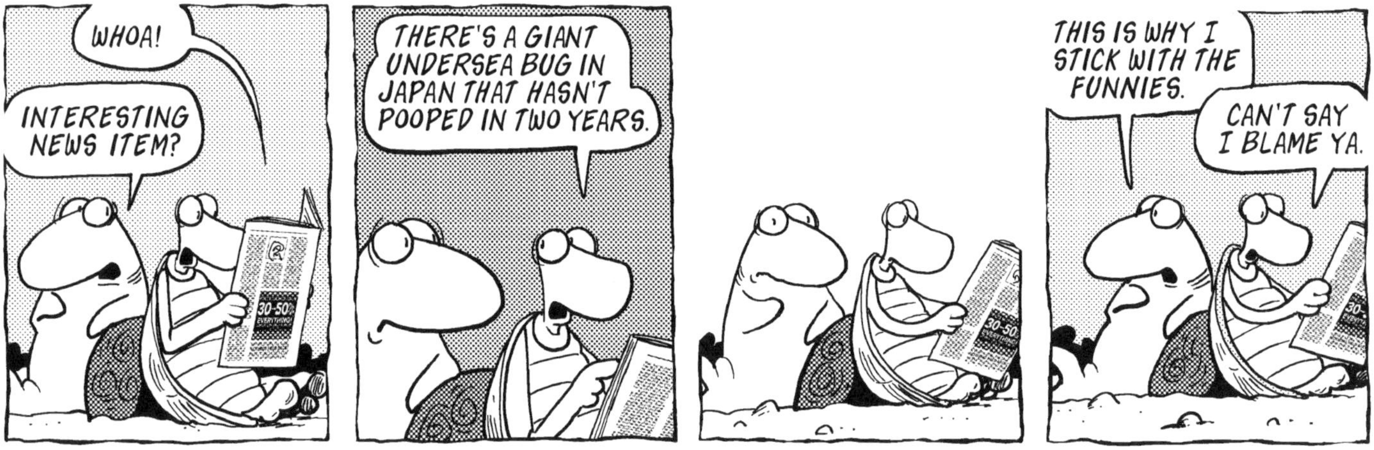
WHOA!
INTERESTING NEWS ITEM?
THERE'S A GIANT UNDERSEA BUG IN JAPAN THAT HASN'T POOPED IN TWO YEARS.
THIS IS WHY I STICK WITH THE FUNNIES.
CAN'T SAY I BLAME YA.

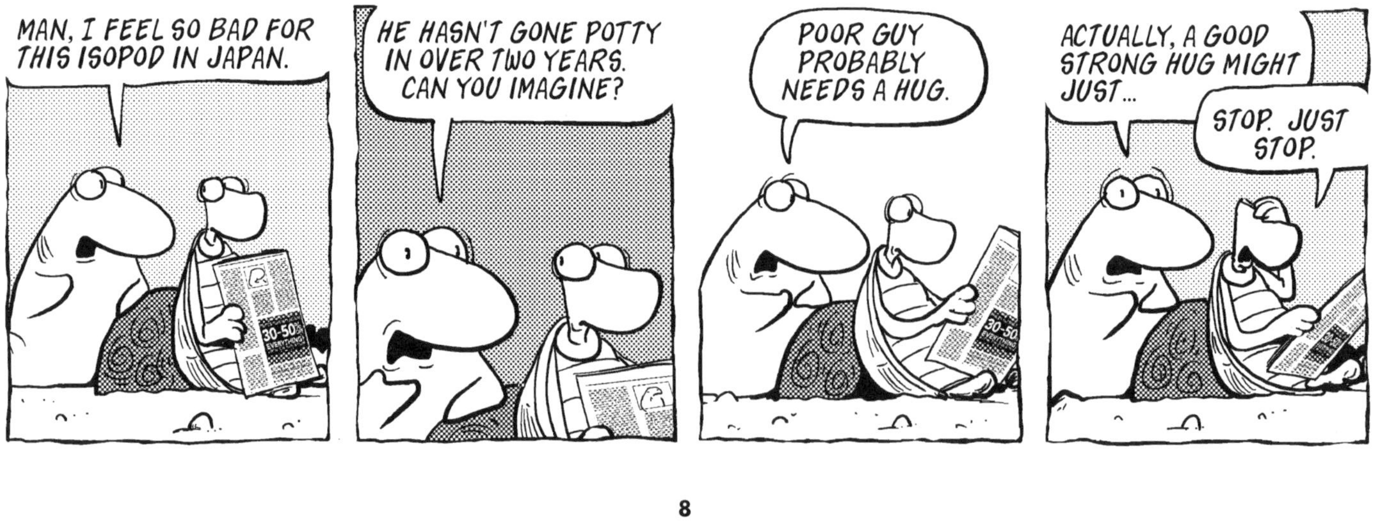
MAN, I FEEL SO BAD FOR THIS ISOPOD IN JAPAN.
HE HASN'T GONE POTTY IN OVER TWO YEARS. CAN YOU IMAGINE?
POOR GUY PROBABLY NEEDS A HUG.
ACTUALLY, A GOOD STRONG HUG MIGHT JUST...
STOP. JUST STOP.

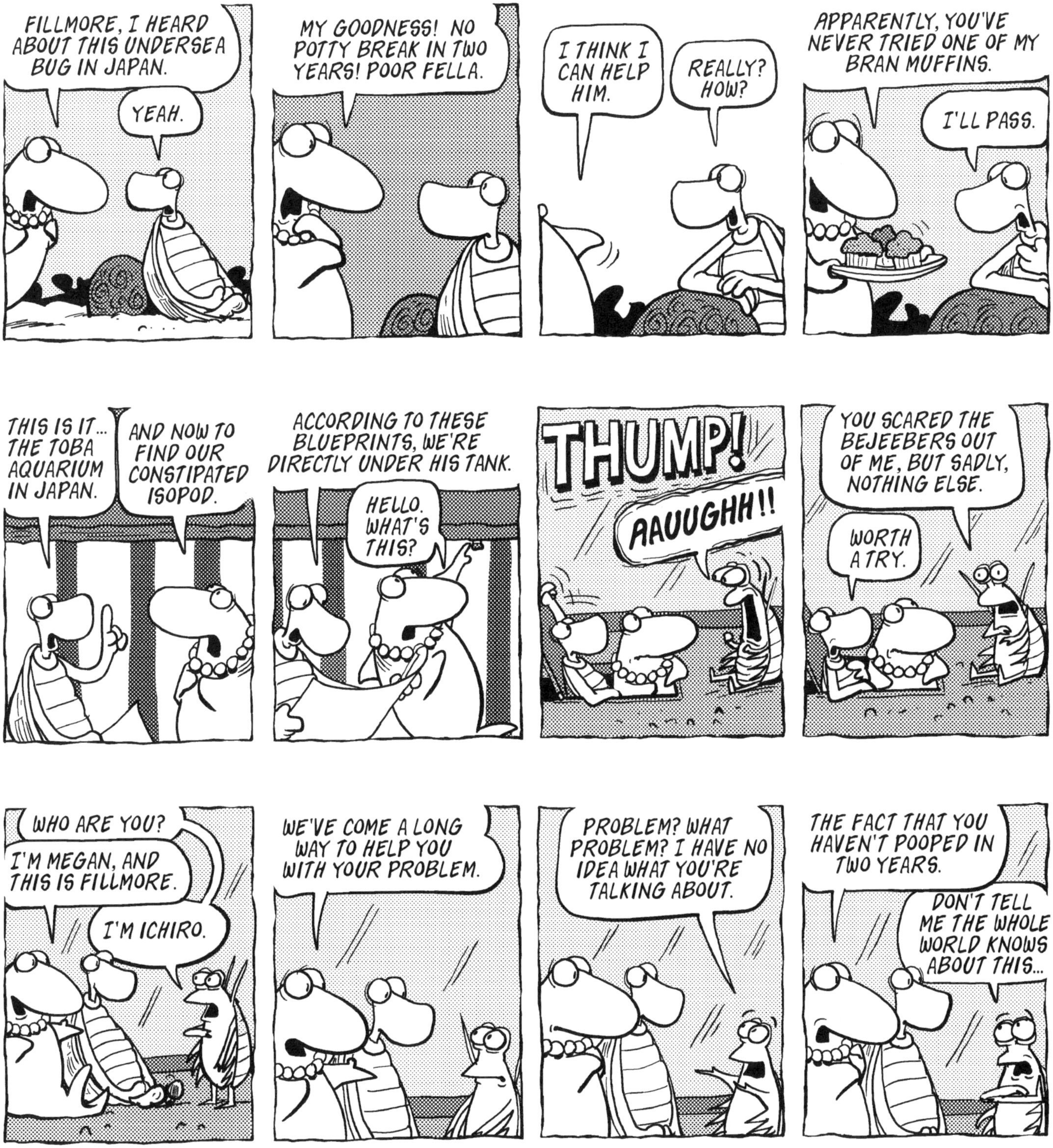
FILLMORE, I HEARD ABOUT THIS UNDERSEA BUG IN JAPAN.
YEAH.
MY GOODNESS! NO POTTY BREAK IN TWO YEARS! POOR FELLA.
I THINK I CAN HELP HIM.
REALLY? HOW?
APPARENTLY, YOU'VE NEVER TRIED ONE OF MY BRAN MUFFINS.
I'LL PASS.
THIS IS IT... THE TOBA AQUARIUM IN JAPAN.
AND NOW TO FIND OUR CONSTIPATED ISOPOD.
ACCORDING TO THESE BLUEPRINTS, WE'RE DIRECTLY UNDER HIS TANK.
HELLO. WHAT'S THIS?
THUMP!
AAUUGHH!!
YOU SCARED THE BEJEEBERS OUT OF ME, BUT SADLY, NOTHING ELSE.
WORTH A TRY.
WHO ARE YOU?
I'M MEGAN, AND THIS IS FILLMORE.
I'M ICHIRO.
WE'VE COME A LONG WAY TO HELP YOU WITH YOUR PROBLEM.
PROBLEM? WHAT PROBLEM? I HAVE NO IDEA WHAT YOU'RE TALKING ABOUT.
THE FACT THAT YOU HAVEN'T POOPED IN TWO YEARS.
DON'T TELL ME THE WHOLE WORLD KNOWS ABOUT THIS...

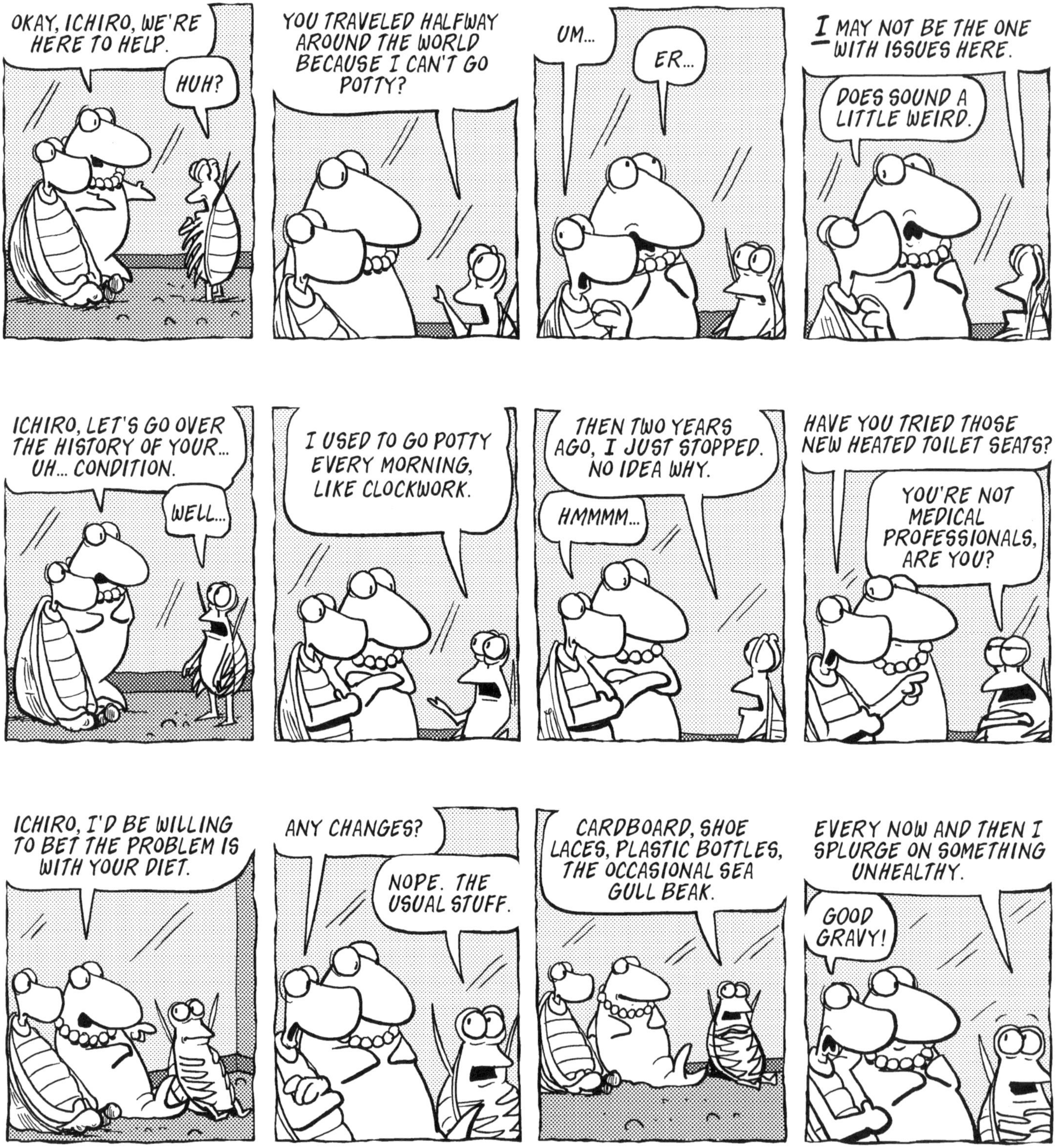
OKAY, ICHIRO, WE'RE HERE TO HELP.
HUH?
YOU TRAVELED HALFWAY AROUND THE WORLD BECAUSE I CAN'T GO POTTY?
UM...
ER...
I MAY NOT BE THE ONE WITH ISSUES HERE.
DOES SOUND A LITTLE WEIRD.
ICHIRO, LET'S GO OVER THE HISTORY OF YOUR... UH... CONDITION.
WELL...
I USED TO GO POTTY EVERY MORNING, LIKE CLOCKWORK.
THEN TWO YEARS AGO, I JUST STOPPED. NO IDEA WHY.
HMMMM...
HAVE YOU TRIED THOSE NEW HEATED TOILET SEATS?
YOU'RE NOT MEDICAL PROFESSIONALS, ARE YOU?
ICHIRO, I'D BE WILLING TO BET THE PROBLEM IS WITH YOUR DIET.
ANY CHANGES?
NOPE. THE USUAL STUFF.
CARDBOARD, SHOE LACES, PLASTIC BOTTLES, THE OCCASIONAL SEA GULL BEAK.
EVERY NOW AND THEN I SPLURGE ON SOMETHING UNHEALTHY.
GOOD GRAVY!

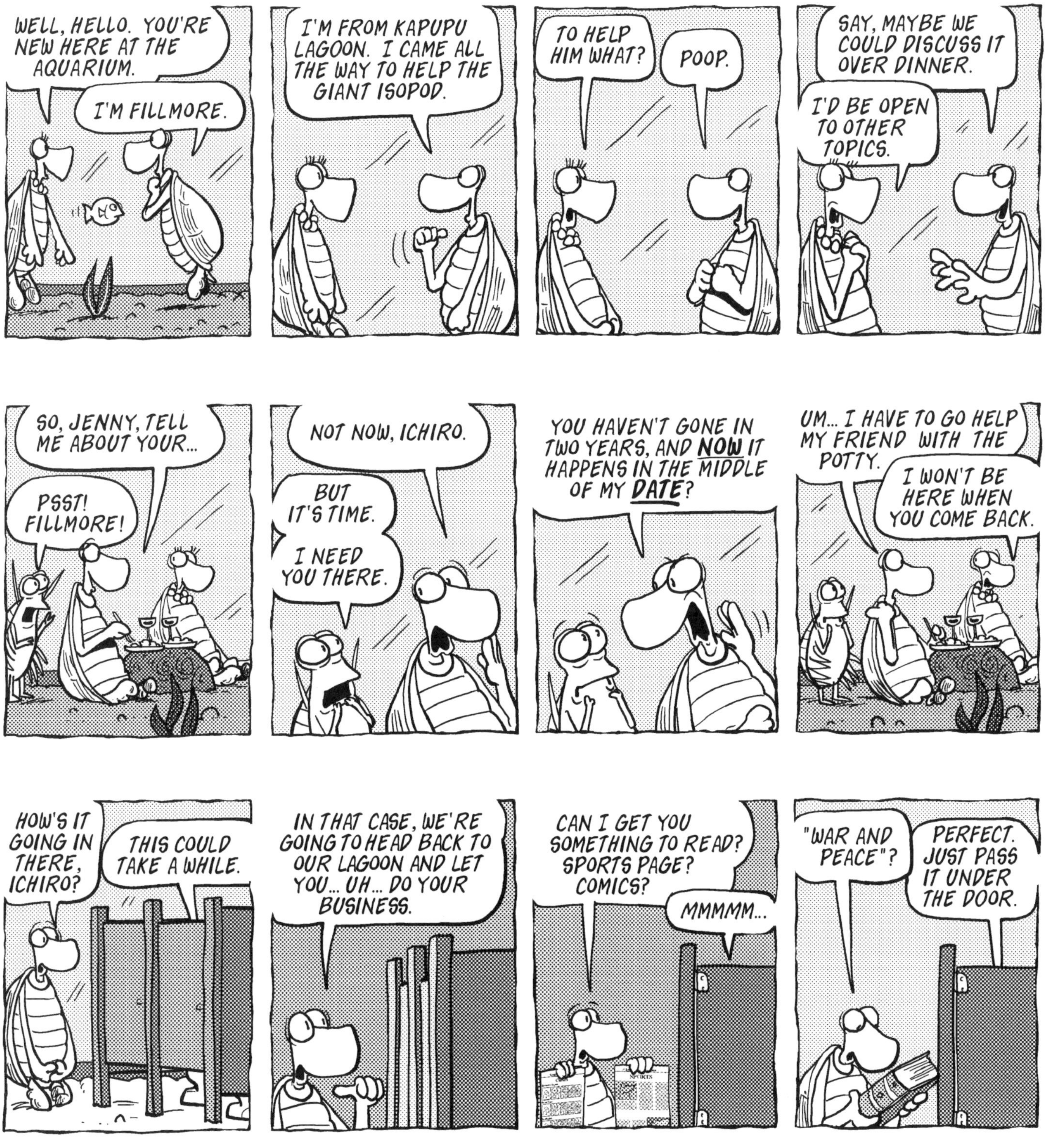
WELL, HELLO. YOU'RE NEW HERE AT THE AQUARIUM.
I'M FILLMORE.
I'M FROM KAPUPU LAGOON. I CAME ALL THE WAY TO HELP THE GIANT ISOPOD.
TO HELP HIM WHAT?
POOP.
SAY, MAYBE WE COULD DISCUSS IT OVER DINNER.
I'D BE OPEN TO OTHER TOPICS.
SO, JENNY, TELL ME ABOUT YOUR...
PSST! FILLMORE!
NOT NOW, ICHIRO.
BUT IT'S TIME.
I NEED YOU THERE.
YOU HAVEN'T GONE IN TWO YEARS, AND NOW IT HAPPENS IN THE MIDDLE OF MY DATE?
UM... I HAVE TO GO HELP MY FRIEND WITH THE POTTY.
I WON'T BE HERE WHEN YOU COME BACK.
HOW'S IT GOING IN THERE, ICHIRO?
THIS COULD TAKE A WHILE.
IN THAT CASE, WE'RE GOING TO HEAD BACK TO OUR LAGOON AND LET YOU... UH... DO YOUR BUSINESS.
CAN I GET YOU SOMETHING TO READ? SPORTS PAGE? COMICS?
MMMMM...
"WAR AND PEACE"?
PERFECT. JUST PASS IT UNDER THE DOOR.

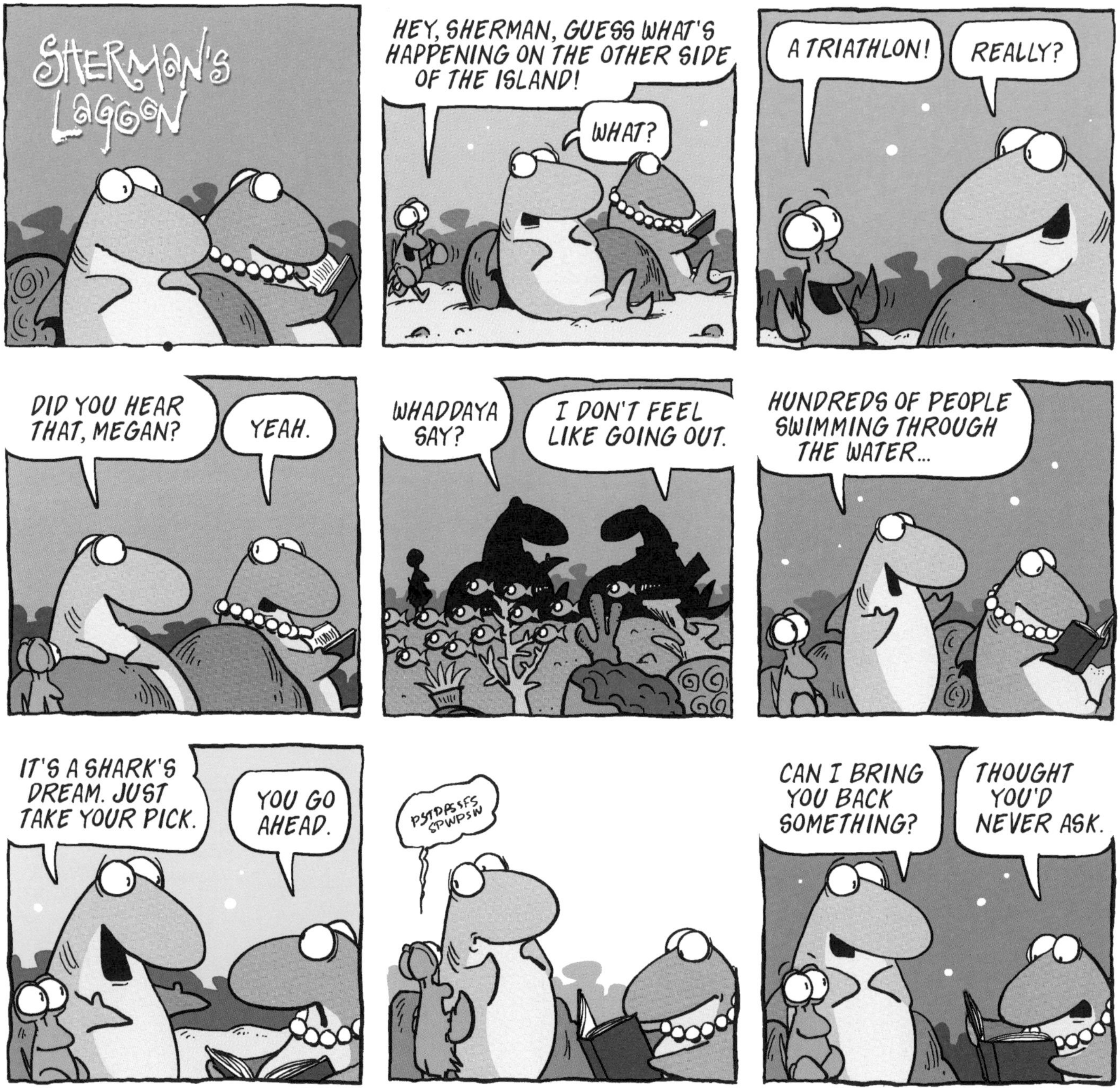
SHERMAN'S LAGOON
HEY, SHERMAN, GUESS WHAT'S HAPPENING ON THE OTHER SIDE OF THE ISLAND!
WHAT?
A TRIATHLON!
REALLY?
DID YOU HEAR THAT, MEGAN?
YEAH.
WHADDAYA SAY?
I DON'T FEEL LIKE GOING OUT.
HUNDREDS OF PEOPLE SWIMMING THROUGH THE WATER...
IT'S A SHARK'S DREAM. JUST TAKE YOUR PICK.
YOU GO AHEAD.
CAN I BRING YOU BACK SOMETHING?
THOUGHT YOU'D NEVER ASK.

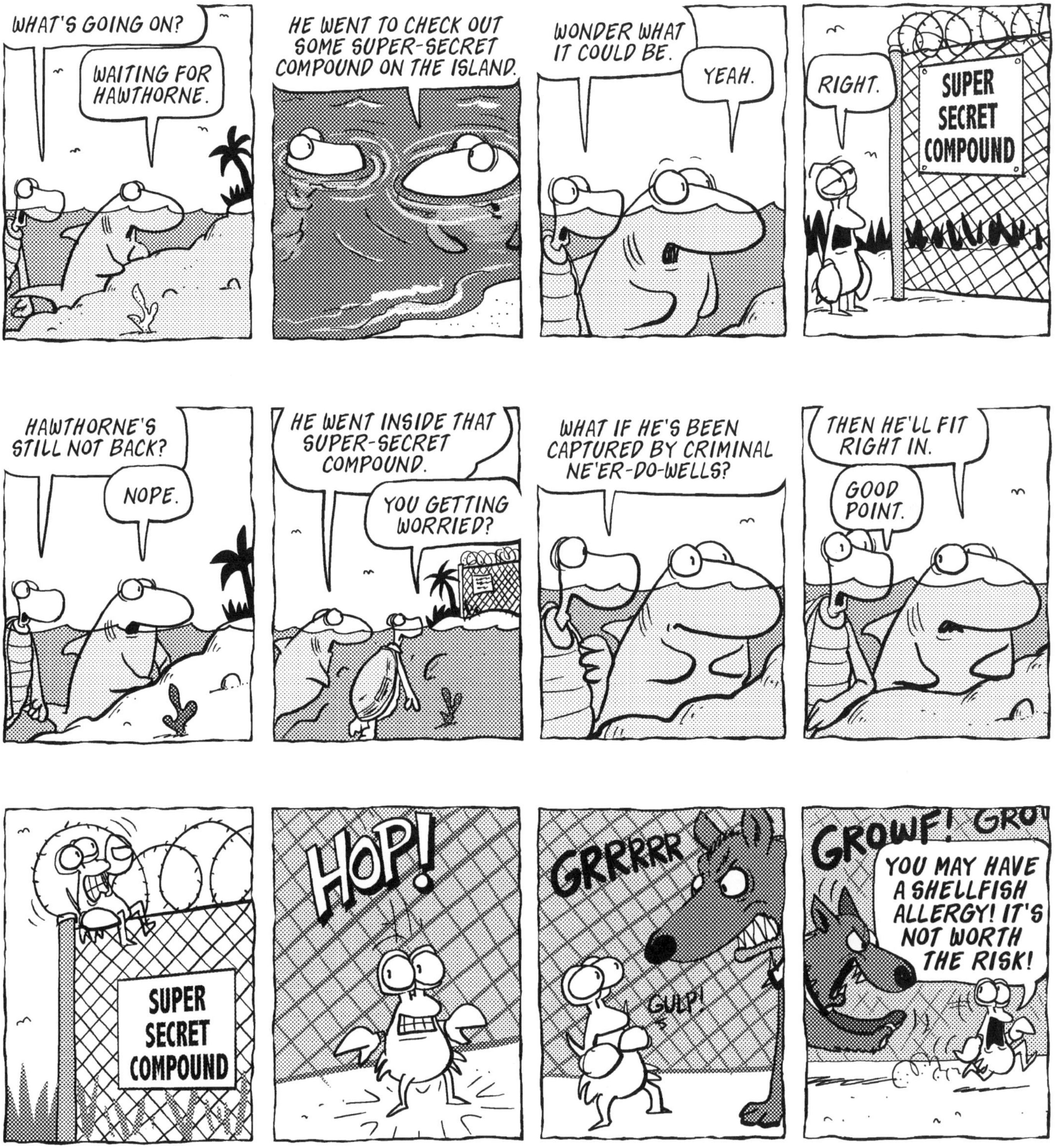
WHAT'S GOING ON?
WAITING FOR HAWTHORNE.
HE WENT TO CHECK OUT SOME SUPER-SECRET COMPOUND ON THE ISLAND.
WONDER WHAT IT COULD BE.
YEAH.
RIGHT.
SUPER SECRET COMPOUND
HAWTHORNE'S STILL NOT BACK?
NOPE.
HE WENT INSIDE THAT SUPER-SECRET COMPOUND.
YOU GETTING WORRIED?
WHAT IF HE'S BEEN CAPTURED BY CRIMINAL NE'ER-DO-WELLS?
THEN HE'LL FIT RIGHT IN.
GOOD POINT.
SUPER SECRET COMPOUND
HOP!
GRRRRR
GULP!
GROWF! GRO
YOU MAY HAVE A SHELLFISH ALLERGY! IT'S NOT WORTH THE RISK!

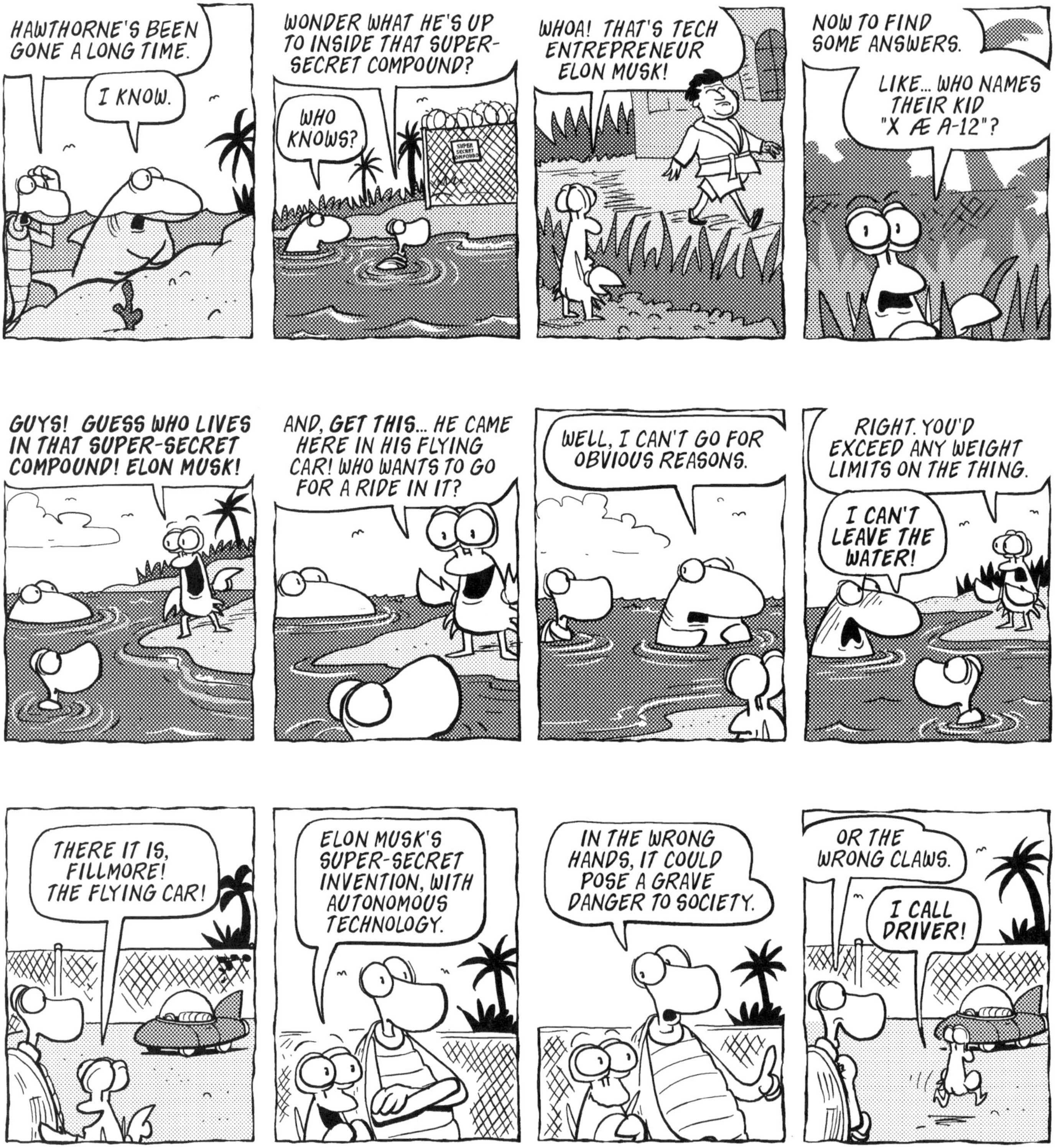
HAWTHORNE'S BEEN GONE A LONG TIME.
I KNOW.
WONDER WHAT HE'S UP TO INSIDE THAT SUPER-SECRET COMPOUND?
WHO KNOWS?
SUPER SECRET COMPOUND
WHOA! THAT'S TECH ENTREPRENEUR ELON MUSK!
NOW TO FIND SOME ANSWERS.
LIKE... WHO NAMES THEIR KID "X Æ A-12"?
GUYS! GUESS WHO LIVES IN THAT SUPER-SECRET COMPOUND! ELON MUSK!
AND, GET THIS... HE CAME HERE IN HIS FLYING CAR! WHO WANTS TO GO FOR A RIDE IN IT?
WELL, I CAN'T GO FOR OBVIOUS REASONS.
RIGHT. YOU'D EXCEED ANY WEIGHT LIMITS ON THE THING.
I CAN'T LEAVE THE WATER!
THERE IT IS, FILLMORE! THE FLYING CAR!
ELON MUSK'S SUPER-SECRET INVENTION, WITH AUTONOMOUS TECHNOLOGY.
IN THE WRONG HANDS, IT COULD POSE A GRAVE DANGER TO SOCIETY.
OR THE WRONG CLAWS.
I CALL DRIVER!

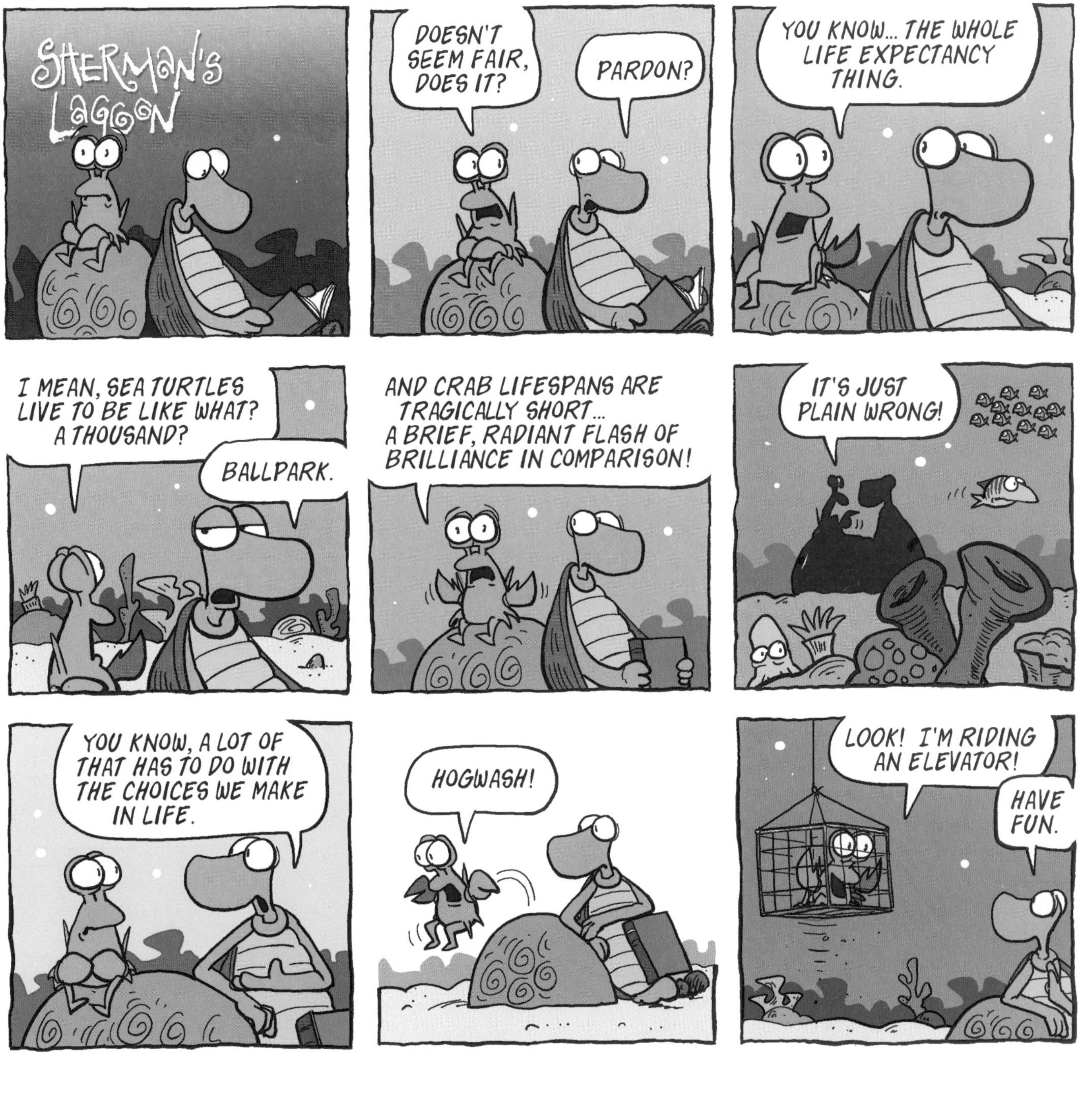
SHERMAN'S LAGOON
DOESN'T SEEM FAIR, DOES IT?
PARDON?
YOU KNOW... THE WHOLE LIFE EXPECTANCY THING.
I MEAN, SEA TURTLES LIVE TO BE LIKE WHAT? A THOUSAND?
BALLPARK.
AND CRAB LIFESPANS ARE TRAGICALLY SHORT... A BRIEF, RADIANT FLASH OF BRILLIANCE IN COMPARISON!
IT'S JUST PLAIN WRONG!
YOU KNOW, A LOT OF THAT HAS TO DO WITH THE CHOICES WE MAKE IN LIFE.
HOGWASH!
LOOK! I'M RIDING AN ELEVATOR!
HAVE FUN.

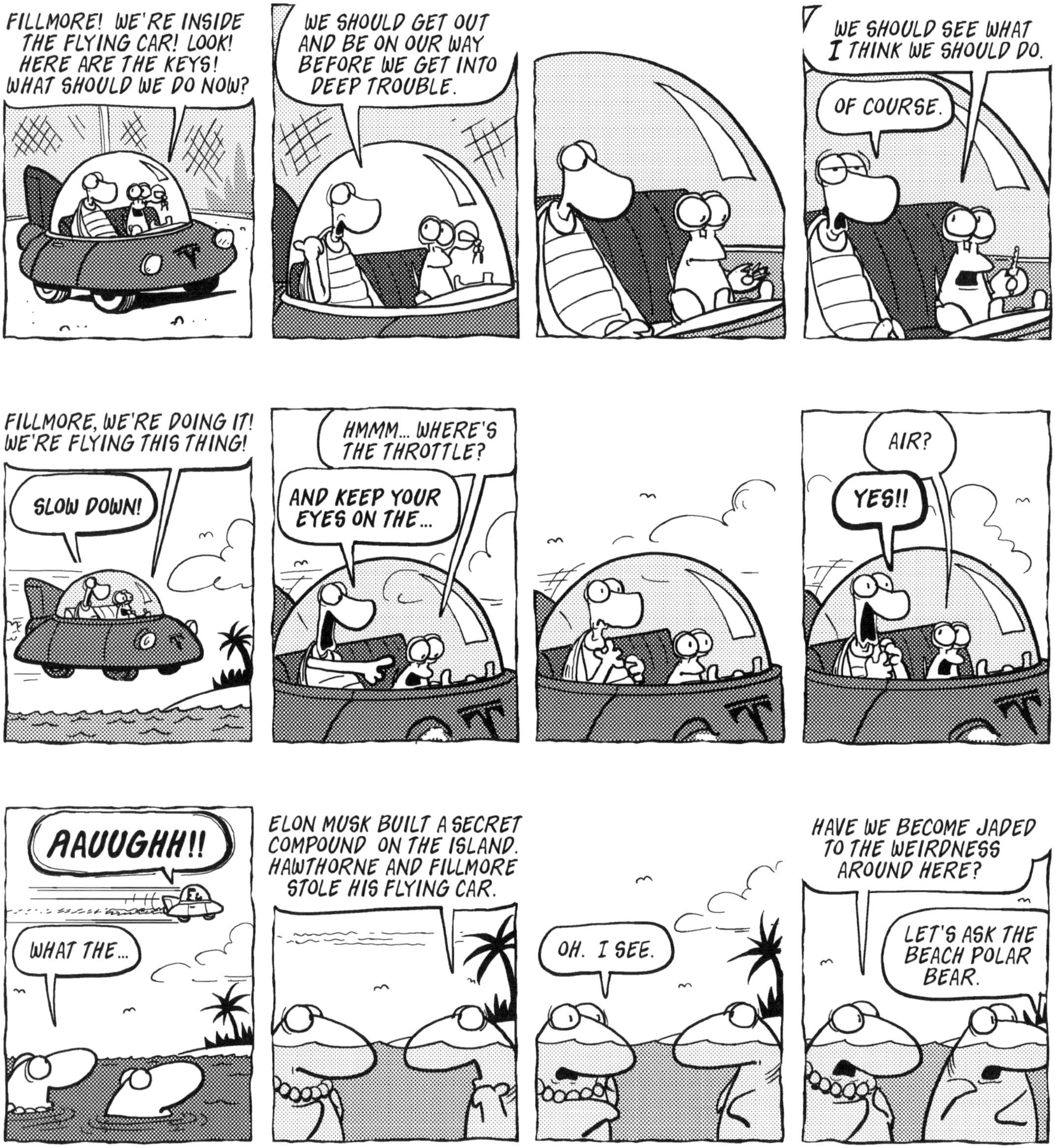
FILLMORE! WE'RE INSIDE THE FLYING CAR! LOOK! HERE ARE THE KEYS! WHAT SHOULD WE DO NOW?
WE SHOULD GET OUT AND BE ON OUR WAY BEFORE WE GET INTO DEEP TROUBLE.
WE SHOULD SEE WHAT I THINK WE SHOULD DO.
OF COURSE.
FILLMORE, WE'RE DOING IT! WE'RE FLYING THIS THING!
SLOW DOWN!
HMMM... WHERE'S THE THROTTLE?
AND KEEP YOUR EYES ON THE...
AIR?
YES!!
AAUUGHH!!
WHAT THE...
ELON MUSK BUILT A SECRET COMPOUND ON THE ISLAND. HAWTHORNE AND FILLMORE STOLE HIS FLYING CAR.
OH. I SEE.
HAVE WE BECOME JADED TO THE WEIRDNESS AROUND HERE?
LET'S ASK THE BEACH POLAR BEAR.

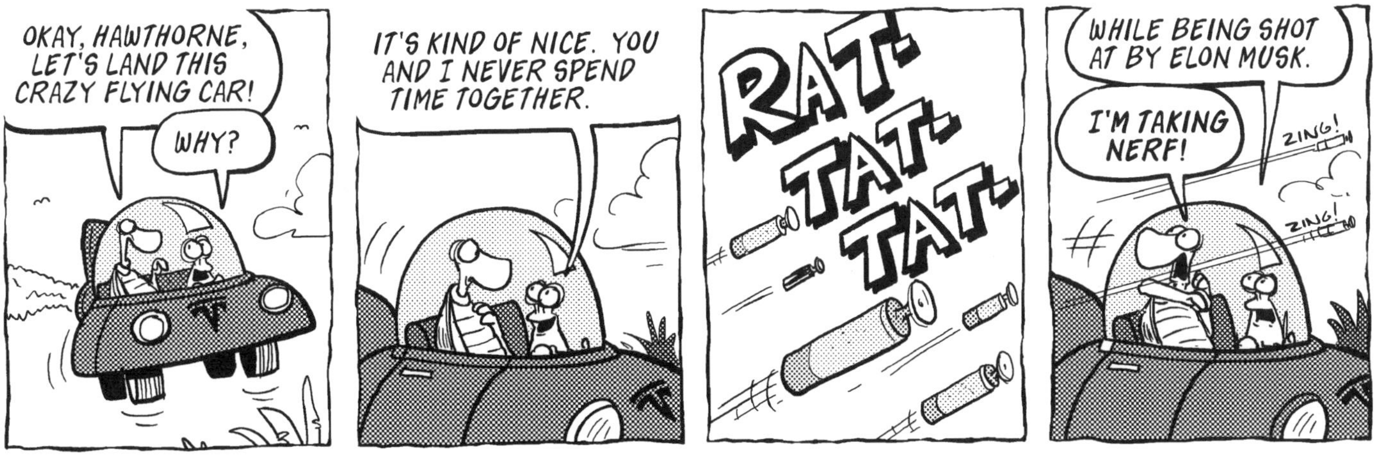
OKAY, HAWTHORNE, LET'S LAND THIS CRAZY FLYING CAR!
WHY?
IT'S KIND OF NICE. YOU AND I NEVER SPEND TIME TOGETHER.
RAT-TAT-TAT-
WHILE BEING SHOT AT BY ELON MUSK.
I'M TAKING NERF!
ZING!
ZING!

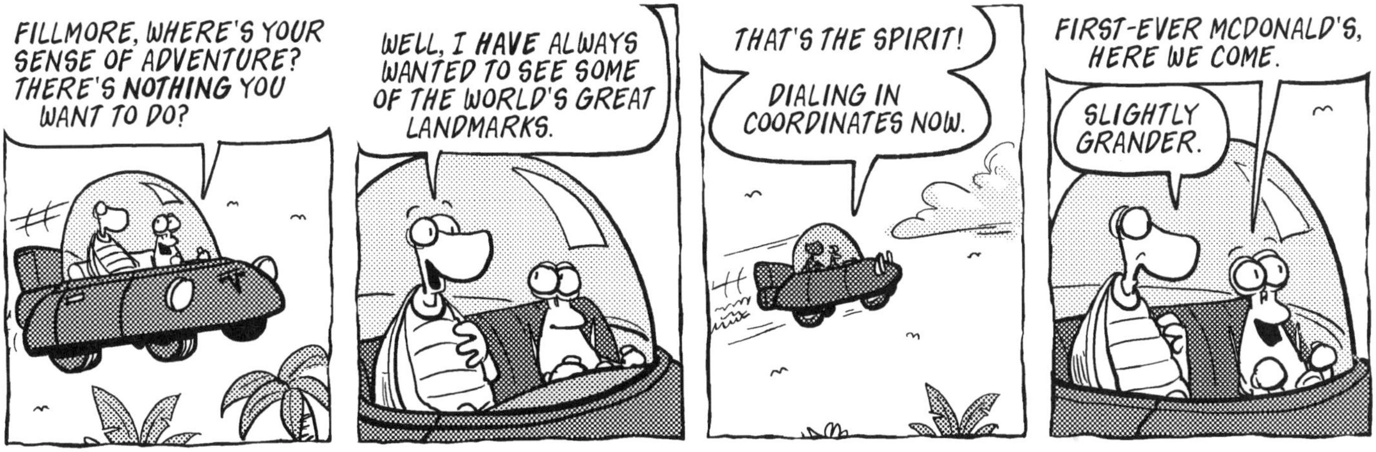
FILLMORE, WHERE'S YOUR SENSE OF ADVENTURE? THERE'S NOTHING YOU WANT TO DO?
WELL, I HAVE ALWAYS WANTED TO SEE SOME OF THE WORLD'S GREAT LANDMARKS.
THAT'S THE SPIRIT!
DIALING IN COORDINATES NOW.
FIRST-EVER MCDONALD'S, HERE WE COME.
SLIGHTLY GRANDER.

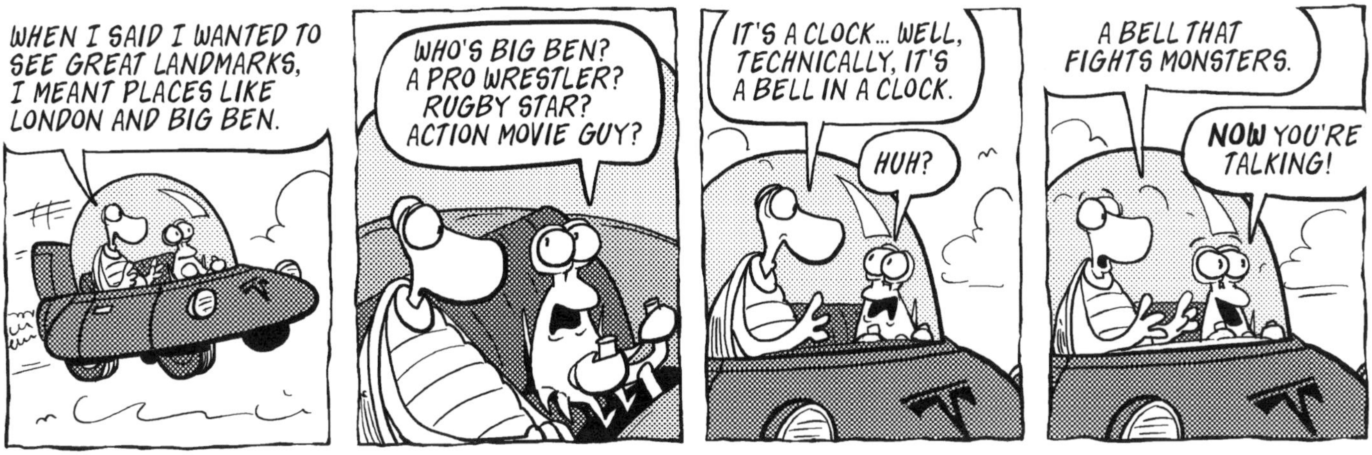
WHEN I SAID I WANTED TO SEE GREAT LANDMARKS, I MEANT PLACES LIKE LONDON AND BIG BEN.
WHO'S BIG BEN? A PRO WRESTLER? RUGBY STAR? ACTION MOVIE GUY?
IT'S A CLOCK... WELL, TECHNICALLY, IT'S A BELL IN A CLOCK.
HUH?
A BELL THAT FIGHTS MONSTERS.
NOW YOU'RE TALKING!

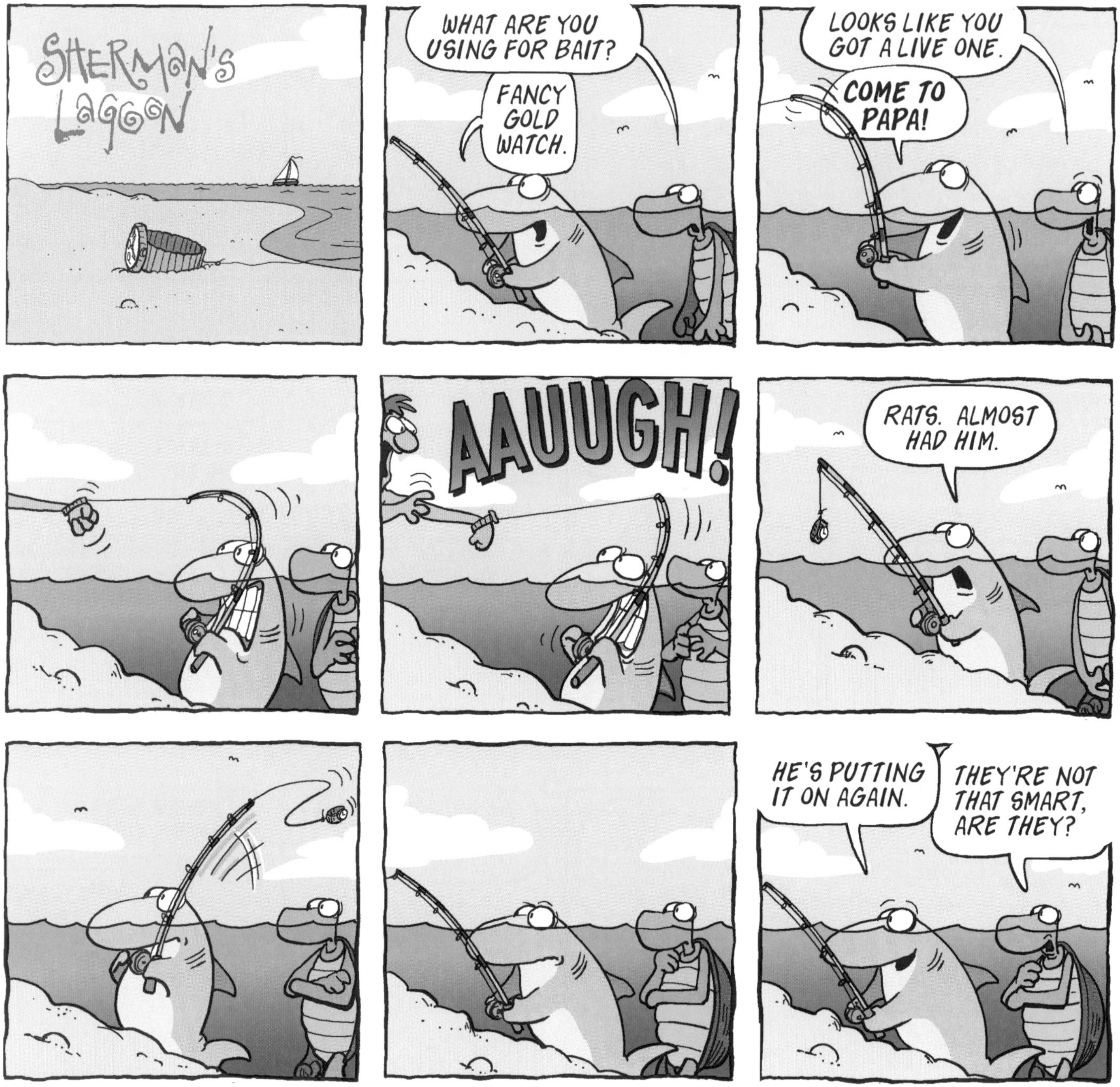
SHERMAN'S LAGOON
WHAT ARE YOU USING FOR BAIT?
FANCY GOLD WATCH.
LOOKS LIKE YOU GOT A LIVE ONE.
COME TO PAPA!
AAUUGH!
RATS. ALMOST HAD HIM.
HE'S PUTTING IT ON AGAIN.
THEY'RE NOT THAT SMART, ARE THEY?

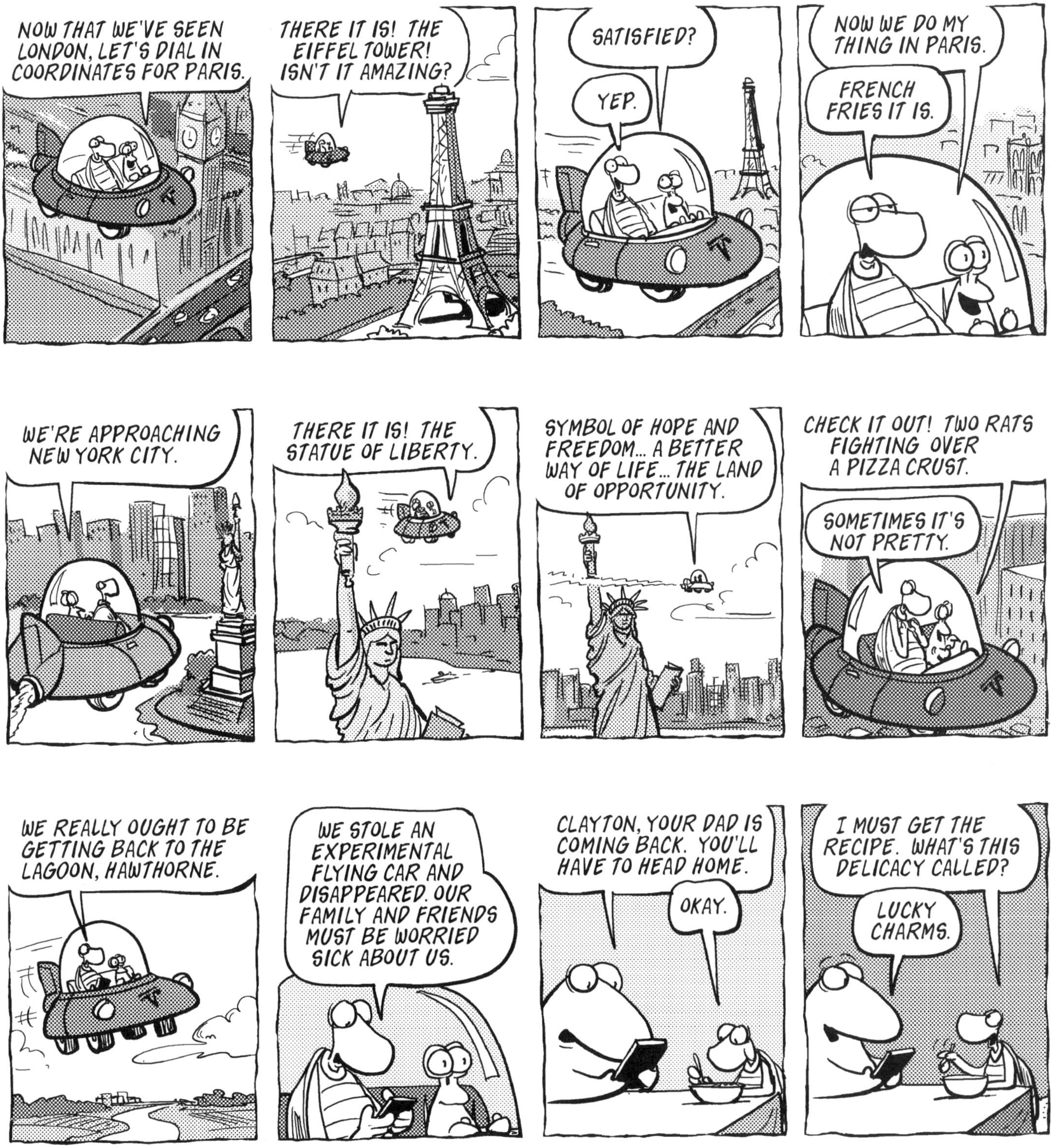
NOW THAT WE'VE SEEN LONDON, LET'S DIAL IN COORDINATES FOR PARIS.
THERE IT IS! THE EIFFEL TOWER! ISN'T IT AMAZING?
SATISFIED?
YEP.
NOW WE DO MY THING IN PARIS.
FRENCH FRIES IT IS.
WE'RE APPROACHING NEW YORK CITY.
THERE IT IS! THE STATUE OF LIBERTY.
SYMBOL OF HOPE AND FREEDOM... A BETTER WAY OF LIFE... THE LAND OF OPPORTUNITY.
CHECK IT OUT! TWO RATS FIGHTING OVER A PIZZA CRUST.
SOMETIMES IT'S NOT PRETTY.
WE REALLY OUGHT TO BE GETTING BACK TO THE LAGOON, HAWTHORNE.
WE STOLE AN EXPERIMENTAL FLYING CAR AND DISAPPEARED. OUR FAMILY AND FRIENDS MUST BE WORRIED SICK ABOUT US.
CLAYTON, YOUR DAD IS COMING BACK. YOU'LL HAVE TO HEAD HOME.
OKAY.
I MUST GET THE RECIPE. WHAT'S THIS DELICACY CALLED?
LUCKY CHARMS.

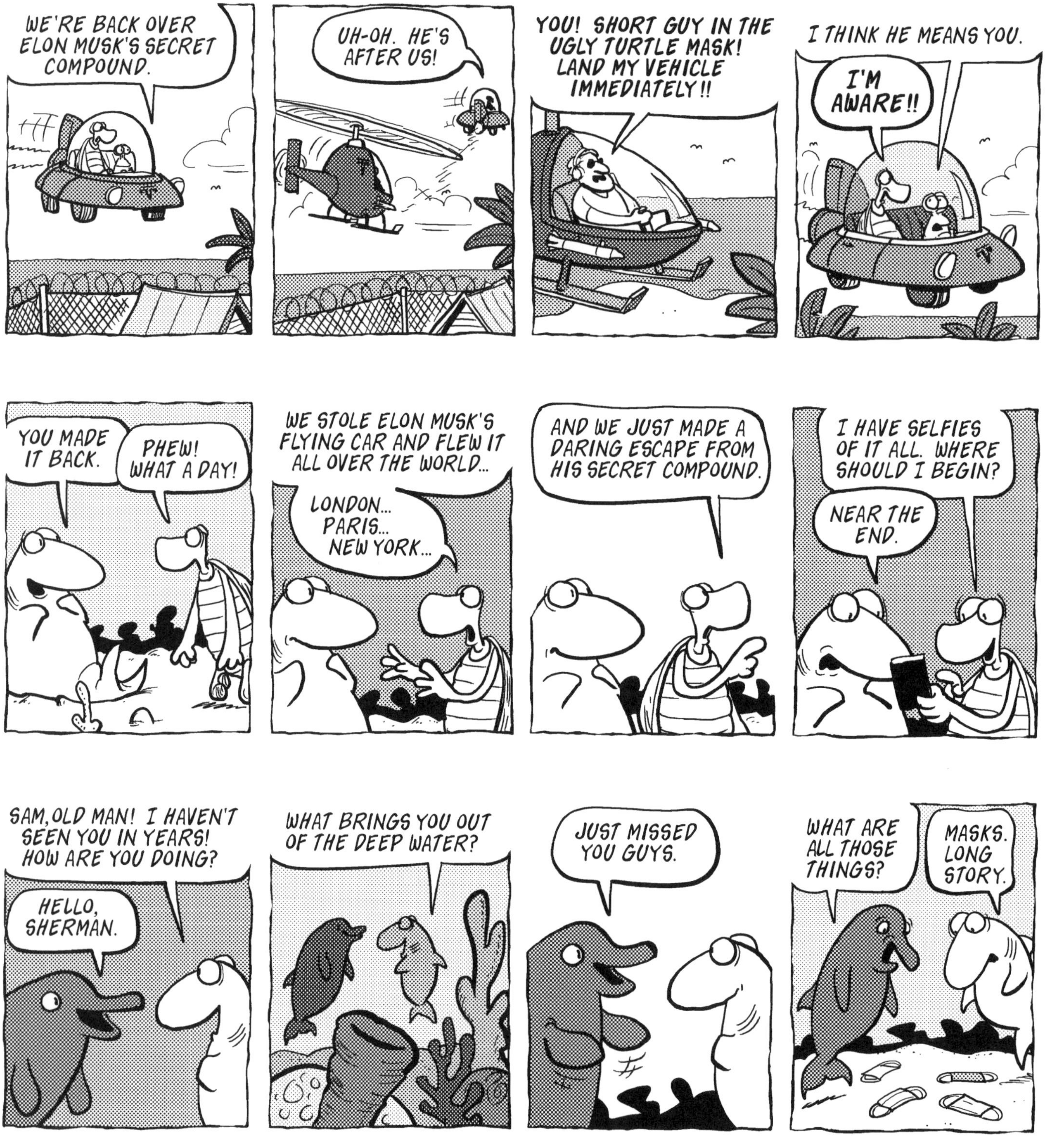
WE'RE BACK OVER ELON MUSK'S SECRET COMPOUND.
UH-OH. HE'S AFTER US!
YOU! SHORT GUY IN THE UGLY TURTLE MASK! LAND MY VEHICLE IMMEDIATELY!!
I THINK HE MEANS YOU.
I'M AWARE!!
YOU MADE IT BACK.
PHEW! WHAT A DAY!
WE STOLE ELON MUSK'S FLYING CAR AND FLEW IT ALL OVER THE WORLD...
LONDON... PARIS... NEW YORK...
AND WE JUST MADE A DARING ESCAPE FROM HIS SECRET COMPOUND.
I HAVE SELFIES OF IT ALL. WHERE SHOULD I BEGIN?
NEAR THE END.
SAM, OLD MAN! I HAVEN'T SEEN YOU IN YEARS! HOW ARE YOU DOING?
HELLO, SHERMAN.
WHAT BRINGS YOU OUT OF THE DEEP WATER?
JUST MISSED YOU GUYS.
WHAT ARE ALL THOSE THINGS?
MASKS. LONG STORY.

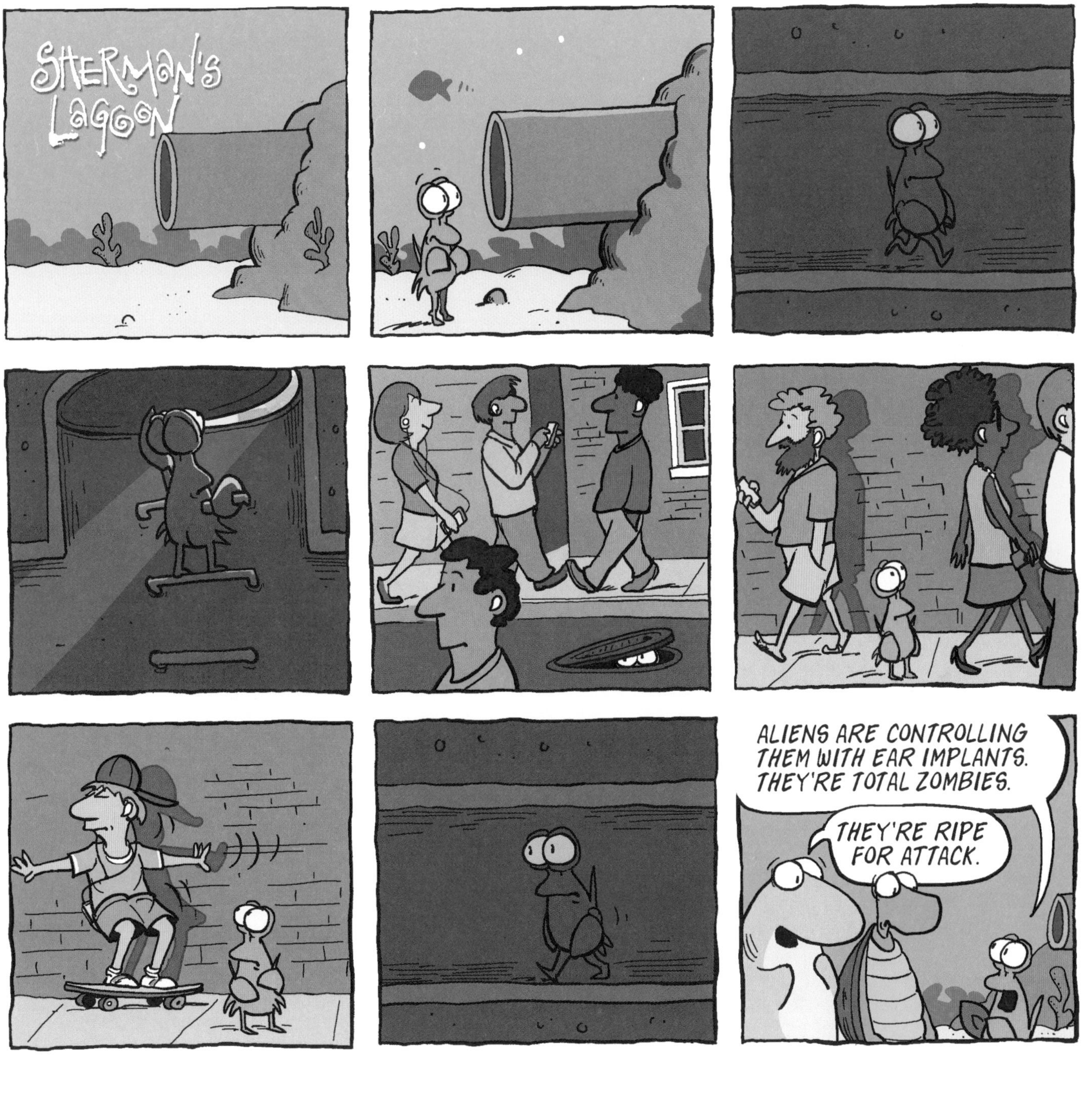
SHERMAN'S LAGOON
ALIENS ARE CONTROLLING THEM WITH EAR IMPLANTS. THEY'RE TOTAL ZOMBIES.
THEY'RE RIPE FOR ATTACK.

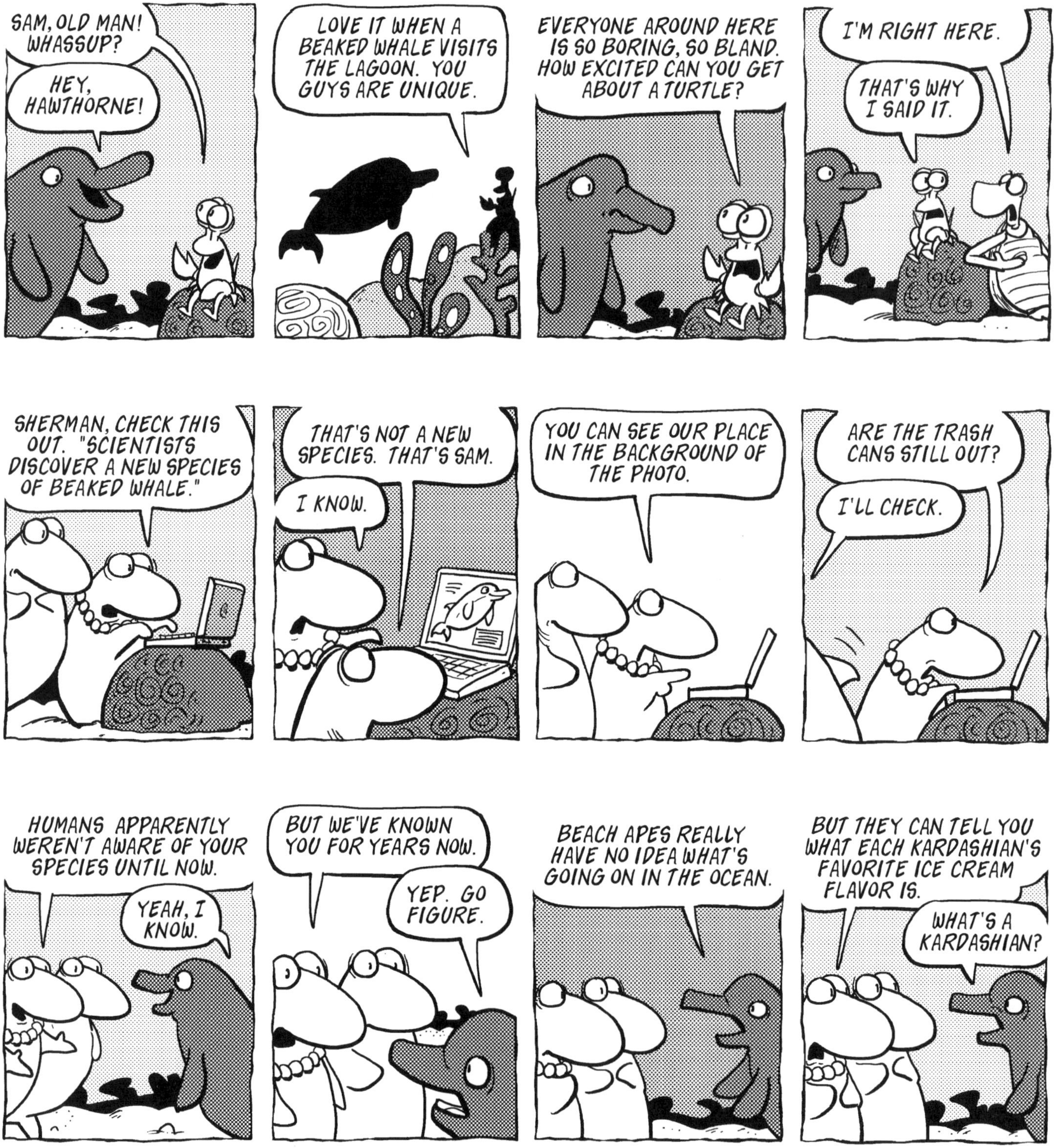
SAM, OLD MAN! WHASSUP?
HEY, HAWTHORNE!
LOVE IT WHEN A BEAKED WHALE VISITS THE LAGOON. YOU GUYS ARE UNIQUE.
EVERYONE AROUND HERE IS SO BORING, SO BLAND. HOW EXCITED CAN YOU GET ABOUT A TURTLE?
I'M RIGHT HERE.
THAT'S WHY I SAID IT.
SHERMAN, CHECK THIS OUT. "SCIENTISTS DISCOVER A NEW SPECIES OF BEAKED WHALE."
THAT'S NOT A NEW SPECIES. THAT'S SAM.
I KNOW.
YOU CAN SEE OUR PLACE IN THE BACKGROUND OF THE PHOTO.
ARE THE TRASH CANS STILL OUT?
I'LL CHECK.
HUMANS APPARENTLY WEREN'T AWARE OF YOUR SPECIES UNTIL NOW.
YEAH, I KNOW.
BUT WE'VE KNOWN YOU FOR YEARS NOW.
YEP. GO FIGURE.
BEACH APES REALLY HAVE NO IDEA WHAT'S GOING ON IN THE OCEAN.
BUT THEY CAN TELL YOU WHAT EACH KARDASHIAN'S FAVORITE ICE CREAM FLAVOR IS.
WHAT'S A KARDASHIAN?

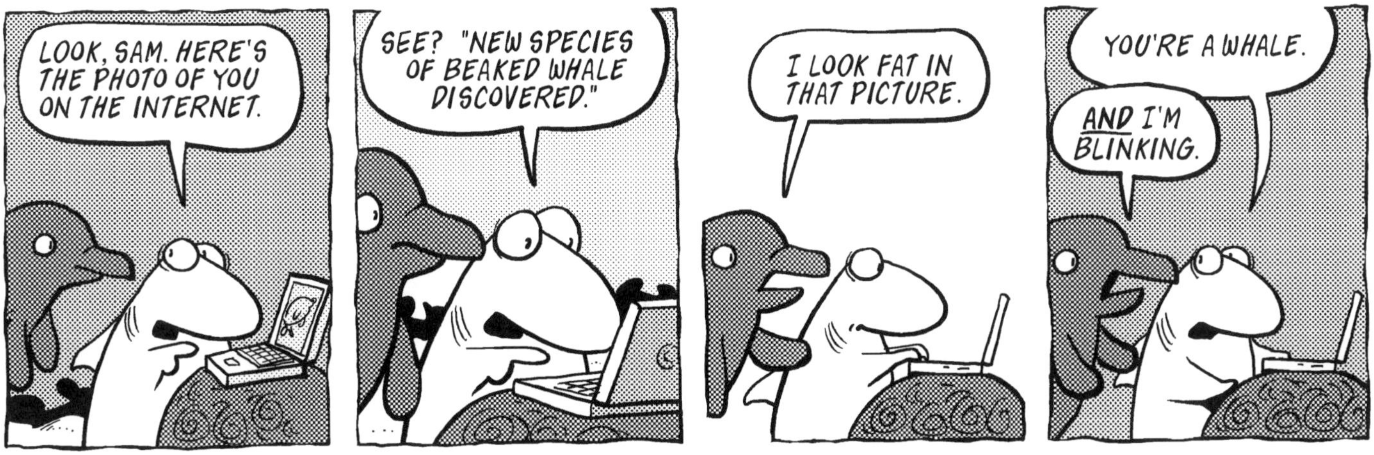
LOOK, SAM. HERE'S THE PHOTO OF YOU ON THE INTERNET.
SEE? "NEW SPECIES OF BEAKED WHALE DISCOVERED."
I LOOK FAT IN THAT PICTURE.
YOU'RE A WHALE.
AND I'M BLINKING.

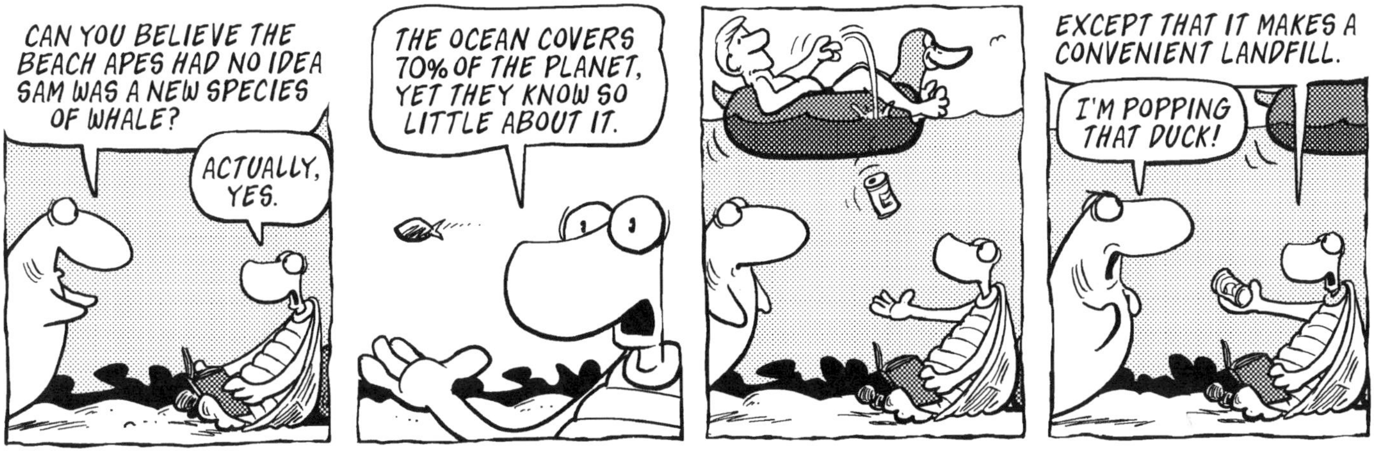
CAN YOU BELIEVE THE BEACH APES HAD NO IDEA SAM WAS A NEW SPECIES OF WHALE?
ACTUALLY, YES.
THE OCEAN COVERS 70% OF THE PLANET, YET THEY KNOW SO LITTLE ABOUT IT.
EXCEPT THAT IT MAKES A CONVENIENT LANDFILL.
I'M POPPING THAT DUCK!

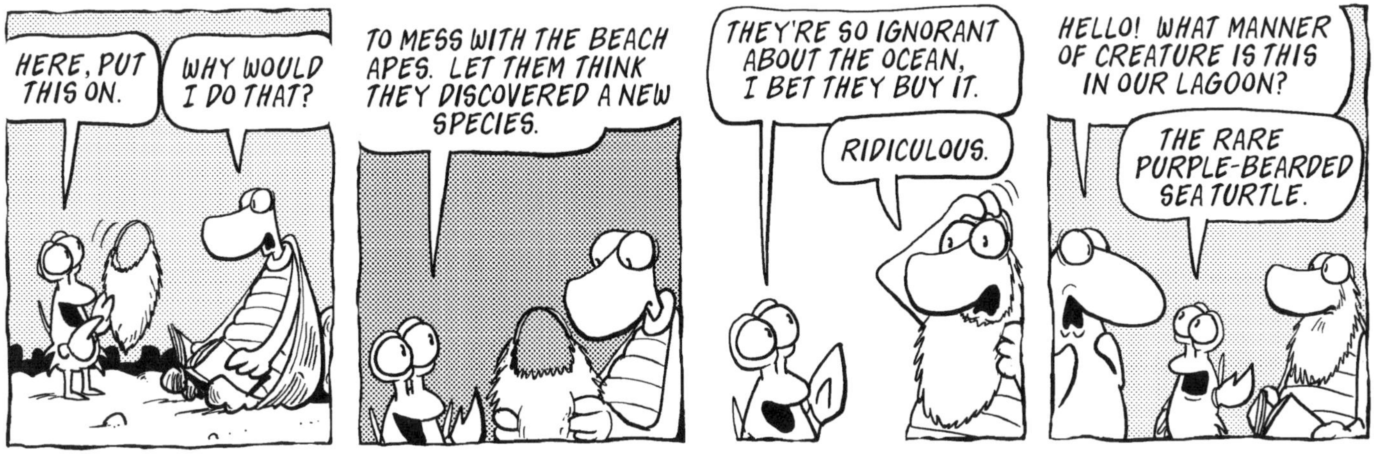
HERE, PUT THIS ON.
WHY WOULD I DO THAT?
TO MESS WITH THE BEACH APES. LET THEM THINK THEY DISCOVERED A NEW SPECIES.
THEY'RE SO IGNORANT ABOUT THE OCEAN, I BET THEY BUY IT.
RIDICULOUS.
HELLO! WHAT MANNER OF CREATURE IS THIS IN OUR LAGOON?
THE RARE PURPLE-BEARDED SEA TURTLE.

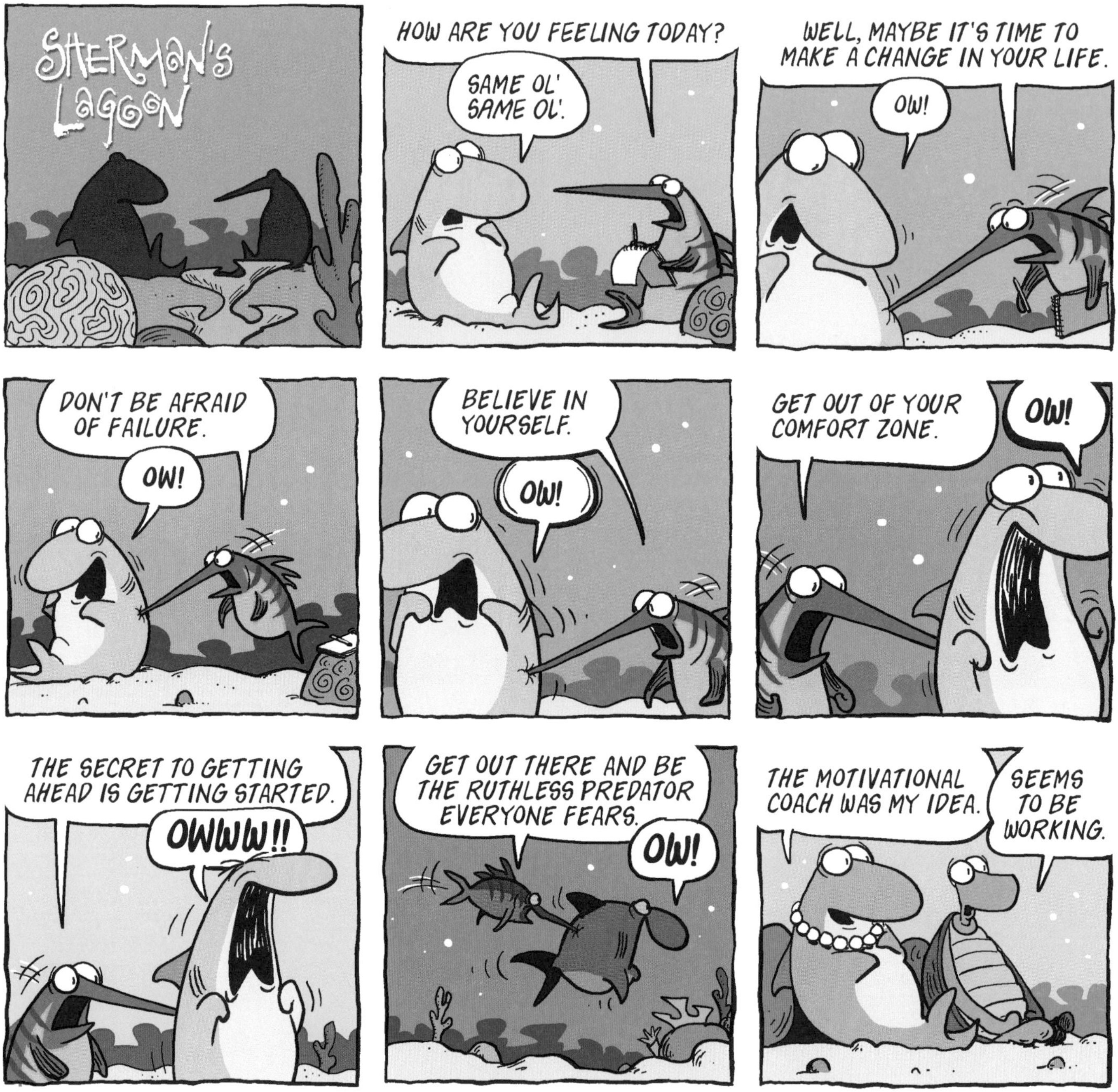
SHERMAN'S LAGOON
HOW ARE YOU FEELING TODAY?
SAME OL' SAME OL'.
WELL, MAYBE IT'S TIME TO MAKE A CHANGE IN YOUR LIFE.
OW!
DON'T BE AFRAID OF FAILURE.
OW!
BELIEVE IN YOURSELF.
OW!
GET OUT OF YOUR COMFORT ZONE.
OW!
THE SECRET TO GETTING AHEAD IS GETTING STARTED.
OWWW!!
GET OUT THERE AND BE THE RUTHLESS PREDATOR EVERYONE FEARS.
OW!
THE MOTIVATIONAL COACH WAS MY IDEA.
SEEMS TO BE WORKING.

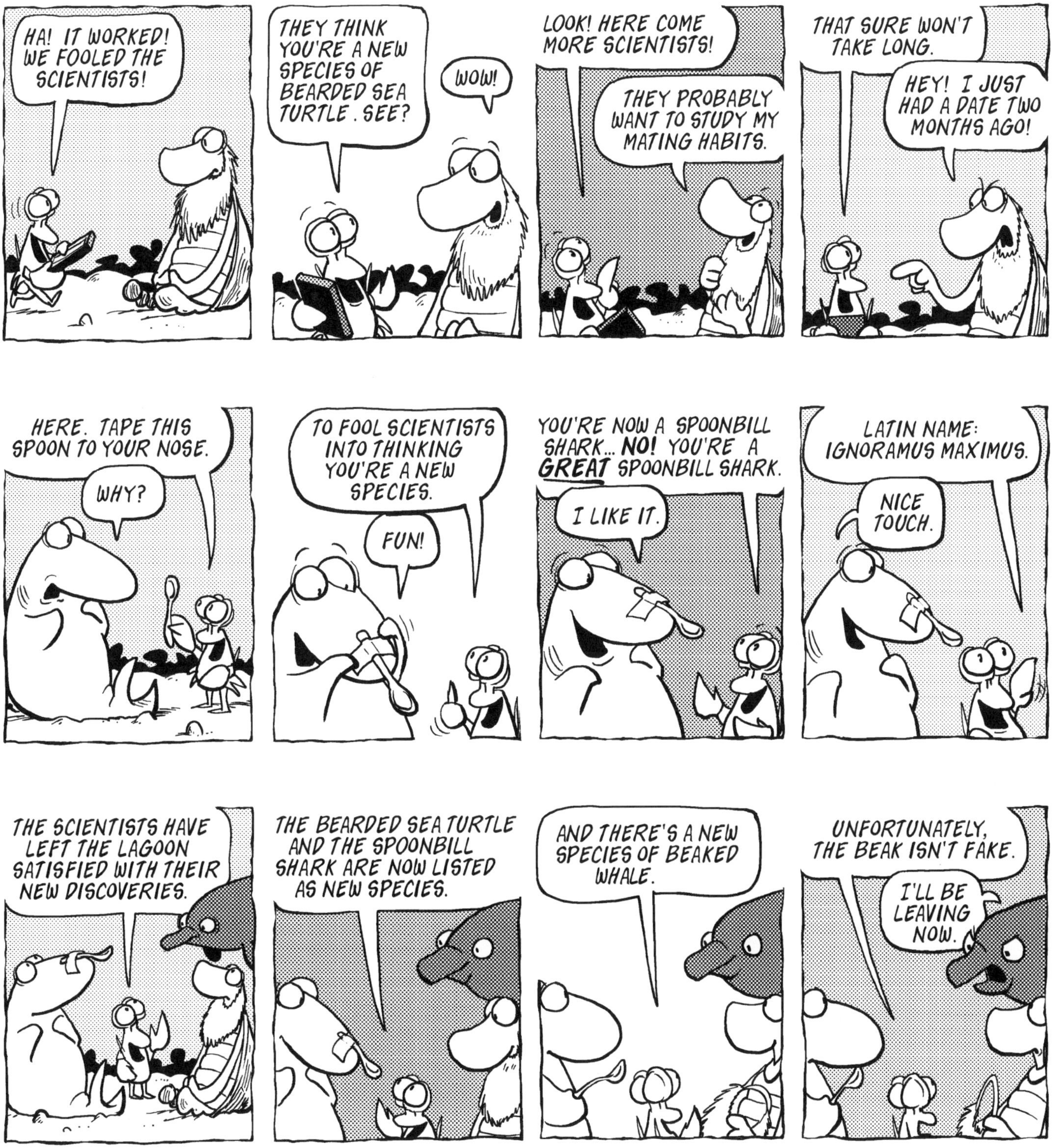

HA! IT WORKED! WE FOOLED THE SCIENTISTS!
THEY THINK YOU'RE A NEW SPECIES OF BEARDED SEA TURTLE . SEE?
WOW!
LOOK! HERE COME MORE SCIENTISTS!
THEY PROBABLY WANT TO STUDY MY MATING HABITS.
THAT SURE WON'T TAKE LONG.
HEY! I JUST HAD A DATE TWO MONTHS AGO!
HERE. TAPE THIS SPOON TO YOUR NOSE.
WHY?
TO FOOL SCIENTISTS INTO THINKING YOU'RE A NEW SPECIES.
FUN!
YOU'RE NOW A SPOONBILL SHARK... NO! YOU'RE A GREAT SPOONBILL SHARK.
I LIKE IT.
LATIN NAME: IGNORAMUS MAXIMUS.
NICE TOUCH.
THE SCIENTISTS HAVE LEFT THE LAGOON SATISFIED WITH THEIR NEW DISCOVERIES.
THE BEARDED SEA TURTLE AND THE SPOONBILL SHARK ARE NOW LISTED AS NEW SPECIES.
AND THERE'S A NEW SPECIES OF BEAKED WHALE.
UNFORTUNATELY, THE BEAK ISN'T FAKE.
I'LL BE LEAVING NOW.

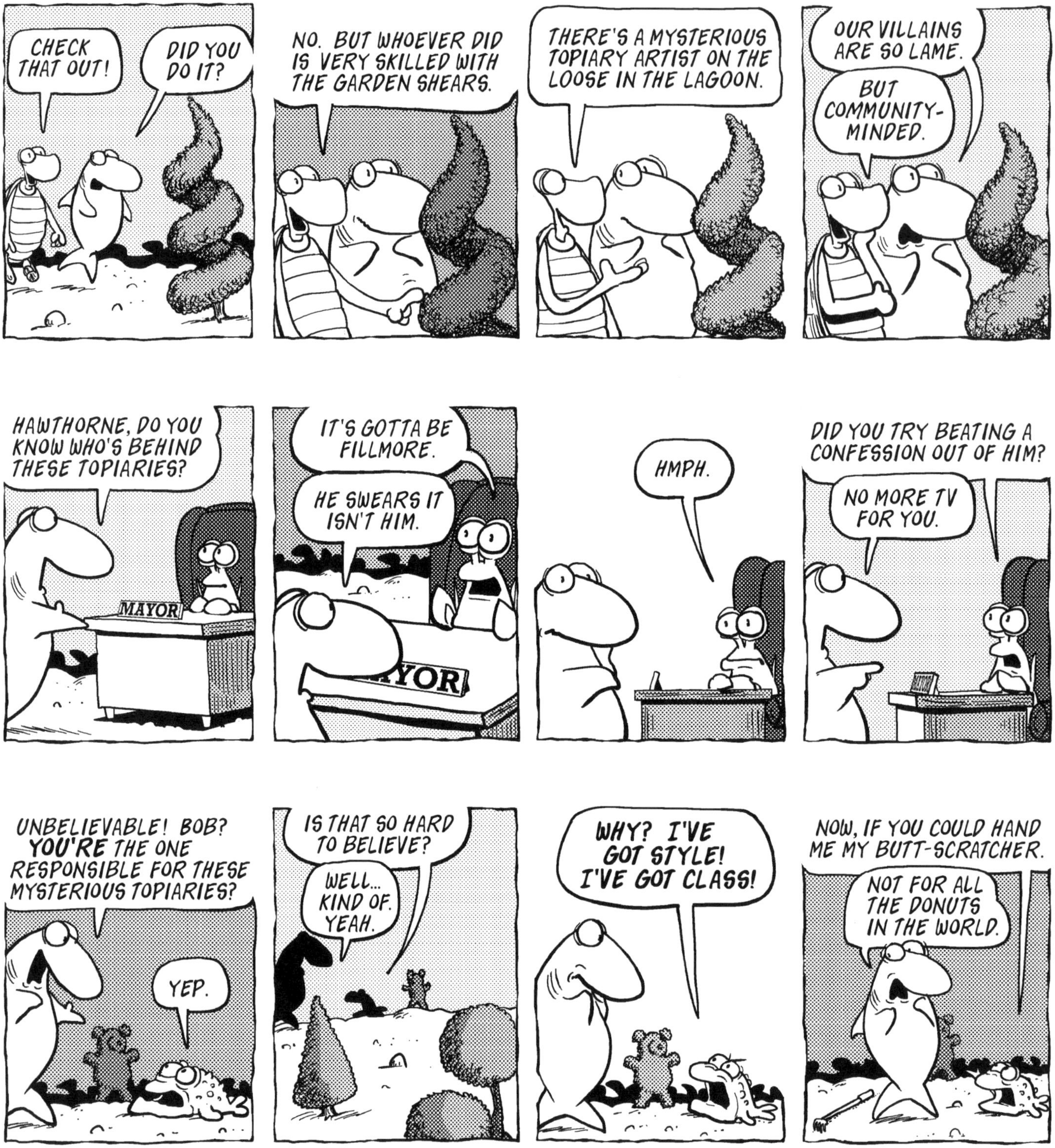
CHECK THAT OUT!
DID YOU DO IT?
NO. BUT WHOEVER DID IS VERY SKILLED WITH THE GARDEN SHEARS.
THERE'S A MYSTERIOUS TOPIARY ARTIST ON THE LOOSE IN THE LAGOON.
OUR VILLAINS ARE SO LAME.
BUT COMMUNITY-MINDED.
HAWTHORNE, DO YOU KNOW WHO'S BEHIND THESE TOPIARIES?
MAYOR
IT'S GOTTA BE FILLMORE.
HE SWEARS IT ISN'T HIM.
HMPH.
DID YOU TRY BEATING A CONFESSION OUT OF HIM?
NO MORE TV FOR YOU.
UNBELIEVABLE! BOB? YOU'RE THE ONE RESPONSIBLE FOR THESE MYSTERIOUS TOPIARIES?
YEP.
IS THAT SO HARD TO BELIEVE?
WELL... KIND OF. YEAH.
WHY? I'VE GOT STYLE! I'VE GOT CLASS!
NOW, IF YOU COULD HAND ME MY BUTT-SCRATCHER.
NOT FOR ALL THE DONUTS IN THE WORLD.

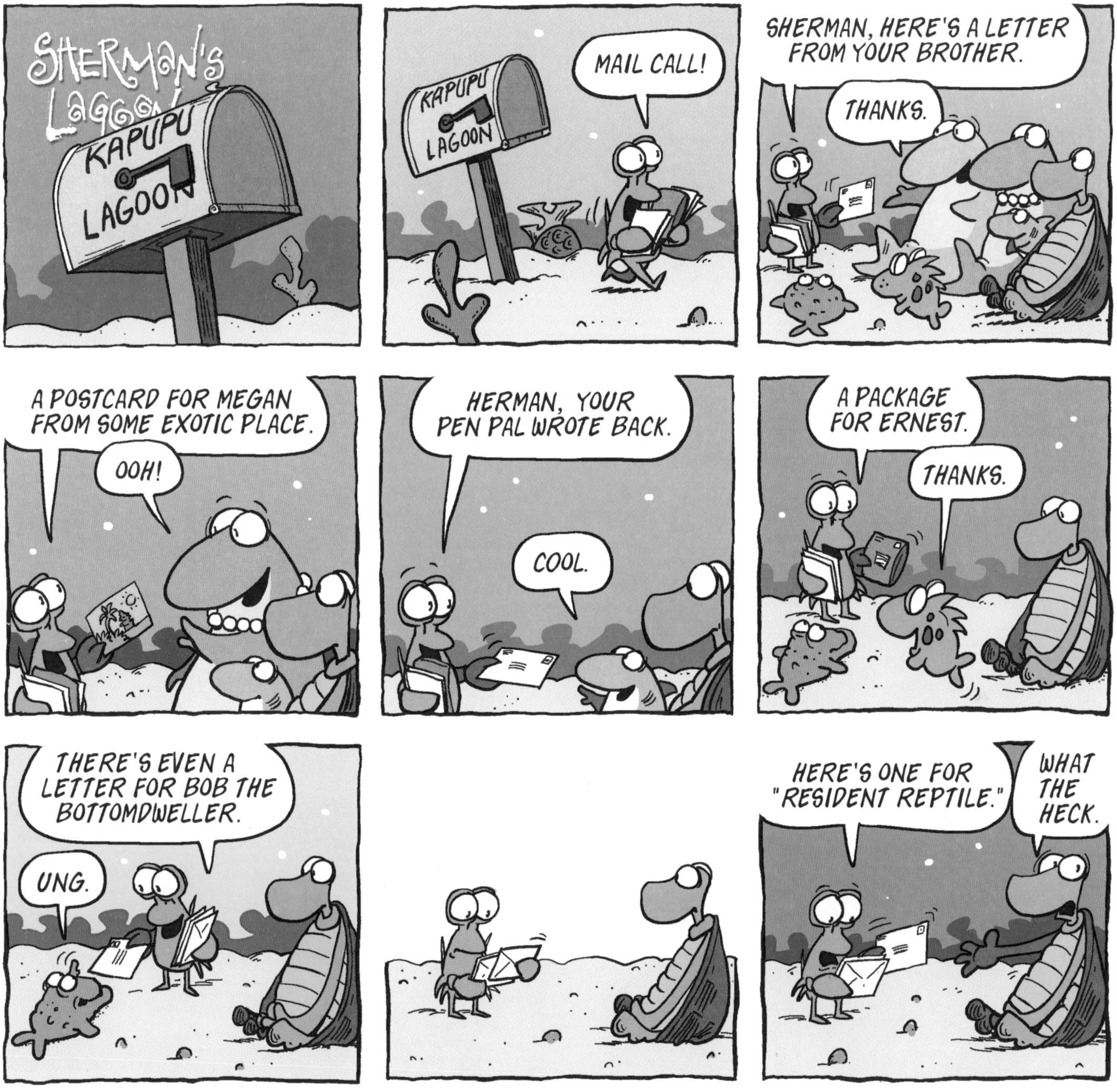
SHERMAN'S LAGOON
KAPUPU LAGOON
KAPUPU LAGOON
MAIL CALL!
SHERMAN, HERE'S A LETTER FROM YOUR BROTHER.
THANKS.
A POSTCARD FOR MEGAN FROM SOME EXOTIC PLACE.
OOH!
HERMAN, YOUR PEN PAL WROTE BACK.
COOL.
A PACKAGE FOR ERNEST.
THANKS.
THERE'S EVEN A LETTER FOR BOB THE BOTTOMDWELLER.
UNG.
HERE'S ONE FOR "RESIDENT REPTILE."
WHAT THE HECK.

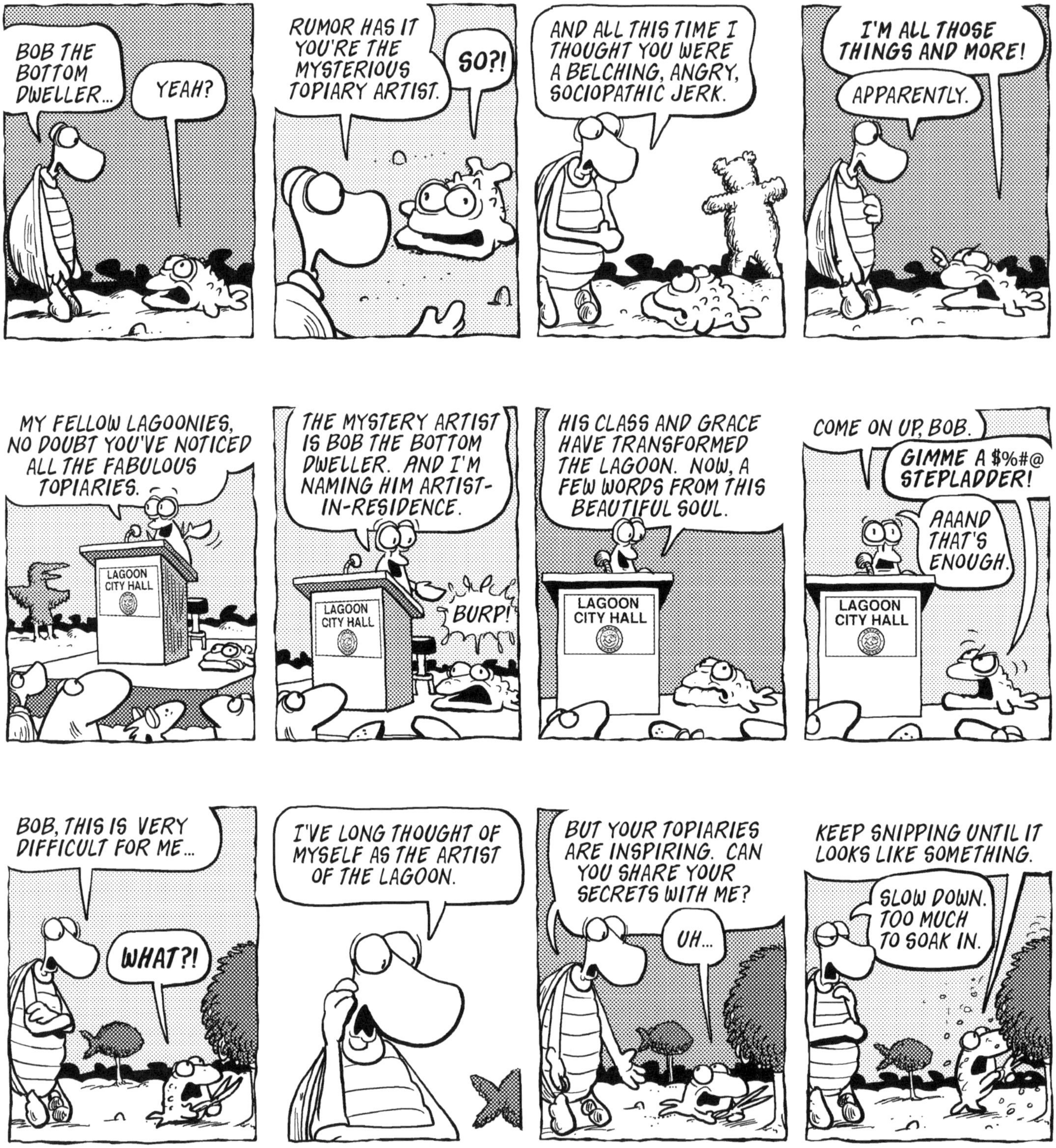
BOB THE BOTTOM DWELLER...
YEAH?
RUMOR HAS IT YOU'RE THE MYSTERIOUS TOPIARY ARTIST.
SO?!
AND ALL THIS TIME I THOUGHT YOU WERE A BELCHING, ANGRY, SOCIOPATHIC JERK.
I'M ALL THOSE THINGS AND MORE!
APPARENTLY.
MY FELLOW LAGOONIES, NO DOUBT YOU'VE NOTICED ALL THE FABULOUS TOPIARIES.
LAGOON CITY HALL
THE MYSTERY ARTIST IS BOB THE BOTTOM DWELLER. AND I'M NAMING HIM ARTIST-IN-RESIDENCE.
LAGOON CITY HALL
BURP!
HIS CLASS AND GRACE HAVE TRANSFORMED THE LAGOON. NOW, A FEW WORDS FROM THIS BEAUTIFUL SOUL.
LAGOON CITY HALL
COME ON UP, BOB.
GIMME A $%#@ STEPLADDER!
AAAND THAT'S ENOUGH.
LAGOON CITY HALL
BOB, THIS IS VERY DIFFICULT FOR ME...
WHAT?!
I'VE LONG THOUGHT OF MYSELF AS THE ARTIST OF THE LAGOON.
BUT YOUR TOPIARIES ARE INSPIRING. CAN YOU SHARE YOUR SECRETS WITH ME?
UH...
KEEP SNIPPING UNTIL IT LOOKS LIKE SOMETHING.
SLOW DOWN. TOO MUCH TO SOAK IN.

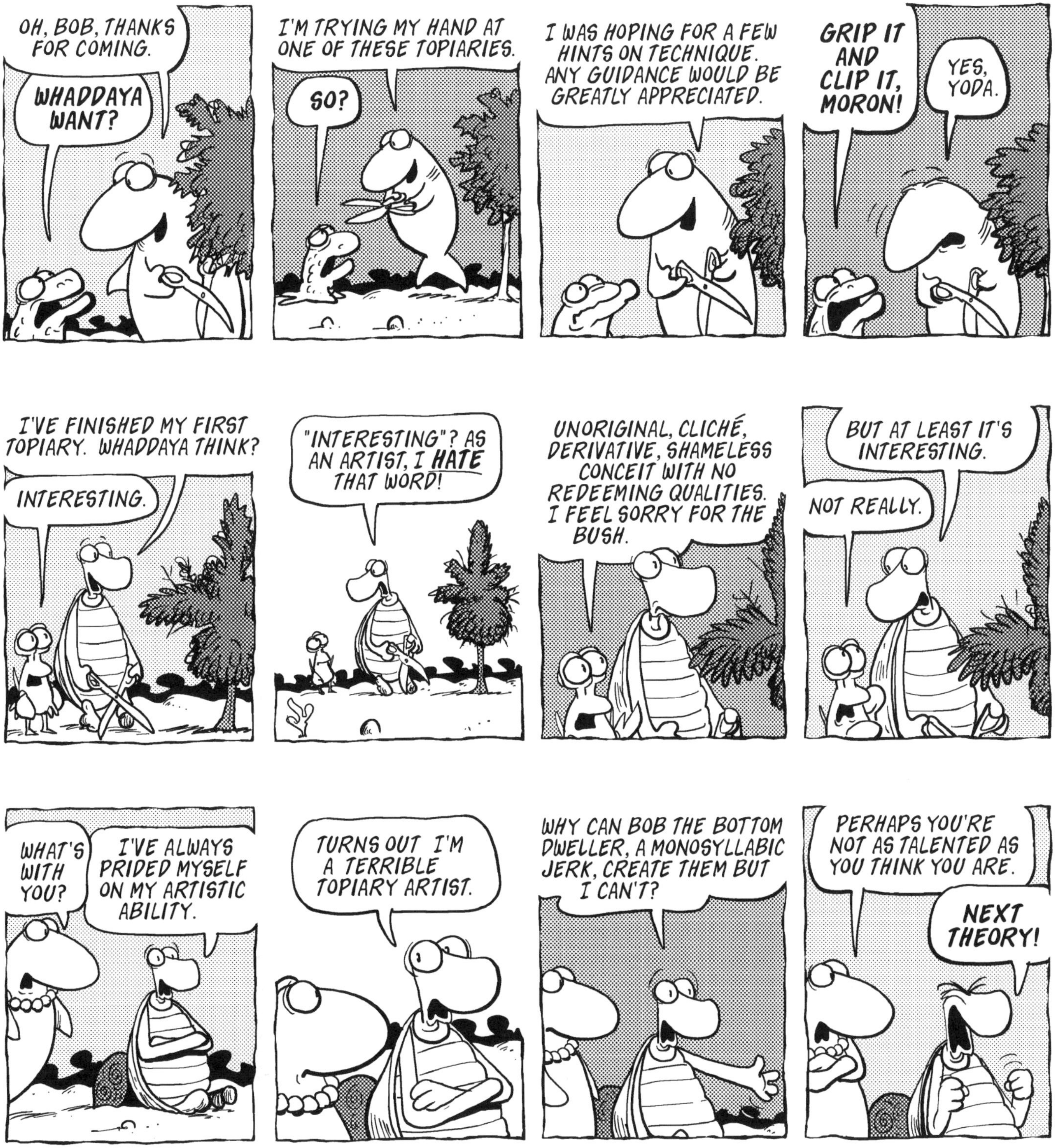
OH, BOB, THANKS FOR COMING.
WHADDAYA WANT?
I'M TRYING MY HAND AT ONE OF THESE TOPIARIES.
SO?
I WAS HOPING FOR A FEW HINTS ON TECHNIQUE. ANY GUIDANCE WOULD BE GREATLY APPRECIATED.
GRIP IT AND CLIP IT, MORON!
YES, YODA.
I'VE FINISHED MY FIRST TOPIARY. WHADDAYA THINK?
INTERESTING.
"INTERESTING"? AS AN ARTIST, I HATE THAT WORD!
UNORIGINAL, CLICHÉ, DERIVATIVE, SHAMELESS CONCEIT WITH NO REDEEMING QUALITIES. I FEEL SORRY FOR THE BUSH.
BUT AT LEAST IT'S INTERESTING.
NOT REALLY.
WHAT'S WITH YOU?
I'VE ALWAYS PRIDED MYSELF ON MY ARTISTIC ABILITY.
TURNS OUT I'M A TERRIBLE TOPIARY ARTIST.
WHY CAN BOB THE BOTTOM DWELLER, A MONOSYLLABIC JERK, CREATE THEM BUT I CAN'T?
PERHAPS YOU'RE NOT AS TALENTED AS YOU THINK YOU ARE.
NEXT THEORY!

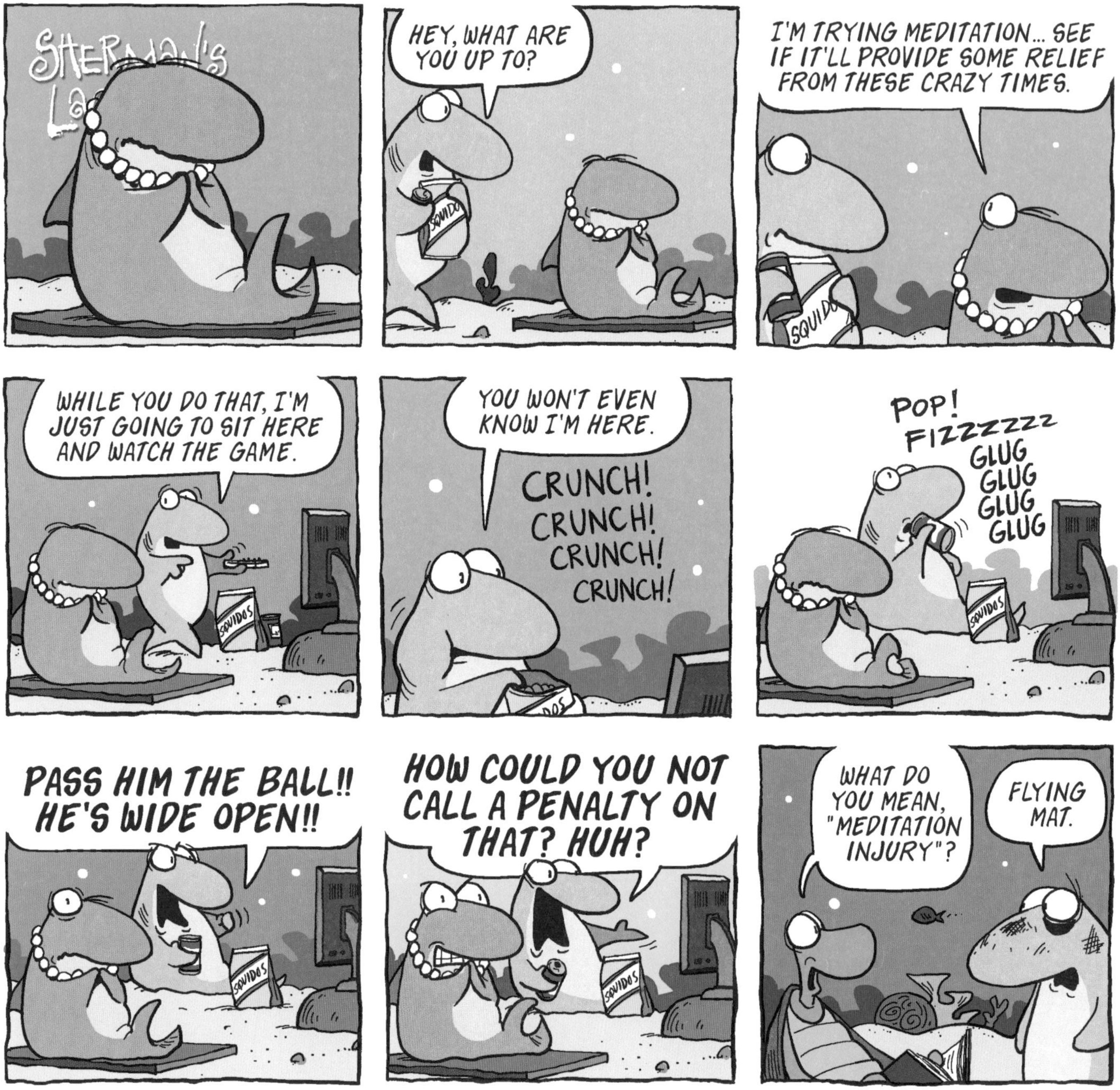
SHERMAN'S LAGOON
HEY, WHAT ARE YOU UP TO?
SQUIDOS
I'M TRYING MEDITATION... SEE IF IT'LL PROVIDE SOME RELIEF FROM THESE CRAZY TIMES.
SQUIDOS
WHILE YOU DO THAT, I'M JUST GOING TO SIT HERE AND WATCH THE GAME.
SQUIDOS
YOU WON'T EVEN KNOW I'M HERE.
CRUNCH! CRUNCH! CRUNCH! CRUNCH!
POP! FIZZZZZZ
GLUG GLUG GLUG GLUG
SQUIDOS
PASS HIM THE BALL!! HE'S WIDE OPEN!!
SQUIDOS
HOW COULD YOU NOT CALL A PENALTY ON THAT? HUH?
SQUIDOS
WHAT DO YOU MEAN, "MEDITATION INJURY"?
FLYING MAT.

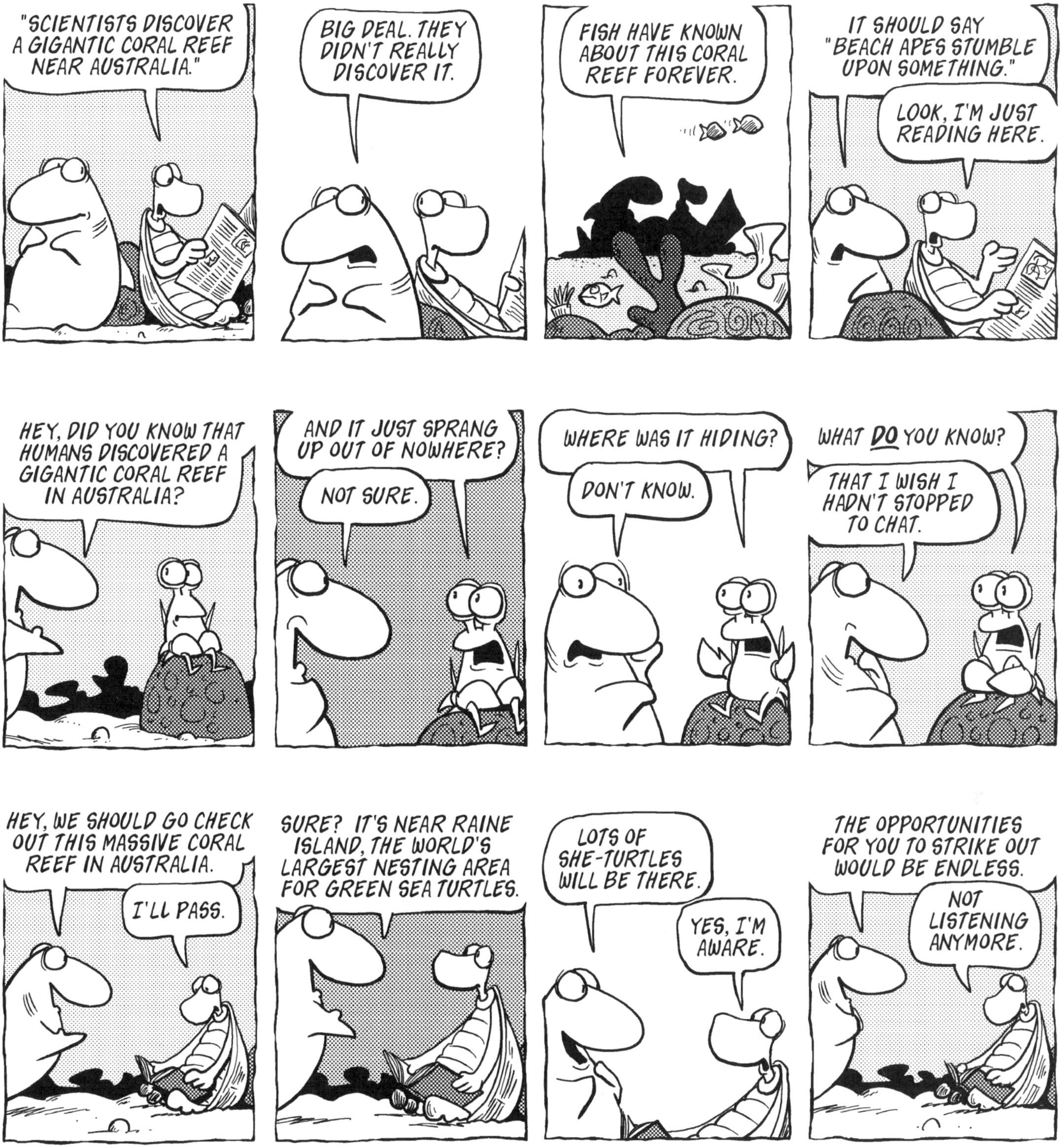
"SCIENTISTS DISCOVER A GIGANTIC CORAL REEF NEAR AUSTRALIA."
BIG DEAL. THEY DIDN'T REALLY DISCOVER IT.
FISH HAVE KNOWN ABOUT THIS CORAL REEF FOREVER.
IT SHOULD SAY "BEACH APES STUMBLE UPON SOMETHING."
LOOK, I'M JUST READING HERE.
HEY, DID YOU KNOW THAT HUMANS DISCOVERED A GIGANTIC CORAL REEF IN AUSTRALIA?
AND IT JUST SPRANG UP OUT OF NOWHERE?
NOT SURE.
WHERE WAS IT HIDING?
DON'T KNOW.
WHAT **DO** YOU KNOW?
THAT I WISH I HADN'T STOPPED TO CHAT.
HEY, WE SHOULD GO CHECK OUT THIS MASSIVE CORAL REEF IN AUSTRALIA.
I'LL PASS.
SURE? IT'S NEAR RAINE ISLAND, THE WORLD'S LARGEST NESTING AREA FOR GREEN SEA TURTLES.
LOTS OF SHE-TURTLES WILL BE THERE.
YES, I'M AWARE.
THE OPPORTUNITIES FOR YOU TO STRIKE OUT WOULD BE ENDLESS.
NOT LISTENING ANYMORE.

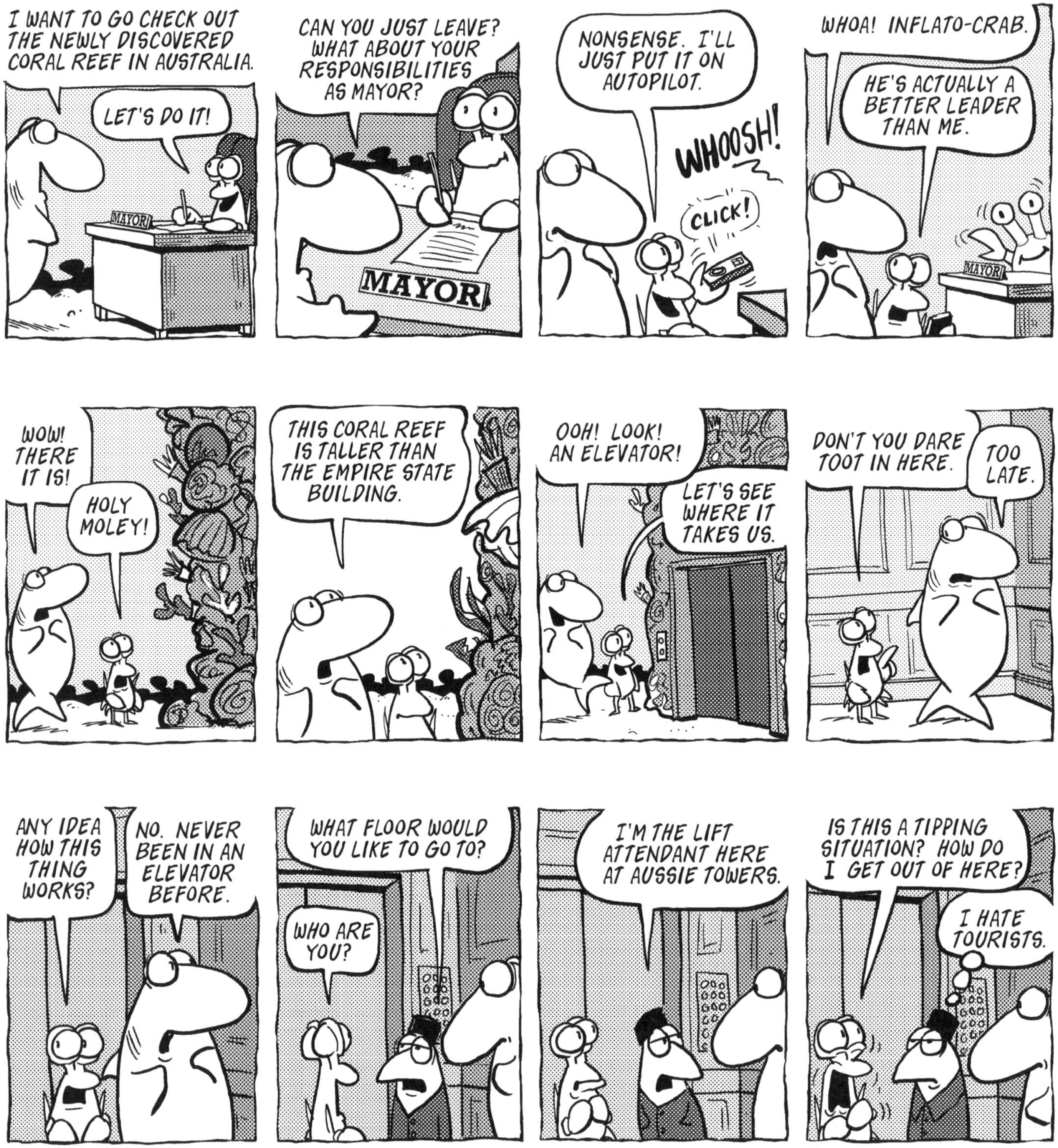
I WANT TO GO CHECK OUT THE NEWLY DISCOVERED CORAL REEF IN AUSTRALIA.
LET'S DO IT!
MAYOR
CAN YOU JUST LEAVE? WHAT ABOUT YOUR RESPONSIBILITIES AS MAYOR?
MAYOR
NONSENSE. I'LL JUST PUT IT ON AUTOPILOT.
WHOOSH!
CLICK!
WHOA! INFLATO-CRAB.
HE'S ACTUALLY A BETTER LEADER THAN ME.
MAYOR
WOW! THERE IT IS!
HOLY MOLEY!
THIS CORAL REEF IS TALLER THAN THE EMPIRE STATE BUILDING.
OOH! LOOK! AN ELEVATOR!
LET'S SEE WHERE IT TAKES US.
DON'T YOU DARE TOOT IN HERE.
TOO LATE.
ANY IDEA HOW THIS THING WORKS?
NO. NEVER BEEN IN AN ELEVATOR BEFORE.
WHAT FLOOR WOULD YOU LIKE TO GO TO?
WHO ARE YOU?
I'M THE LIFT ATTENDANT HERE AT AUSSIE TOWERS.
IS THIS A TIPPING SITUATION? HOW DO I GET OUT OF HERE?
I HATE TOURISTS.

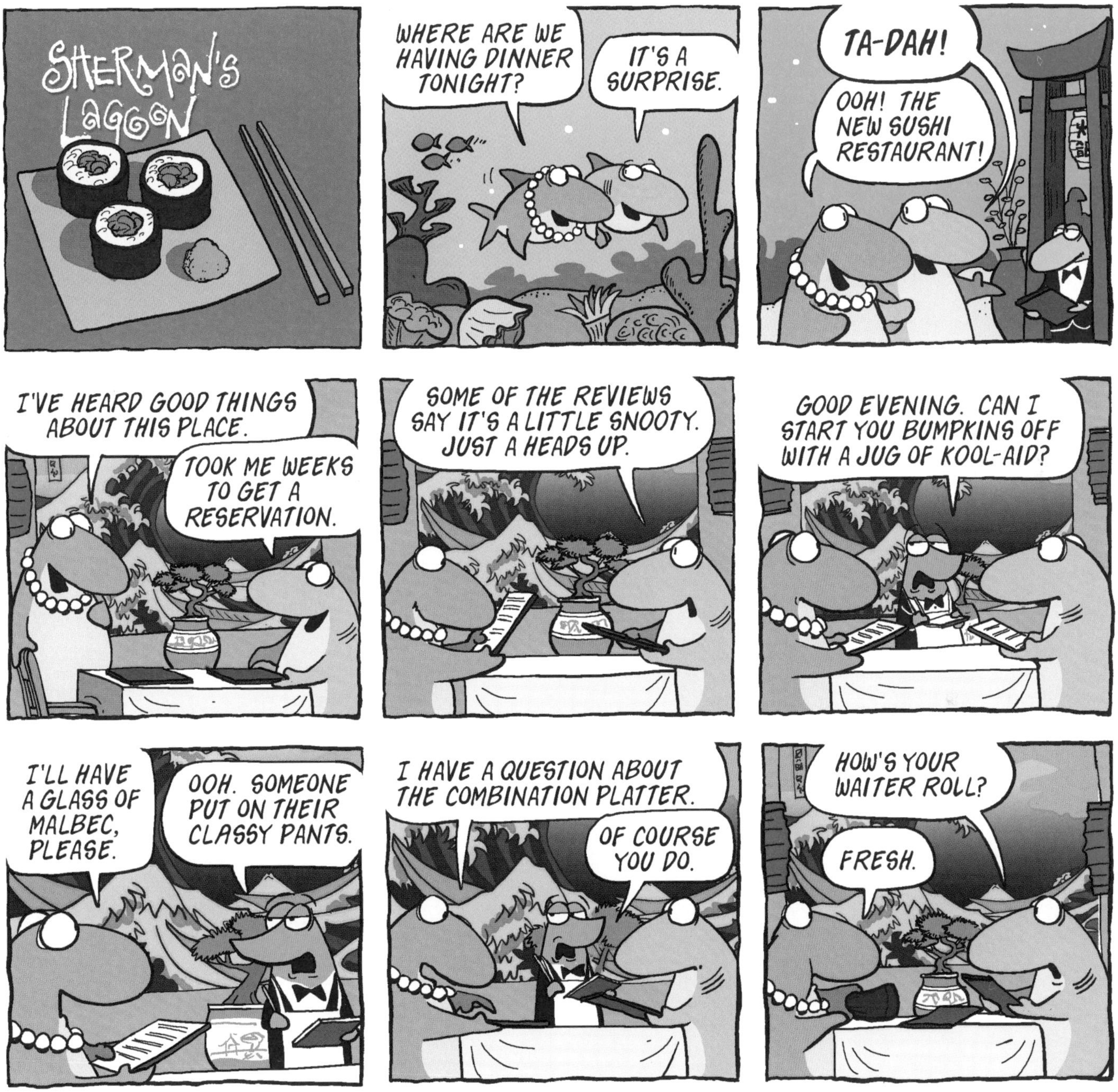
SHERMAN'S LAGOON
WHERE ARE WE HAVING DINNER TONIGHT?
IT'S A SURPRISE.
TA-DAH!
OOH! THE NEW SUSHI RESTAURANT!
I'VE HEARD GOOD THINGS ABOUT THIS PLACE.
TOOK ME WEEKS TO GET A RESERVATION.
SOME OF THE REVIEWS SAY IT'S A LITTLE SNOOTY. JUST A HEADS UP.
GOOD EVENING. CAN I START YOU BUMPKINS OFF WITH A JUG OF KOOL-AID?
I'LL HAVE A GLASS OF MALBEC, PLEASE.
OOH. SOMEONE PUT ON THEIR CLASSY PANTS.
I HAVE A QUESTION ABOUT THE COMBINATION PLATTER.
OF COURSE YOU DO.
HOW'S YOUR WAITER ROLL?
FRESH.

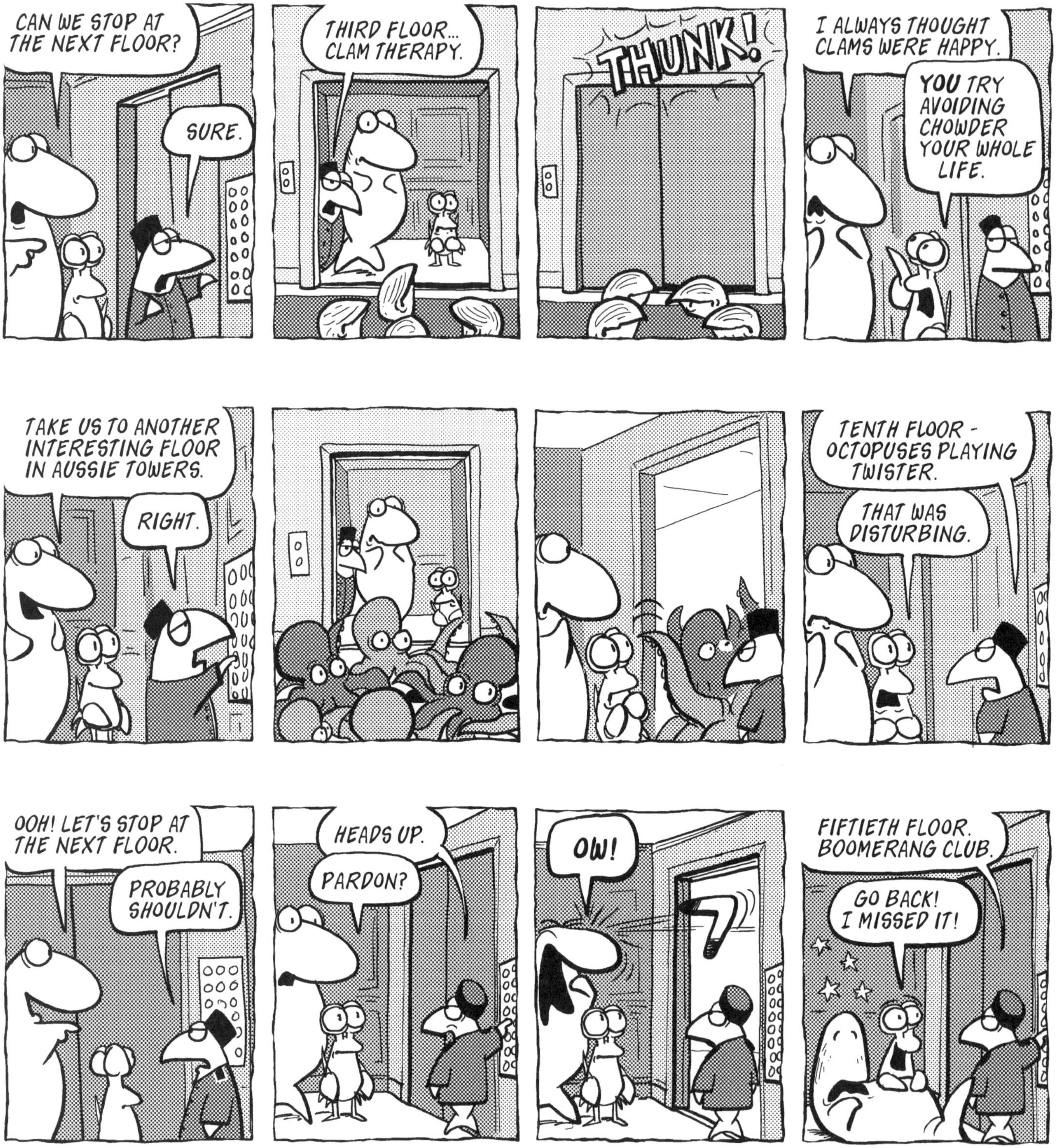
CAN WE STOP AT THE NEXT FLOOR?
SURE.
THIRD FLOOR... CLAM THERAPY.
THUNK!
I ALWAYS THOUGHT CLAMS WERE HAPPY.
YOU TRY AVOIDING CHOWDER YOUR WHOLE LIFE.
TAKE US TO ANOTHER INTERESTING FLOOR IN AUSSIE TOWERS.
RIGHT.
TENTH FLOOR - OCTOPUSES PLAYING TWISTER.
THAT WAS DISTURBING.
OOH! LET'S STOP AT THE NEXT FLOOR.
PROBABLY SHOULDN'T.
HEADS UP.
PARDON?
OW!
FIFTIETH FLOOR. BOOMERANG CLUB.
GO BACK! I MISSED IT!

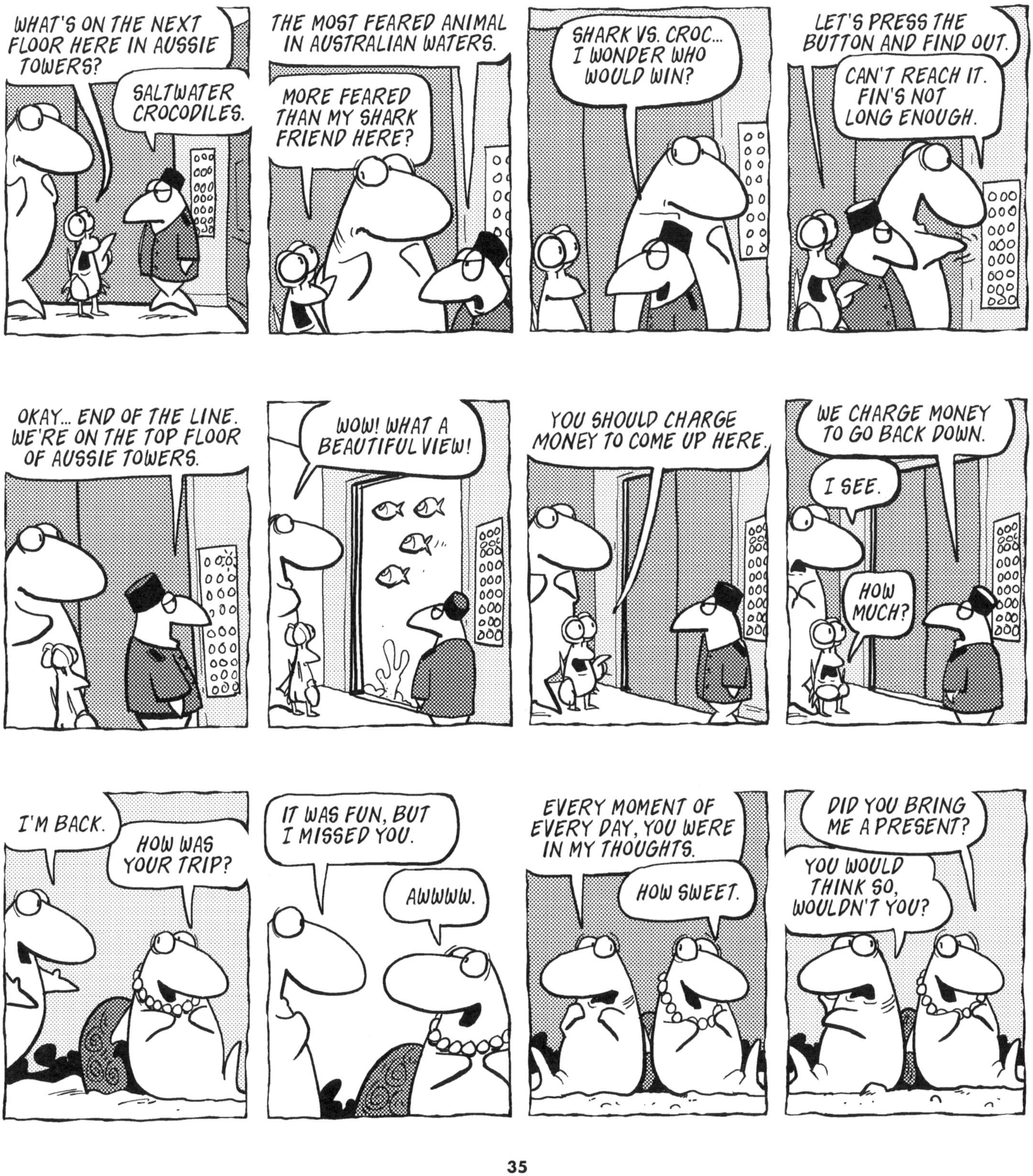
WHAT'S ON THE NEXT FLOOR HERE IN AUSSIE TOWERS?
SALTWATER CROCODILES.
THE MOST FEARED ANIMAL IN AUSTRALIAN WATERS.
MORE FEARED THAN MY SHARK FRIEND HERE?
SHARK VS. CROC... I WONDER WHO WOULD WIN?
LET'S PRESS THE BUTTON AND FIND OUT.
CAN'T REACH IT. FIN'S NOT LONG ENOUGH.
OKAY... END OF THE LINE. WE'RE ON THE TOP FLOOR OF AUSSIE TOWERS.
WOW! WHAT A BEAUTIFUL VIEW!
YOU SHOULD CHARGE MONEY TO COME UP HERE.
WE CHARGE MONEY TO GO BACK DOWN.
I SEE.
HOW MUCH?
I'M BACK.
HOW WAS YOUR TRIP?
IT WAS FUN, BUT I MISSED YOU.
AWWWW.
EVERY MOMENT OF EVERY DAY, YOU WERE IN MY THOUGHTS.
HOW SWEET.
DID YOU BRING ME A PRESENT?
YOU WOULD THINK SO, WOULDN'T YOU?

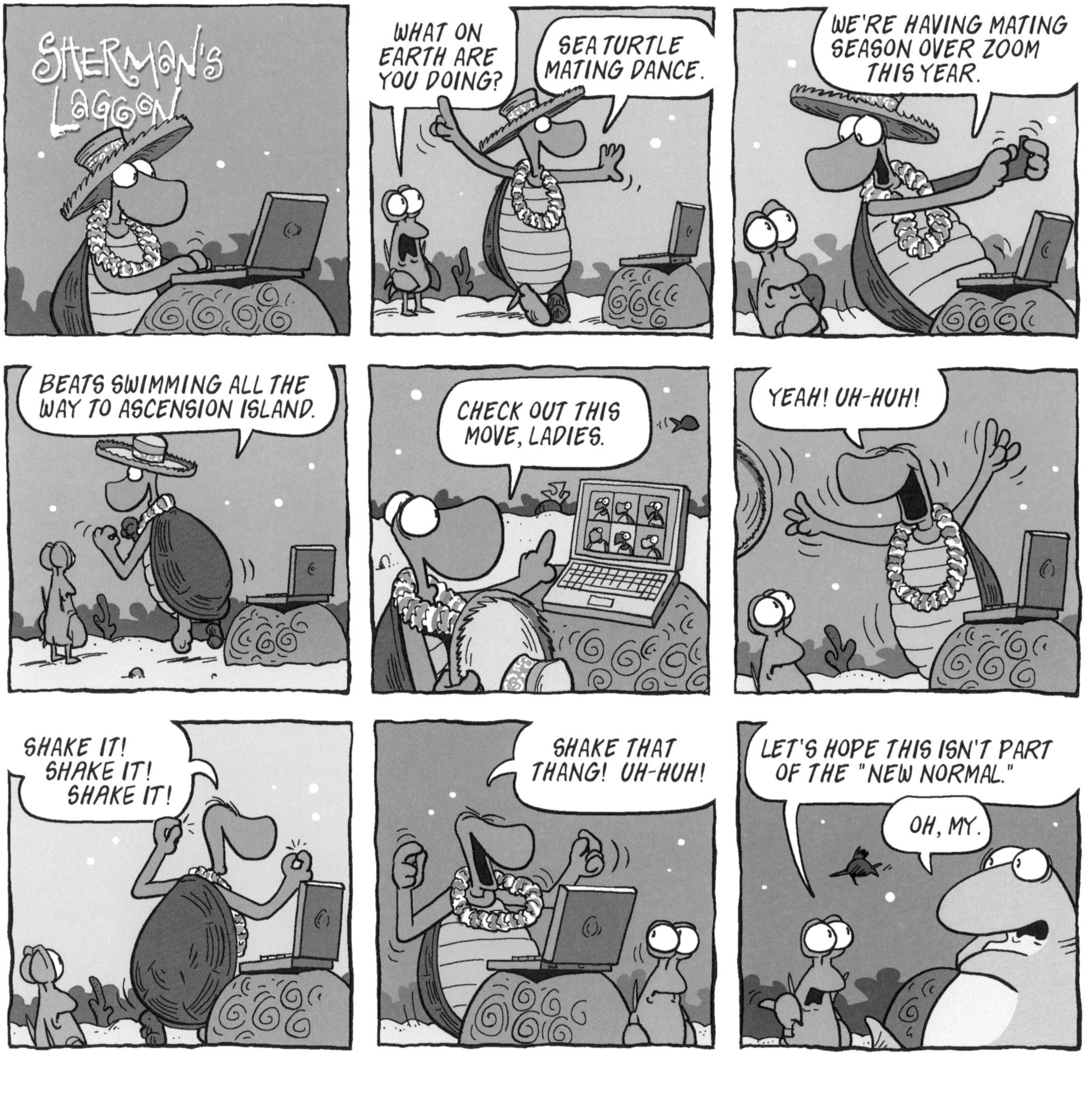
SHERMAN'S LAGOON
WHAT ON EARTH ARE YOU DOING?
SEA TURTLE MATING DANCE.
WE'RE HAVING MATING SEASON OVER ZOOM THIS YEAR.
BEATS SWIMMING ALL THE WAY TO ASCENSION ISLAND.
CHECK OUT THIS MOVE, LADIES.
YEAH! UH-HUH!
SHAKE IT! SHAKE IT! SHAKE IT!
SHAKE THAT THANG! UH-HUH!
LET'S HOPE THIS ISN'T PART OF THE "NEW NORMAL."
OH, MY.

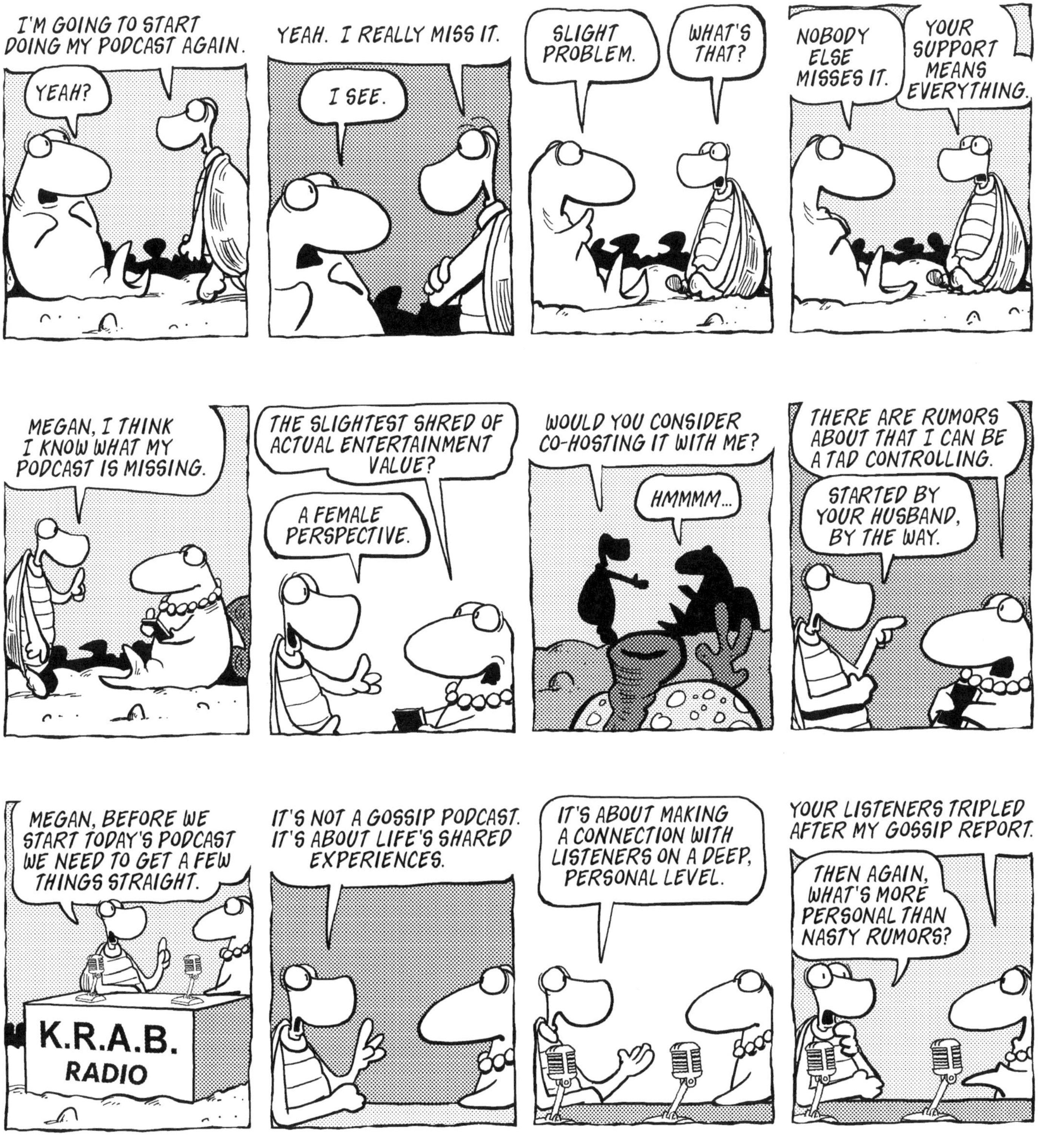
I'M GOING TO START DOING MY PODCAST AGAIN.
YEAH?
YEAH. I REALLY MISS IT.
I SEE.
SLIGHT PROBLEM.
WHAT'S THAT?
NOBODY ELSE MISSES IT.
YOUR SUPPORT MEANS EVERYTHING.
MEGAN, I THINK I KNOW WHAT MY PODCAST IS MISSING.
THE SLIGHTEST SHRED OF ACTUAL ENTERTAINMENT VALUE?
A FEMALE PERSPECTIVE.
WOULD YOU CONSIDER CO-HOSTING IT WITH ME?
HMMMM...
THERE ARE RUMORS ABOUT THAT I CAN BE A TAD CONTROLLING.
STARTED BY YOUR HUSBAND, BY THE WAY.
MEGAN, BEFORE WE START TODAY'S PODCAST WE NEED TO GET A FEW THINGS STRAIGHT.
K.R.A.B.
RADIO
IT'S NOT A GOSSIP PODCAST. IT'S ABOUT LIFE'S SHARED EXPERIENCES.
IT'S ABOUT MAKING A CONNECTION WITH LISTENERS ON A DEEP, PERSONAL LEVEL.
YOUR LISTENERS TRIPLED AFTER MY GOSSIP REPORT.
THEN AGAIN, WHAT'S MORE PERSONAL THAN NASTY RUMORS?

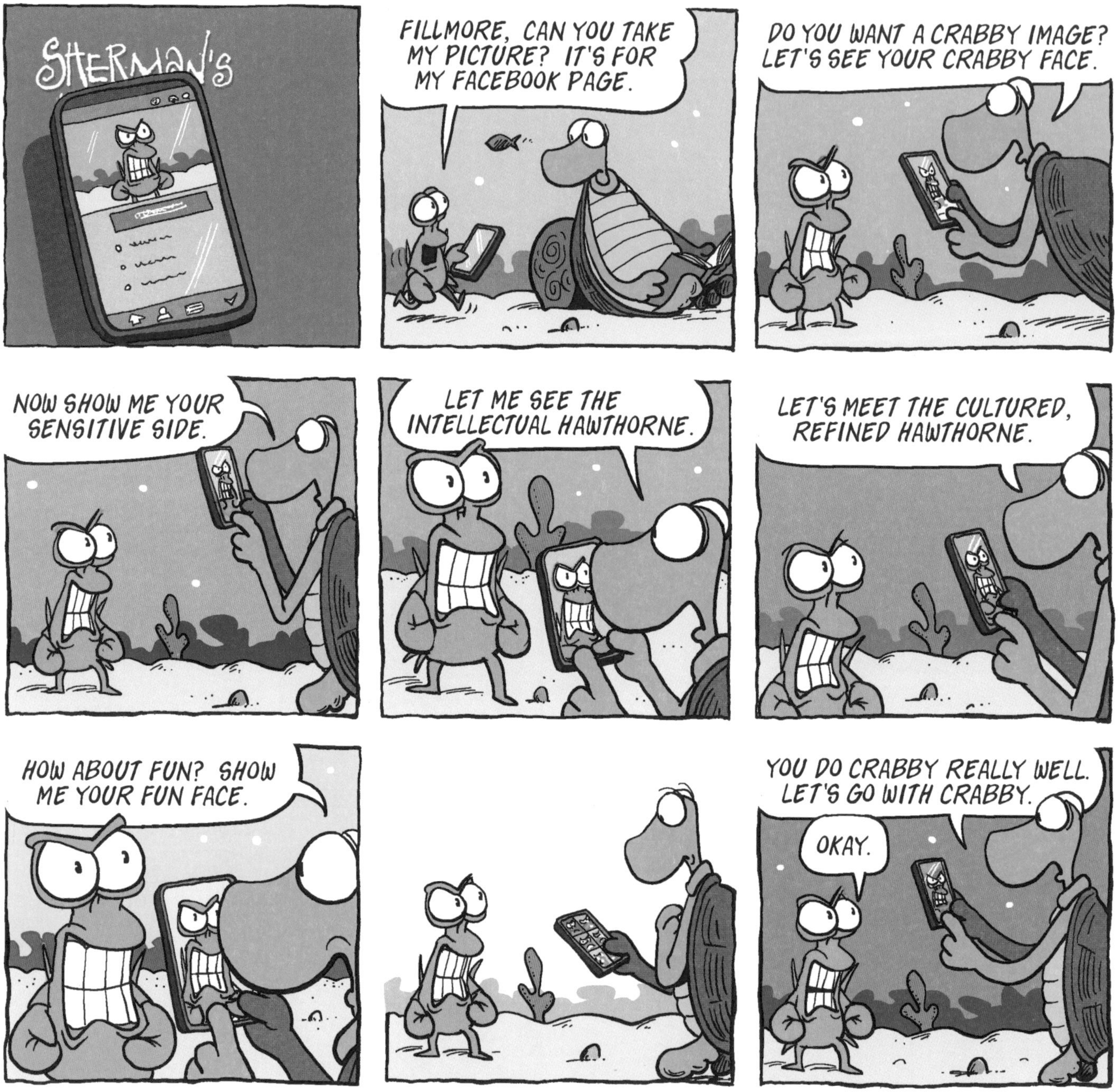
SHERMAN'S
FILLMORE, CAN YOU TAKE MY PICTURE? IT'S FOR MY FACEBOOK PAGE.
DO YOU WANT A CRABBY IMAGE? LET'S SEE YOUR CRABBY FACE.
NOW SHOW ME YOUR SENSITIVE SIDE.
LET ME SEE THE INTELLECTUAL HAWTHORNE.
LET'S MEET THE CULTURED, REFINED HAWTHORNE.
HOW ABOUT FUN? SHOW ME YOUR FUN FACE.
YOU DO CRABBY REALLY WELL. LET'S GO WITH CRABBY.
OKAY.

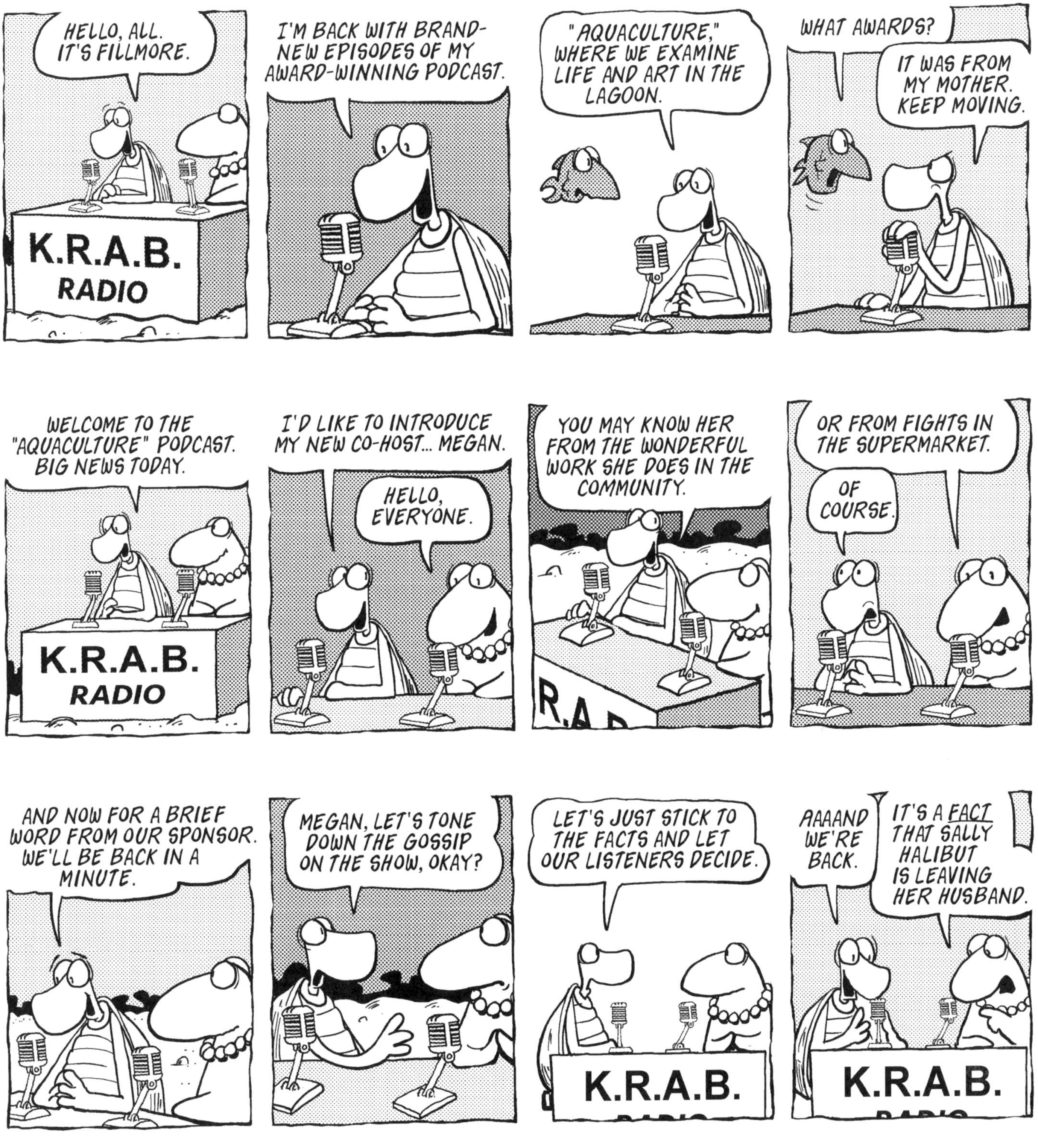
HELLO, ALL. IT'S FILLMORE.
K.R.A.B. RADIO
I'M BACK WITH BRAND-NEW EPISODES OF MY AWARD-WINNING PODCAST.
"AQUACULTURE," WHERE WE EXAMINE LIFE AND ART IN THE LAGOON.
WHAT AWARDS?
IT WAS FROM MY MOTHER. KEEP MOVING.
WELCOME TO THE "AQUACULTURE" PODCAST. BIG NEWS TODAY.
K.R.A.B. RADIO
I'D LIKE TO INTRODUCE MY NEW CO-HOST... MEGAN.
HELLO, EVERYONE.
YOU MAY KNOW HER FROM THE WONDERFUL WORK SHE DOES IN THE COMMUNITY.
OR FROM FIGHTS IN THE SUPERMARKET.
OF COURSE.
AND NOW FOR A BRIEF WORD FROM OUR SPONSOR. WE'LL BE BACK IN A MINUTE.
MEGAN, LET'S TONE DOWN THE GOSSIP ON THE SHOW, OKAY?
LET'S JUST STICK TO THE FACTS AND LET OUR LISTENERS DECIDE.
K.R.A.B.
AAAAND WE'RE BACK.
IT'S A FACT THAT SALLY HALIBUT IS LEAVING HER HUSBAND.
K.R.A.B.

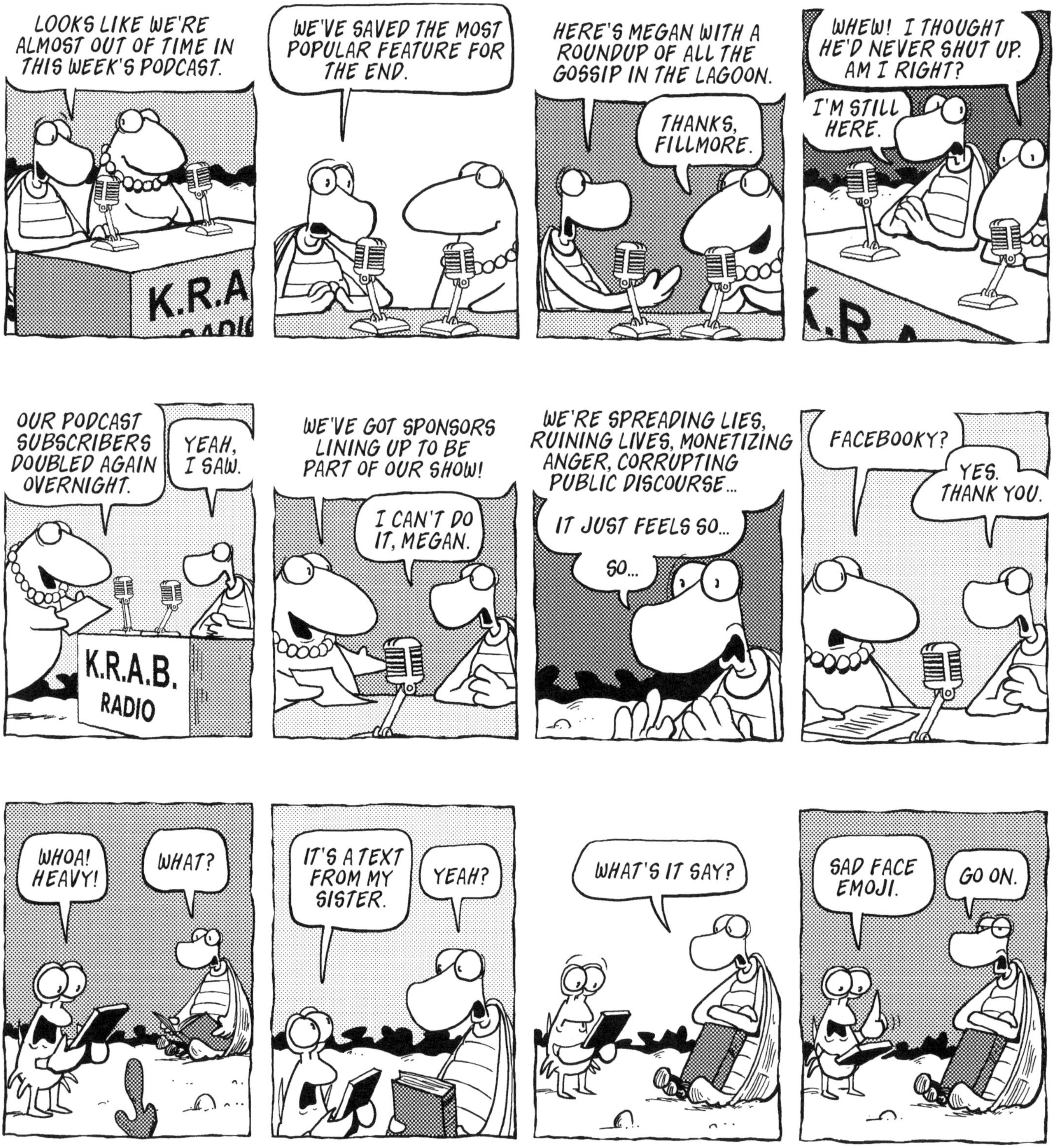
LOOKS LIKE WE'RE ALMOST OUT OF TIME IN THIS WEEK'S PODCAST.
K.R.A
WE'VE SAVED THE MOST POPULAR FEATURE FOR THE END.
HERE'S MEGAN WITH A ROUNDUP OF ALL THE GOSSIP IN THE LAGOON.
THANKS, FILLMORE.
WHEW! I THOUGHT HE'D NEVER SHUT UP. AM I RIGHT?
I'M STILL HERE.
OUR PODCAST SUBSCRIBERS DOUBLED AGAIN OVERNIGHT.
YEAH, I SAW.
K.R.A.B. RADIO
WE'VE GOT SPONSORS LINING UP TO BE PART OF OUR SHOW!
I CAN'T DO IT, MEGAN.
WE'RE SPREADING LIES, RUINING LIVES, MONETIZING ANGER, CORRUPTING PUBLIC DISCOURSE...
IT JUST FEELS SO...
SO...
FACEBOOKY?
YES. THANK YOU.
WHOA! HEAVY!
WHAT?
IT'S A TEXT FROM MY SISTER.
YEAH?
WHAT'S IT SAY?
SAD FACE EMOJI.
GO ON.

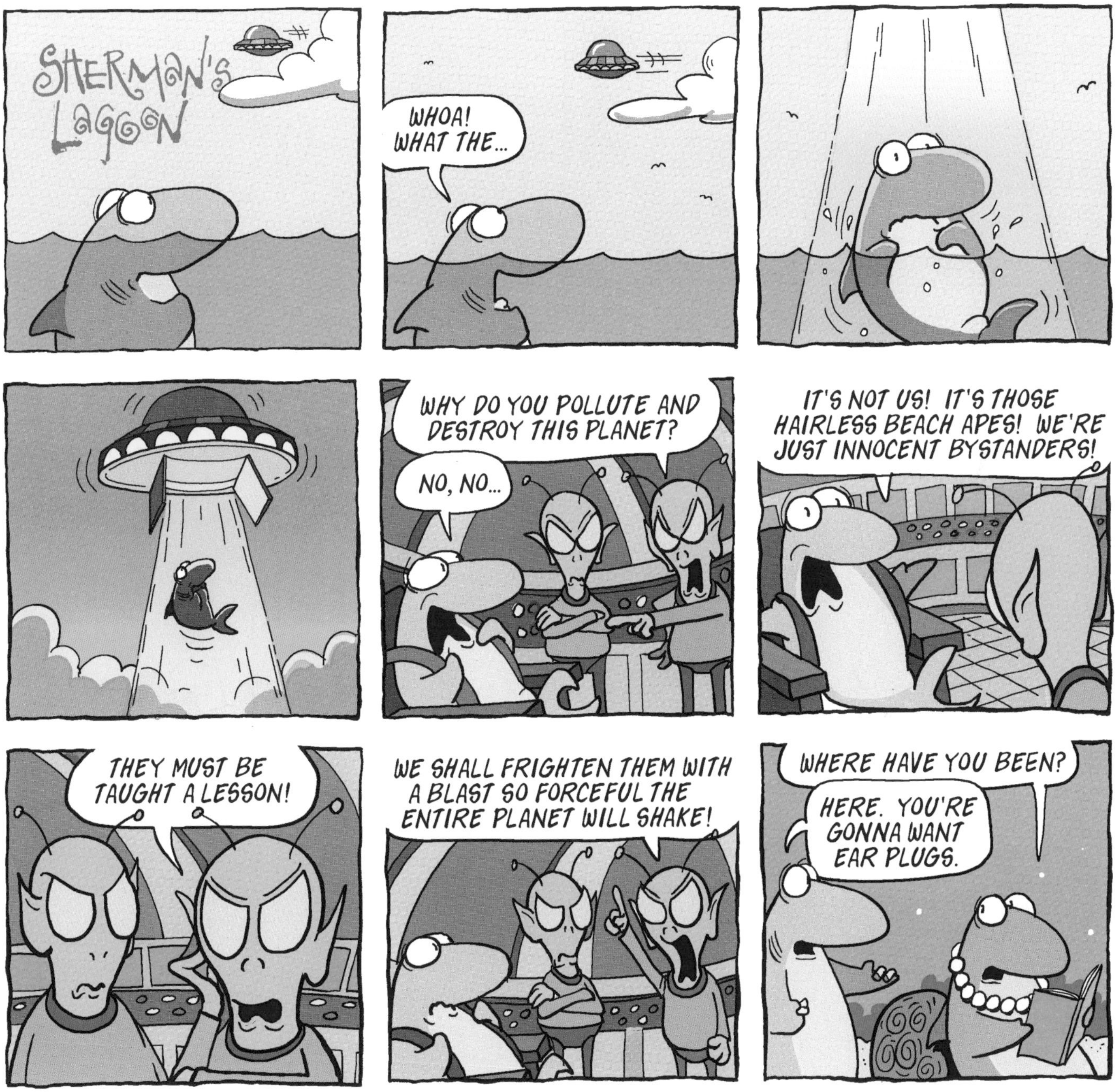
SHERMAN'S LAGOON
WHOA! WHAT THE...
WHY DO YOU POLLUTE AND DESTROY THIS PLANET?
NO, NO...
IT'S NOT US! IT'S THOSE HAIRLESS BEACH APES! WE'RE JUST INNOCENT BYSTANDERS!
THEY MUST BE TAUGHT A LESSON!
WE SHALL FRIGHTEN THEM WITH A BLAST SO FORCEFUL THE ENTIRE PLANET WILL SHAKE!
WHERE HAVE YOU BEEN?
HERE. YOU'RE GONNA WANT EAR PLUGS.

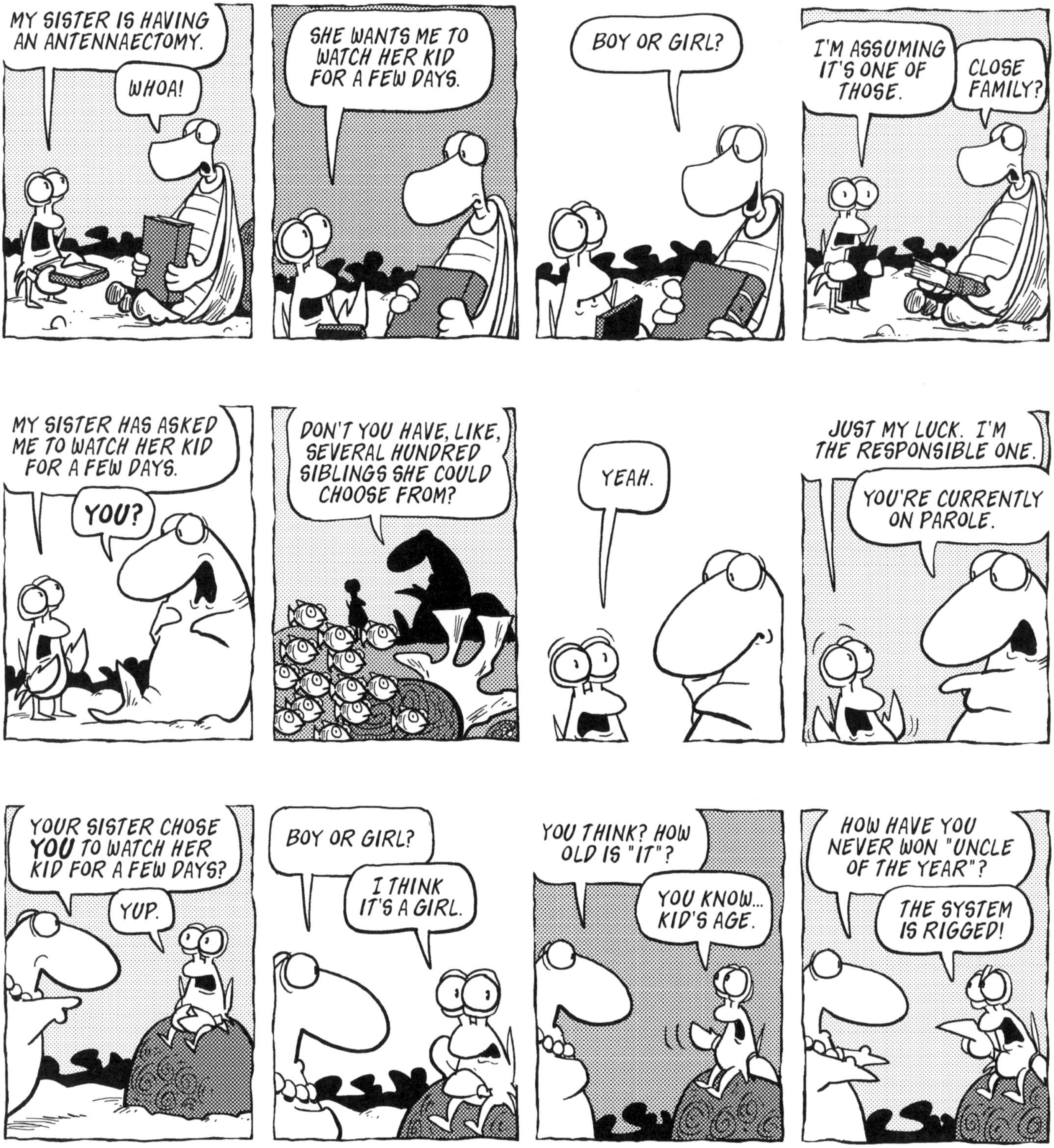
MY SISTER IS HAVING AN ANTENNAECTOMY.
WHOA!
SHE WANTS ME TO WATCH HER KID FOR A FEW DAYS.
BOY OR GIRL?
I'M ASSUMING IT'S ONE OF THOSE.
CLOSE FAMILY?
MY SISTER HAS ASKED ME TO WATCH HER KID FOR A FEW DAYS.
YOU?
DON'T YOU HAVE, LIKE, SEVERAL HUNDRED SIBLINGS SHE COULD CHOOSE FROM?
YEAH.
JUST MY LUCK. I'M THE RESPONSIBLE ONE.
YOU'RE CURRENTLY ON PAROLE.
YOUR SISTER CHOSE **YOU** TO WATCH HER KID FOR A FEW DAYS?
YUP.
BOY OR GIRL?
I THINK IT'S A GIRL.
YOU THINK? HOW OLD IS "IT"?
YOU KNOW... KID'S AGE.
HOW HAVE YOU NEVER WON "UNCLE OF THE YEAR"?
THE SYSTEM IS RIGGED!

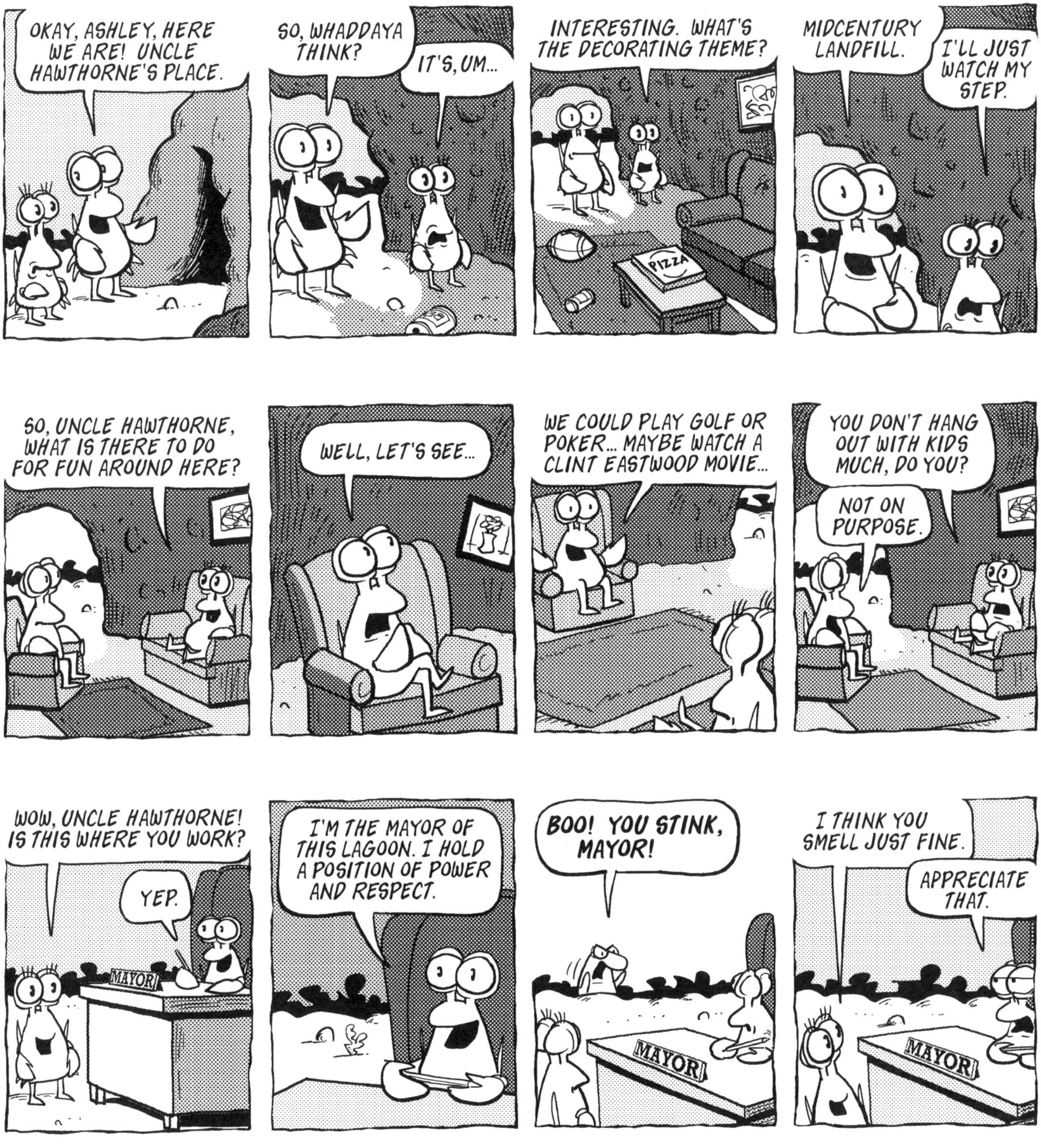

OKAY, ASHLEY, HERE WE ARE! UNCLE HAWTHORNE'S PLACE.
SO, WHADDAYA THINK?
IT'S, UM...
INTERESTING. WHAT'S THE DECORATING THEME?
PIZZA
MIDCENTURY LANDFILL.
I'LL JUST WATCH MY STEP.
SO, UNCLE HAWTHORNE, WHAT IS THERE TO DO FOR FUN AROUND HERE?
WELL, LET'S SEE...
WE COULD PLAY GOLF OR POKER... MAYBE WATCH A CLINT EASTWOOD MOVIE...
YOU DON'T HANG OUT WITH KIDS MUCH, DO YOU?
NOT ON PURPOSE.
WOW, UNCLE HAWTHORNE! IS THIS WHERE YOU WORK?
YEP.
MAYOR
I'M THE MAYOR OF THIS LAGOON. I HOLD A POSITION OF POWER AND RESPECT.
BOO! YOU STINK, MAYOR!
MAYOR
I THINK YOU SMELL JUST FINE.
APPRECIATE THAT.
MAYOR

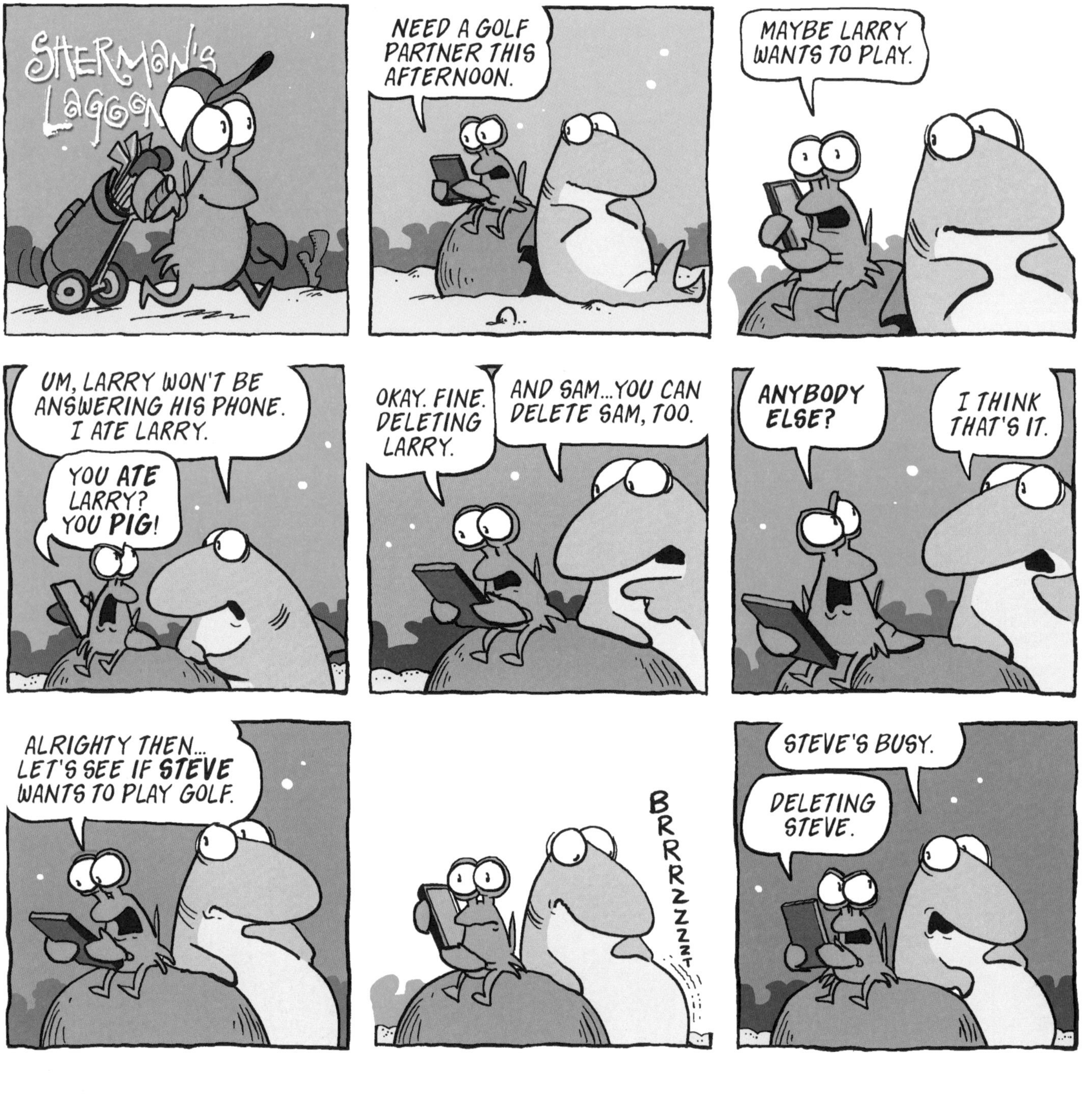
SHERMAN'S LAGOON
NEED A GOLF PARTNER THIS AFTERNOON.
MAYBE LARRY WANTS TO PLAY.
UM, LARRY WON'T BE ANSWERING HIS PHONE. I ATE LARRY.
YOU **ATE** LARRY? YOU **PIG**!
OKAY. FINE. DELETING LARRY.
AND SAM...YOU CAN DELETE SAM, TOO.
ANYBODY ELSE?
I THINK THAT'S IT.
ALRIGHTY THEN... LET'S SEE IF **STEVE** WANTS TO PLAY GOLF.
BRRRZZZZT
STEVE'S BUSY.
DELETING STEVE.

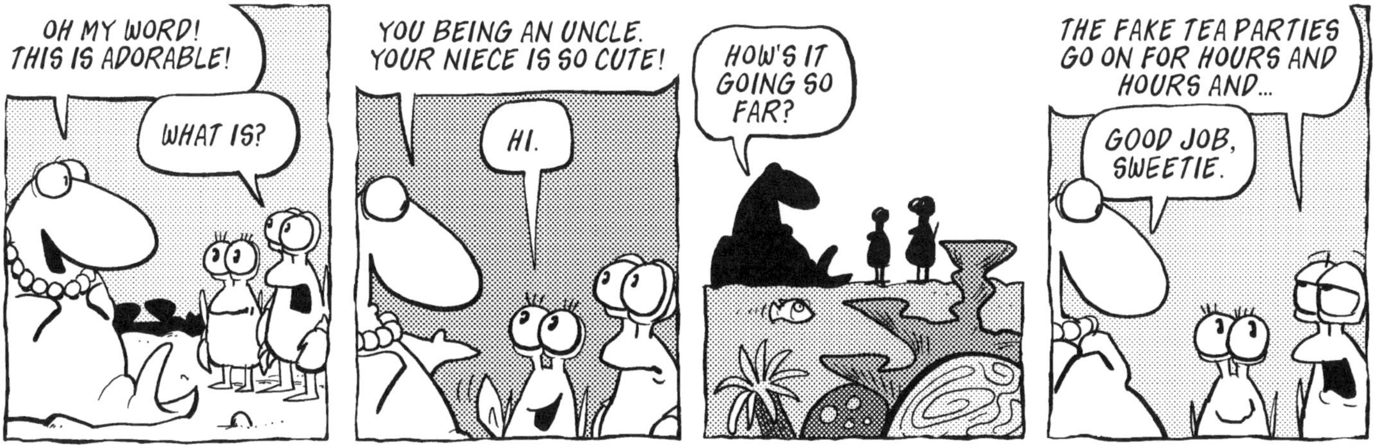
OH MY WORD! THIS IS ADORABLE!
WHAT IS?
YOU BEING AN UNCLE. YOUR NIECE IS SO CUTE!
HI.
HOW'S IT GOING SO FAR?
THE FAKE TEA PARTIES GO ON FOR HOURS AND HOURS AND...
GOOD JOB, SWEETIE.

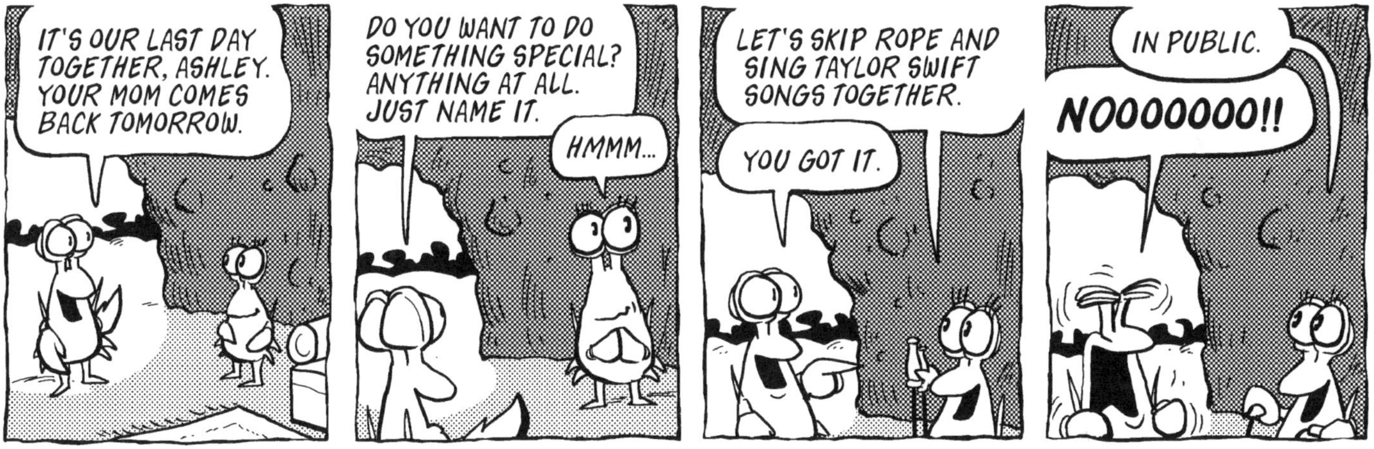
IT'S OUR LAST DAY TOGETHER, ASHLEY. YOUR MOM COMES BACK TOMORROW.
DO YOU WANT TO DO SOMETHING SPECIAL? ANYTHING AT ALL. JUST NAME IT.
HMMM...
LET'S SKIP ROPE AND SING TAYLOR SWIFT SONGS TOGETHER.
YOU GOT IT.
IN PUBLIC.
NOOOOOOO!!

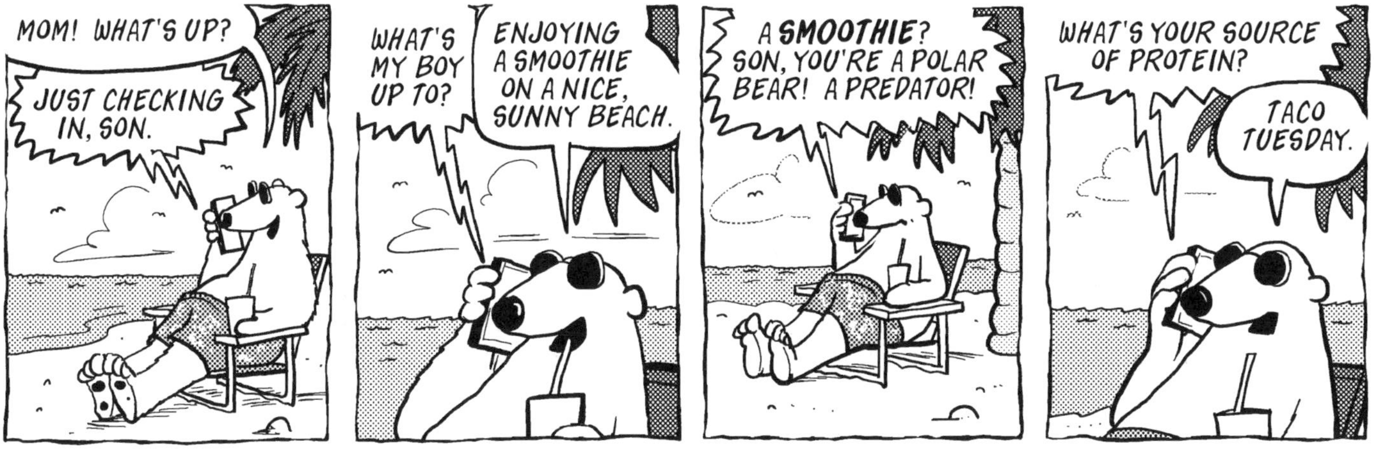
MOM! WHAT'S UP?
JUST CHECKING IN, SON.
WHAT'S MY BOY UP TO?
ENJOYING A SMOOTHIE ON A NICE, SUNNY BEACH.
A SMOOTHIE? SON, YOU'RE A POLAR BEAR! A PREDATOR!
WHAT'S YOUR SOURCE OF PROTEIN?
TACO TUESDAY.

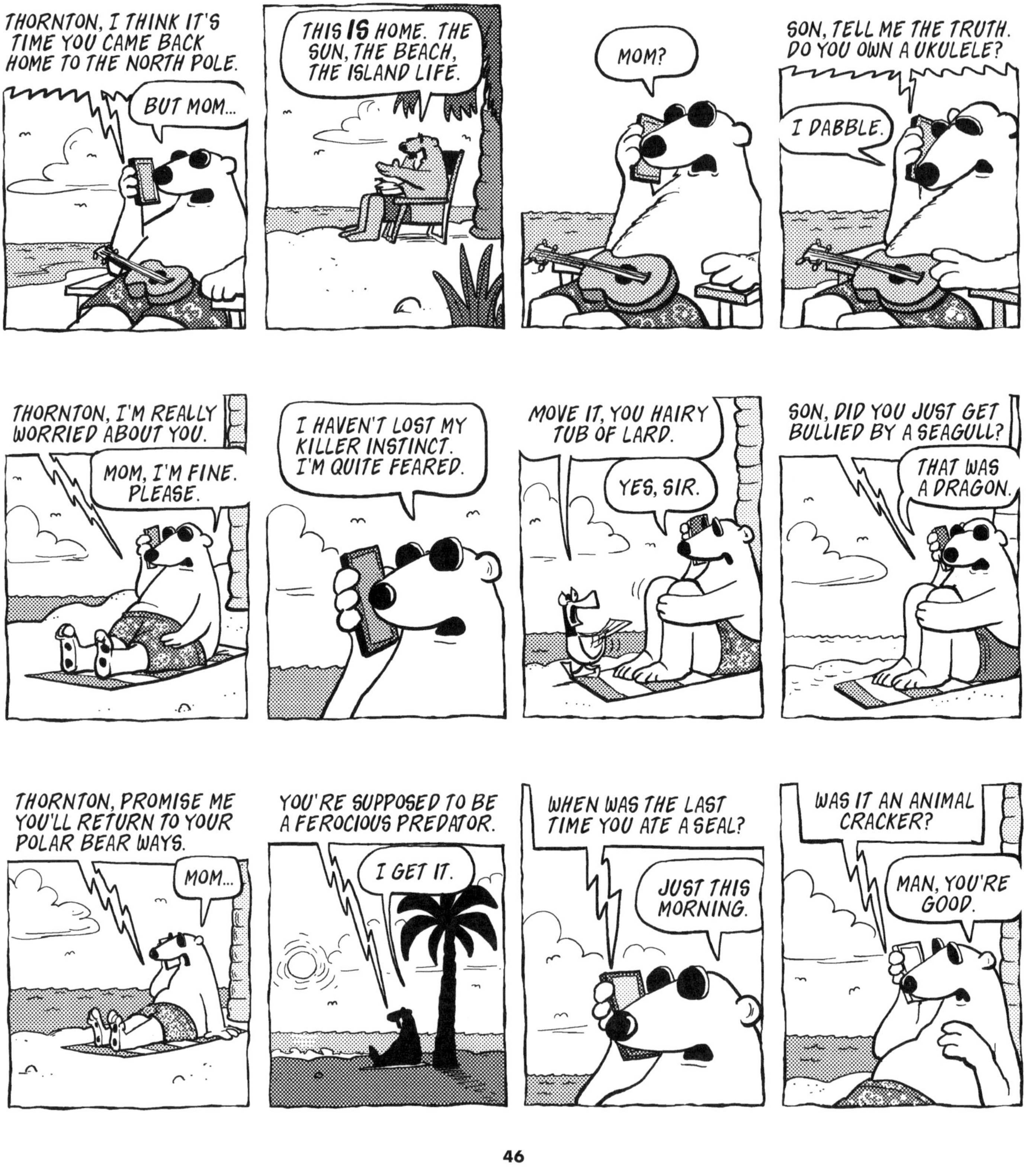
THORNTON, I THINK IT'S TIME YOU CAME BACK HOME TO THE NORTH POLE.
BUT MOM...
THIS IS HOME. THE SUN, THE BEACH, THE ISLAND LIFE.
MOM?
SON, TELL ME THE TRUTH. DO YOU OWN A UKULELE?
I DABBLE.
THORNTON, I'M REALLY WORRIED ABOUT YOU.
MOM, I'M FINE. PLEASE.
I HAVEN'T LOST MY KILLER INSTINCT. I'M QUITE FEARED.
MOVE IT, YOU HAIRY TUB OF LARD.
YES, SIR.
SON, DID YOU JUST GET BULLIED BY A SEAGULL?
THAT WAS A DRAGON.
THORNTON, PROMISE ME YOU'LL RETURN TO YOUR POLAR BEAR WAYS.
MOM...
YOU'RE SUPPOSED TO BE A FEROCIOUS PREDATOR.
I GET IT.
WHEN WAS THE LAST TIME YOU ATE A SEAL?
JUST THIS MORNING.
WAS IT AN ANIMAL CRACKER?
MAN, YOU'RE GOOD.

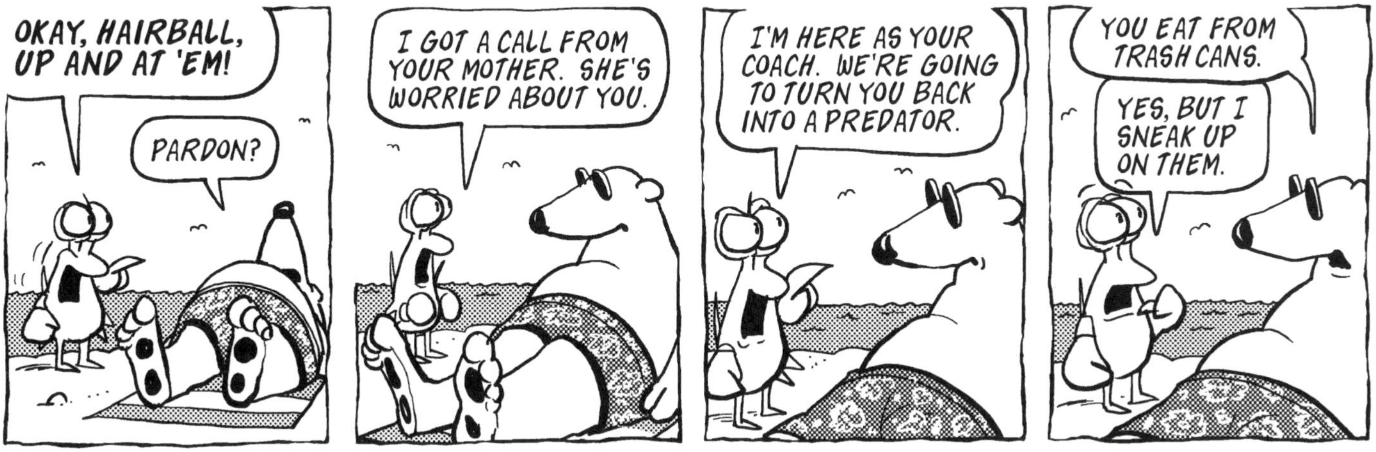
OKAY, HAIRBALL, UP AND AT 'EM!
PARDON?
I GOT A CALL FROM YOUR MOTHER. SHE'S WORRIED ABOUT YOU.
I'M HERE AS YOUR COACH. WE'RE GOING TO TURN YOU BACK INTO A PREDATOR.
YOU EAT FROM TRASH CANS.
YES, BUT I SNEAK UP ON THEM.

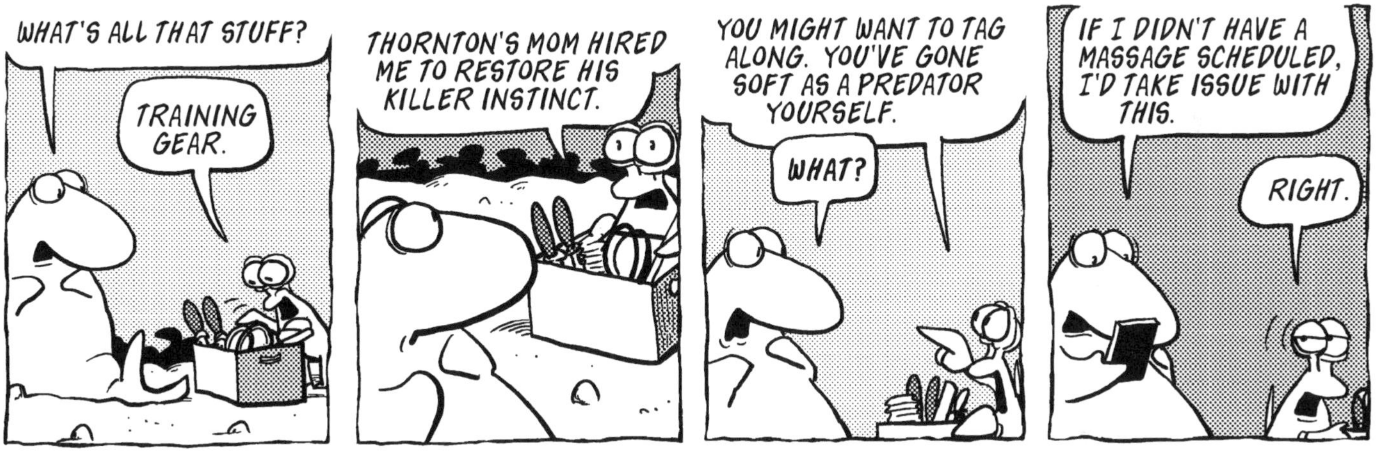
WHAT'S ALL THAT STUFF?
TRAINING GEAR.
THORNTON'S MOM HIRED ME TO RESTORE HIS KILLER INSTINCT.
YOU MIGHT WANT TO TAG ALONG. YOU'VE GONE SOFT AS A PREDATOR YOURSELF.
WHAT?
IF I DIDN'T HAVE A MASSAGE SCHEDULED, I'D TAKE ISSUE WITH THIS.
RIGHT.

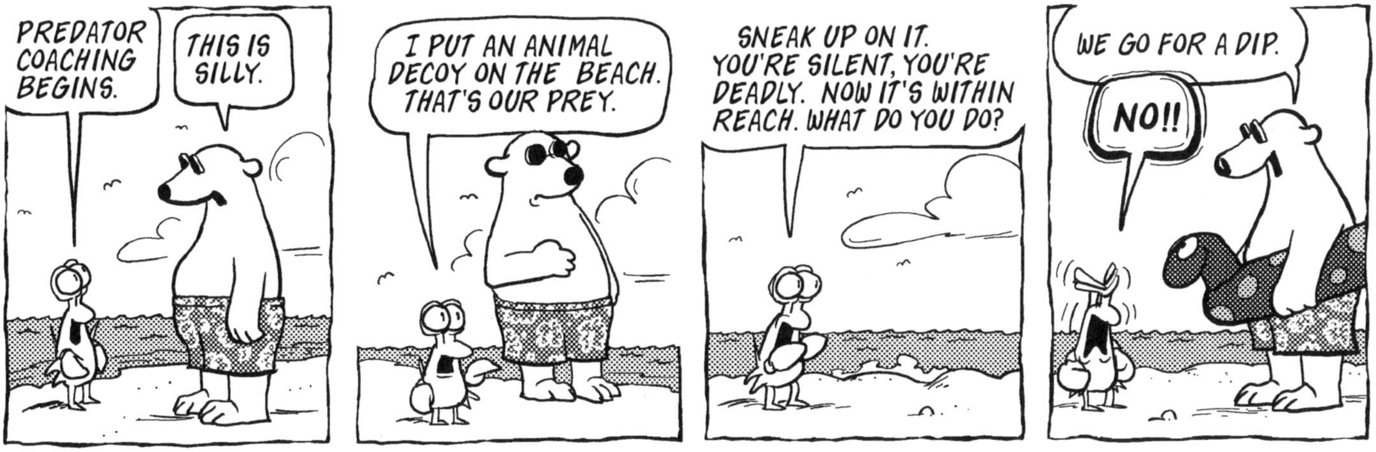
PREDATOR COACHING BEGINS.
THIS IS SILLY.
I PUT AN ANIMAL DECOY ON THE BEACH. THAT'S OUR PREY.
SNEAK UP ON IT. YOU'RE SILENT, YOU'RE DEADLY. NOW IT'S WITHIN REACH. WHAT DO YOU DO?
WE GO FOR A DIP.
NO!!

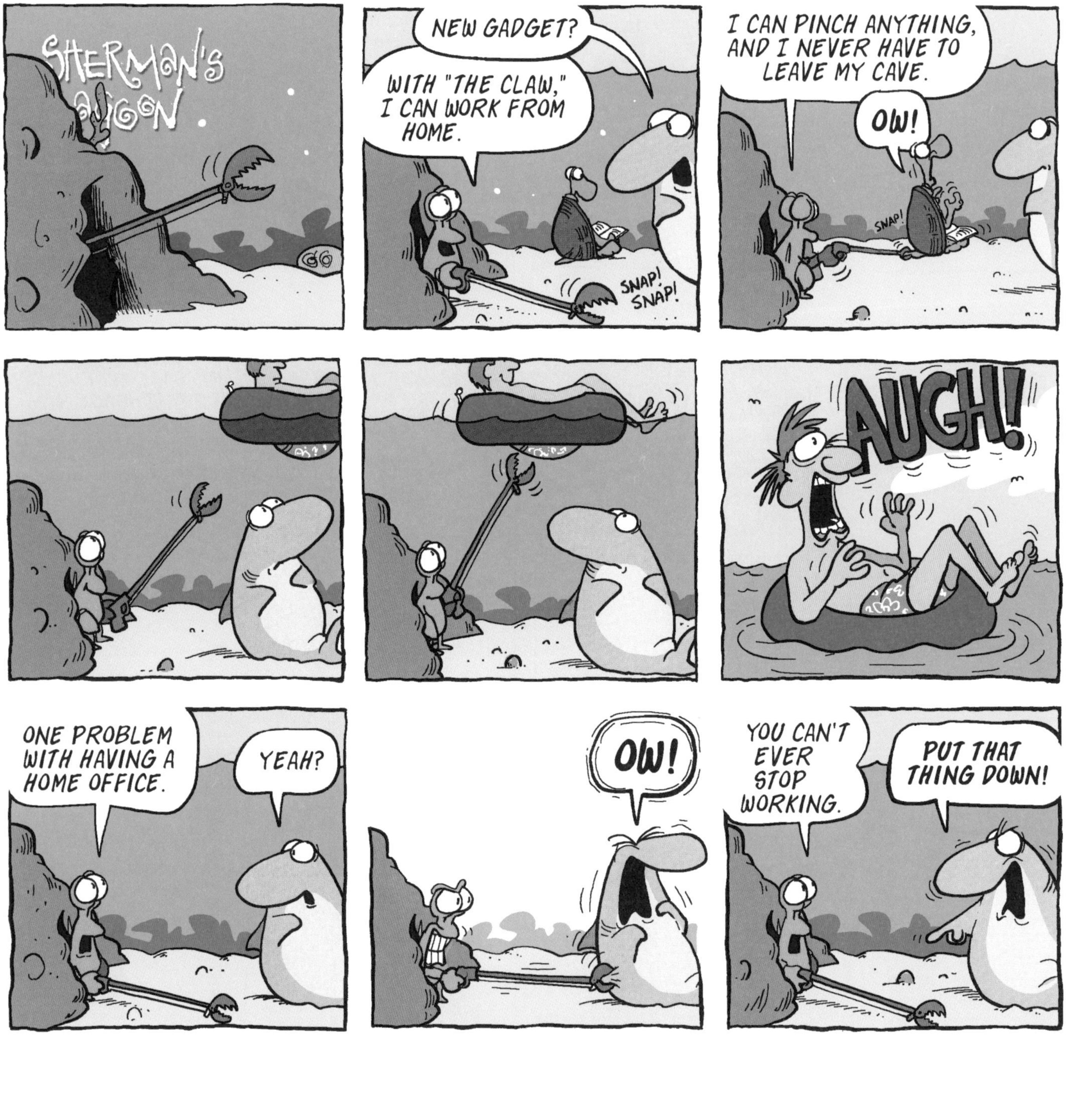
SHERMAN'S LAGOON
NEW GADGET?
WITH "THE CLAW," I CAN WORK FROM HOME.
SNAP! SNAP!
I CAN PINCH ANYTHING, AND I NEVER HAVE TO LEAVE MY CAVE.
OW!
SNAP!
AUGH!
ONE PROBLEM WITH HAVING A HOME OFFICE.
YEAH?
OW!
YOU CAN'T EVER STOP WORKING.
PUT THAT THING DOWN!

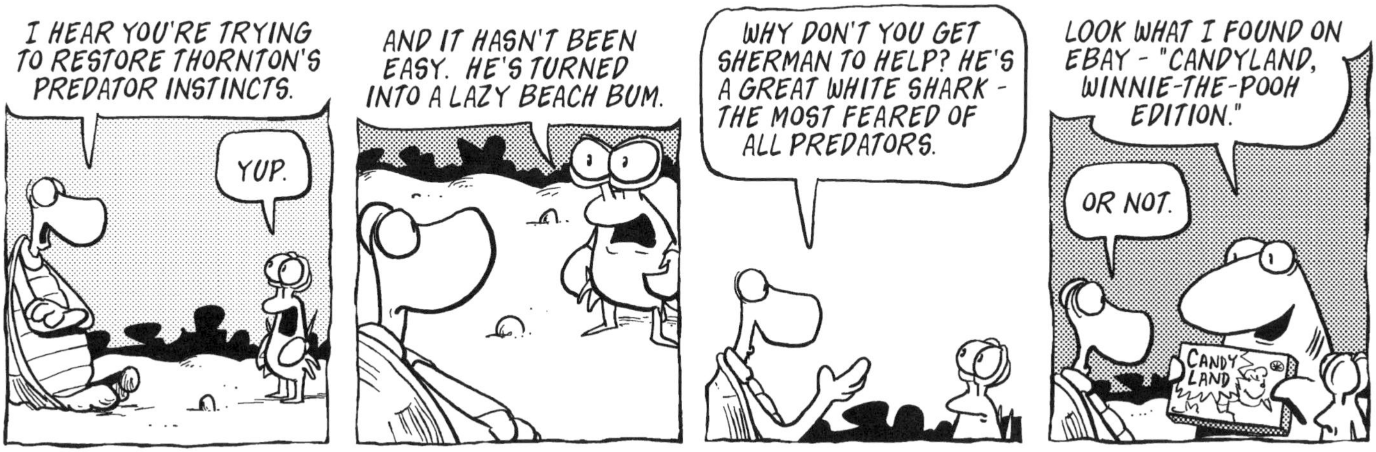
I HEAR YOU'RE TRYING TO RESTORE THORNTON'S PREDATOR INSTINCTS.
YUP.
AND IT HASN'T BEEN EASY. HE'S TURNED INTO A LAZY BEACH BUM.
WHY DON'T YOU GET SHERMAN TO HELP? HE'S A GREAT WHITE SHARK - THE MOST FEARED OF ALL PREDATORS.
LOOK WHAT I FOUND ON EBAY - "CANDYLAND, WINNIE-THE-POOH EDITION."
OR NOT.
CANDY LAND

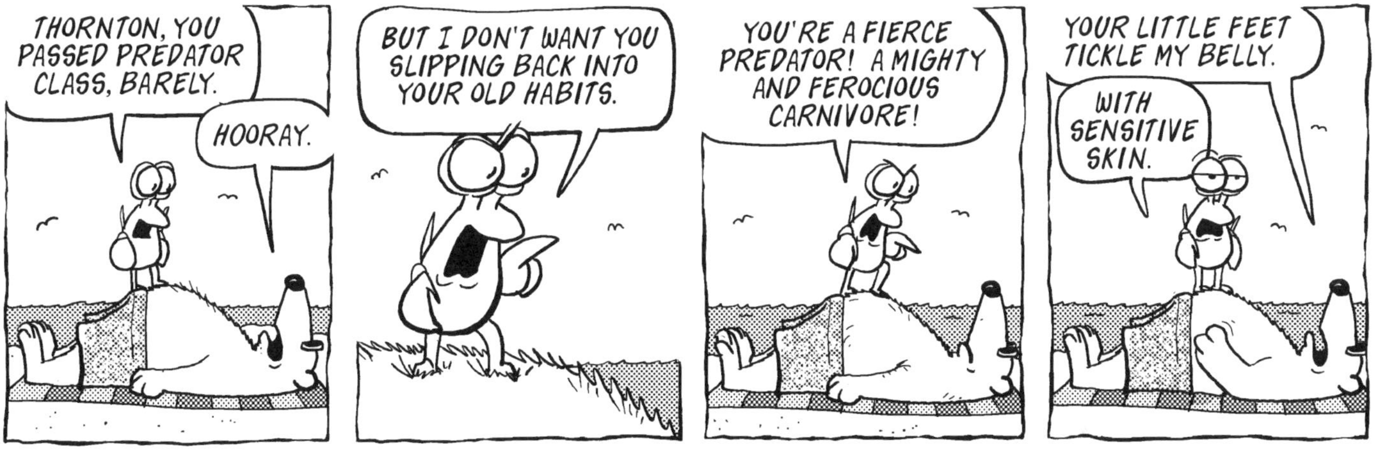
THORNTON, YOU PASSED PREDATOR CLASS, BARELY.
HOORAY.
BUT I DON'T WANT YOU SLIPPING BACK INTO YOUR OLD HABITS.
YOU'RE A FIERCE PREDATOR! A MIGHTY AND FEROCIOUS CARNIVORE!
YOUR LITTLE FEET TICKLE MY BELLY.
WITH SENSITIVE SKIN.

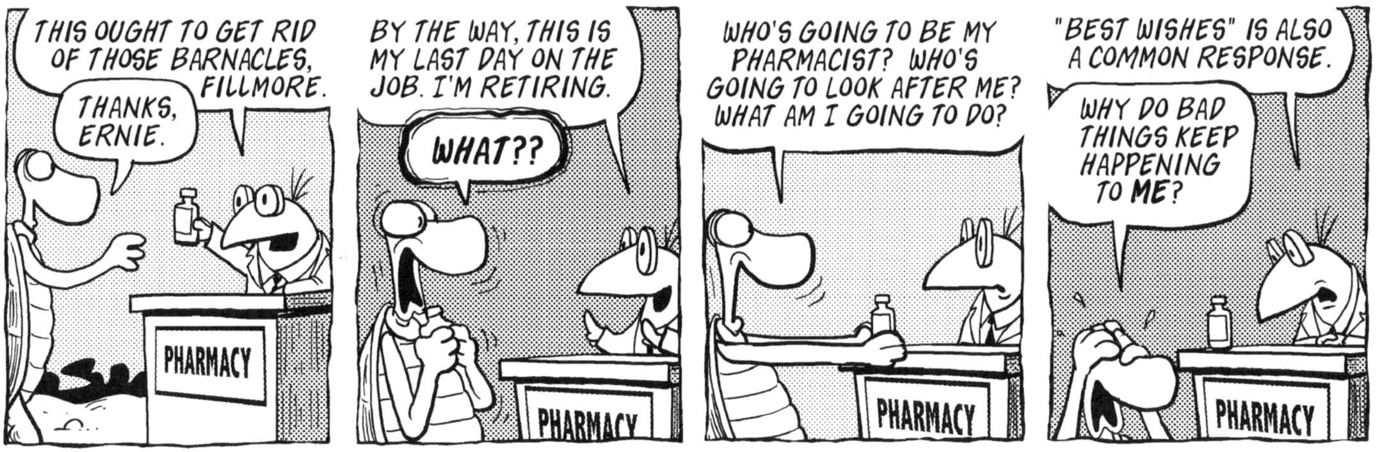
THIS OUGHT TO GET RID OF THOSE BARNACLES, FILLMORE.
THANKS, ERNIE.
PHARMACY
BY THE WAY, THIS IS MY LAST DAY ON THE JOB. I'M RETIRING.
WHAT??
PHARMACY
WHO'S GOING TO BE MY PHARMACIST? WHO'S GOING TO LOOK AFTER ME? WHAT AM I GOING TO DO?
PHARMACY
"BEST WISHES" IS ALSO A COMMON RESPONSE.
WHY DO BAD THINGS KEEP HAPPENING TO **ME**?
PHARMACY

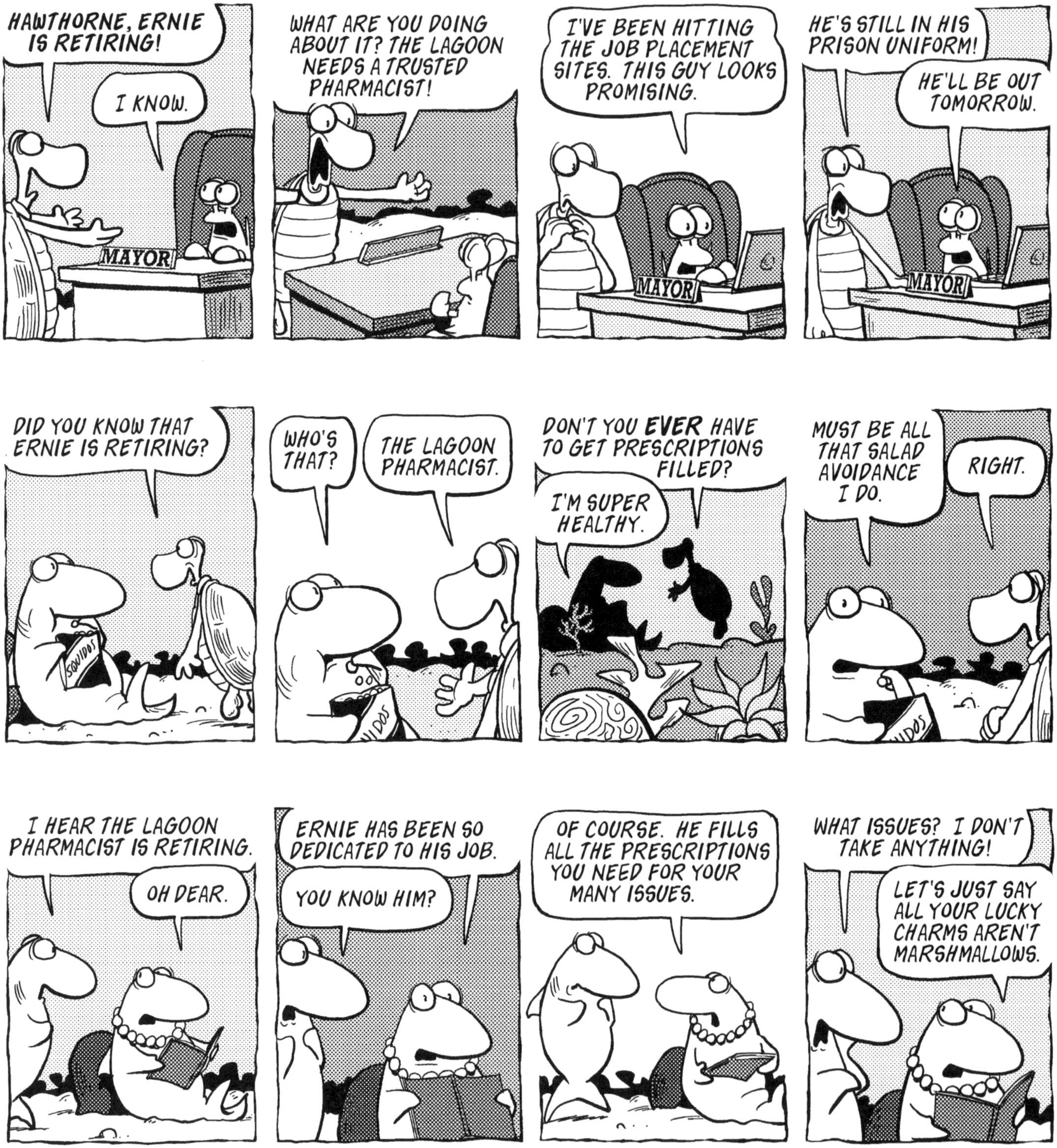
HAWTHORNE, ERNIE IS RETIRING!
I KNOW.
MAYOR
WHAT ARE YOU DOING ABOUT IT? THE LAGOON NEEDS A TRUSTED PHARMACIST!
I'VE BEEN HITTING THE JOB PLACEMENT SITES. THIS GUY LOOKS PROMISING.
MAYOR
HE'S STILL IN HIS PRISON UNIFORM!
HE'LL BE OUT TOMORROW.
MAYOR
DID YOU KNOW THAT ERNIE IS RETIRING?
SQUIDOS
WHO'S THAT?
THE LAGOON PHARMACIST.
DON'T YOU EVER HAVE TO GET PRESCRIPTIONS FILLED?
I'M SUPER HEALTHY.
MUST BE ALL THAT SALAD AVOIDANCE I DO.
RIGHT.
I HEAR THE LAGOON PHARMACIST IS RETIRING.
OH DEAR.
ERNIE HAS BEEN SO DEDICATED TO HIS JOB.
YOU KNOW HIM?
OF COURSE. HE FILLS ALL THE PRESCRIPTIONS YOU NEED FOR YOUR MANY ISSUES.
WHAT ISSUES? I DON'T TAKE ANYTHING!
LET'S JUST SAY ALL YOUR LUCKY CHARMS AREN'T MARSHMALLOWS.

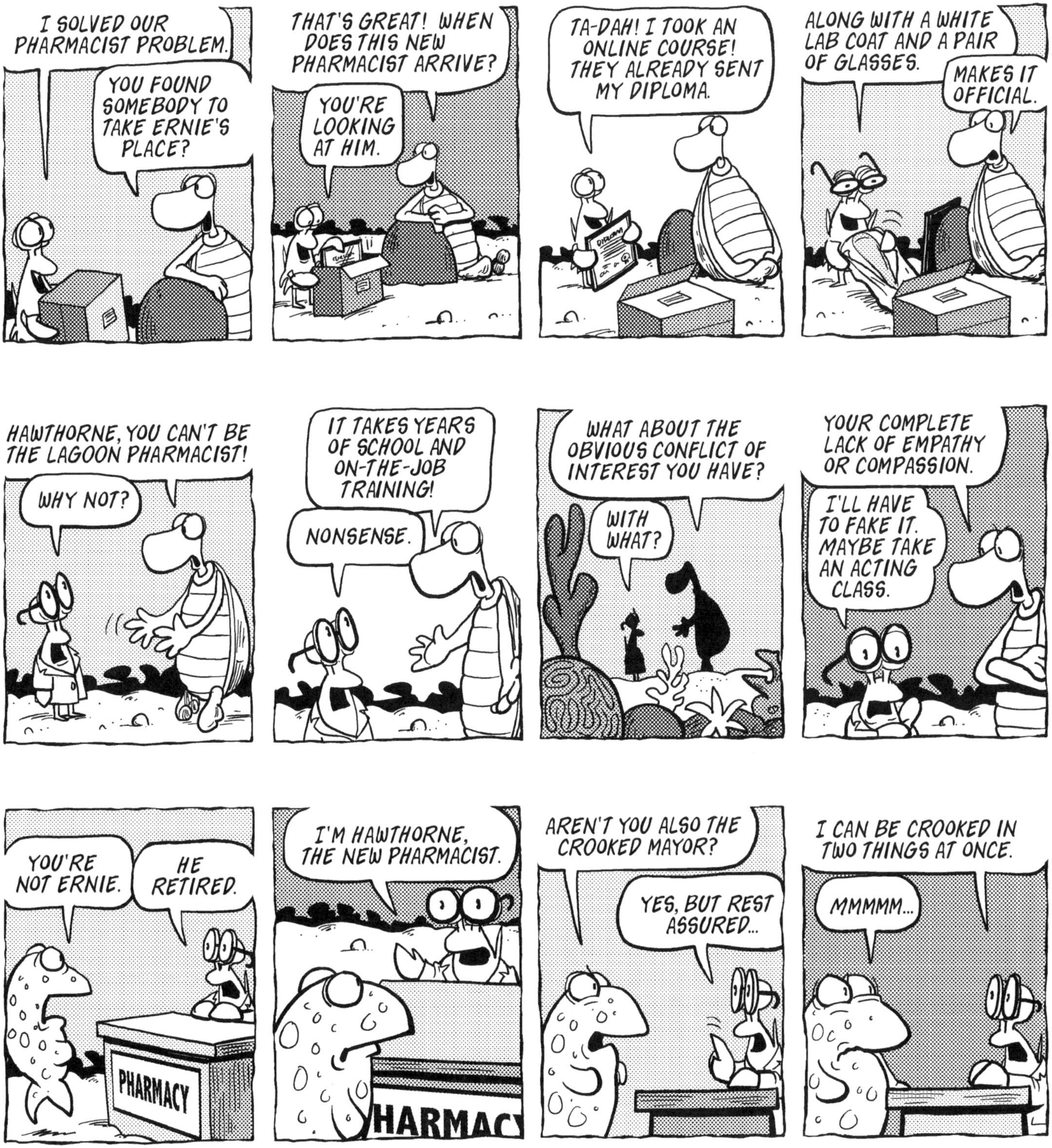
I SOLVED OUR PHARMACIST PROBLEM.
YOU FOUND SOMEBODY TO TAKE ERNIE'S PLACE?
THAT'S GREAT! WHEN DOES THIS NEW PHARMACIST ARRIVE?
YOU'RE LOOKING AT HIM.
TA-DAH! I TOOK AN ONLINE COURSE! THEY ALREADY SENT MY DIPLOMA.
ALONG WITH A WHITE LAB COAT AND A PAIR OF GLASSES.
MAKES IT OFFICIAL.
HAWTHORNE, YOU CAN'T BE THE LAGOON PHARMACIST!
WHY NOT?
IT TAKES YEARS OF SCHOOL AND ON-THE-JOB TRAINING!
NONSENSE.
WHAT ABOUT THE OBVIOUS CONFLICT OF INTEREST YOU HAVE?
WITH WHAT?
YOUR COMPLETE LACK OF EMPATHY OR COMPASSION.
I'LL HAVE TO FAKE IT. MAYBE TAKE AN ACTING CLASS.
YOU'RE NOT ERNIE.
HE RETIRED.
PHARMACY
I'M HAWTHORNE, THE NEW PHARMACIST.
HARMACY
AREN'T YOU ALSO THE CROOKED MAYOR?
YES, BUT REST ASSURED...
I CAN BE CROOKED IN TWO THINGS AT ONCE.
MMMMM...

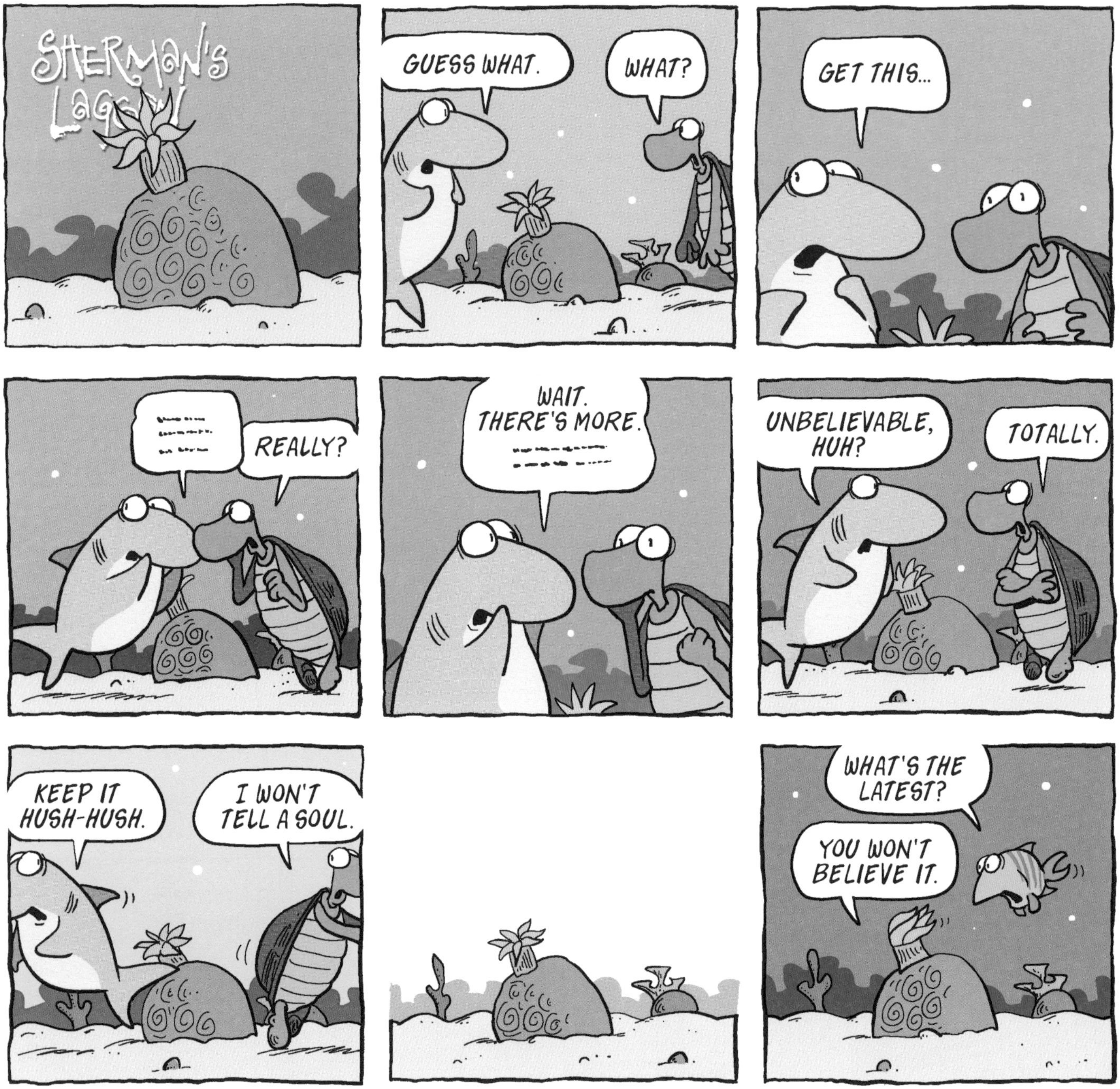
SHERMAN'S
GUESS WHAT.
WHAT?
GET THIS...
REALLY?
WAIT. THERE'S MORE.
UNBELIEVABLE, HUH?
TOTALLY.
KEEP IT HUSH-HUSH.
I WON'T TELL A SOUL.
WHAT'S THE LATEST?
YOU WON'T BELIEVE IT.

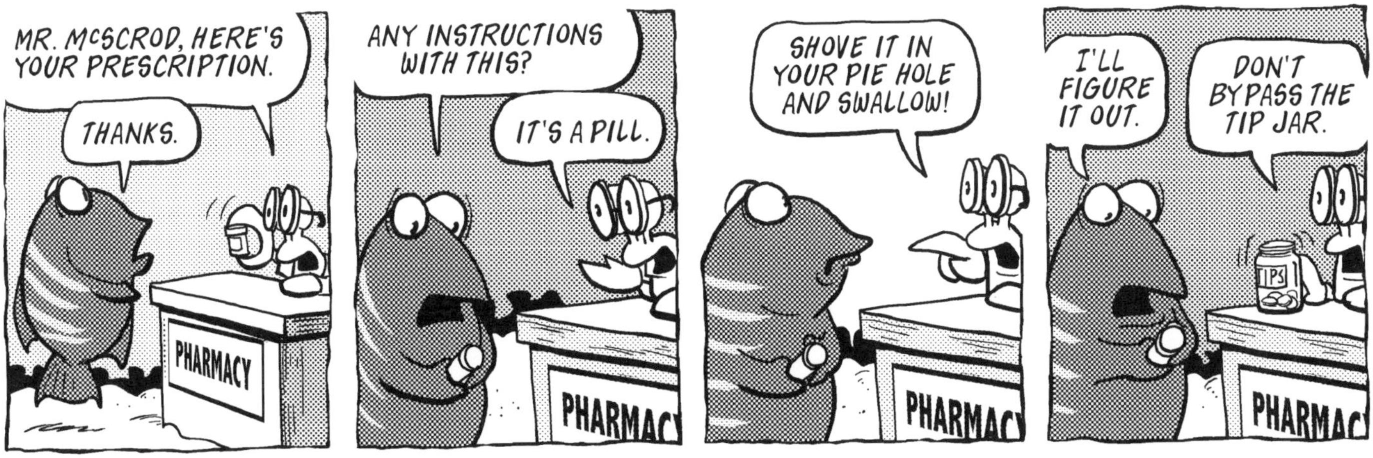
MR. McSCROD, HERE'S YOUR PRESCRIPTION.
THANKS.
PHARMACY
ANY INSTRUCTIONS WITH THIS?
IT'S A PILL.
PHARMACY
SHOVE IT IN YOUR PIE HOLE AND SWALLOW!
PHARMACY
I'LL FIGURE IT OUT.
DON'T BYPASS THE TIP JAR.
TIPS
PHARMACY

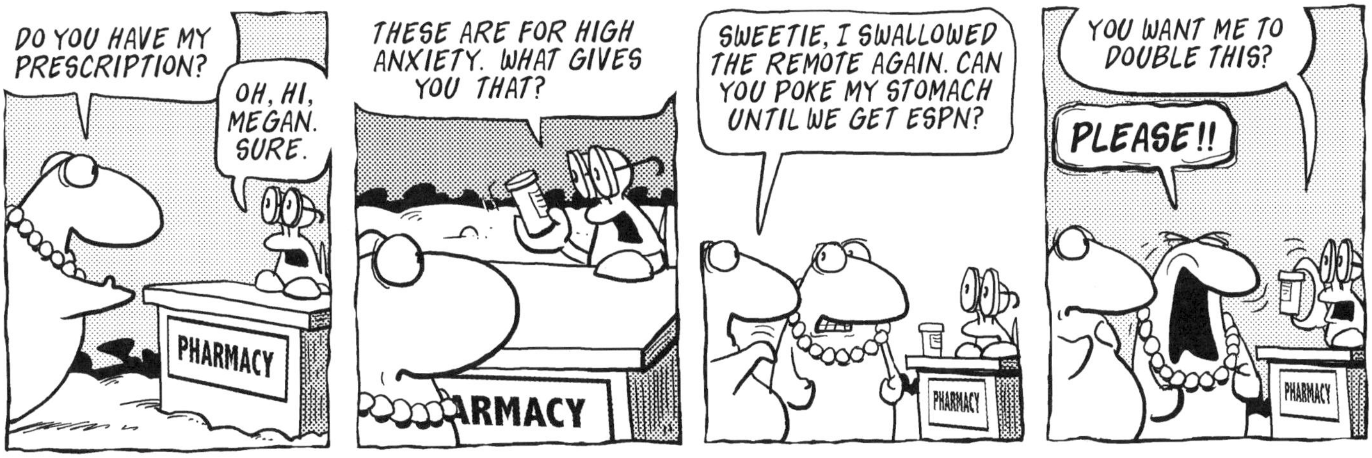
DO YOU HAVE MY PRESCRIPTION?
OH, HI, MEGAN. SURE.
PHARMACY
THESE ARE FOR HIGH ANXIETY. WHAT GIVES YOU THAT?
ARMACY
SWEETIE, I SWALLOWED THE REMOTE AGAIN. CAN YOU POKE MY STOMACH UNTIL WE GET ESPN?
PHARMACY
YOU WANT ME TO DOUBLE THIS?
PLEASE!!
PHARMACY

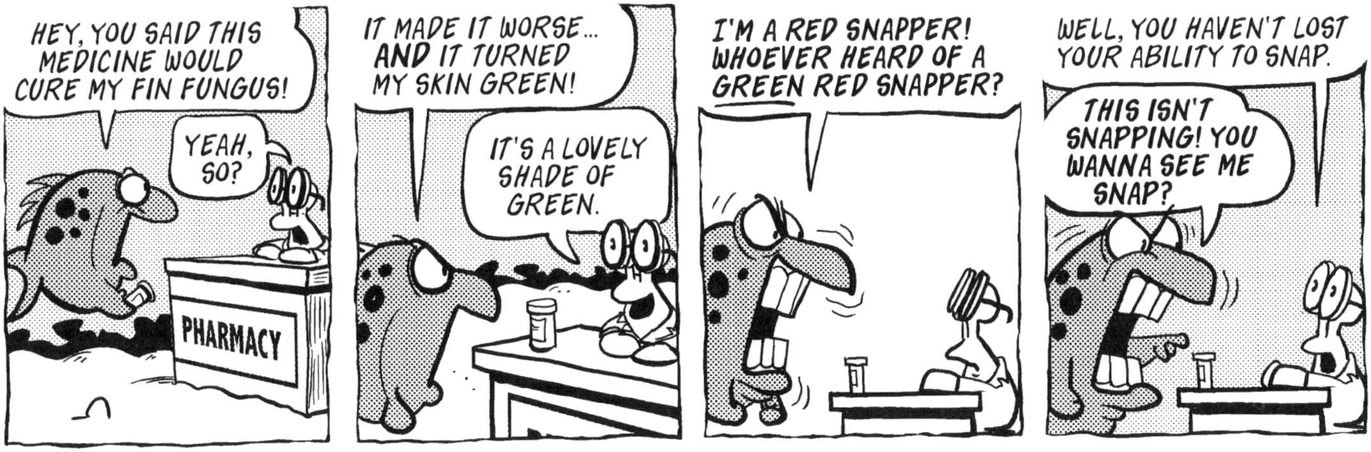
HEY, YOU SAID THIS MEDICINE WOULD CURE MY FIN FUNGUS!
YEAH, SO?
PHARMACY
IT MADE IT WORSE... AND IT TURNED MY SKIN GREEN!
IT'S A LOVELY SHADE OF GREEN.
I'M A RED SNAPPER! WHOEVER HEARD OF A GREEN RED SNAPPER?
WELL, YOU HAVEN'T LOST YOUR ABILITY TO SNAP.
THIS ISN'T SNAPPING! YOU WANNA SEE ME SNAP?

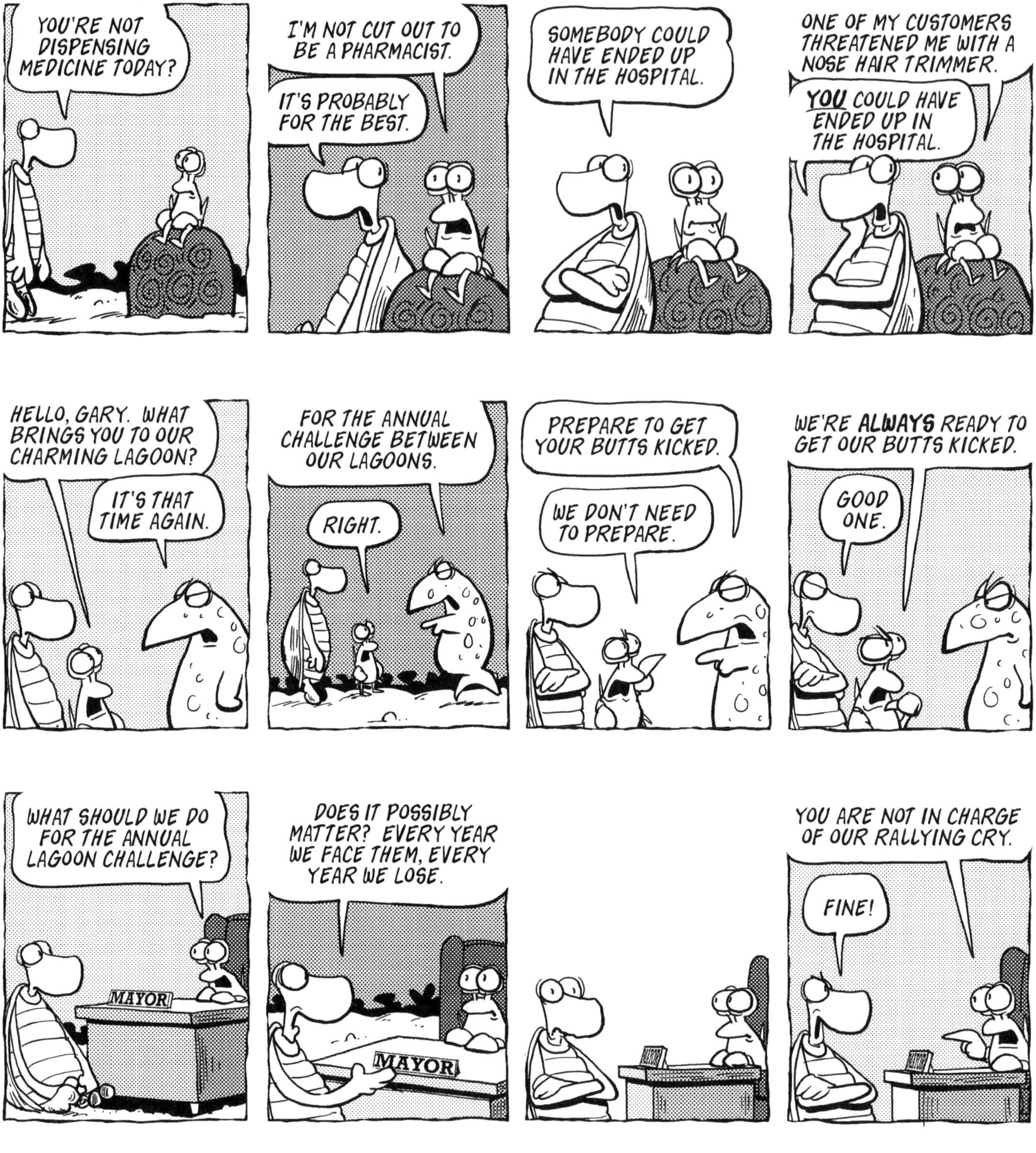
YOU'RE NOT DISPENSING MEDICINE TODAY?
I'M NOT CUT OUT TO BE A PHARMACIST.
IT'S PROBABLY FOR THE BEST.
SOMEBODY COULD HAVE ENDED UP IN THE HOSPITAL.
ONE OF MY CUSTOMERS THREATENED ME WITH A NOSE HAIR TRIMMER.
YOU COULD HAVE ENDED UP IN THE HOSPITAL.
HELLO, GARY. WHAT BRINGS YOU TO OUR CHARMING LAGOON?
IT'S THAT TIME AGAIN.
FOR THE ANNUAL CHALLENGE BETWEEN OUR LAGOONS.
RIGHT.
PREPARE TO GET YOUR BUTTS KICKED.
WE DON'T NEED TO PREPARE.
WE'RE ALWAYS READY TO GET OUR BUTTS KICKED.
GOOD ONE.
WHAT SHOULD WE DO FOR THE ANNUAL LAGOON CHALLENGE?
MAYOR
DOES IT POSSIBLY MATTER? EVERY YEAR WE FACE THEM, EVERY YEAR WE LOSE.
MAYOR
YOU ARE NOT IN CHARGE OF OUR RALLYING CRY.
FINE!

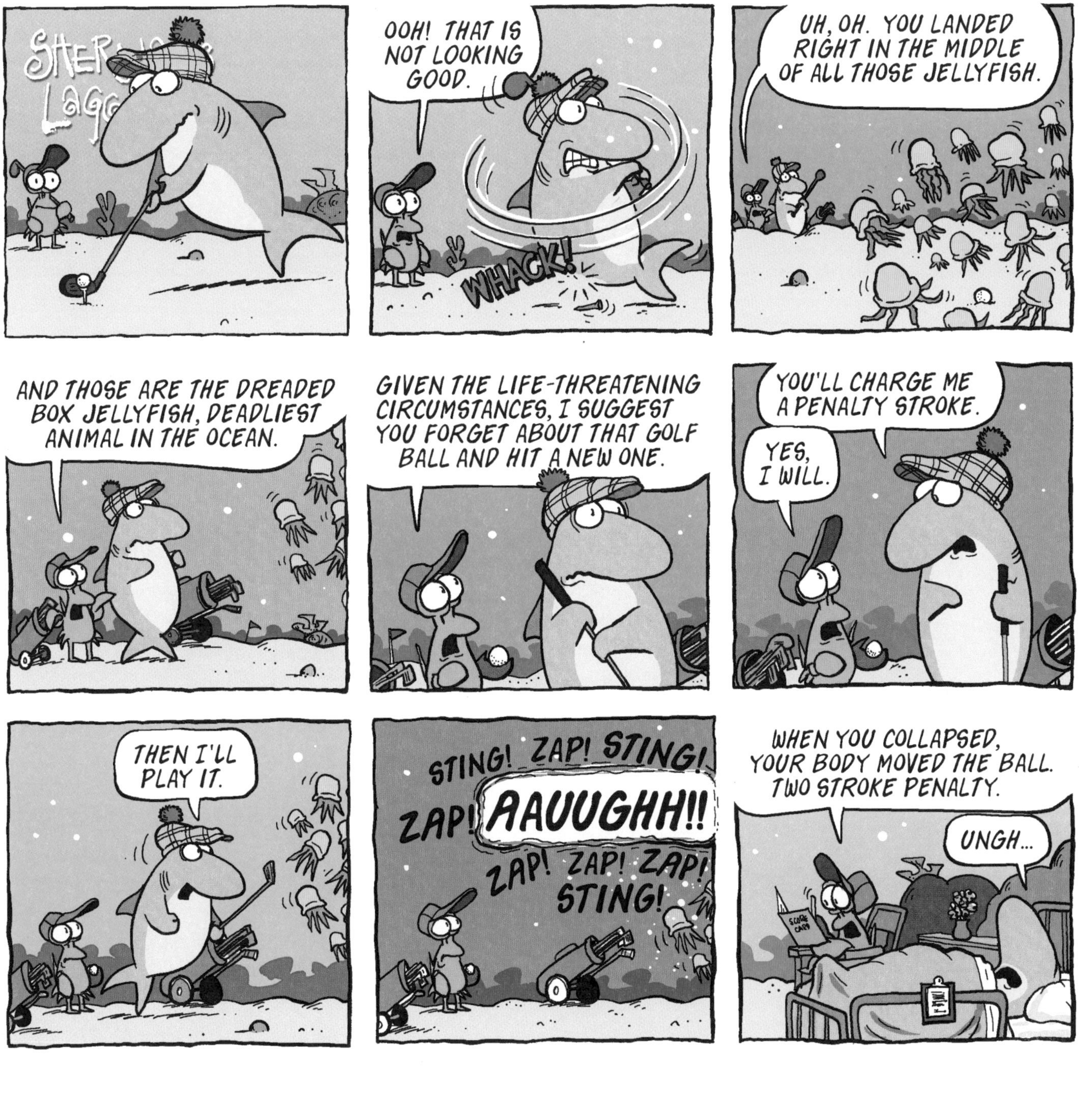
OOH! THAT IS NOT LOOKING GOOD.
WHACK!
UH, OH. YOU LANDED RIGHT IN THE MIDDLE OF ALL THOSE JELLYFISH.
AND THOSE ARE THE DREADED BOX JELLYFISH, DEADLIEST ANIMAL IN THE OCEAN.
GIVEN THE LIFE-THREATENING CIRCUMSTANCES, I SUGGEST YOU FORGET ABOUT THAT GOLF BALL AND HIT A NEW ONE.
YOU'LL CHARGE ME A PENALTY STROKE.
YES, I WILL.
THEN I'LL PLAY IT.
STING! ZAP! STING!
ZAP! AAUUGHH!!
ZAP! ZAP! ZAP!
STING!
WHEN YOU COLLAPSED, YOUR BODY MOVED THE BALL. TWO STROKE PENALTY.
UNGH...

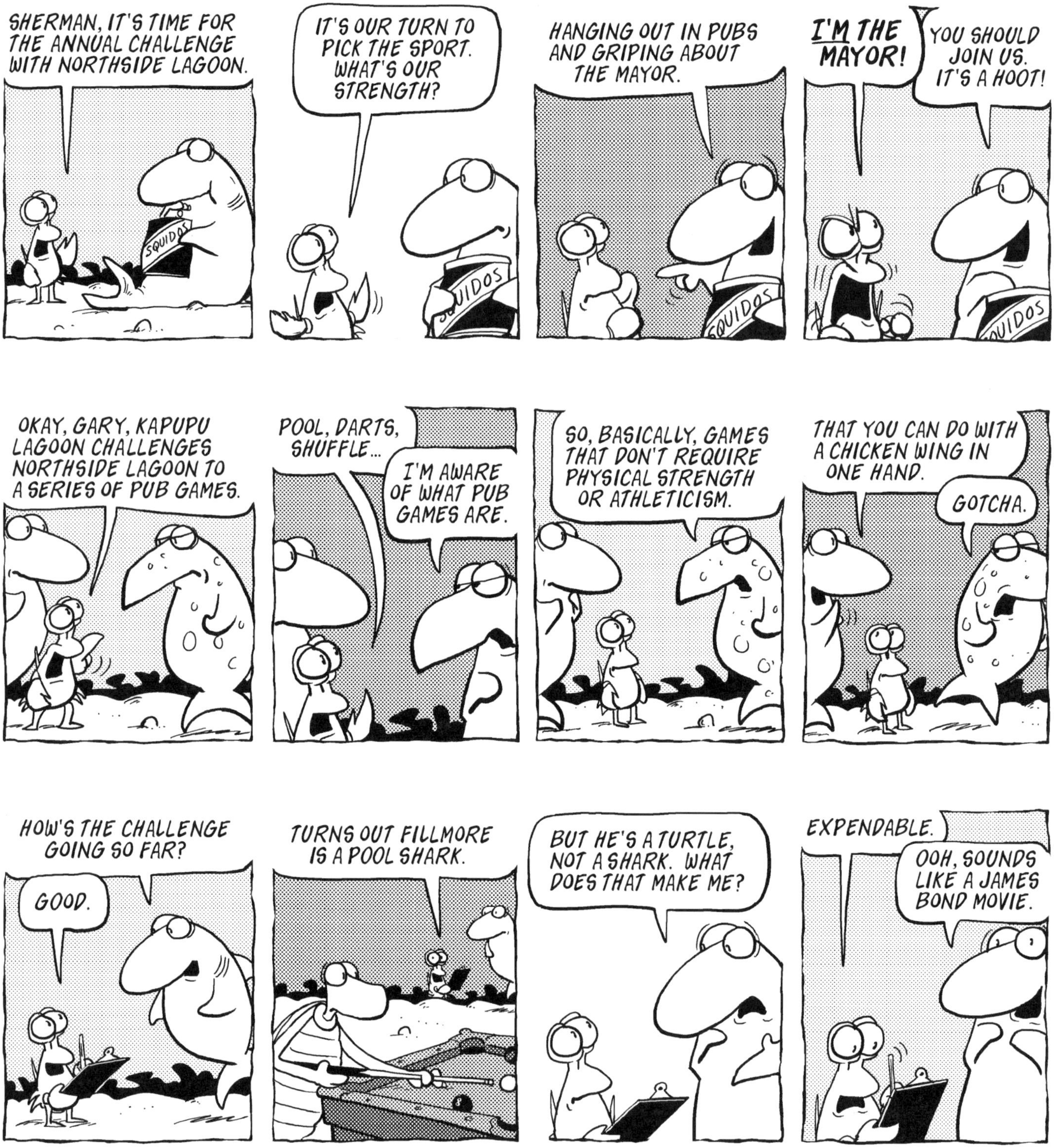
SHERMAN, IT'S TIME FOR THE ANNUAL CHALLENGE WITH NORTHSIDE LAGOON.
SQUIDOS
IT'S OUR TURN TO PICK THE SPORT. WHAT'S OUR STRENGTH?
SQUIDOS
HANGING OUT IN PUBS AND GRIPING ABOUT THE MAYOR.
SQUIDOS
I'M THE MAYOR!
YOU SHOULD JOIN US. IT'S A HOOT!
SQUIDOS
OKAY, GARY, KAPUPU LAGOON CHALLENGES NORTHSIDE LAGOON TO A SERIES OF PUB GAMES.
POOL, DARTS, SHUFFLE...
I'M AWARE OF WHAT PUB GAMES ARE.
SO, BASICALLY, GAMES THAT DON'T REQUIRE PHYSICAL STRENGTH OR ATHLETICISM.
THAT YOU CAN DO WITH A CHICKEN WING IN ONE HAND.
GOTCHA.
HOW'S THE CHALLENGE GOING SO FAR?
GOOD.
TURNS OUT FILLMORE IS A POOL SHARK.
BUT HE'S A TURTLE, NOT A SHARK. WHAT DOES THAT MAKE ME?
EXPENDABLE.
OOH, SOUNDS LIKE A JAMES BOND MOVIE.

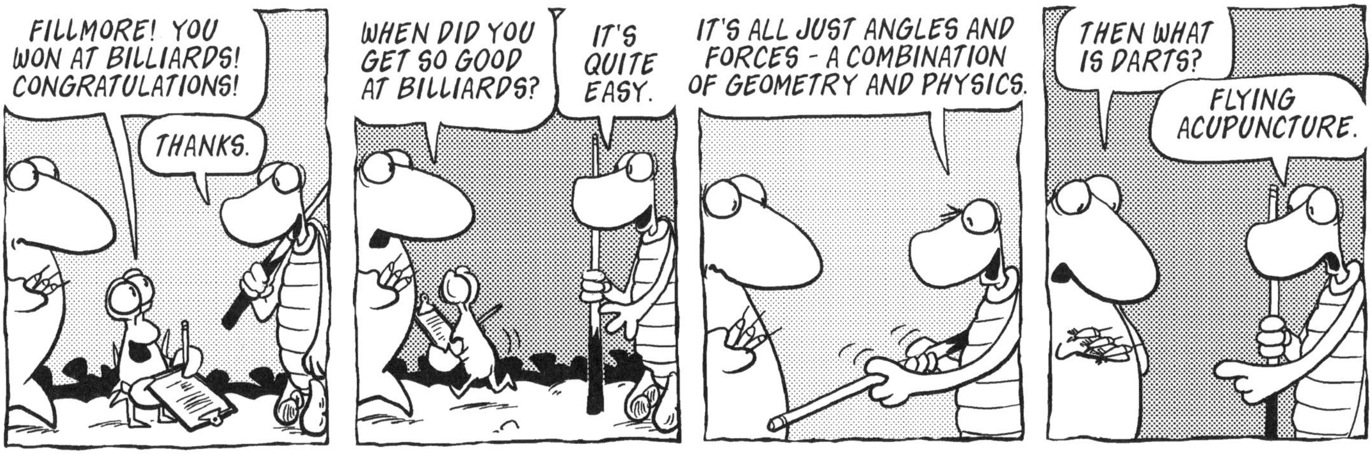
FILLMORE! YOU WON AT BILLIARDS! CONGRATULATIONS!
THANKS.
WHEN DID YOU GET SO GOOD AT BILLIARDS?
IT'S QUITE EASY.
IT'S ALL JUST ANGLES AND FORCES - A COMBINATION OF GEOMETRY AND PHYSICS.
THEN WHAT IS DARTS?
FLYING ACUPUNCTURE.

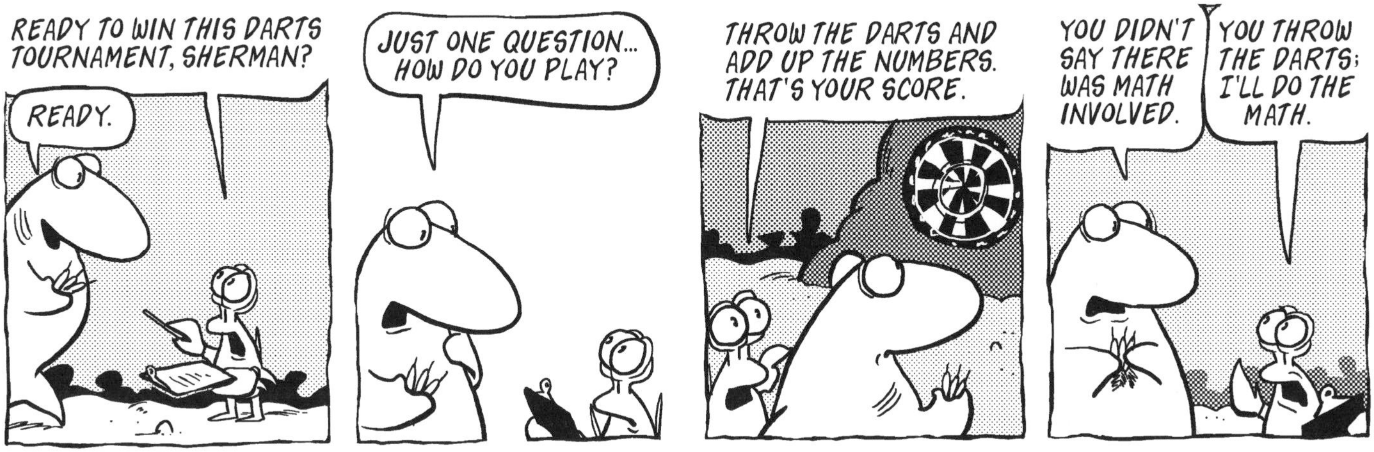
READY TO WIN THIS DARTS TOURNAMENT, SHERMAN?
READY.
JUST ONE QUESTION... HOW DO YOU PLAY?
THROW THE DARTS AND ADD UP THE NUMBERS. THAT'S YOUR SCORE.
YOU DIDN'T SAY THERE WAS MATH INVOLVED.
YOU THROW THE DARTS; I'LL DO THE MATH.

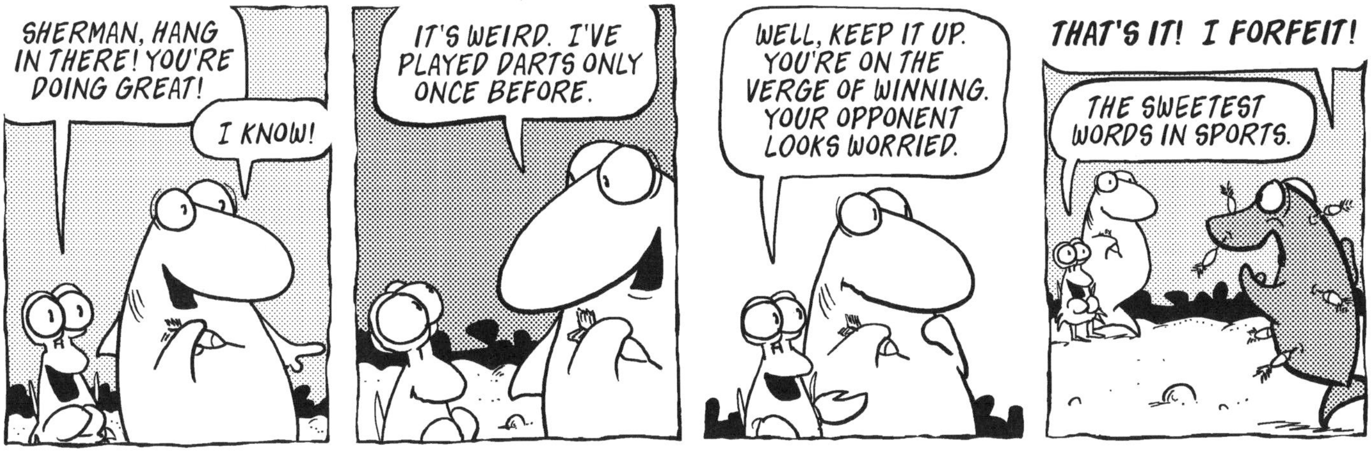
SHERMAN, HANG IN THERE! YOU'RE DOING GREAT!
I KNOW!
IT'S WEIRD. I'VE PLAYED DARTS ONLY ONCE BEFORE.
WELL, KEEP IT UP. YOU'RE ON THE VERGE OF WINNING. YOUR OPPONENT LOOKS WORRIED.
THAT'S IT! I FORFEIT!
THE SWEETEST WORDS IN SPORTS.

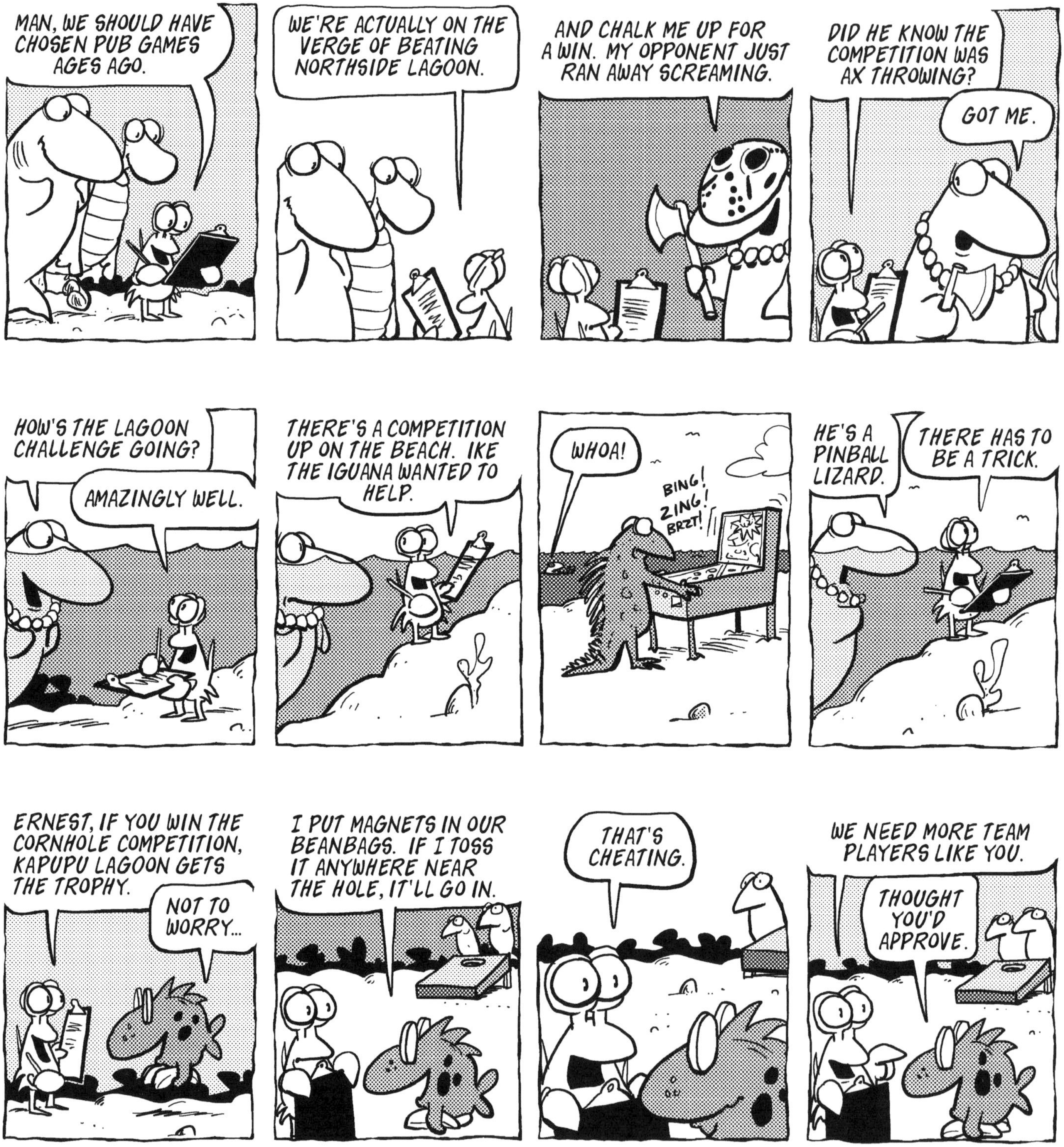
MAN, WE SHOULD HAVE CHOSEN PUB GAMES AGES AGO.
WE'RE ACTUALLY ON THE VERGE OF BEATING NORTHSIDE LAGOON.
AND CHALK ME UP FOR A WIN. MY OPPONENT JUST RAN AWAY SCREAMING.
DID HE KNOW THE COMPETITION WAS AX THROWING?
GOT ME.
HOW'S THE LAGOON CHALLENGE GOING?
AMAZINGLY WELL.
THERE'S A COMPETITION UP ON THE BEACH. IKE THE IGUANA WANTED TO HELP.
WHOA!
BING! ZING! BRZT!
HE'S A PINBALL LIZARD.
THERE HAS TO BE A TRICK.
ERNEST, IF YOU WIN THE CORNHOLE COMPETITION, KAPUPU LAGOON GETS THE TROPHY.
NOT TO WORRY...
I PUT MAGNETS IN OUR BEANBAGS. IF I TOSS IT ANYWHERE NEAR THE HOLE, IT'LL GO IN.
THAT'S CHEATING.
WE NEED MORE TEAM PLAYERS LIKE YOU.
THOUGHT YOU'D APPROVE.

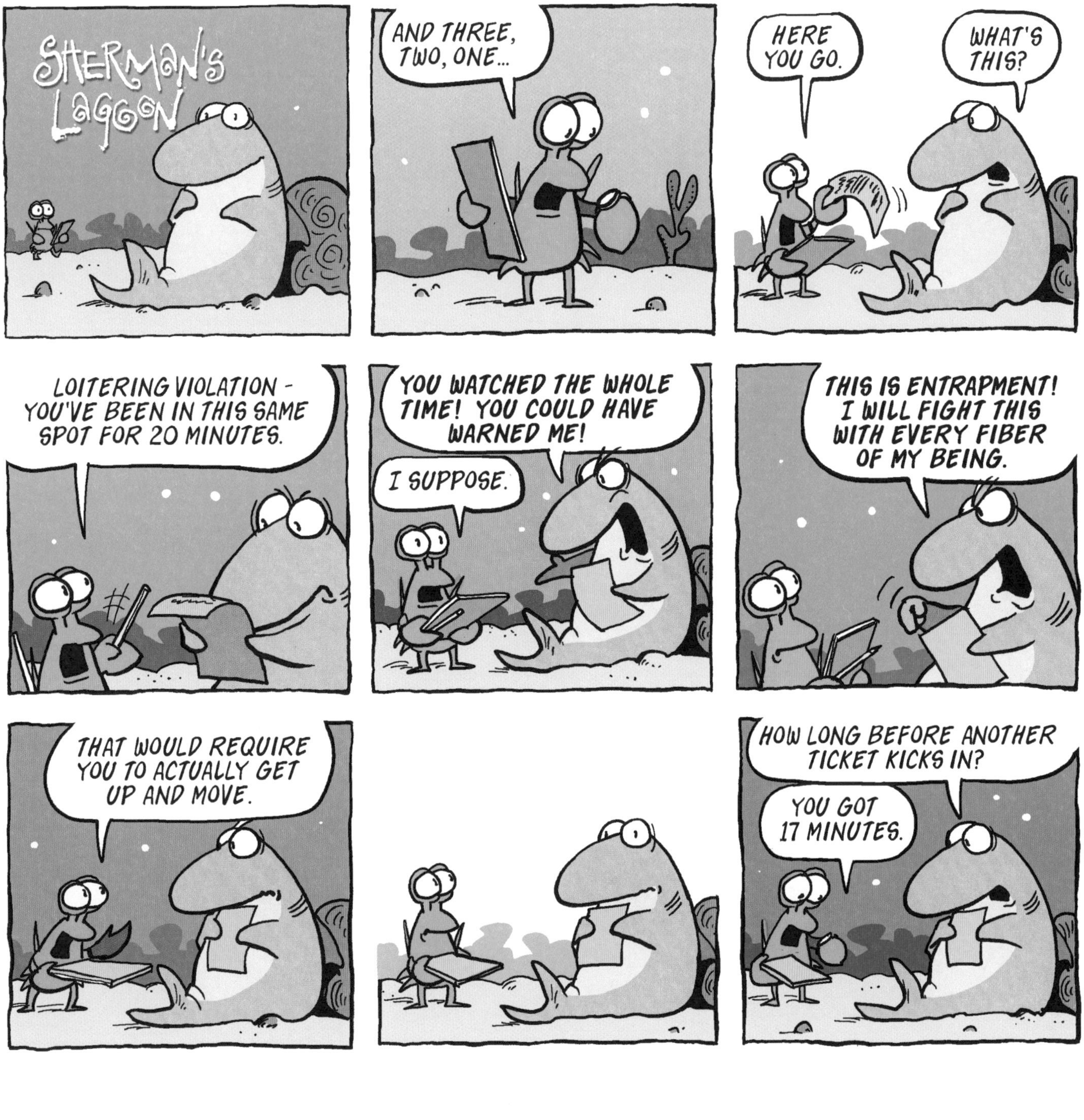
SHERMAN'S LAGOON
AND THREE, TWO, ONE...
HERE YOU GO.
WHAT'S THIS?
LOITERING VIOLATION - YOU'VE BEEN IN THIS SAME SPOT FOR 20 MINUTES.
YOU WATCHED THE WHOLE TIME! YOU COULD HAVE WARNED ME!
I SUPPOSE.
THIS IS ENTRAPMENT! I WILL FIGHT THIS WITH EVERY FIBER OF MY BEING.
THAT WOULD REQUIRE YOU TO ACTUALLY GET UP AND MOVE.
HOW LONG BEFORE ANOTHER TICKET KICKS IN?
YOU GOT 17 MINUTES.

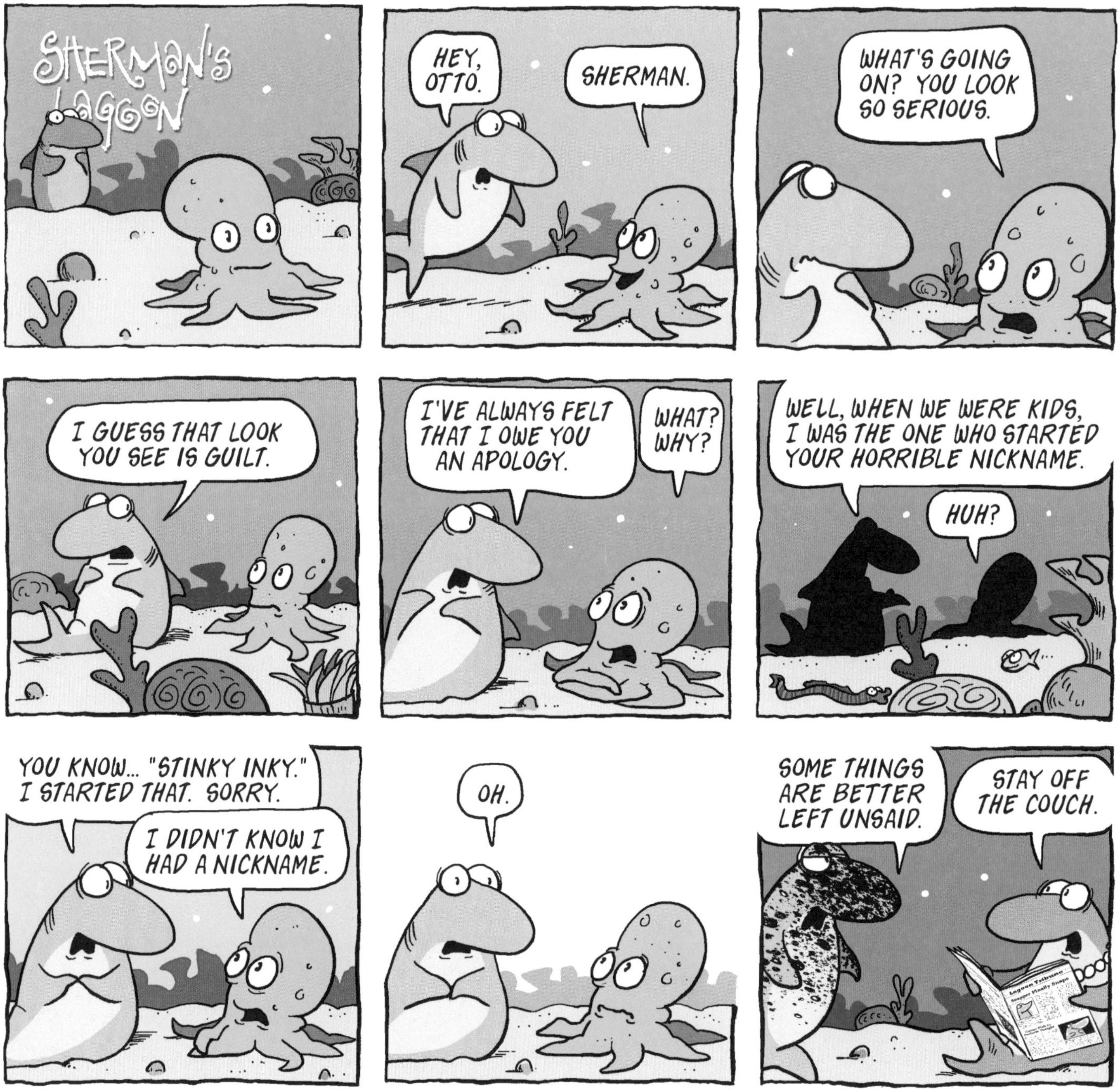
SHERMAN'S LAGOON
HEY, OTTO.
SHERMAN.
WHAT'S GOING ON? YOU LOOK SO SERIOUS.
I GUESS THAT LOOK YOU SEE IS GUILT.
I'VE ALWAYS FELT THAT I OWE YOU AN APOLOGY.
WHAT? WHY?
WELL, WHEN WE WERE KIDS, I WAS THE ONE WHO STARTED YOUR HORRIBLE NICKNAME.
HUH?
YOU KNOW... "STINKY INKY." I STARTED THAT. SORRY.
I DIDN'T KNOW I HAD A NICKNAME.
OH.
SOME THINGS ARE BETTER LEFT UNSAID.
STAY OFF THE COUCH.
Lagoon Tribune
Snapper Finally Snaps

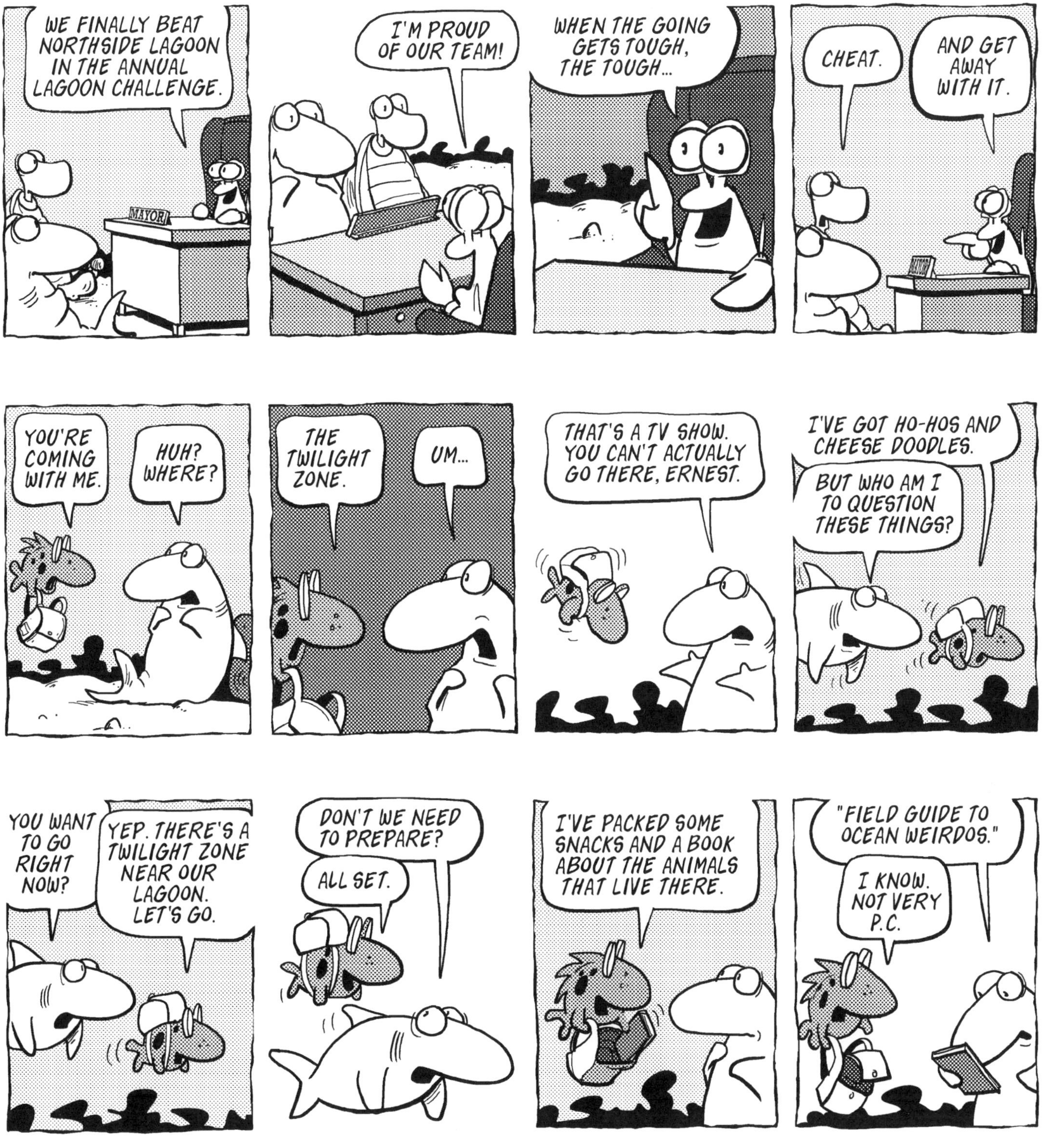
WE FINALLY BEAT NORTHSIDE LAGOON IN THE ANNUAL LAGOON CHALLENGE.
MAYOR
I'M PROUD OF OUR TEAM!
WHEN THE GOING GETS TOUGH, THE TOUGH...
CHEAT.
AND GET AWAY WITH IT.
YOU'RE COMING WITH ME.
HUH? WHERE?
THE TWILIGHT ZONE.
UM...
THAT'S A TV SHOW. YOU CAN'T ACTUALLY GO THERE, ERNEST.
I'VE GOT HO-HOS AND CHEESE DOODLES.
BUT WHO AM I TO QUESTION THESE THINGS?
YOU WANT TO GO RIGHT NOW?
YEP. THERE'S A TWILIGHT ZONE NEAR OUR LAGOON. LET'S GO.
DON'T WE NEED TO PREPARE?
ALL SET.
I'VE PACKED SOME SNACKS AND A BOOK ABOUT THE ANIMALS THAT LIVE THERE.
"FIELD GUIDE TO OCEAN WEIRDOS."
I KNOW. NOT VERY P.C.

ERNEST, WHAT'S THIS "TWILIGHT ZONE" YOU'RE TALKING ABOUT?
IT'S THE MIDDLE OF THE OCEAN WATER COLUMN, NOT THE BOTTOM AND NOT THE SURFACE.
IT'S A PART OF THE OCEAN WHERE WEIRD ANIMALS LIVE.
NOT LIKE WE'RE LACKING WEIRDNESS AROUND HERE.
HEY! I'M COLLECTING SEAGULL TEETH. GOT ANY?
IT'S GETTING DARK.
WE'RE ENTERING THE TWILIGHT ZONE.
THIS PART OF THE OCEAN PLAYS A KEY ROLE IN REMOVING CARBON FROM THE ATMOSPHERE.
IT SHOULD BE STUDIED IN GREATER DEPTH BEFORE HUMANS CHANGE IT OR IRREPARABLY DAMAGE IT.
BUT THAT'S WHAT THEY DO BEST.
I'M AWARE.
WHOA! CHECK IT OUT! IT'S AN ANGLERFISH!
IT'S FREAKY-LOOKING.
IT'S GOT A MOUTH FULL OF JAGGED TEETH AND A FLASHLIGHT ON ITS FOREHEAD.
IT'S ALSO RIGHT HERE.
AND GOOD HEARING.

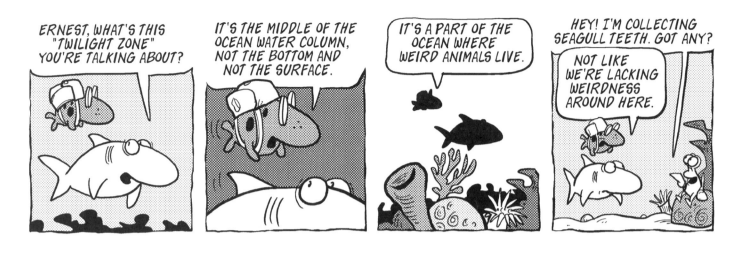

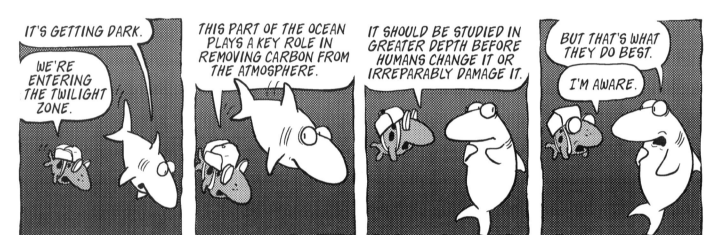

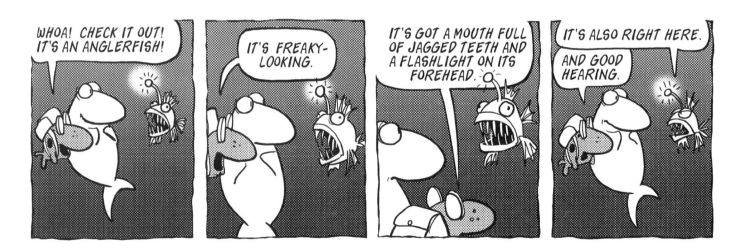

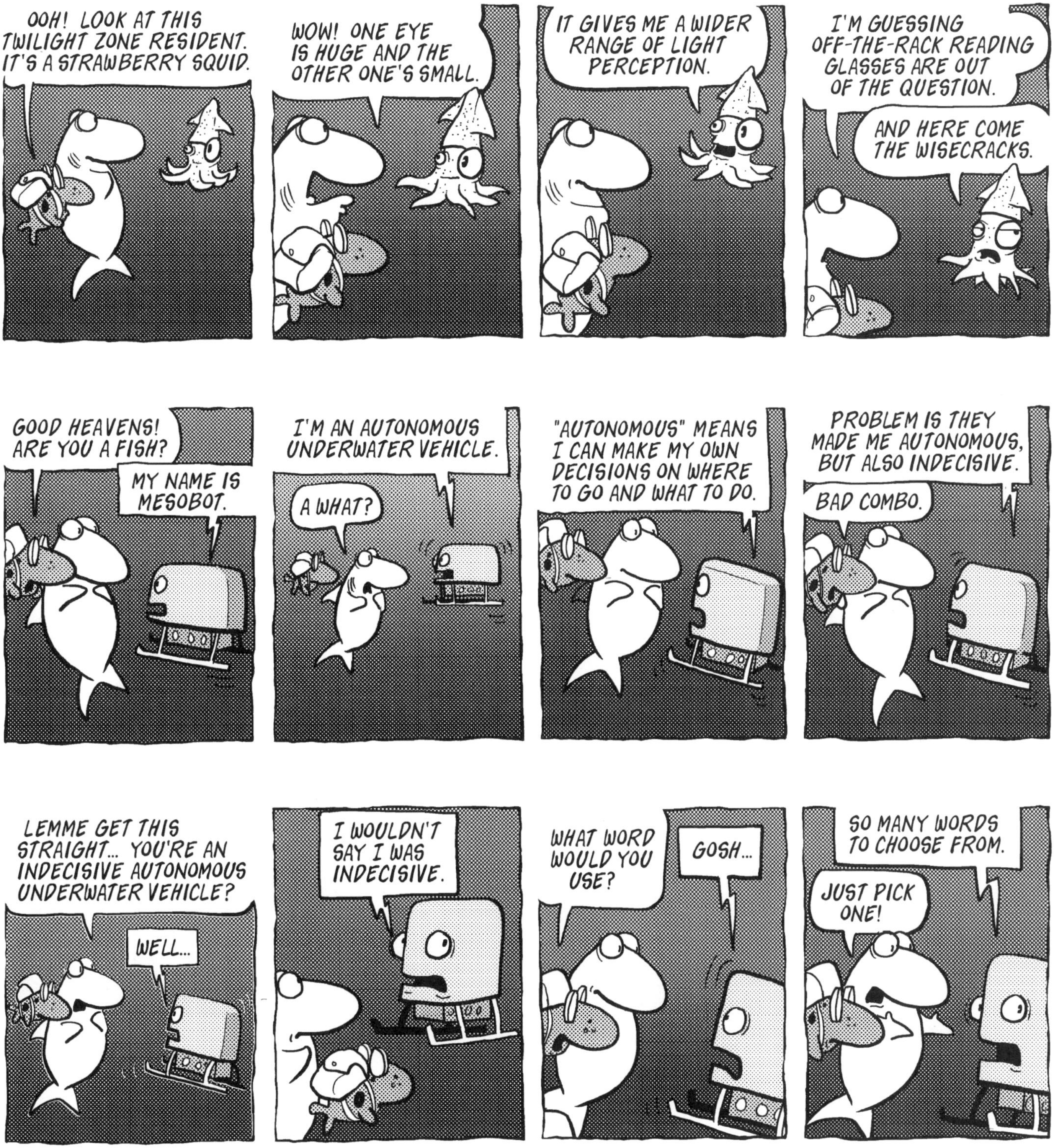
OOH! LOOK AT THIS TWILIGHT ZONE RESIDENT. IT'S A STRAWBERRY SQUID.
WOW! ONE EYE IS HUGE AND THE OTHER ONE'S SMALL.
IT GIVES ME A WIDER RANGE OF LIGHT PERCEPTION.
I'M GUESSING OFF-THE-RACK READING GLASSES ARE OUT OF THE QUESTION.
AND HERE COME THE WISECRACKS.
GOOD HEAVENS! ARE YOU A FISH?
MY NAME IS MESOBOT.
I'M AN AUTONOMOUS UNDERWATER VEHICLE.
A WHAT?
"AUTONOMOUS" MEANS I CAN MAKE MY OWN DECISIONS ON WHERE TO GO AND WHAT TO DO.
PROBLEM IS THEY MADE ME AUTONOMOUS, BUT ALSO INDECISIVE.
BAD COMBO.
LEMME GET THIS STRAIGHT... YOU'RE AN INDECISIVE AUTONOMOUS UNDERWATER VEHICLE?
WELL...
I WOULDN'T SAY I WAS INDECISIVE.
WHAT WORD WOULD YOU USE?
GOSH...
SO MANY WORDS TO CHOOSE FROM.
JUST PICK ONE!

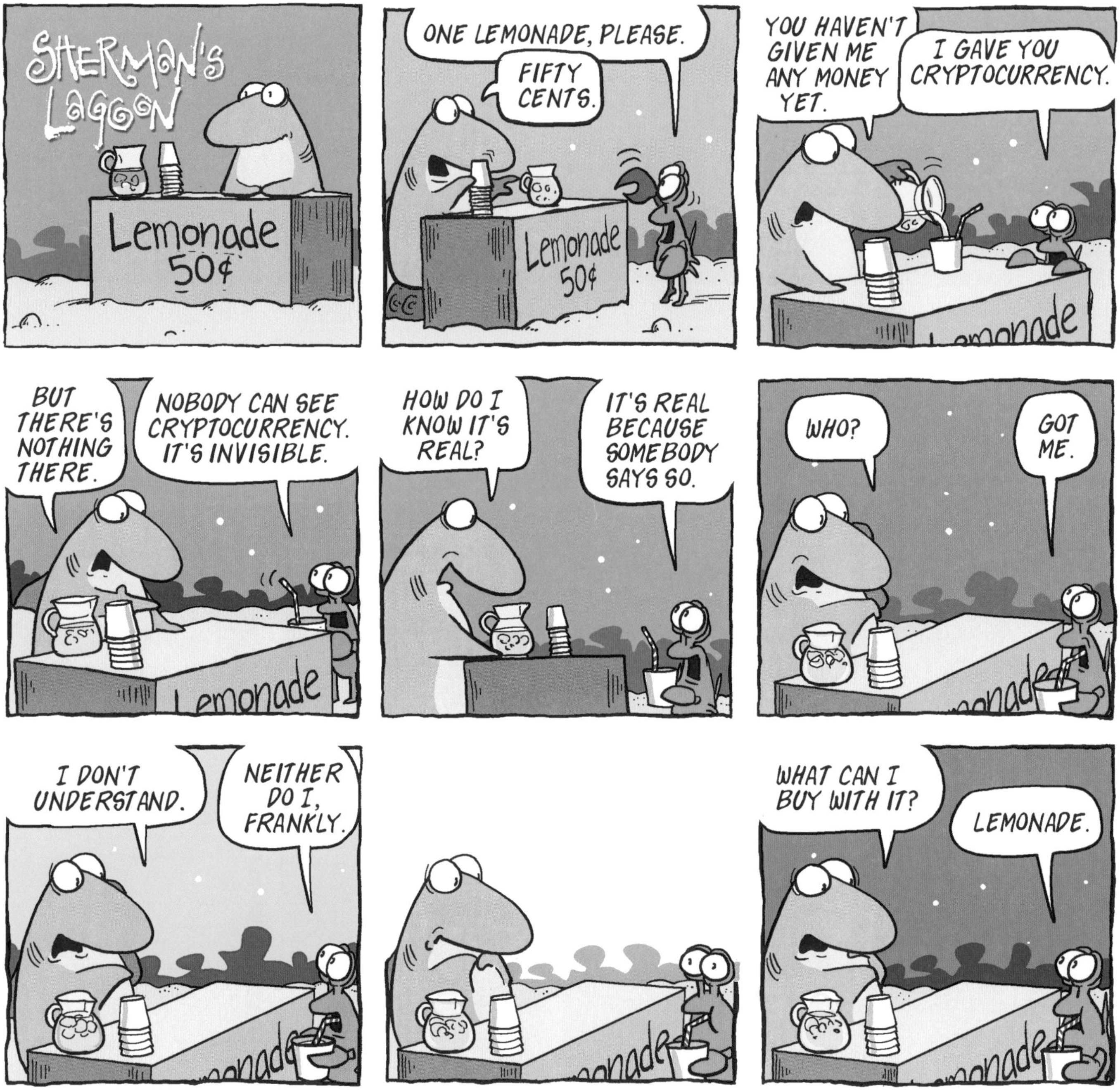
SHERMAN'S LAGOON
Lemonade 50¢
ONE LEMONADE, PLEASE.
FIFTY CENTS.
Lemonade 50¢
YOU HAVEN'T GIVEN ME ANY MONEY YET.
I GAVE YOU CRYPTOCURRENCY.
BUT THERE'S NOTHING THERE.
NOBODY CAN SEE CRYPTOCURRENCY. IT'S INVISIBLE.
HOW DO I KNOW IT'S REAL?
IT'S REAL BECAUSE SOMEBODY SAYS SO.
WHO?
GOT ME.
I DON'T UNDERSTAND.
NEITHER DO I, FRANKLY.
WHAT CAN I BUY WITH IT?
LEMONADE.

MESOBOT, WHAT ARE YOU DOING HERE IN THE OCEAN TWILIGHT ZONE?

I'M STUDYING ALL THE WEIRD ANIMALS THAT LIVE HERE.

HEY! WHO ARE YOU CALLING WEIRD?

NOT YOU.

MR. BOJANGLES IS WONDERING IF YOU WERE TALKING ABOUT HIM.

NO, NOT YOUR SOCK PUPPET EITHER.

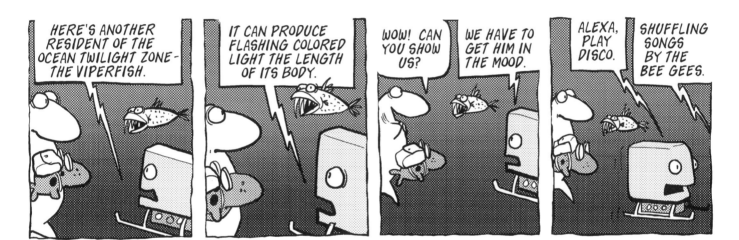

HERE'S ANOTHER RESIDENT OF THE OCEAN TWILIGHT ZONE— THE VIPERFISH.

IT CAN PRODUCE FLASHING COLORED LIGHT THE LENGTH OF ITS BODY.

WOW! CAN YOU SHOW US?

WE HAVE TO GET HIM IN THE MOOD.

ALEXA, PLAY DISCO.

SHUFFLING SONGS BY THE BEE GEES.

WHOA! IS THAT A CRAB? IT'S SO SMALL!

SMALL, BUT FEROCIOUS.

NICKNAMED THE "PRAM BUG," THIS LITTLE MONSTER SKEWERS ITS VICTIMS WITH ITS RAZOR-SHARP CLAWS.

GOOD HEAVENS!

THEN HE CRAWLS INSIDE THEIR HOLLOWED-OUT BODIES.

GROSS! HE'S A PSYCHO!

THEN HE DOES CELEBRITY IMPERSONATIONS.

HE'S A TALENTED PSYCHO.

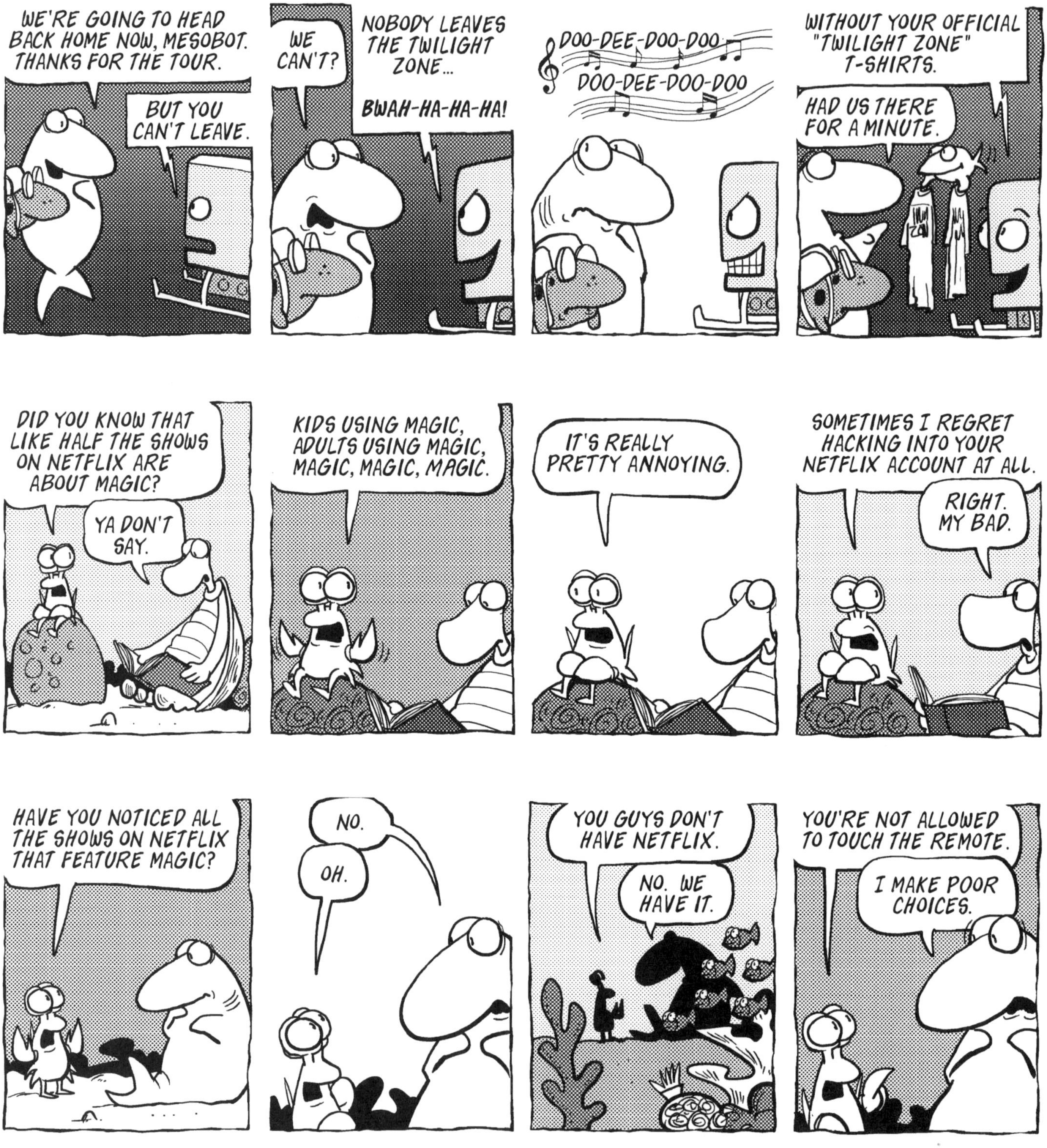
WE'RE GOING TO HEAD BACK HOME NOW, MESOBOT. THANKS FOR THE TOUR.
BUT YOU CAN'T LEAVE.
WE CAN'T?
NOBODY LEAVES THE TWILIGHT ZONE...
BWAH-HA-HA-HA!
DOO-DEE-DOO-DOO
DOO-DEE-DOO-DOO
WITHOUT YOUR OFFICIAL "TWILIGHT ZONE" T-SHIRTS.
HAD US THERE FOR A MINUTE.
DID YOU KNOW THAT LIKE HALF THE SHOWS ON NETFLIX ARE ABOUT MAGIC?
YA DON'T SAY.
KIDS USING MAGIC, ADULTS USING MAGIC, MAGIC, MAGIC, MAGIC.
IT'S REALLY PRETTY ANNOYING.
SOMETIMES I REGRET HACKING INTO YOUR NETFLIX ACCOUNT AT ALL.
RIGHT. MY BAD.
HAVE YOU NOTICED ALL THE SHOWS ON NETFLIX THAT FEATURE MAGIC?
NO.
OH.
YOU GUYS DON'T HAVE NETFLIX.
NO. WE HAVE IT.
YOU'RE NOT ALLOWED TO TOUCH THE REMOTE.
I MAKE POOR CHOICES.

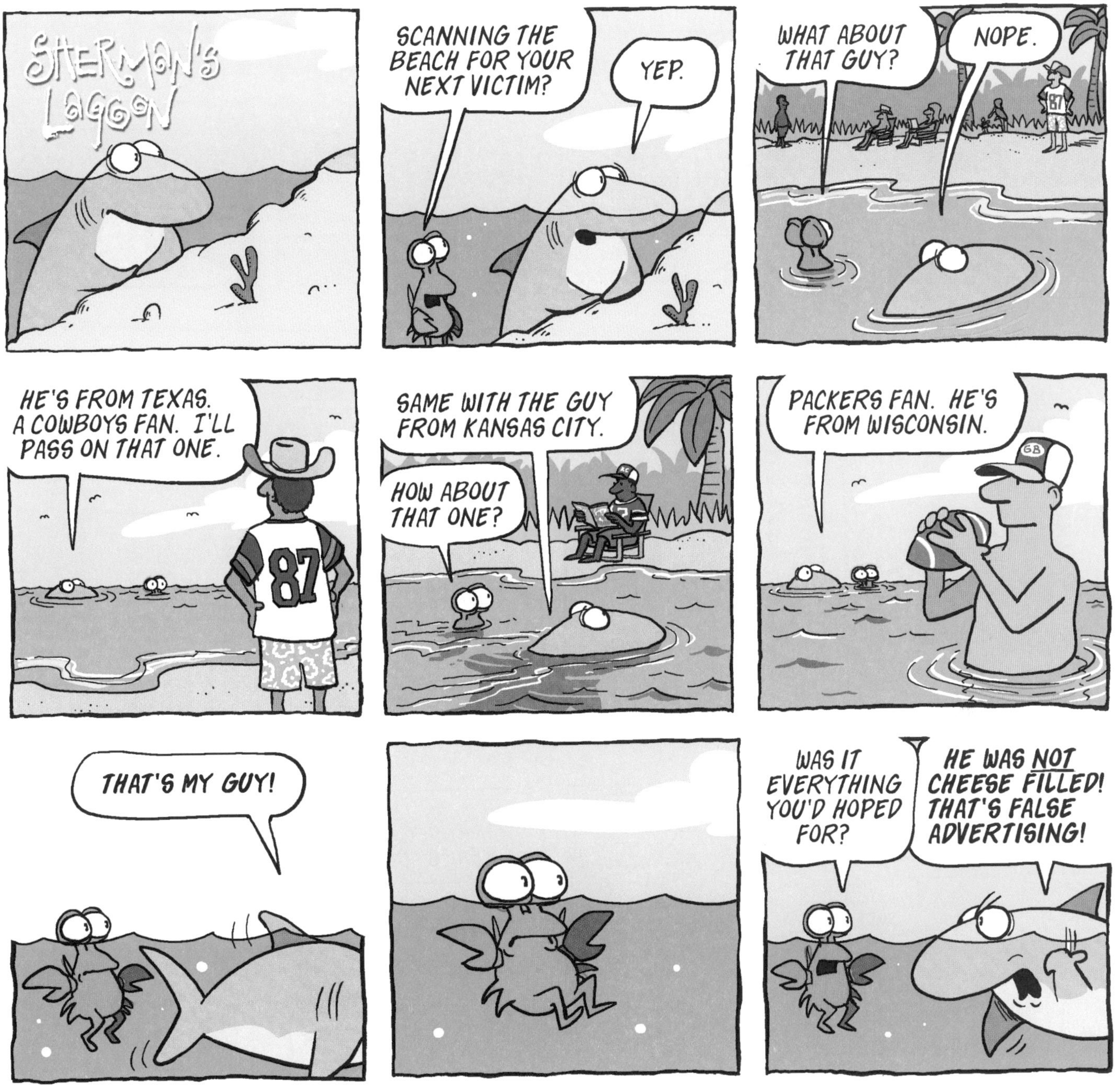
SHERMAN'S LAGOON
SCANNING THE BEACH FOR YOUR NEXT VICTIM?
YEP.
WHAT ABOUT THAT GUY?
NOPE.
HE'S FROM TEXAS. A COWBOYS FAN. I'LL PASS ON THAT ONE.
SAME WITH THE GUY FROM KANSAS CITY.
HOW ABOUT THAT ONE?
PACKERS FAN. HE'S FROM WISCONSIN.
THAT'S MY GUY!
WAS IT EVERYTHING YOU'D HOPED FOR?
HE WAS NOT CHEESE FILLED! THAT'S FALSE ADVERTISING!

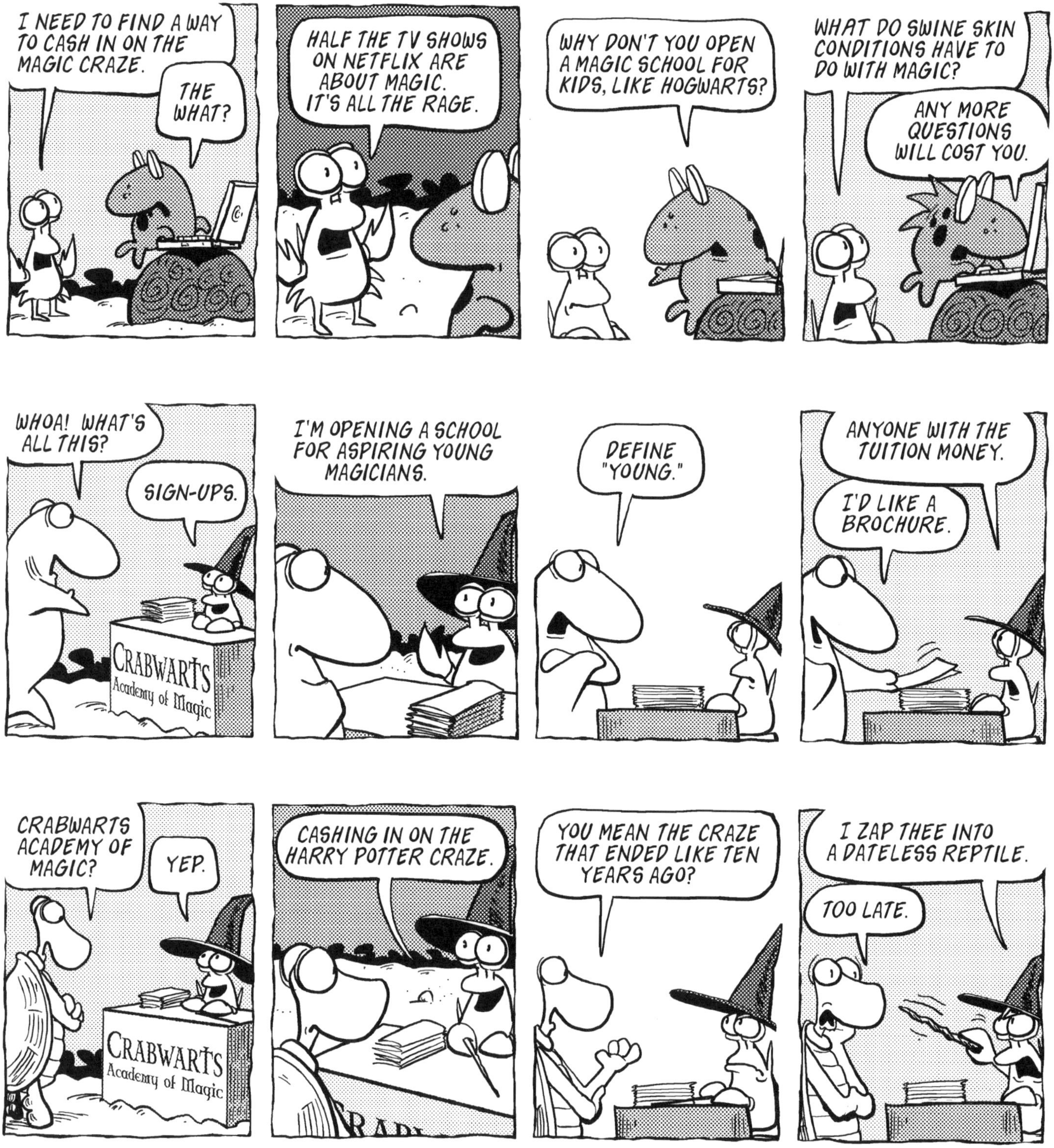
I NEED TO FIND A WAY TO CASH IN ON THE MAGIC CRAZE.
THE WHAT?
HALF THE TV SHOWS ON NETFLIX ARE ABOUT MAGIC. IT'S ALL THE RAGE.
WHY DON'T YOU OPEN A MAGIC SCHOOL FOR KIDS, LIKE HOGWARTS?
WHAT DO SWINE SKIN CONDITIONS HAVE TO DO WITH MAGIC?
ANY MORE QUESTIONS WILL COST YOU.
WHOA! WHAT'S ALL THIS?
SIGN-UPS.
CRABWARTS Academy of Magic
I'M OPENING A SCHOOL FOR ASPIRING YOUNG MAGICIANS.
DEFINE "YOUNG."
ANYONE WITH THE TUITION MONEY.
I'D LIKE A BROCHURE.
CRABWARTS ACADEMY OF MAGIC?
YEP.
CRABWARTS Academy of Magic
CASHING IN ON THE HARRY POTTER CRAZE.
YOU MEAN THE CRAZE THAT ENDED LIKE TEN YEARS AGO?
I ZAP THEE INTO A DATELESS REPTILE.
TOO LATE.

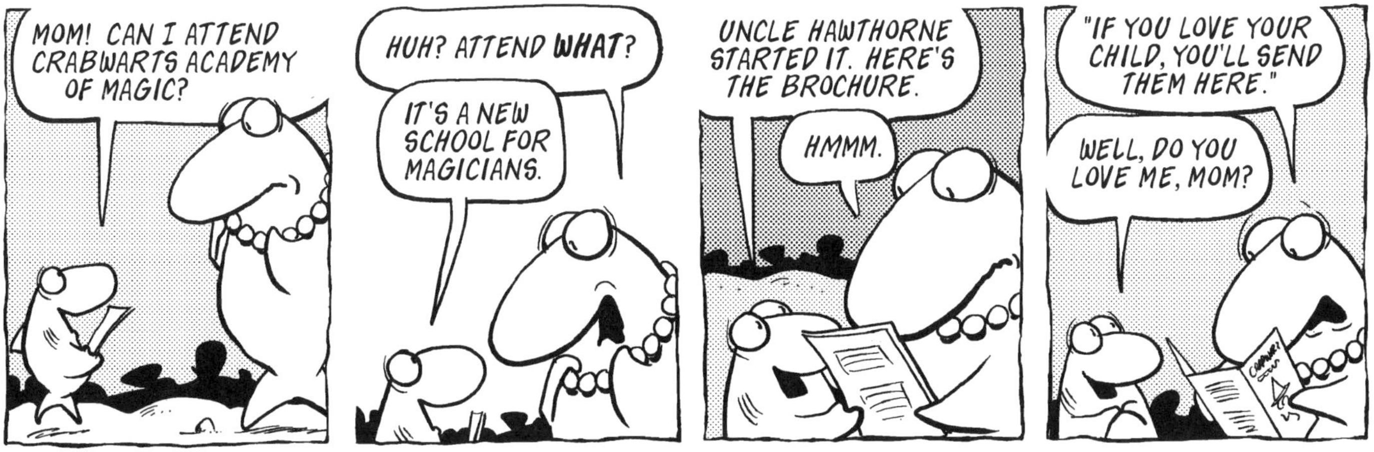
MOM! CAN I ATTEND CRABWARTS ACADEMY OF MAGIC?
HUH? ATTEND **WHAT**?
IT'S A NEW SCHOOL FOR MAGICIANS.
UNCLE HAWTHORNE STARTED IT. HERE'S THE BROCHURE.
HMMM.
"IF YOU LOVE YOUR CHILD, YOU'LL SEND THEM HERE."
WELL, DO YOU LOVE ME, MOM?

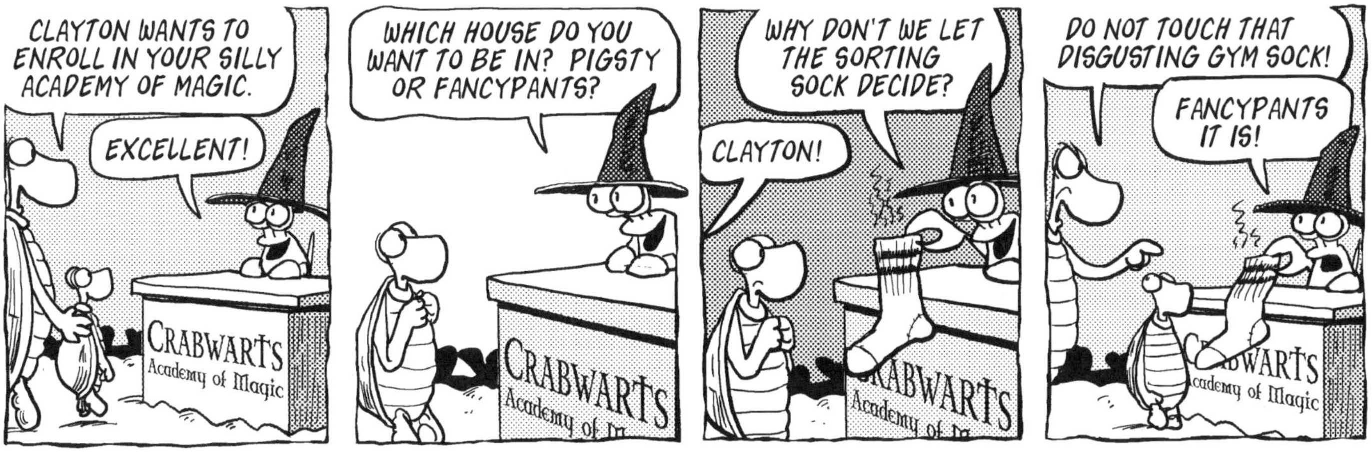
CLAYTON WANTS TO ENROLL IN YOUR SILLY ACADEMY OF MAGIC.
EXCELLENT!
CRABWARTS
Academy of Magic
WHICH HOUSE DO YOU WANT TO BE IN? PIGSTY OR FANCYPANTS?
CRABWARTS
WHY DON'T WE LET THE SORTING SOCK DECIDE?
CLAYTON!
DO NOT TOUCH THAT DISGUSTING GYM SOCK!
FANCYPANTS IT IS!

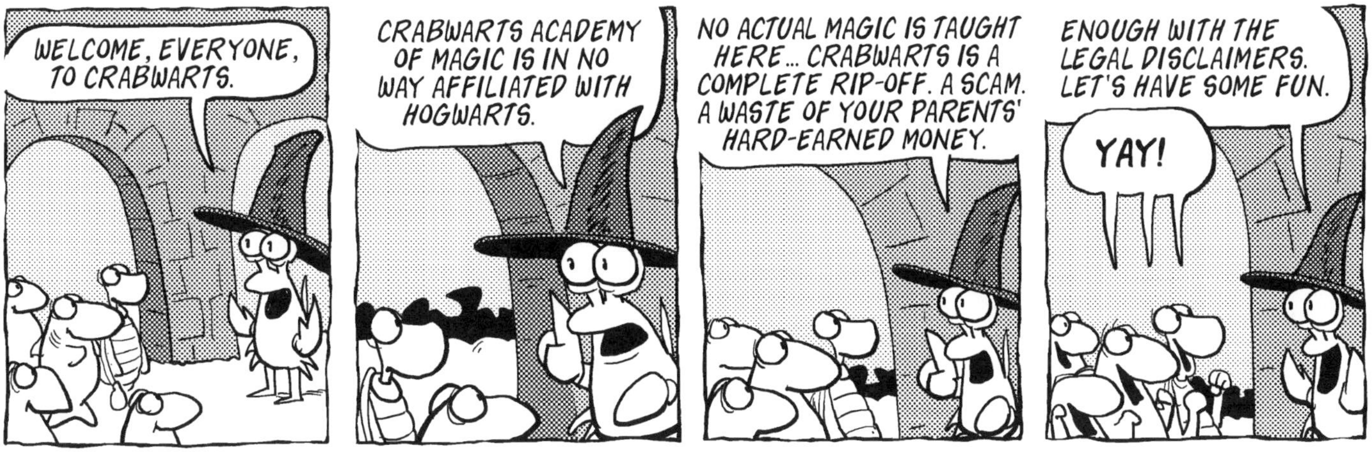
WELCOME, EVERYONE, TO CRABWARTS.
CRABWARTS ACADEMY OF MAGIC IS IN NO WAY AFFILIATED WITH HOGWARTS.
NO ACTUAL MAGIC IS TAUGHT HERE... CRABWARTS IS A COMPLETE RIP-OFF. A SCAM. A WASTE OF YOUR PARENTS' HARD-EARNED MONEY.
ENOUGH WITH THE LEGAL DISCLAIMERS. LET'S HAVE SOME FUN.
YAY!

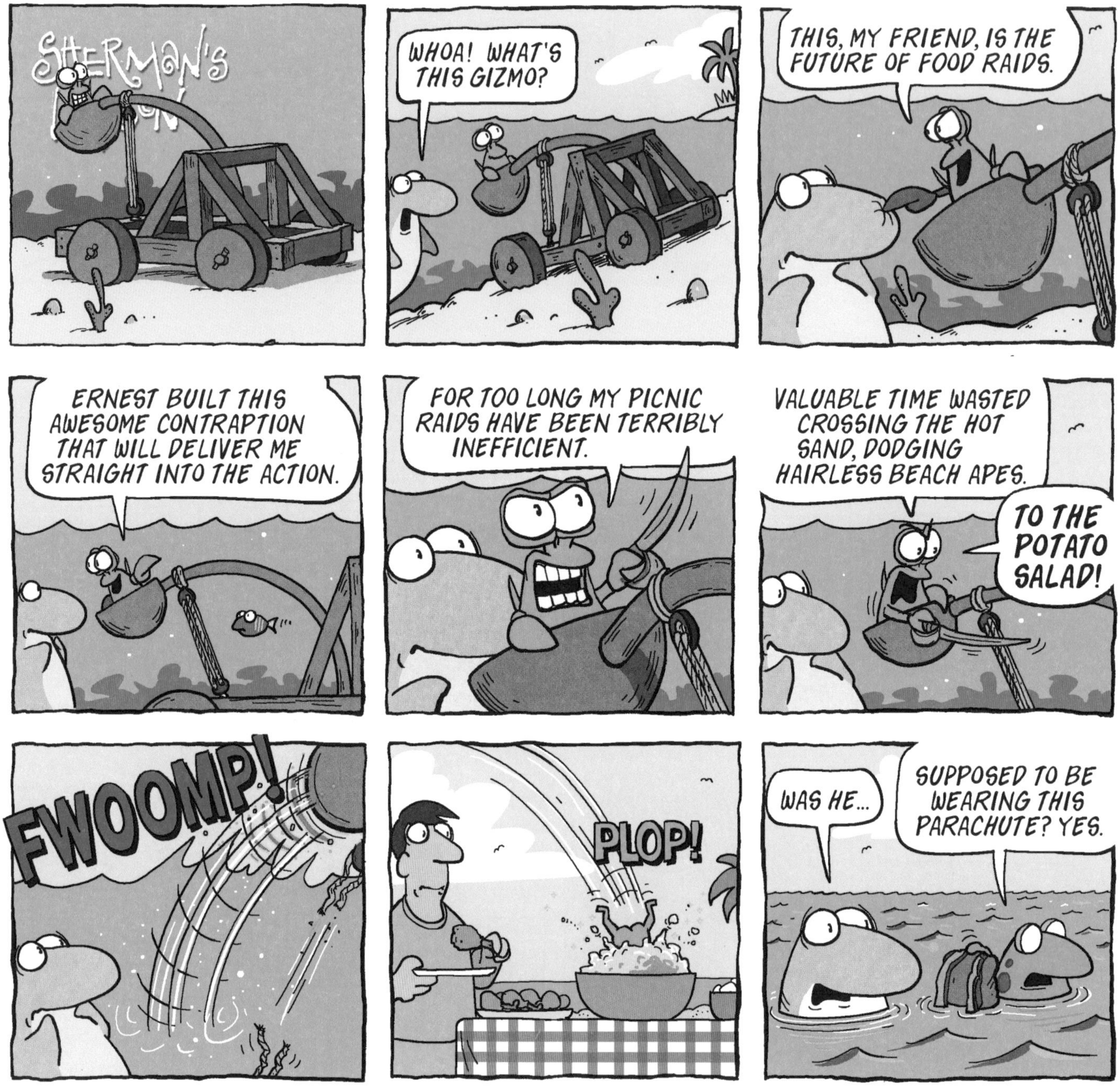
SHERMAN'S LAGOON
WHOA! WHAT'S THIS GIZMO?
THIS, MY FRIEND, IS THE FUTURE OF FOOD RAIDS.
ERNEST BUILT THIS AWESOME CONTRAPTION THAT WILL DELIVER ME STRAIGHT INTO THE ACTION.
FOR TOO LONG MY PICNIC RAIDS HAVE BEEN TERRIBLY INEFFICIENT.
VALUABLE TIME WASTED CROSSING THE HOT SAND, DODGING HAIRLESS BEACH APES.
TO THE POTATO SALAD!
FWOOMP!
PLOP!
WAS HE...
SUPPOSED TO BE WEARING THIS PARACHUTE? YES.

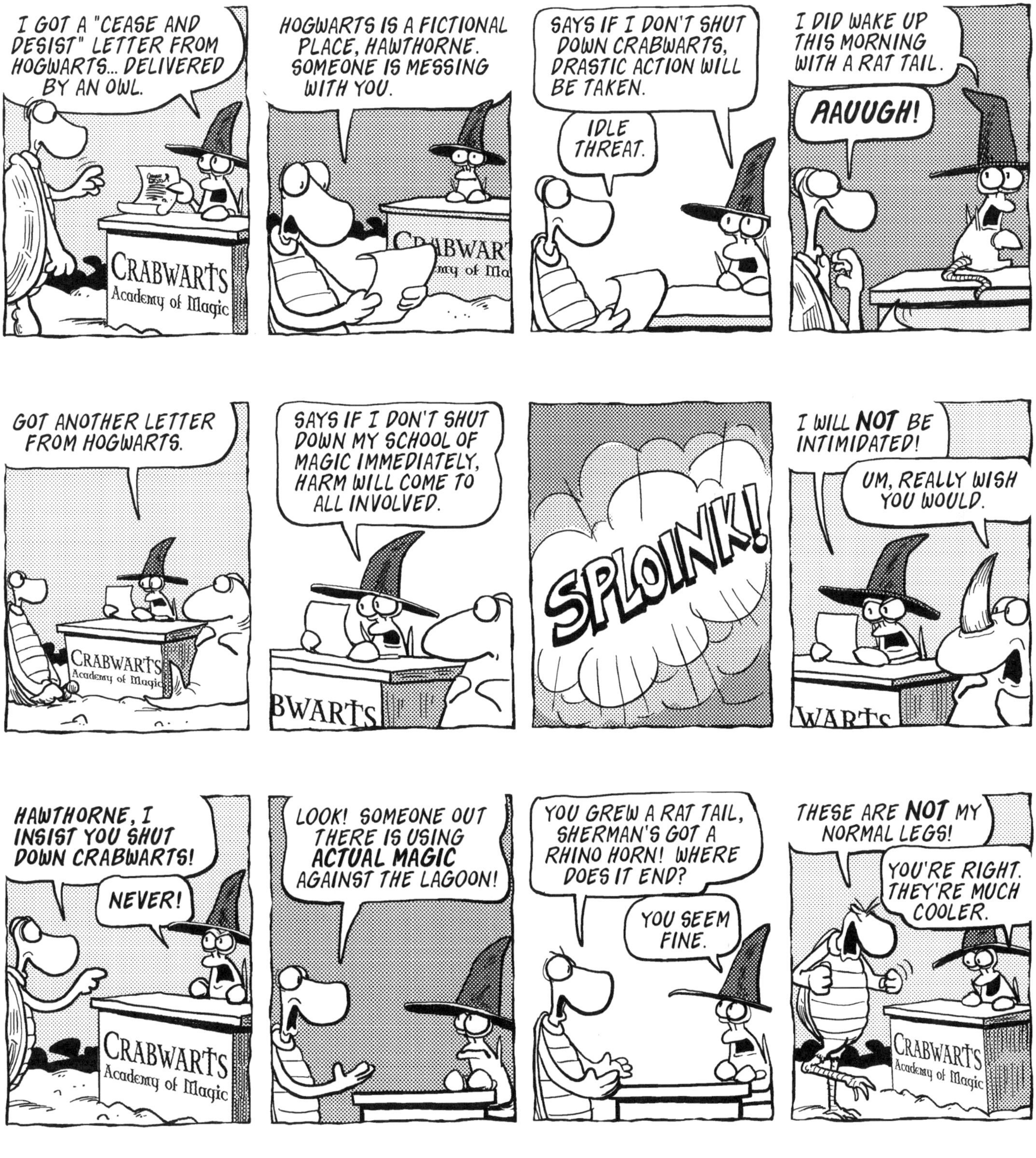
I GOT A "CEASE AND DESIST" LETTER FROM HOGWARTS... DELIVERED BY AN OWL.
HOGWARTS IS A FICTIONAL PLACE, HAWTHORNE. SOMEONE IS MESSING WITH YOU.
CRABWARTS Academy of Magic
SAYS IF I DON'T SHUT DOWN CRABWARTS, DRASTIC ACTION WILL BE TAKEN.
IDLE THREAT.
I DID WAKE UP THIS MORNING WITH A RAT TAIL.
AAUUGH!
GOT ANOTHER LETTER FROM HOGWARTS.
CRABWARTS Academy of Magic
SAYS IF I DON'T SHUT DOWN MY SCHOOL OF MAGIC IMMEDIATELY, HARM WILL COME TO ALL INVOLVED.
BWARTS
SPLOINK!
I WILL **NOT** BE INTIMIDATED!
UM, REALLY WISH YOU WOULD.
WARTS
HAWTHORNE, I INSIST YOU SHUT DOWN CRABWARTS!
NEVER!
CRABWARTS Academy of Magic
LOOK! SOMEONE OUT THERE IS USING **ACTUAL MAGIC** AGAINST THE LAGOON!
YOU GREW A RAT TAIL, SHERMAN'S GOT A RHINO HORN! WHERE DOES IT END?
YOU SEEM FINE.
THESE ARE **NOT** MY NORMAL LEGS!
YOU'RE RIGHT. THEY'RE MUCH COOLER.
CRABWARTS Academy of Magic

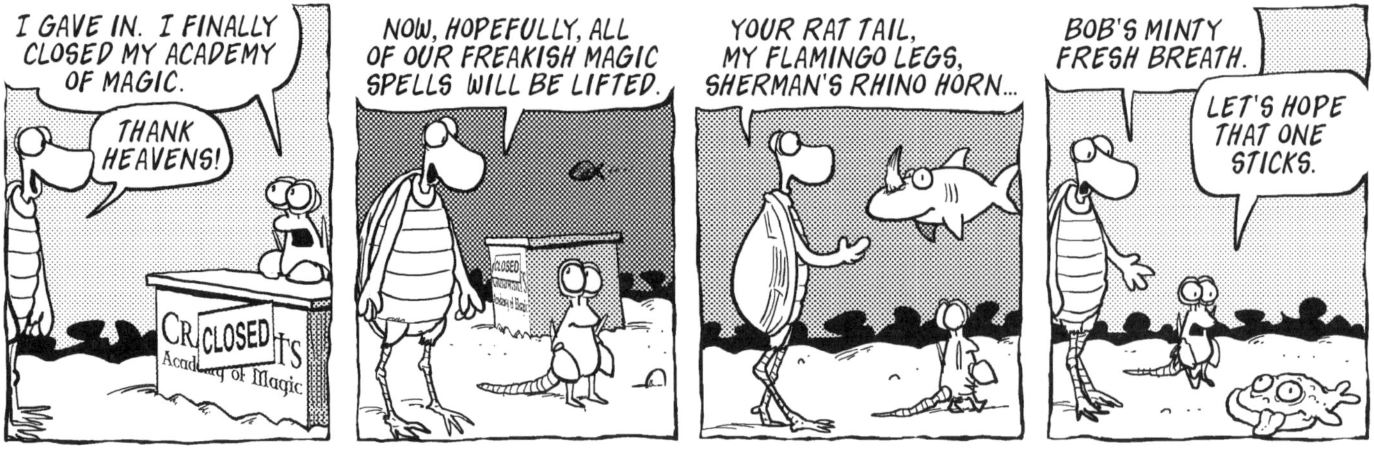
I GAVE IN. I FINALLY CLOSED MY ACADEMY OF MAGIC.
THANK HEAVENS!
CLOSED
NOW, HOPEFULLY, ALL OF OUR FREAKISH MAGIC SPELLS WILL BE LIFTED.
YOUR RAT TAIL, MY FLAMINGO LEGS, SHERMAN'S RHINO HORN...
BOB'S MINTY FRESH BREATH.
LET'S HOPE THAT ONE STICKS.

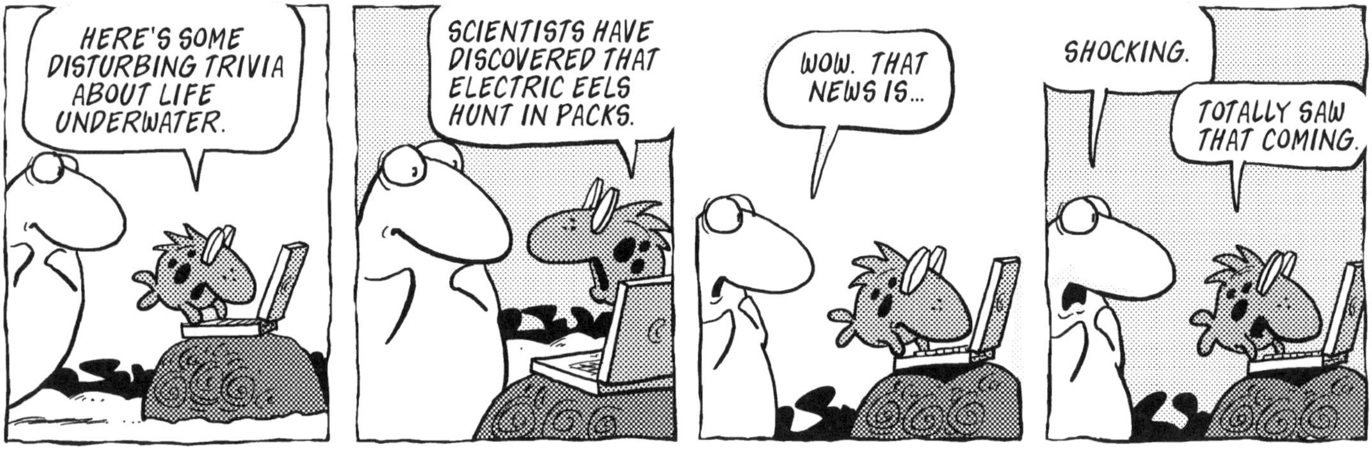
HERE'S SOME DISTURBING TRIVIA ABOUT LIFE UNDERWATER.
SCIENTISTS HAVE DISCOVERED THAT ELECTRIC EELS HUNT IN PACKS.
WOW. THAT NEWS IS...
SHOCKING.
TOTALLY SAW THAT COMING.

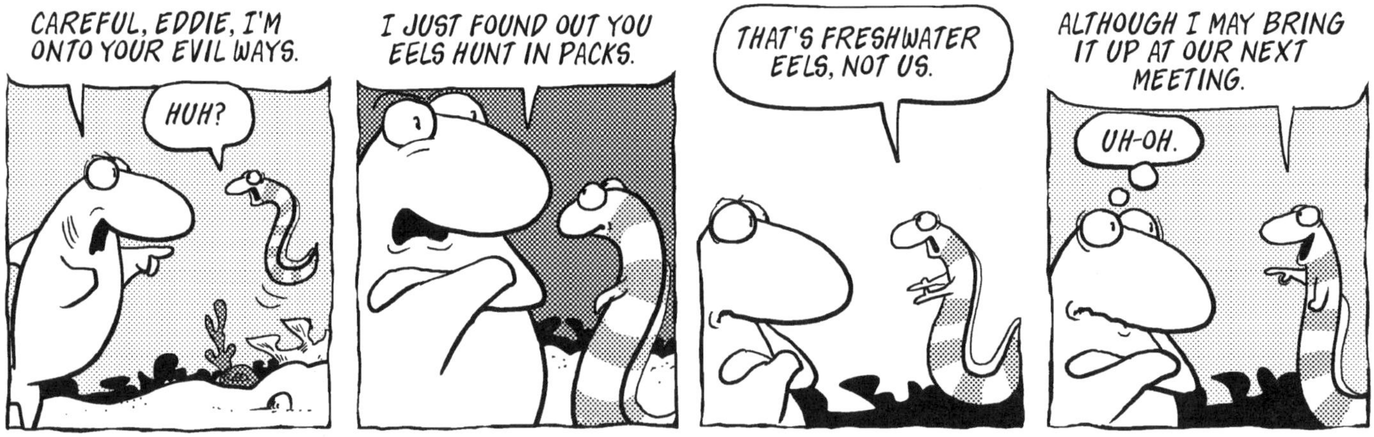
CAREFUL, EDDIE, I'M ONTO YOUR EVIL WAYS.
HUH?
I JUST FOUND OUT YOU EELS HUNT IN PACKS.
THAT'S FRESHWATER EELS, NOT US.
ALTHOUGH I MAY BRING IT UP AT OUR NEXT MEETING.
UH-OH.

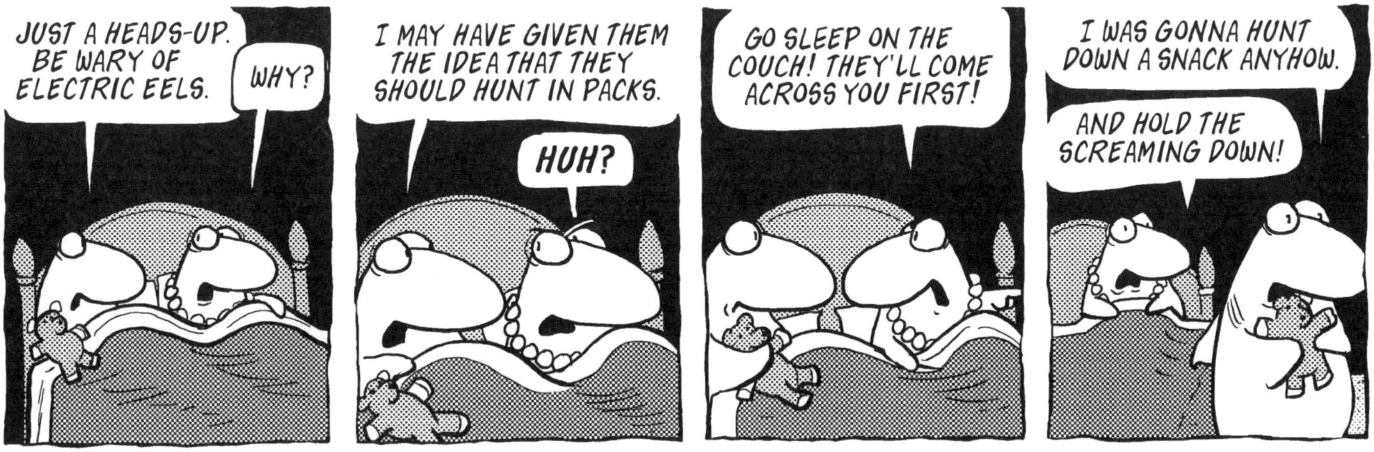
JUST A HEADS-UP. BE WARY OF ELECTRIC EELS.
WHY?
I MAY HAVE GIVEN THEM THE IDEA THAT THEY SHOULD HUNT IN PACKS.
HUH?
GO SLEEP ON THE COUCH! THEY'LL COME ACROSS YOU FIRST!
I WAS GONNA HUNT DOWN A SNACK ANYHOW.
AND HOLD THE SCREAMING DOWN!

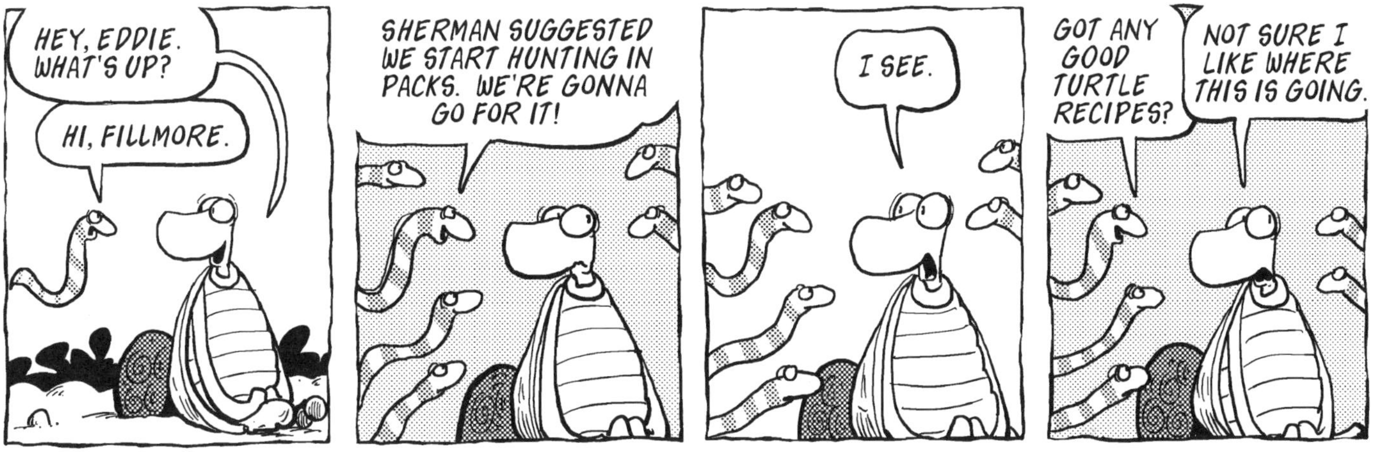
HEY, EDDIE. WHAT'S UP?
HI, FILLMORE.
SHERMAN SUGGESTED WE START HUNTING IN PACKS. WE'RE GONNA GO FOR IT!
I SEE.
GOT ANY GOOD TURTLE RECIPES?
NOT SURE I LIKE WHERE THIS IS GOING.

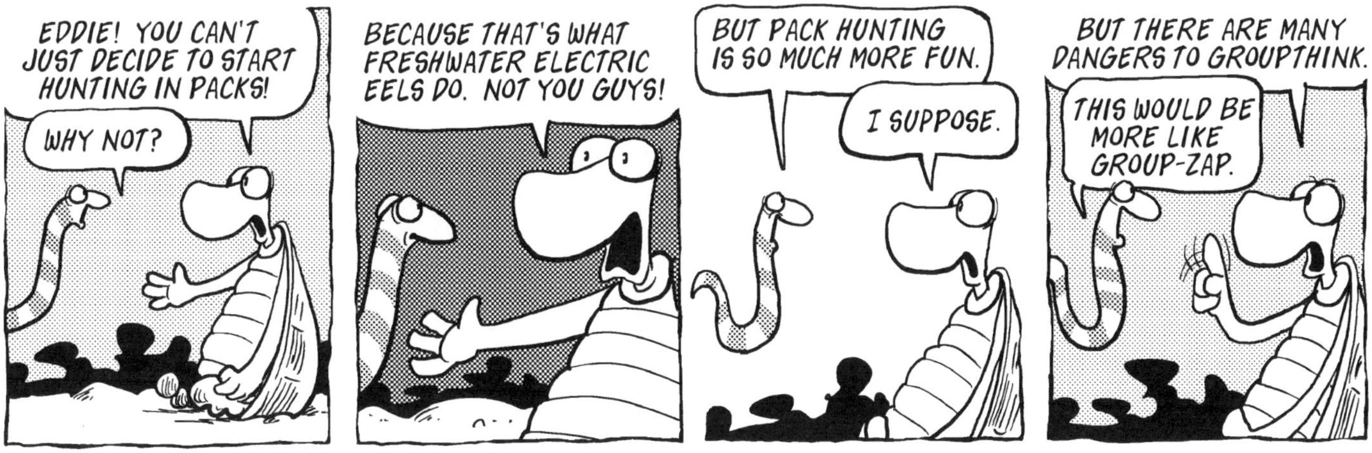
EDDIE! YOU CAN'T JUST DECIDE TO START HUNTING IN PACKS!
WHY NOT?
BECAUSE THAT'S WHAT FRESHWATER ELECTRIC EELS DO. NOT YOU GUYS!
BUT PACK HUNTING IS SO MUCH MORE FUN.
I SUPPOSE.
BUT THERE ARE MANY DANGERS TO GROUPTHINK.
THIS WOULD BE MORE LIKE GROUP-ZAP.

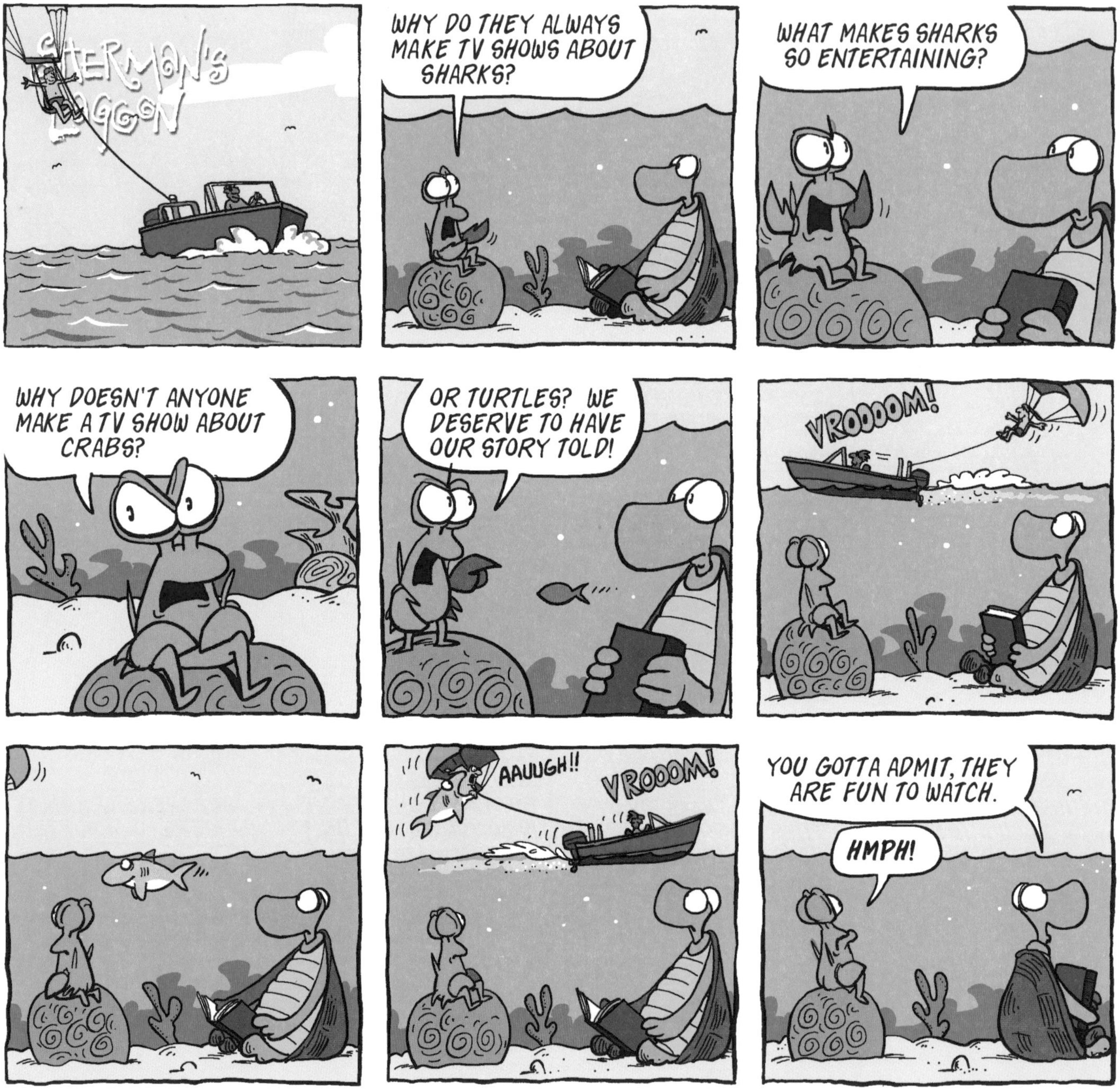
SHERMAN'S LAGOON
WHY DO THEY ALWAYS MAKE TV SHOWS ABOUT SHARKS?
WHAT MAKES SHARKS SO ENTERTAINING?
WHY DOESN'T ANYONE MAKE A TV SHOW ABOUT CRABS?
OR TURTLES? WE DESERVE TO HAVE OUR STORY TOLD!
VROOOOM!
AAUUGH!!
VROOOM!
YOU GOTTA ADMIT, THEY ARE FUN TO WATCH.
HMPH!

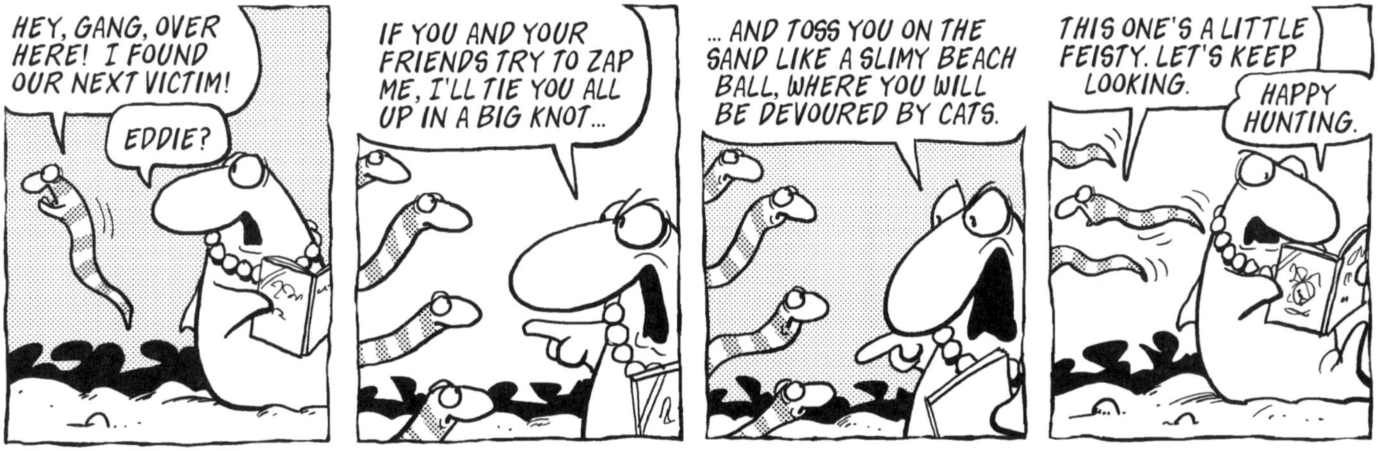
HEY, GANG, OVER HERE! I FOUND OUR NEXT VICTIM!
EDDIE?
IF YOU AND YOUR FRIENDS TRY TO ZAP ME, I'LL TIE YOU ALL UP IN A BIG KNOT...
... AND TOSS YOU ON THE SAND LIKE A SLIMY BEACH BALL, WHERE YOU WILL BE DEVOURED BY CATS.
THIS ONE'S A LITTLE FEISTY. LET'S KEEP LOOKING.
HAPPY HUNTING.

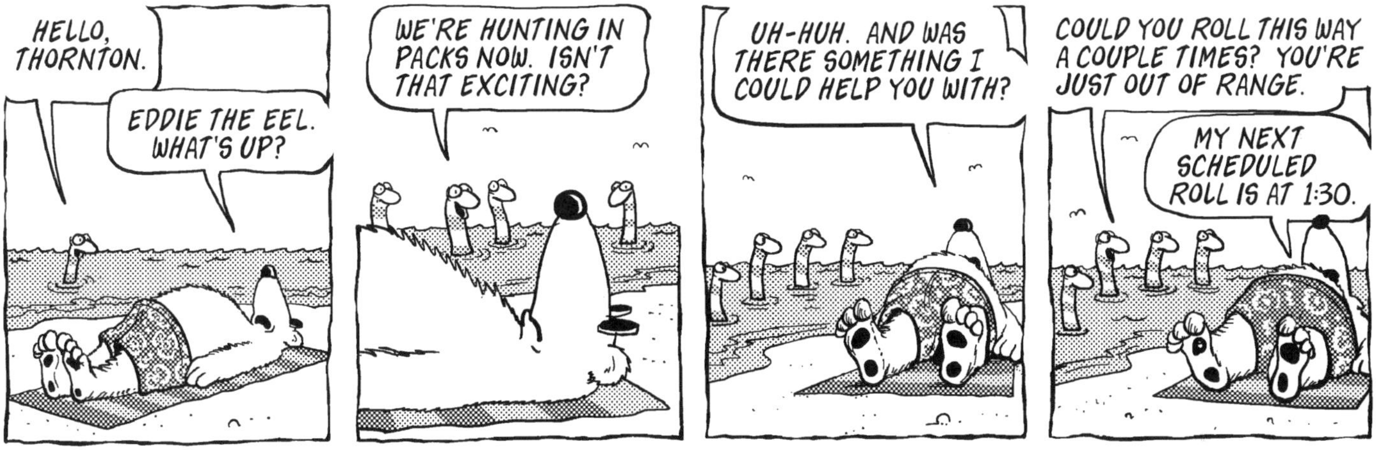
HELLO, THORNTON.
EDDIE THE EEL. WHAT'S UP?
WE'RE HUNTING IN PACKS NOW. ISN'T THAT EXCITING?
UH-HUH. AND WAS THERE SOMETHING I COULD HELP YOU WITH?
COULD YOU ROLL THIS WAY A COUPLE TIMES? YOU'RE JUST OUT OF RANGE.
MY NEXT SCHEDULED ROLL IS AT 1:30.

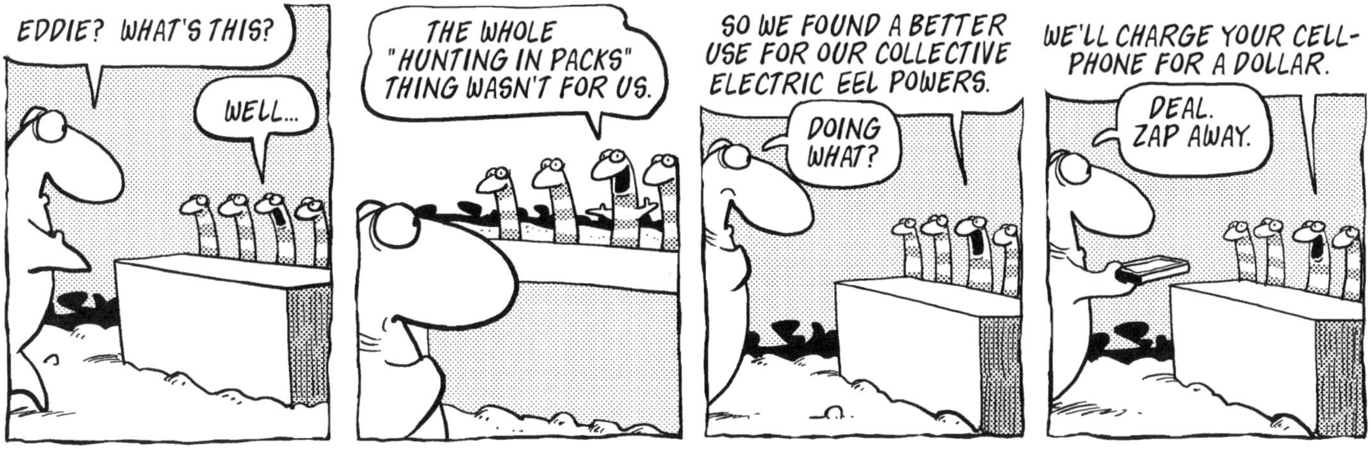
EDDIE? WHAT'S THIS?
WELL...
THE WHOLE "HUNTING IN PACKS" THING WASN'T FOR US.
SO WE FOUND A BETTER USE FOR OUR COLLECTIVE ELECTRIC EEL POWERS.
DOING WHAT?
WE'LL CHARGE YOUR CELL-PHONE FOR A DOLLAR.
DEAL. ZAP AWAY.

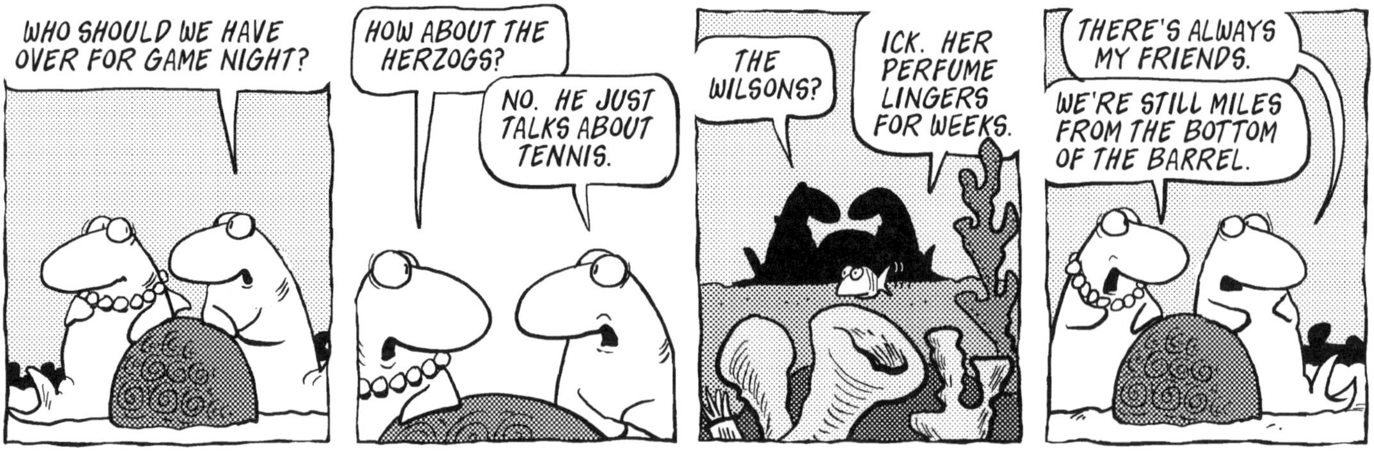
WHO SHOULD WE HAVE OVER FOR GAME NIGHT?
HOW ABOUT THE HERZOGS?
NO. HE JUST TALKS ABOUT TENNIS.
THE WILSONS?
ICK. HER PERFUME LINGERS FOR WEEKS.
THERE'S ALWAYS MY FRIENDS.
WE'RE STILL MILES FROM THE BOTTOM OF THE BARREL.

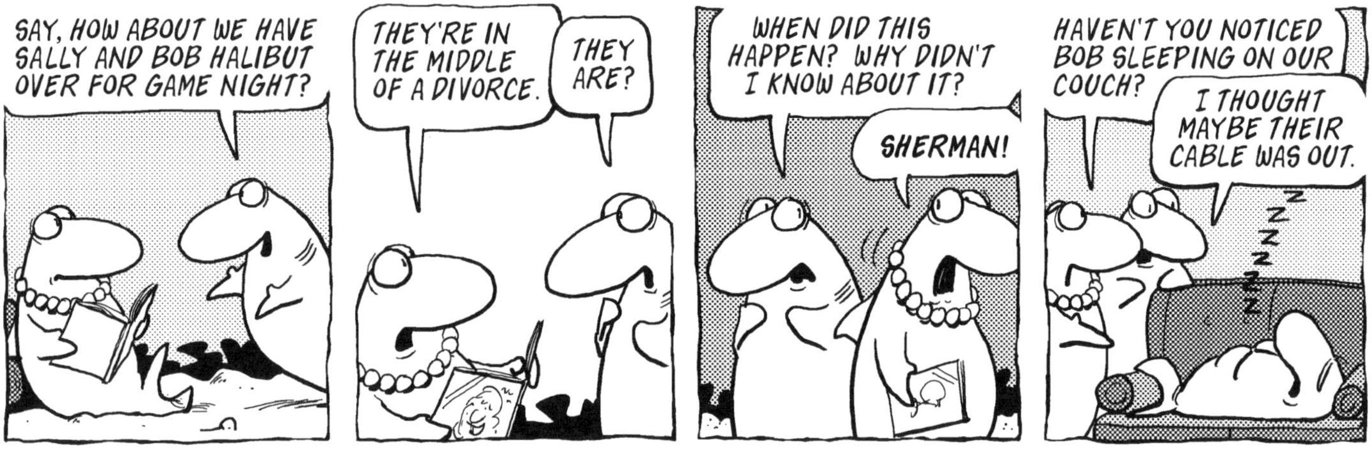
SAY, HOW ABOUT WE HAVE SALLY AND BOB HALIBUT OVER FOR GAME NIGHT?
THEY'RE IN THE MIDDLE OF A DIVORCE.
THEY ARE?
WHEN DID THIS HAPPEN? WHY DIDN'T I KNOW ABOUT IT?
SHERMAN!
HAVEN'T YOU NOTICED BOB SLEEPING ON OUR COUCH?
I THOUGHT MAYBE THEIR CABLE WAS OUT.
Z Z Z Z Z

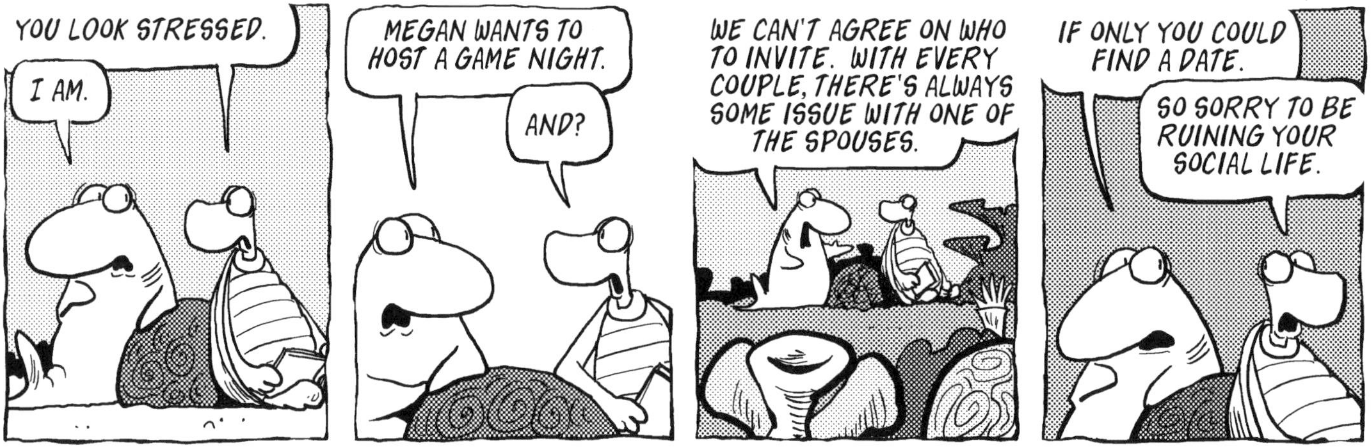
YOU LOOK STRESSED.
I AM.
MEGAN WANTS TO HOST A GAME NIGHT.
AND?
WE CAN'T AGREE ON WHO TO INVITE. WITH EVERY COUPLE, THERE'S ALWAYS SOME ISSUE WITH ONE OF THE SPOUSES.
IF ONLY YOU COULD FIND A DATE.
SO SORRY TO BE RUINING YOUR SOCIAL LIFE.

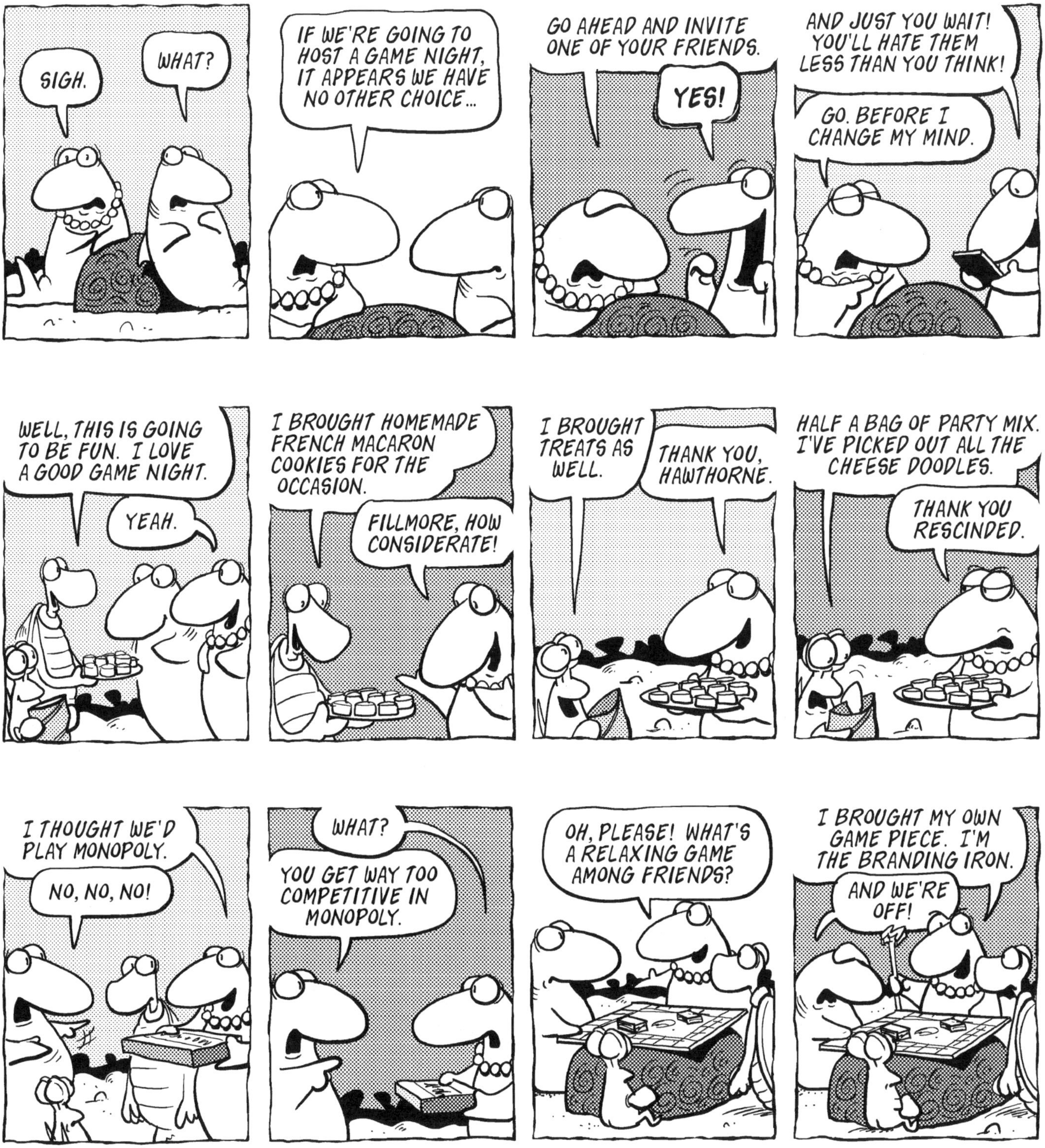
SIGH.
WHAT?
IF WE'RE GOING TO HOST A GAME NIGHT, IT APPEARS WE HAVE NO OTHER CHOICE...
GO AHEAD AND INVITE ONE OF YOUR FRIENDS.
YES!
AND JUST YOU WAIT! YOU'LL HATE THEM LESS THAN YOU THINK!
GO. BEFORE I CHANGE MY MIND.
WELL, THIS IS GOING TO BE FUN. I LOVE A GOOD GAME NIGHT.
YEAH.
I BROUGHT HOMEMADE FRENCH MACARON COOKIES FOR THE OCCASION.
FILLMORE, HOW CONSIDERATE!
I BROUGHT TREATS AS WELL.
THANK YOU, HAWTHORNE.
HALF A BAG OF PARTY MIX. I'VE PICKED OUT ALL THE CHEESE DOODLES.
THANK YOU RESCINDED.
I THOUGHT WE'D PLAY MONOPOLY.
NO, NO, NO!
WHAT?
YOU GET WAY TOO COMPETITIVE IN MONOPOLY.
OH, PLEASE! WHAT'S A RELAXING GAME AMONG FRIENDS?
I BROUGHT MY OWN GAME PIECE. I'M THE BRANDING IRON.
AND WE'RE OFF!

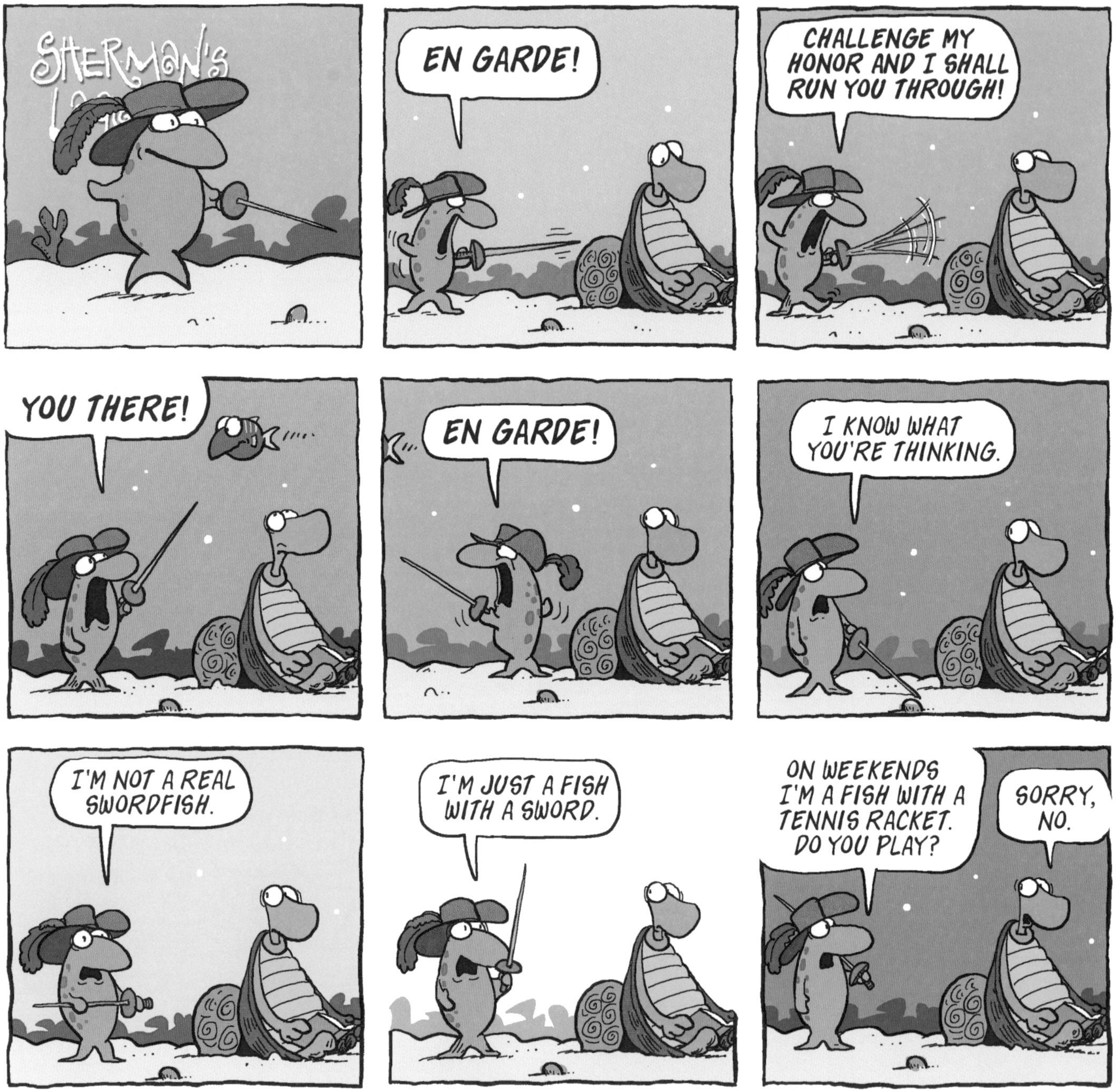
SHERMAN'S LAGOON
EN GARDE!
CHALLENGE MY HONOR AND I SHALL RUN YOU THROUGH!
YOU THERE!
EN GARDE!
I KNOW WHAT YOU'RE THINKING.
I'M NOT A REAL SWORDFISH.
I'M JUST A FISH WITH A SWORD.
ON WEEKENDS I'M A FISH WITH A TENNIS RACKET. DO YOU PLAY?
SORRY, NO.

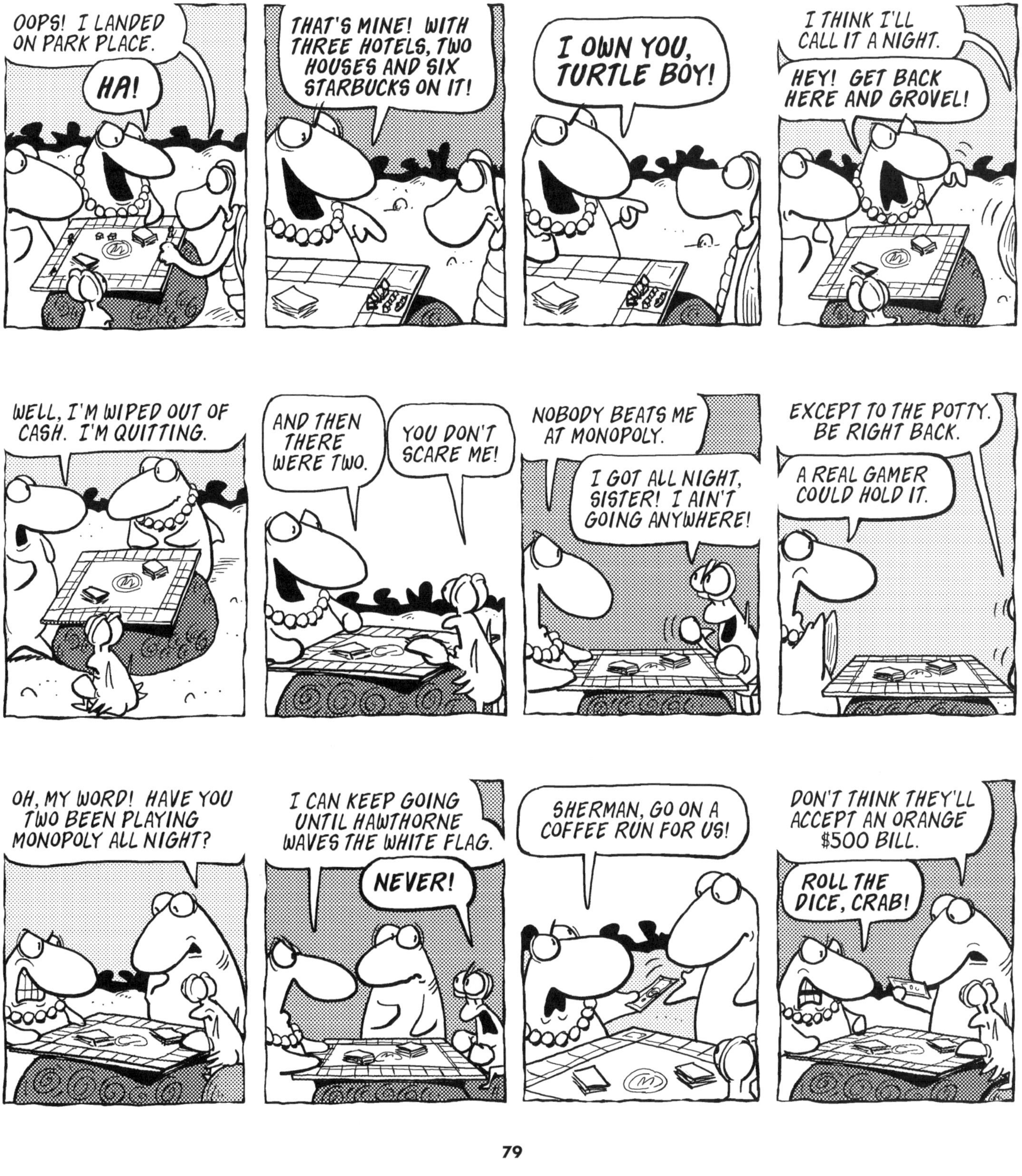
OOPS! I LANDED ON PARK PLACE.
HA!
THAT'S MINE! WITH THREE HOTELS, TWO HOUSES AND SIX STARBUCKS ON IT!
I OWN YOU, TURTLE BOY!
I THINK I'LL CALL IT A NIGHT.
HEY! GET BACK HERE AND GROVEL!
WELL, I'M WIPED OUT OF CASH. I'M QUITTING.
AND THEN THERE WERE TWO.
YOU DON'T SCARE ME!
NOBODY BEATS ME AT MONOPOLY.
I GOT ALL NIGHT, SISTER! I AIN'T GOING ANYWHERE!
EXCEPT TO THE POTTY. BE RIGHT BACK.
A REAL GAMER COULD HOLD IT.
OH, MY WORD! HAVE YOU TWO BEEN PLAYING MONOPOLY ALL NIGHT?
I CAN KEEP GOING UNTIL HAWTHORNE WAVES THE WHITE FLAG.
NEVER!
SHERMAN, GO ON A COFFEE RUN FOR US!
DON'T THINK THEY'LL ACCEPT AN ORANGE $500 BILL.
ROLL THE DICE, CRAB!

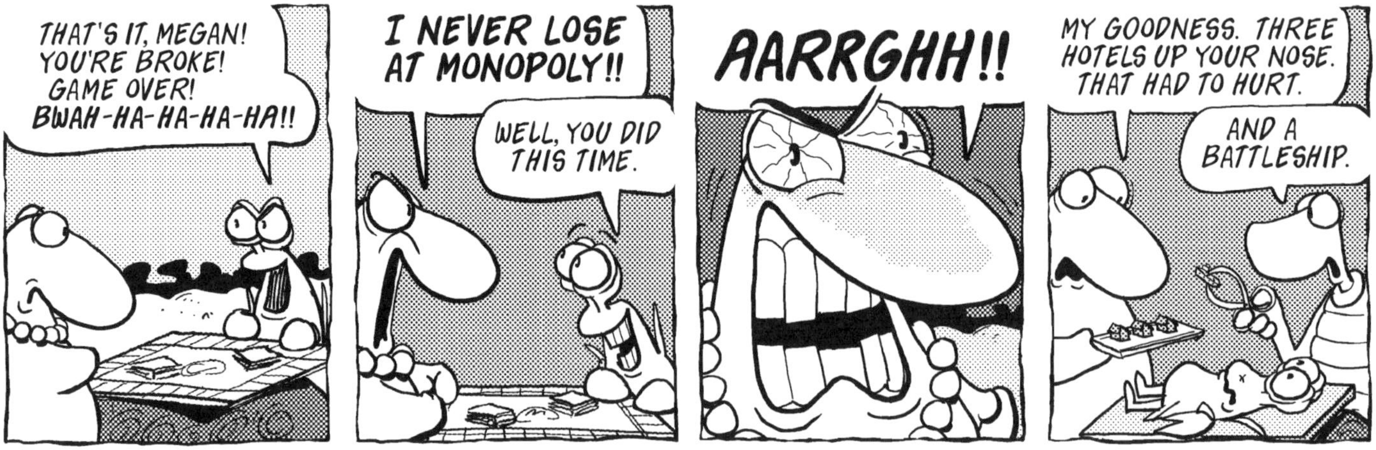
THAT'S IT, MEGAN! YOU'RE BROKE! GAME OVER! BWAH-HA-HA-HA-HA!!
I NEVER LOSE AT MONOPOLY!!
WELL, YOU DID THIS TIME.
AARRGHH!!
MY GOODNESS. THREE HOTELS UP YOUR NOSE. THAT HAD TO HURT.
AND A BATTLESHIP.

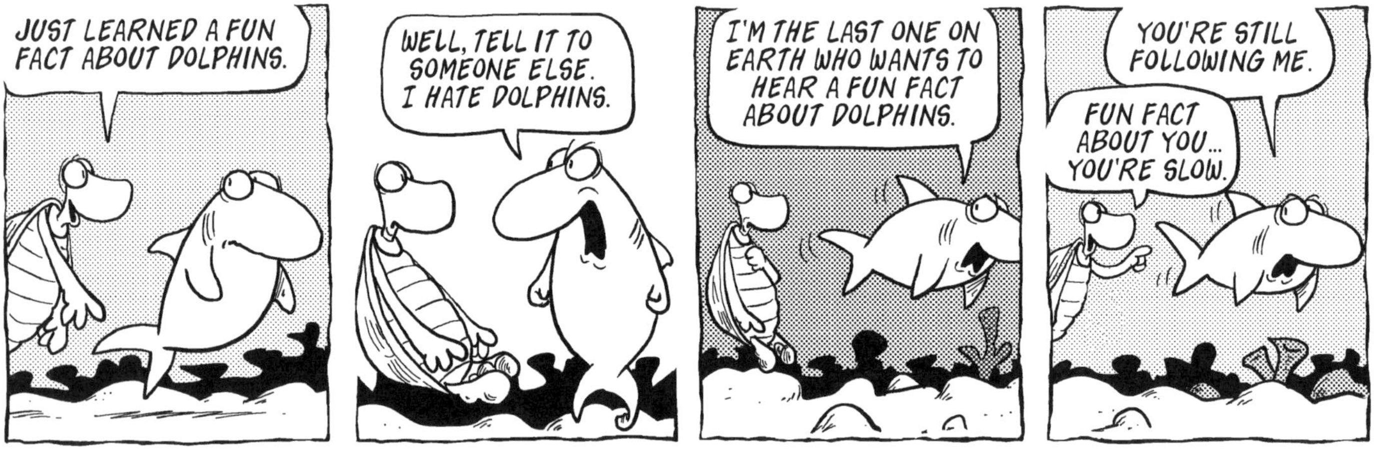
JUST LEARNED A FUN FACT ABOUT DOLPHINS.
WELL, TELL IT TO SOMEONE ELSE. I HATE DOLPHINS.
I'M THE LAST ONE ON EARTH WHO WANTS TO HEAR A FUN FACT ABOUT DOLPHINS.
YOU'RE STILL FOLLOWING ME.
FUN FACT ABOUT YOU... YOU'RE SLOW.

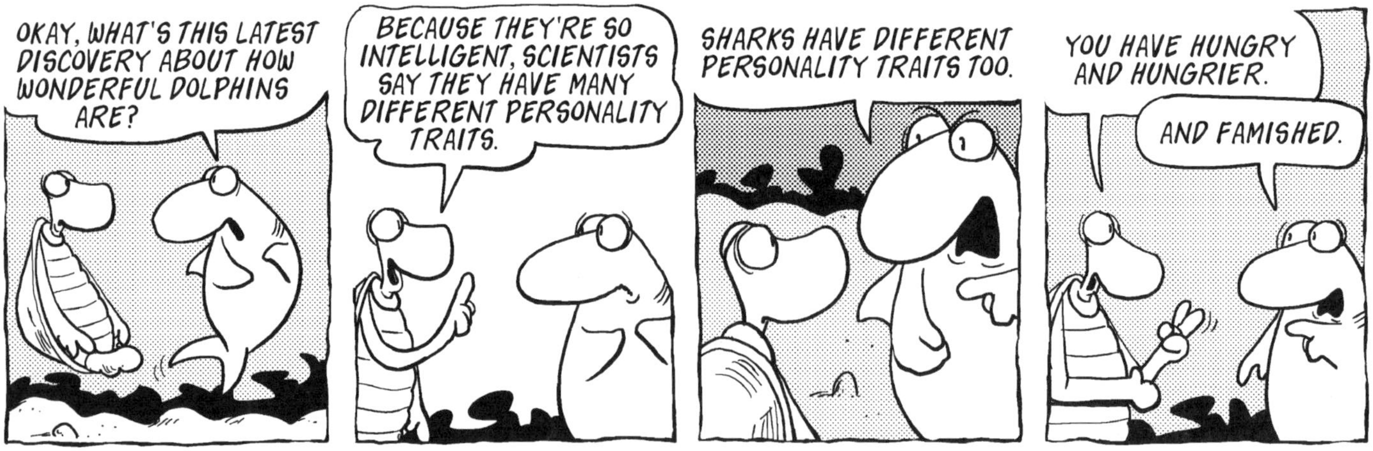
OKAY, WHAT'S THIS LATEST DISCOVERY ABOUT HOW WONDERFUL DOLPHINS ARE?
BECAUSE THEY'RE SO INTELLIGENT, SCIENTISTS SAY THEY HAVE MANY DIFFERENT PERSONALITY TRAITS.
SHARKS HAVE DIFFERENT PERSONALITY TRAITS TOO.
YOU HAVE HUNGRY AND HUNGRIER.
AND FAMISHED.

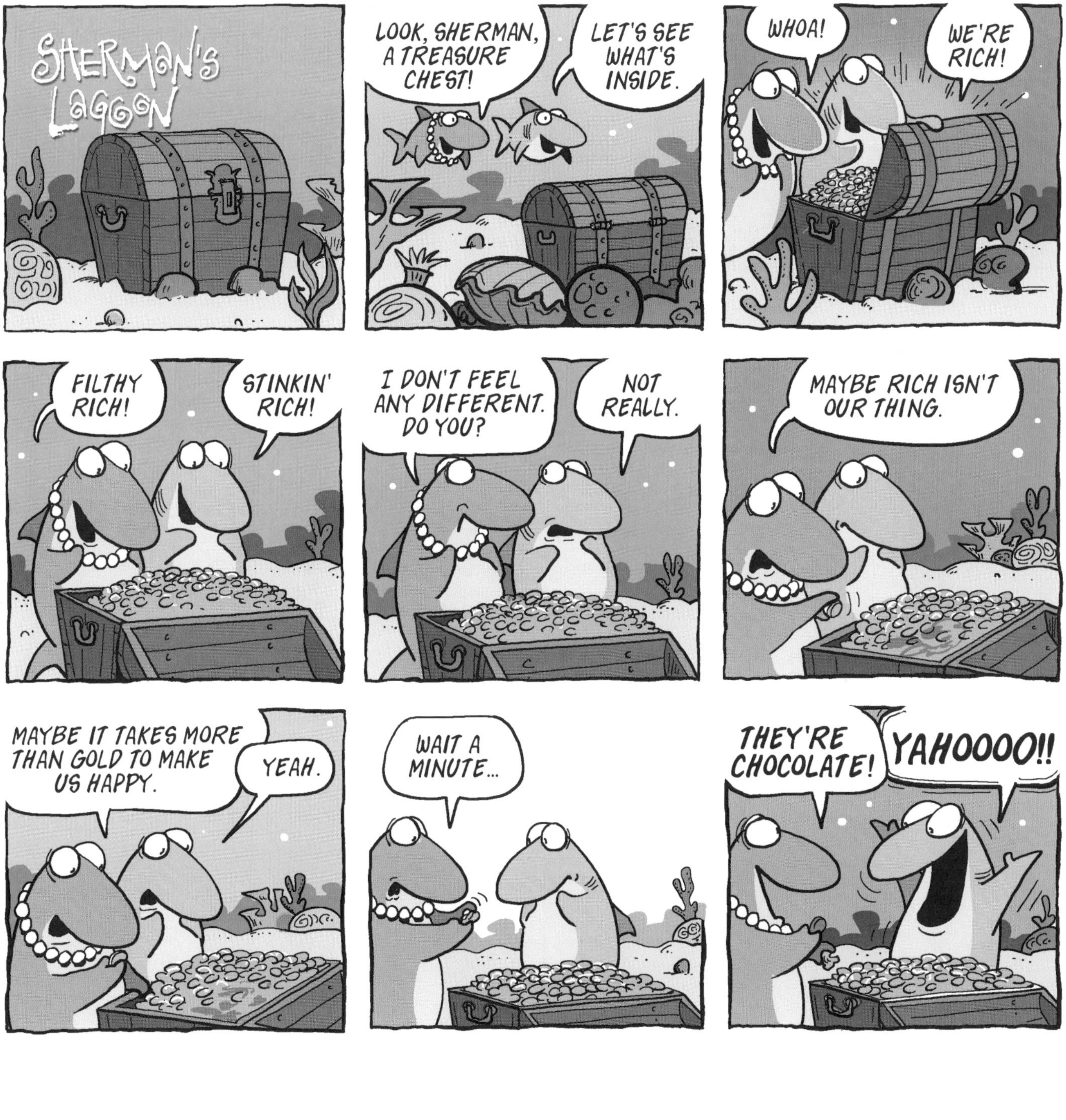
SHERMAN'S LAGOON
LOOK, SHERMAN, A TREASURE CHEST!
LET'S SEE WHAT'S INSIDE.
WHOA!
WE'RE RICH!
FILTHY RICH!
STINKIN' RICH!
I DON'T FEEL ANY DIFFERENT. DO YOU?
NOT REALLY.
MAYBE RICH ISN'T OUR THING.
MAYBE IT TAKES MORE THAN GOLD TO MAKE US HAPPY.
YEAH.
WAIT A MINUTE...
THEY'RE CHOCOLATE!
YAHOOOO!!

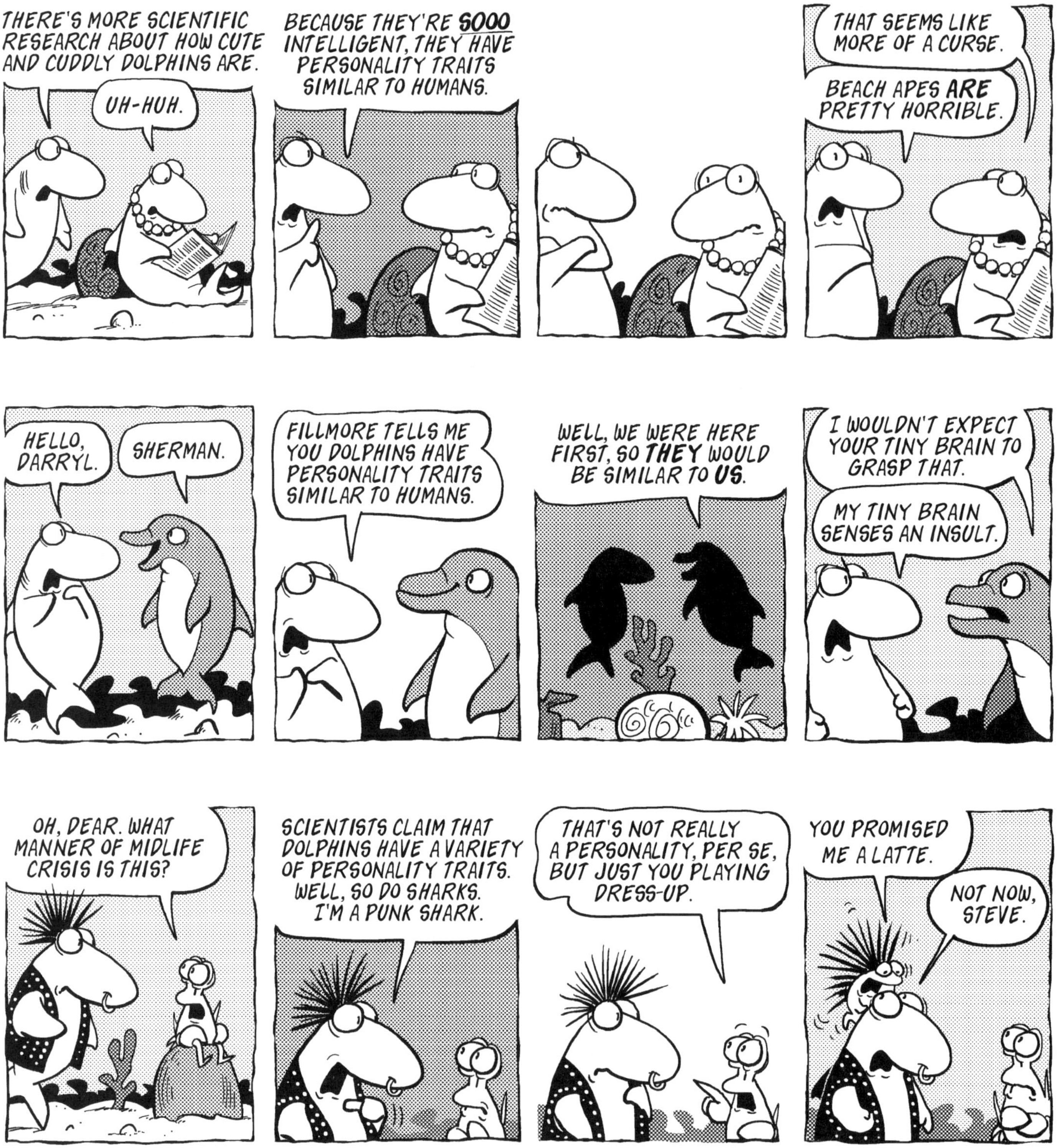
THERE'S MORE SCIENTIFIC RESEARCH ABOUT HOW CUTE AND CUDDLY DOLPHINS ARE.
UH-HUH.
BECAUSE THEY'RE SOOO INTELLIGENT, THEY HAVE PERSONALITY TRAITS SIMILAR TO HUMANS.
THAT SEEMS LIKE MORE OF A CURSE.
BEACH APES ARE PRETTY HORRIBLE.
HELLO, DARRYL.
SHERMAN.
FILLMORE TELLS ME YOU DOLPHINS HAVE PERSONALITY TRAITS SIMILAR TO HUMANS.
WELL, WE WERE HERE FIRST, SO THEY WOULD BE SIMILAR TO US.
I WOULDN'T EXPECT YOUR TINY BRAIN TO GRASP THAT.
MY TINY BRAIN SENSES AN INSULT.
OH, DEAR. WHAT MANNER OF MIDLIFE CRISIS IS THIS?
SCIENTISTS CLAIM THAT DOLPHINS HAVE A VARIETY OF PERSONALITY TRAITS. WELL, SO DO SHARKS. I'M A PUNK SHARK.
THAT'S NOT REALLY A PERSONALITY, PER SE, BUT JUST YOU PLAYING DRESS-UP.
YOU PROMISED ME A LATTE.
NOT NOW, STEVE.

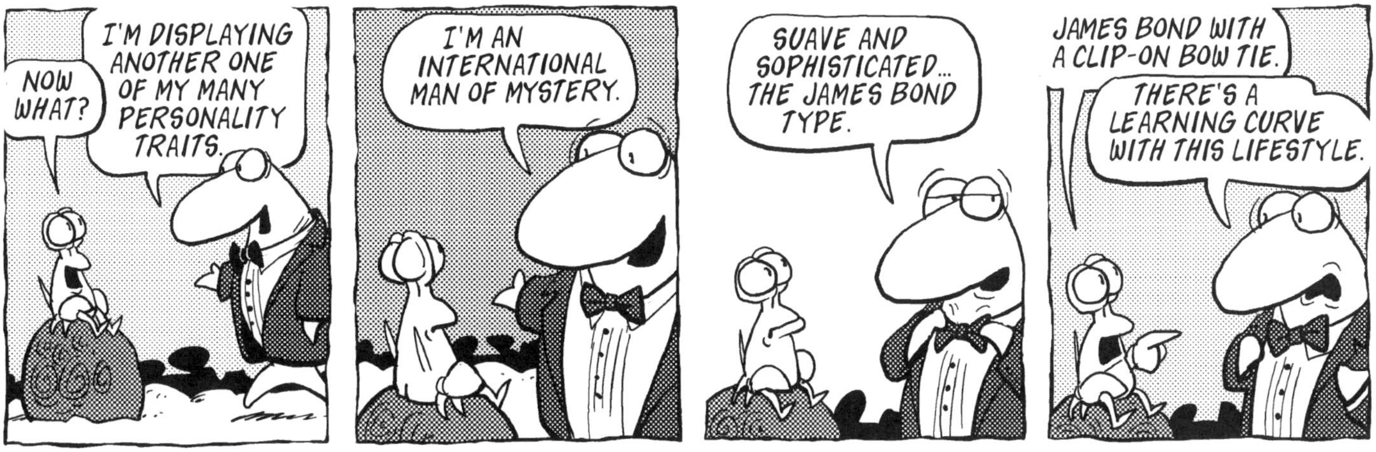
I'M DISPLAYING ANOTHER ONE OF MY MANY PERSONALITY TRAITS.
NOW WHAT?
I'M AN INTERNATIONAL MAN OF MYSTERY.
SUAVE AND SOPHISTICATED... THE JAMES BOND TYPE.
JAMES BOND WITH A CLIP-ON BOW TIE.
THERE'S A LEARNING CURVE WITH THIS LIFESTYLE.

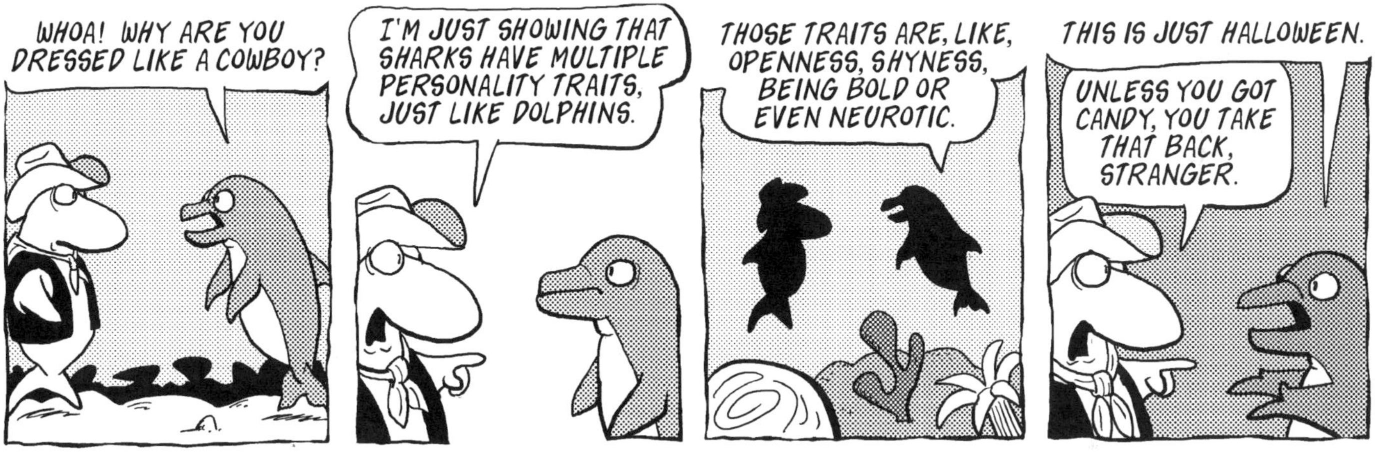
WHOA! WHY ARE YOU DRESSED LIKE A COWBOY?
I'M JUST SHOWING THAT SHARKS HAVE MULTIPLE PERSONALITY TRAITS, JUST LIKE DOLPHINS.
THOSE TRAITS ARE, LIKE, OPENNESS, SHYNESS, BEING BOLD OR EVEN NEUROTIC.
THIS IS JUST HALLOWEEN.
UNLESS YOU GOT CANDY, YOU TAKE THAT BACK, STRANGER.

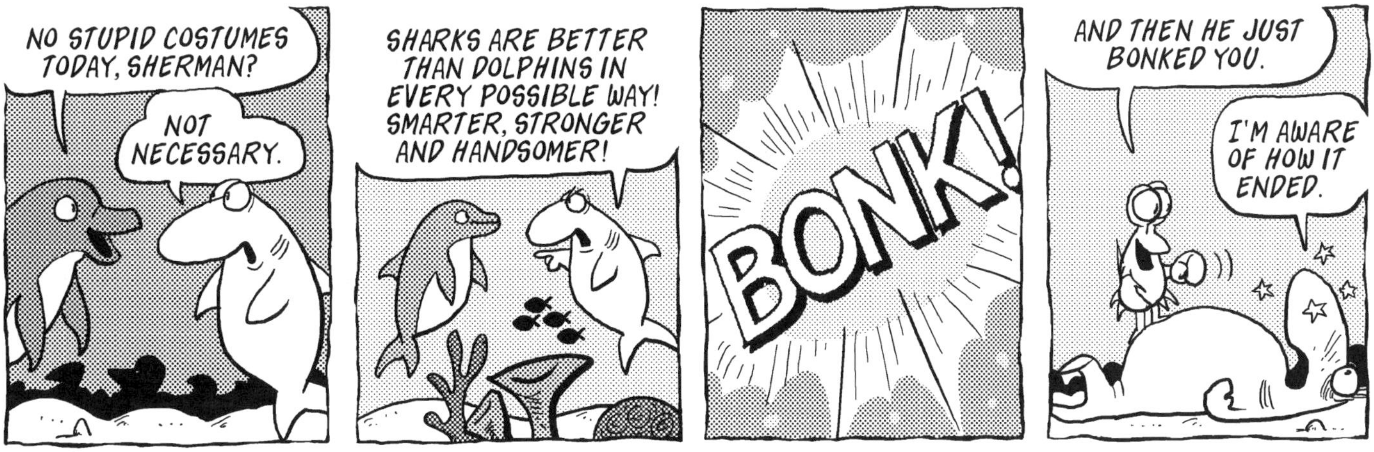
NO STUPID COSTUMES TODAY, SHERMAN?
NOT NECESSARY.
SHARKS ARE BETTER THAN DOLPHINS IN EVERY POSSIBLE WAY! SMARTER, STRONGER AND HANDSOMER!
BONK!
AND THEN HE JUST BONKED YOU.
I'M AWARE OF HOW IT ENDED.

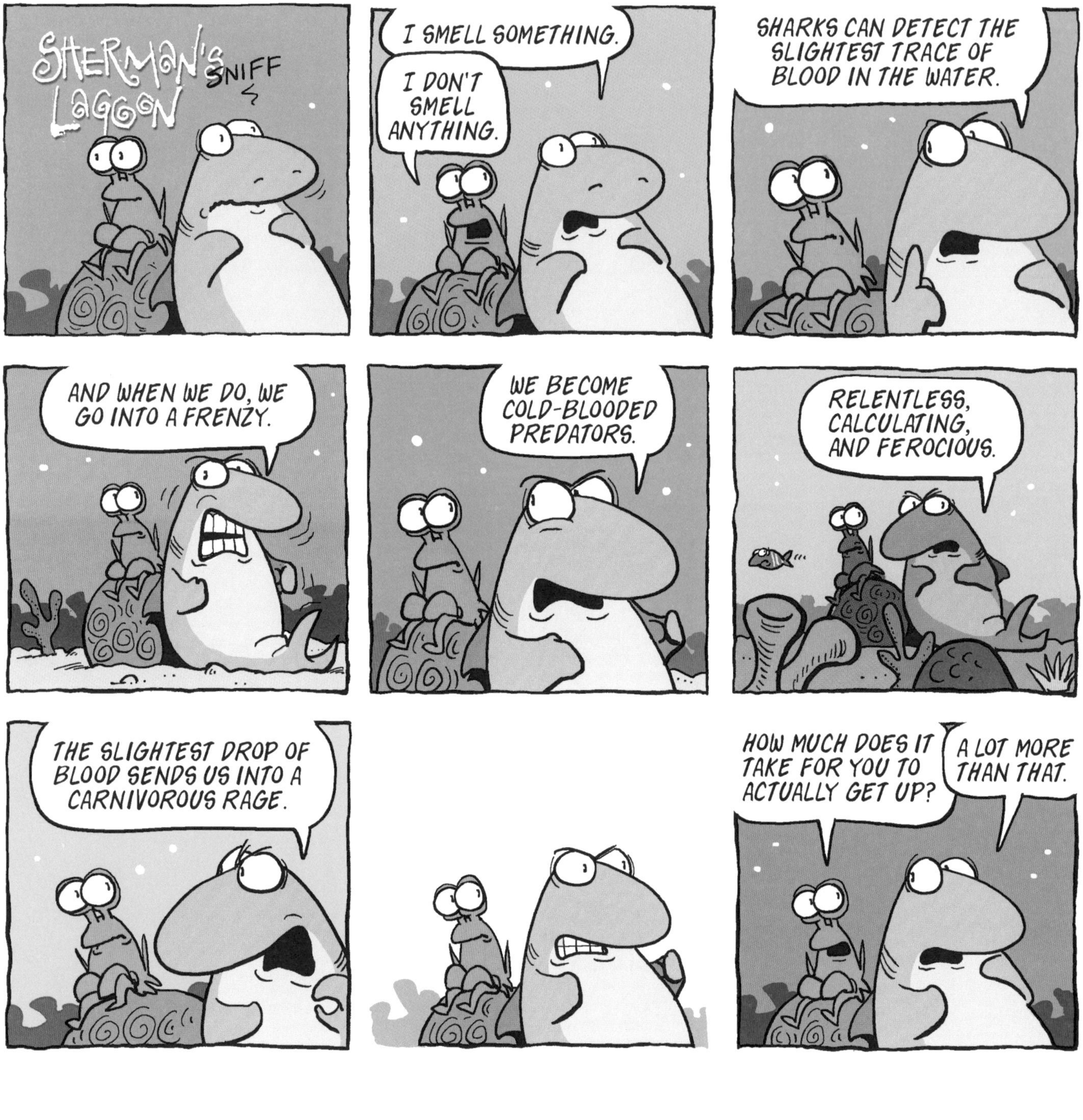
SHERMAN'S LAGOON
SNIFF
I SMELL SOMETHING.
I DON'T SMELL ANYTHING.
SHARKS CAN DETECT THE SLIGHTEST TRACE OF BLOOD IN THE WATER.
AND WHEN WE DO, WE GO INTO A FRENZY.
WE BECOME COLD-BLOODED PREDATORS.
RELENTLESS, CALCULATING, AND FEROCIOUS.
THE SLIGHTEST DROP OF BLOOD SENDS US INTO A CARNIVOROUS RAGE.
HOW MUCH DOES IT TAKE FOR YOU TO ACTUALLY GET UP?
A LOT MORE THAN THAT.

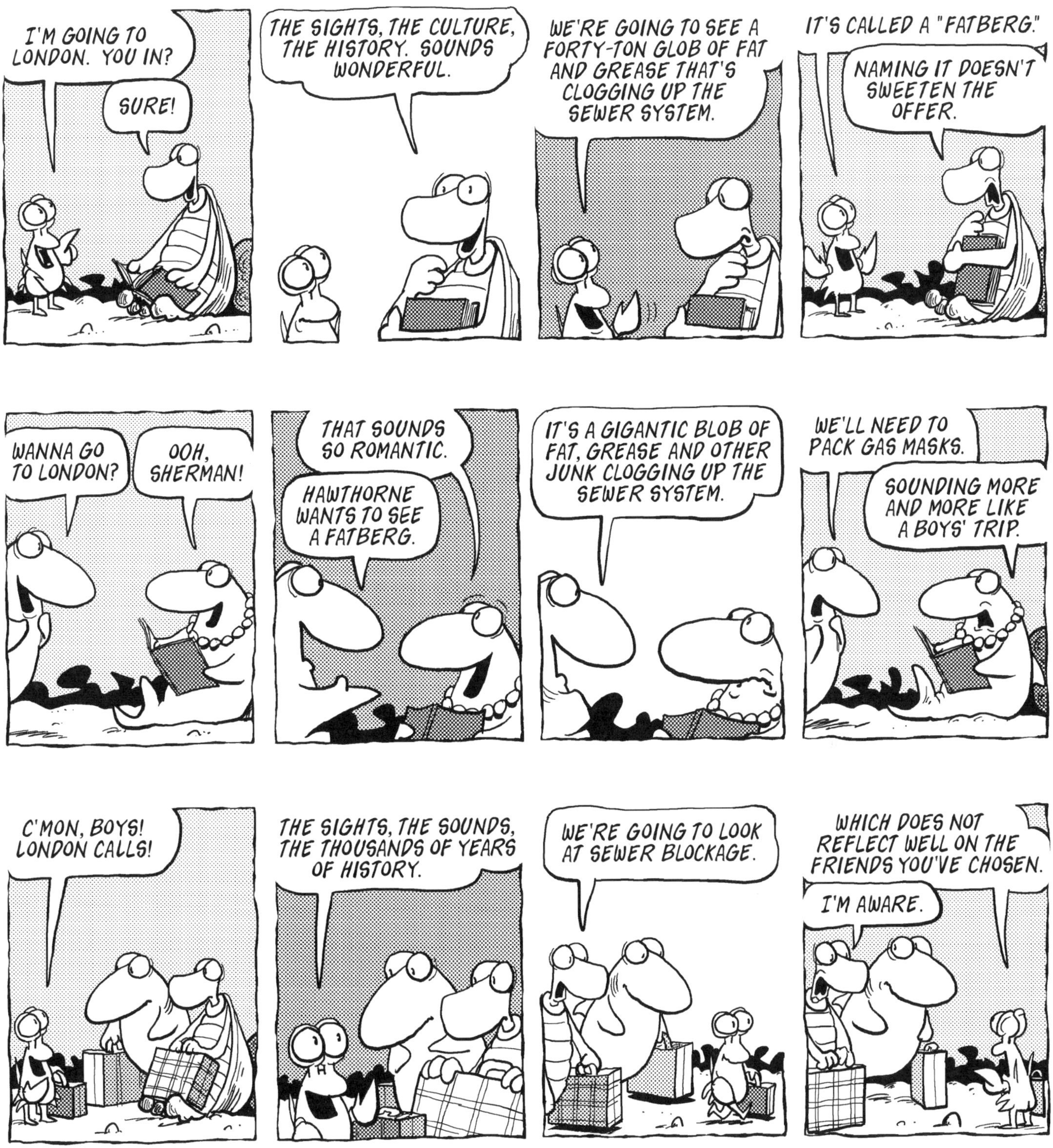
I'M GOING TO LONDON. YOU IN?
SURE!
THE SIGHTS, THE CULTURE, THE HISTORY. SOUNDS WONDERFUL.
WE'RE GOING TO SEE A FORTY-TON GLOB OF FAT AND GREASE THAT'S CLOGGING UP THE SEWER SYSTEM.
IT'S CALLED A "FATBERG."
NAMING IT DOESN'T SWEETEN THE OFFER.
WANNA GO TO LONDON?
OOH, SHERMAN!
THAT SOUNDS SO ROMANTIC.
HAWTHORNE WANTS TO SEE A FATBERG.
IT'S A GIGANTIC BLOB OF FAT, GREASE AND OTHER JUNK CLOGGING UP THE SEWER SYSTEM.
WE'LL NEED TO PACK GAS MASKS.
SOUNDING MORE AND MORE LIKE A BOYS' TRIP.
C'MON, BOYS! LONDON CALLS!
THE SIGHTS, THE SOUNDS, THE THOUSANDS OF YEARS OF HISTORY.
WE'RE GOING TO LOOK AT SEWER BLOCKAGE.
WHICH DOES NOT REFLECT WELL ON THE FRIENDS YOU'VE CHOSEN.
I'M AWARE.

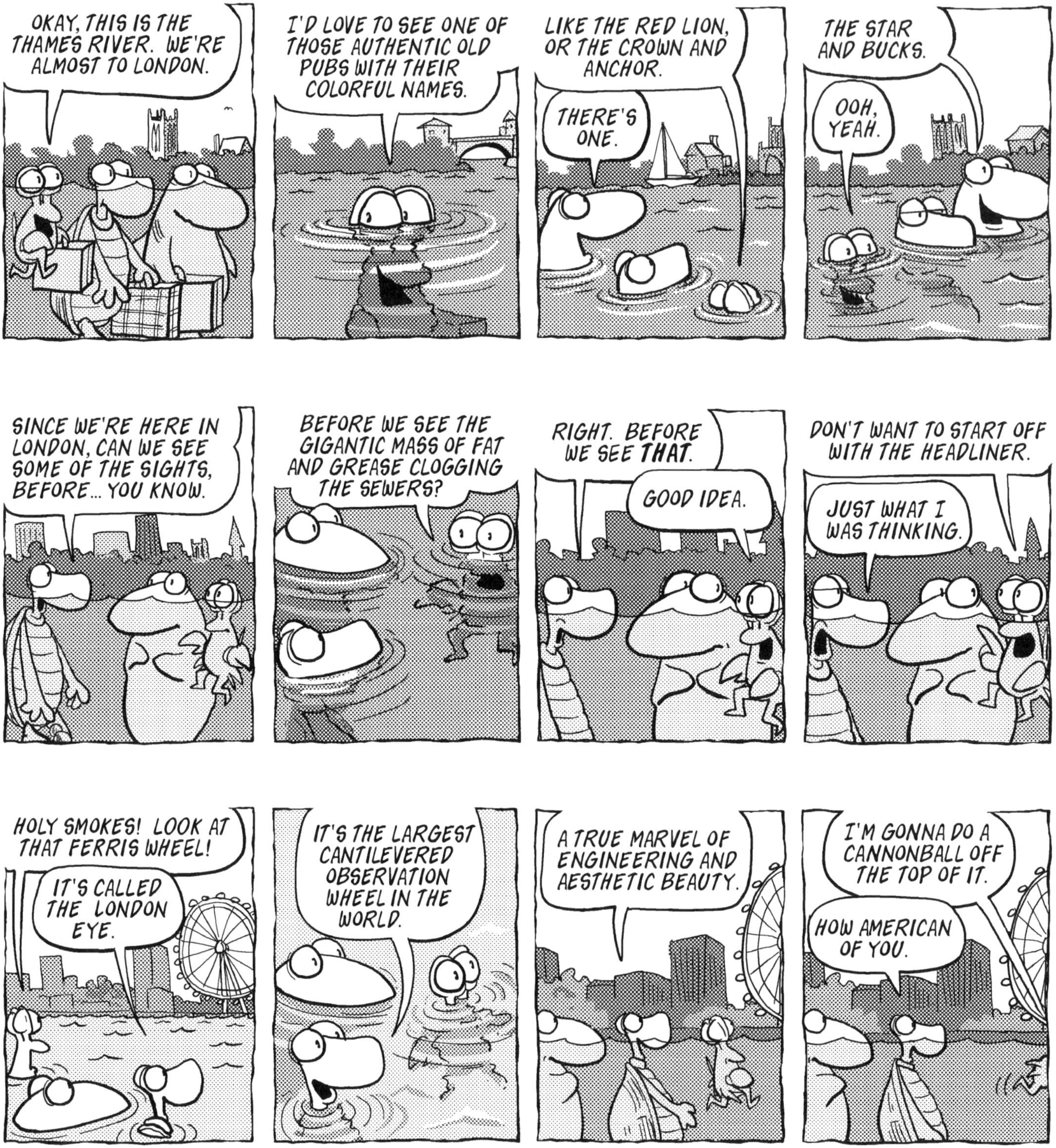
OKAY, THIS IS THE THAMES RIVER. WE'RE ALMOST TO LONDON.
I'D LOVE TO SEE ONE OF THOSE AUTHENTIC OLD PUBS WITH THEIR COLORFUL NAMES.
LIKE THE RED LION, OR THE CROWN AND ANCHOR.
THERE'S ONE.
THE STAR AND BUCKS.
OOH, YEAH.
SINCE WE'RE HERE IN LONDON, CAN WE SEE SOME OF THE SIGHTS, BEFORE... YOU KNOW.
BEFORE WE SEE THE GIGANTIC MASS OF FAT AND GREASE CLOGGING THE SEWERS?
RIGHT. BEFORE WE SEE THAT.
GOOD IDEA.
DON'T WANT TO START OFF WITH THE HEADLINER.
JUST WHAT I WAS THINKING.
HOLY SMOKES! LOOK AT THAT FERRIS WHEEL!
IT'S CALLED THE LONDON EYE.
IT'S THE LARGEST CANTILEVERED OBSERVATION WHEEL IN THE WORLD.
A TRUE MARVEL OF ENGINEERING AND AESTHETIC BEAUTY.
I'M GONNA DO A CANNONBALL OFF THE TOP OF IT.
HOW AMERICAN OF YOU.

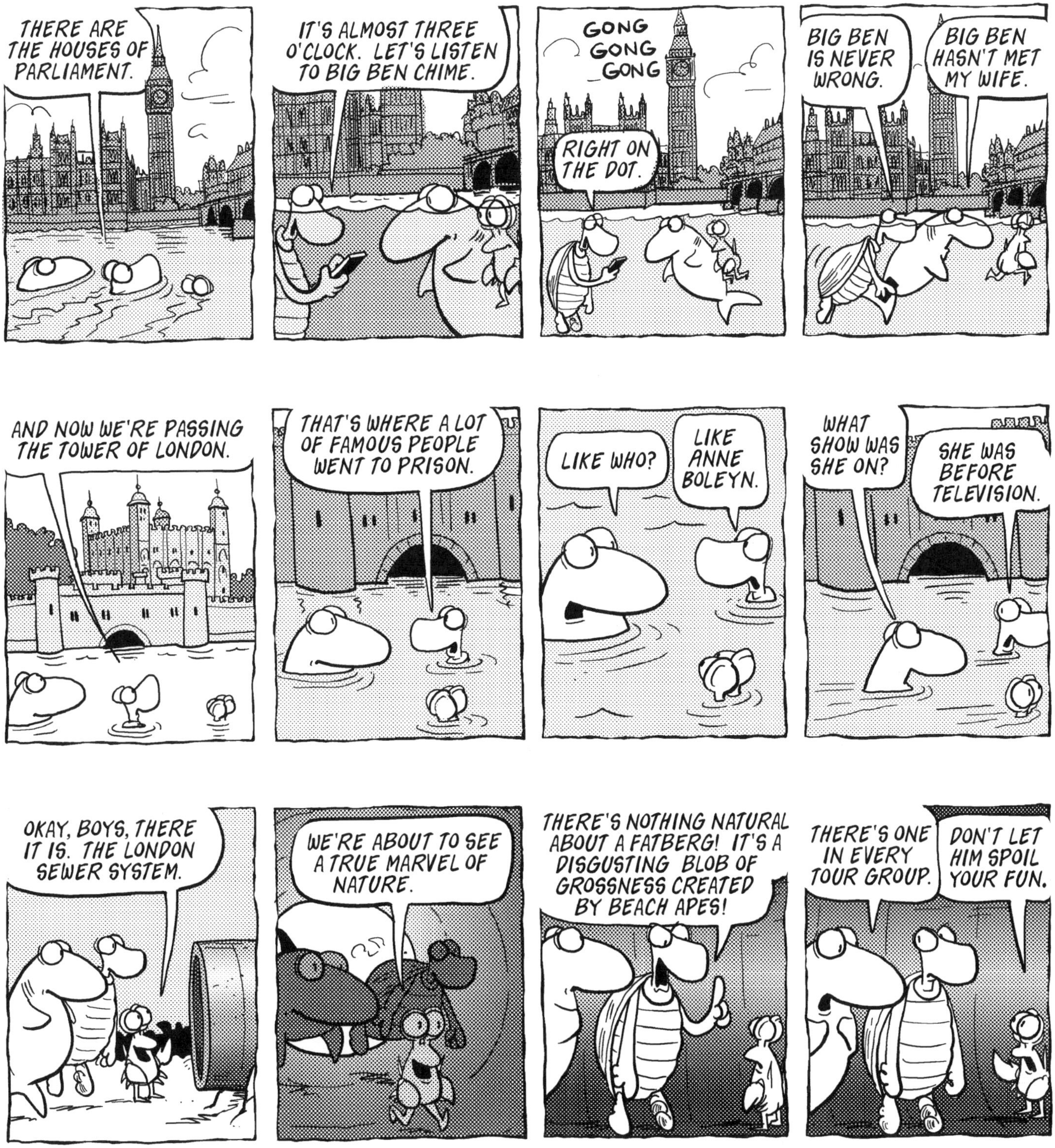
THERE ARE THE HOUSES OF PARLIAMENT.
IT'S ALMOST THREE O'CLOCK. LET'S LISTEN TO BIG BEN CHIME.
GONG GONG GONG
RIGHT ON THE DOT.
BIG BEN IS NEVER WRONG.
BIG BEN HASN'T MET MY WIFE.
AND NOW WE'RE PASSING THE TOWER OF LONDON.
THAT'S WHERE A LOT OF FAMOUS PEOPLE WENT TO PRISON.
LIKE WHO?
LIKE ANNE BOLEYN.
WHAT SHOW WAS SHE ON?
SHE WAS BEFORE TELEVISION.
OKAY, BOYS, THERE IT IS. THE LONDON SEWER SYSTEM.
WE'RE ABOUT TO SEE A TRUE MARVEL OF NATURE.
THERE'S NOTHING NATURAL ABOUT A FATBERG! IT'S A DISGUSTING BLOB OF GROSSNESS CREATED BY BEACH APES!
THERE'S ONE IN EVERY TOUR GROUP.
DON'T LET HIM SPOIL YOUR FUN.

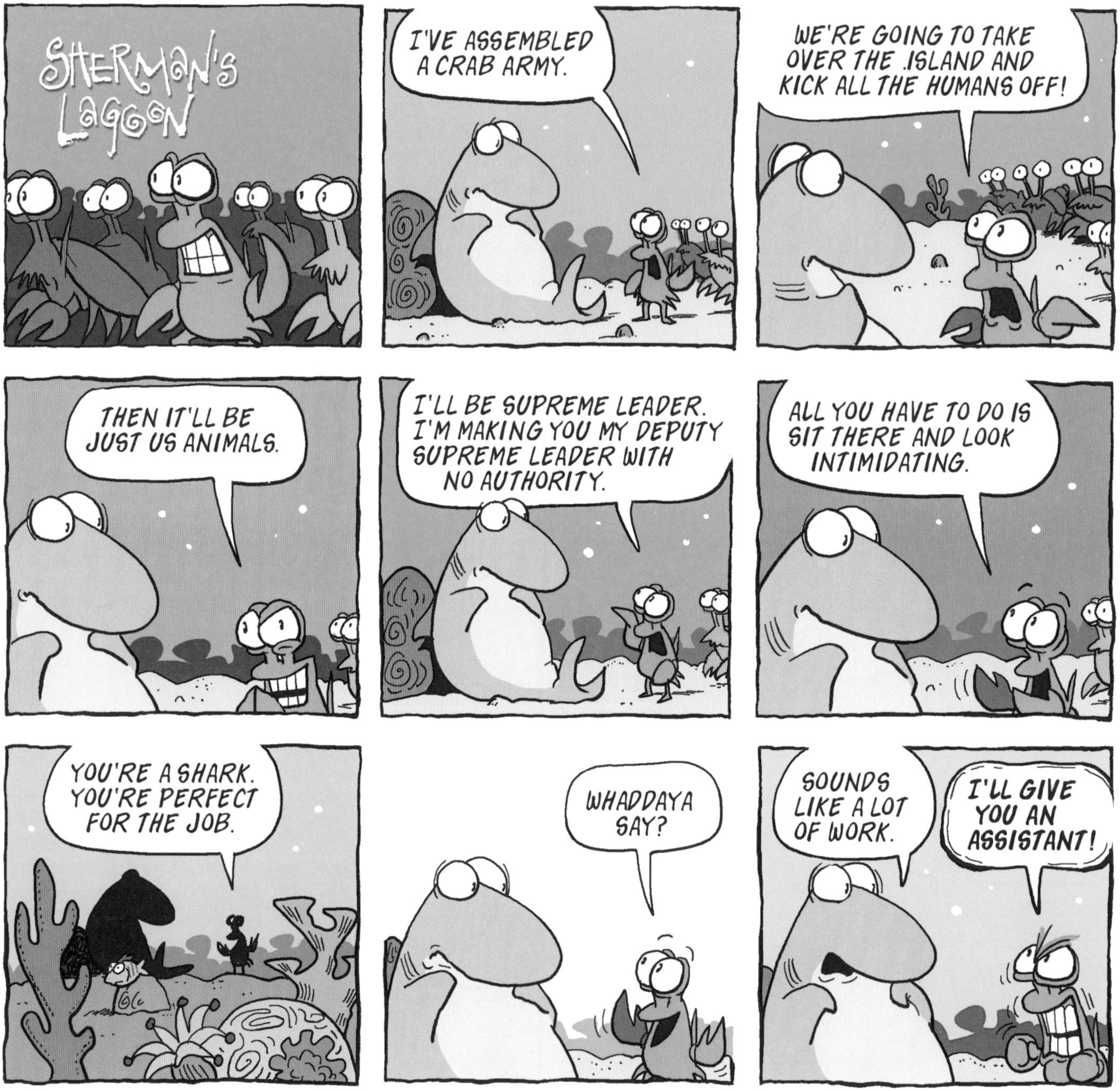
Sherman's Lagoon
I'VE ASSEMBLED A CRAB ARMY.
WE'RE GOING TO TAKE OVER THE ISLAND AND KICK ALL THE HUMANS OFF!
THEN IT'LL BE JUST US ANIMALS.
I'LL BE SUPREME LEADER. I'M MAKING YOU MY DEPUTY SUPREME LEADER WITH NO AUTHORITY.
ALL YOU HAVE TO DO IS SIT THERE AND LOOK INTIMIDATING.
YOU'RE A SHARK. YOU'RE PERFECT FOR THE JOB.
WHADDAYA SAY?
SOUNDS LIKE A LOT OF WORK.
I'LL GIVE YOU AN ASSISTANT!

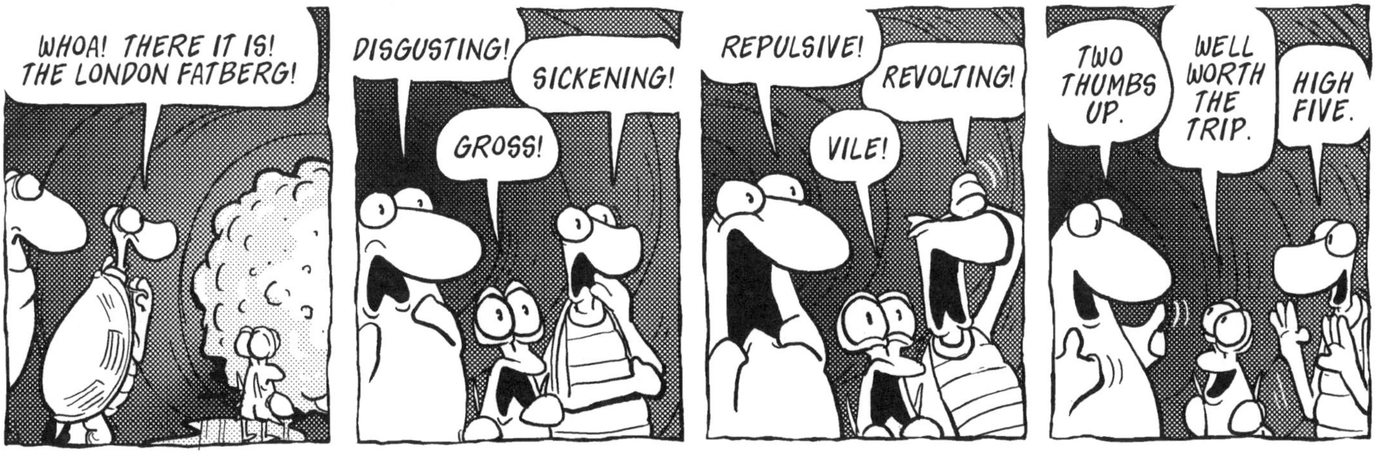
WHOA! THERE IT IS! THE LONDON FATBERG!
DISGUSTING!
SICKENING!
GROSS!
REPULSIVE!
REVOLTING!
VILE!
TWO THUMBS UP.
WELL WORTH THE TRIP.
HIGH FIVE.

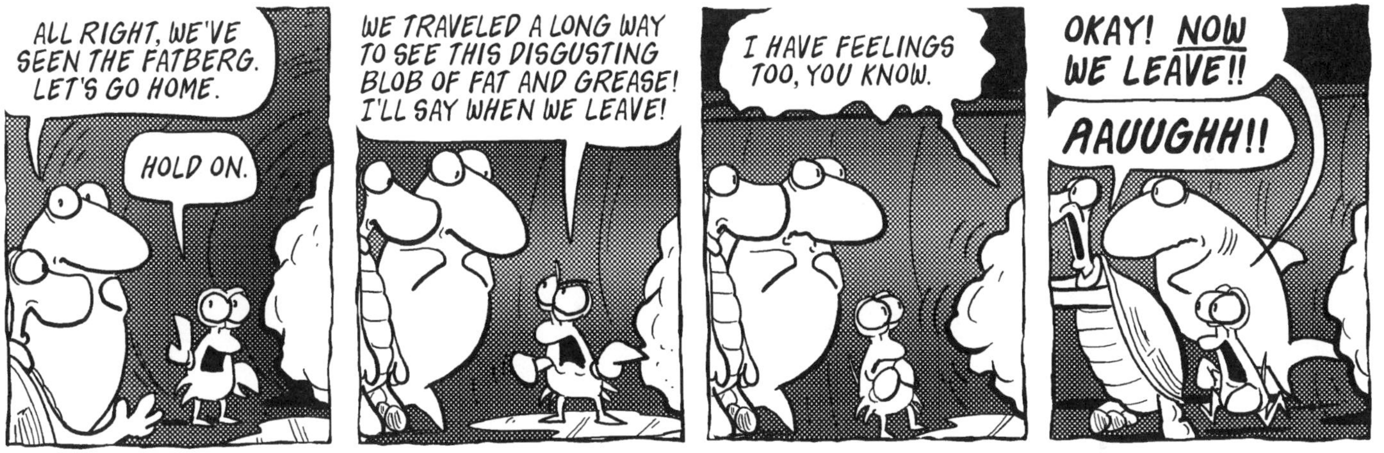
ALL RIGHT, WE'VE SEEN THE FATBERG. LET'S GO HOME.
HOLD ON.
WE TRAVELED A LONG WAY TO SEE THIS DISGUSTING BLOB OF FAT AND GREASE! I'LL SAY WHEN WE LEAVE!
I HAVE FEELINGS TOO, YOU KNOW.
OKAY! NOW WE LEAVE!!
AAUUGHH!!

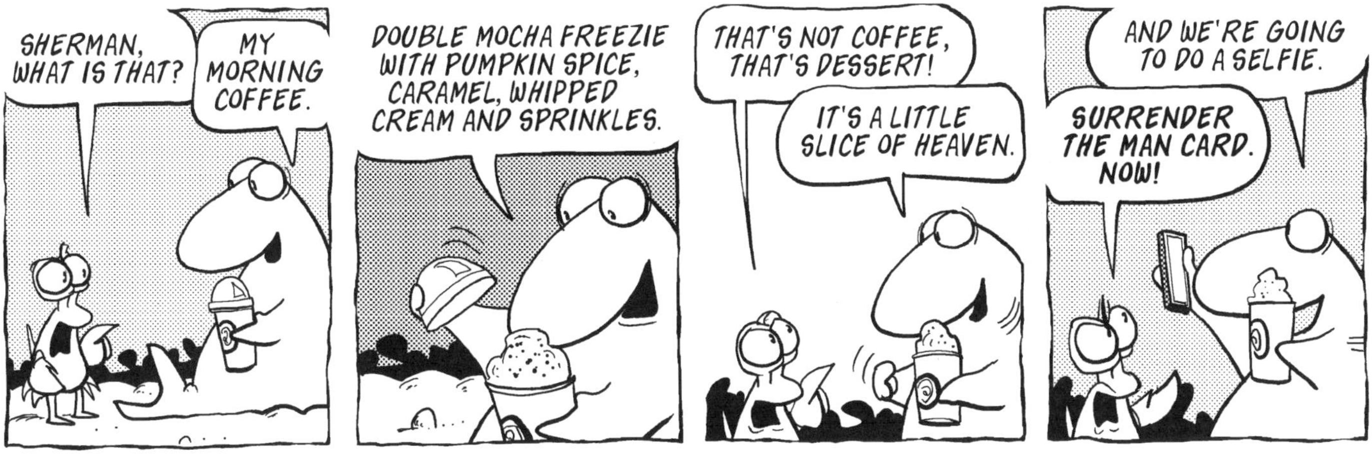
SHERMAN, WHAT IS THAT?
MY MORNING COFFEE.
DOUBLE MOCHA FREEZIE WITH PUMPKIN SPICE, CARAMEL, WHIPPED CREAM AND SPRINKLES.
THAT'S NOT COFFEE, THAT'S DESSERT!
IT'S A LITTLE SLICE OF HEAVEN.
AND WE'RE GOING TO DO A SELFIE.
SURRENDER THE MAN CARD. NOW!

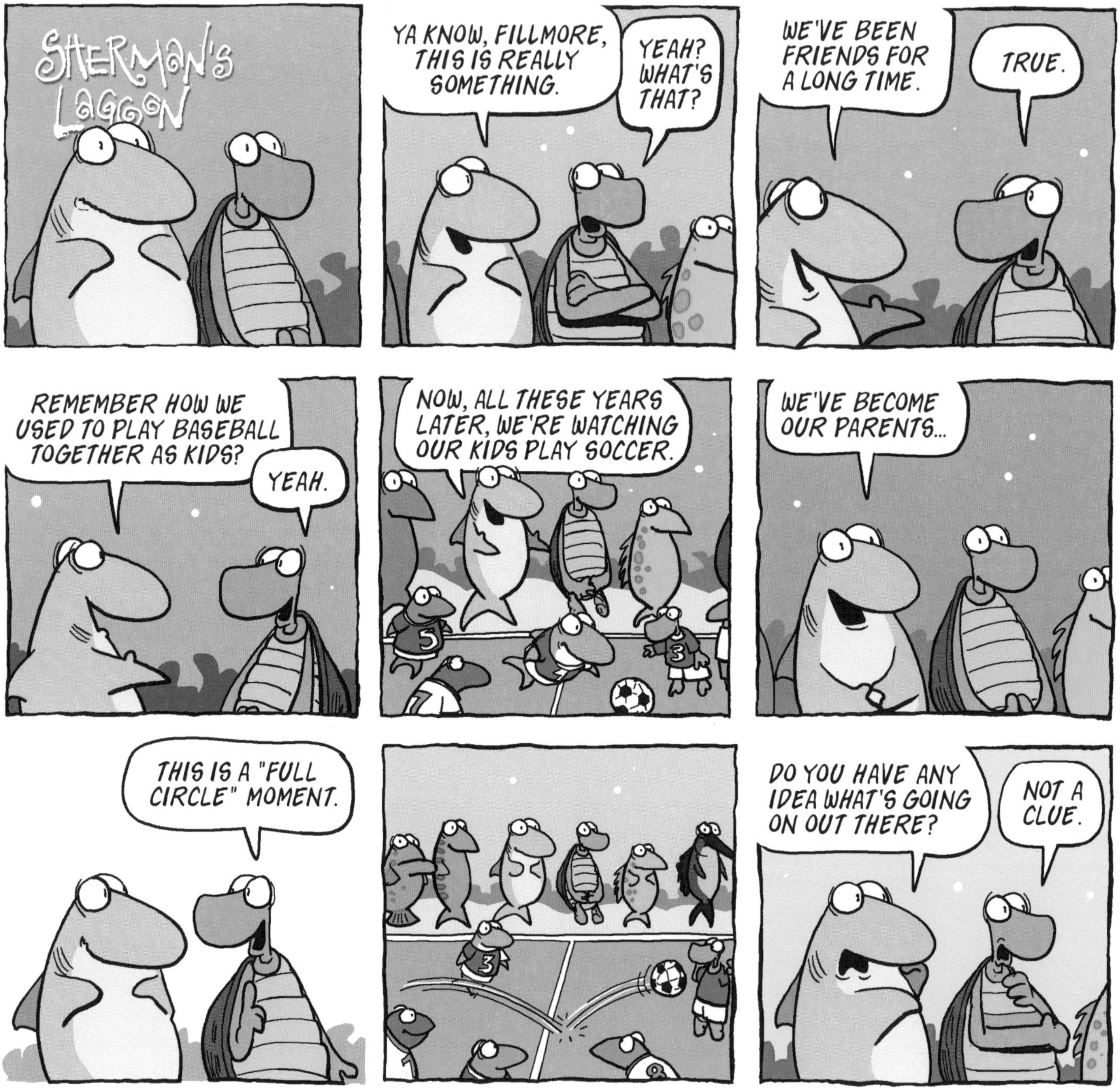
SHERMAN'S LAGOON
YA KNOW, FILLMORE, THIS IS REALLY SOMETHING.
YEAH? WHAT'S THAT?
WE'VE BEEN FRIENDS FOR A LONG TIME.
TRUE.
REMEMBER HOW WE USED TO PLAY BASEBALL TOGETHER AS KIDS?
YEAH.
NOW, ALL THESE YEARS LATER, WE'RE WATCHING OUR KIDS PLAY SOCCER.
WE'VE BECOME OUR PARENTS...
THIS IS A "FULL CIRCLE" MOMENT.
DO YOU HAVE ANY IDEA WHAT'S GOING ON OUT THERE?
NOT A CLUE.

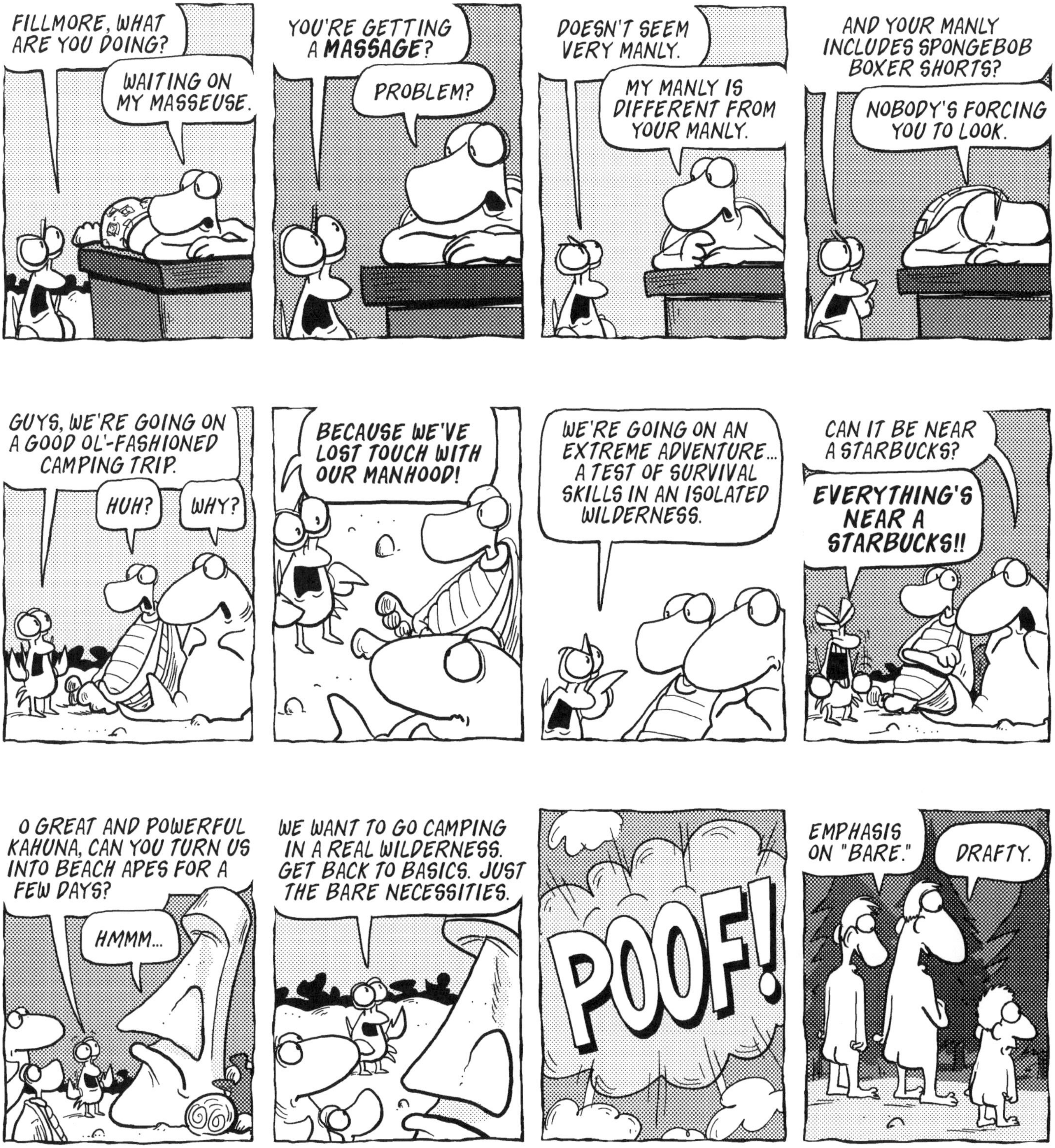
FILLMORE, WHAT ARE YOU DOING?
WAITING ON MY MASSEUSE.
YOU'RE GETTING A **MASSAGE**?
PROBLEM?
DOESN'T SEEM VERY MANLY.
MY MANLY IS DIFFERENT FROM YOUR MANLY.
AND YOUR MANLY INCLUDES SPONGEBOB BOXER SHORTS?
NOBODY'S FORCING YOU TO LOOK.
GUYS, WE'RE GOING ON A GOOD OL'-FASHIONED CAMPING TRIP.
HUH?
WHY?
BECAUSE WE'VE LOST TOUCH WITH OUR MANHOOD!
WE'RE GOING ON AN EXTREME ADVENTURE... A TEST OF SURVIVAL SKILLS IN AN ISOLATED WILDERNESS.
CAN IT BE NEAR A STARBUCKS?
EVERYTHING'S NEAR A STARBUCKS!!
O GREAT AND POWERFUL KAHUNA, CAN YOU TURN US INTO BEACH APES FOR A FEW DAYS?
HMMM...
WE WANT TO GO CAMPING IN A REAL WILDERNESS. GET BACK TO BASICS. JUST THE BARE NECESSITIES.
POOF!
EMPHASIS ON "BARE."
DRAFTY.

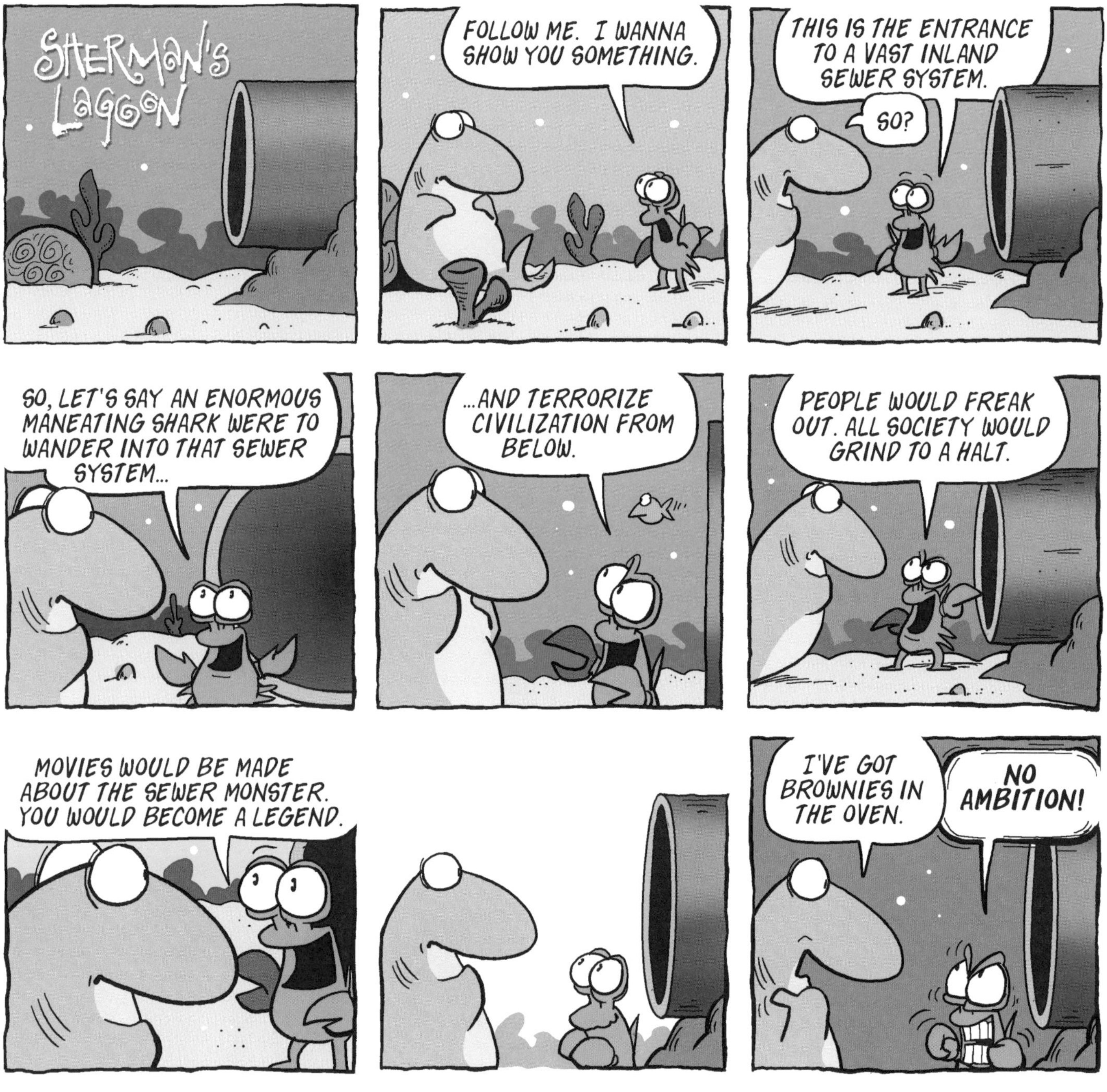
Sherman's Lagoon
FOLLOW ME. I WANNA SHOW YOU SOMETHING.
THIS IS THE ENTRANCE TO A VAST INLAND SEWER SYSTEM.
SO?
SO, LET'S SAY AN ENORMOUS MANEATING SHARK WERE TO WANDER INTO THAT SEWER SYSTEM...
...AND TERRORIZE CIVILIZATION FROM BELOW.
PEOPLE WOULD FREAK OUT. ALL SOCIETY WOULD GRIND TO A HALT.
MOVIES WOULD BE MADE ABOUT THE SEWER MONSTER. YOU WOULD BECOME A LEGEND.
I'VE GOT BROWNIES IN THE OVEN.
NO AMBITION!

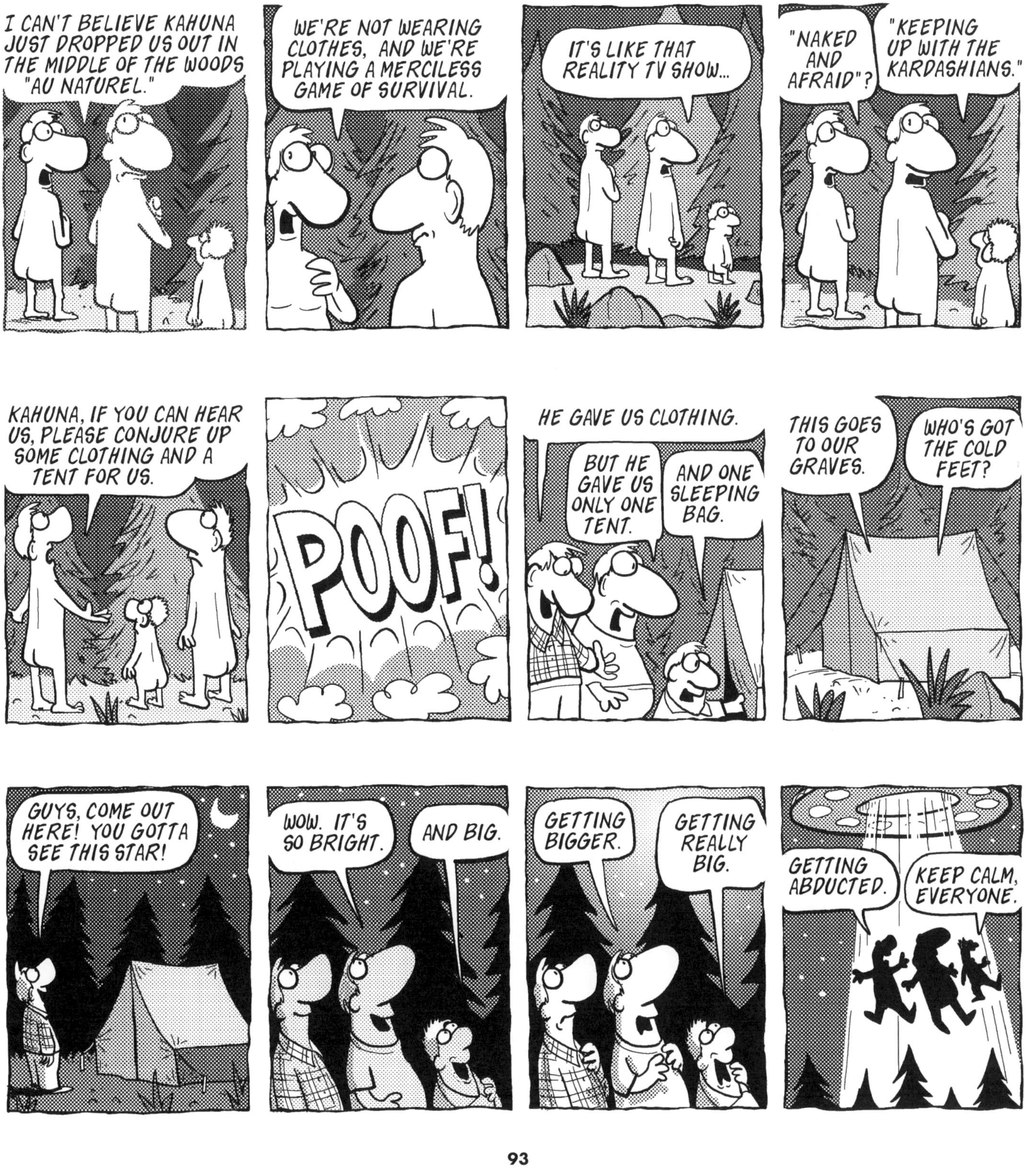
I CAN'T BELIEVE KAHUNA JUST DROPPED US OUT IN THE MIDDLE OF THE WOODS "AU NATUREL."
WE'RE NOT WEARING CLOTHES, AND WE'RE PLAYING A MERCILESS GAME OF SURVIVAL.
IT'S LIKE THAT REALITY TV SHOW...
"NAKED AND AFRAID"?
"KEEPING UP WITH THE KARDASHIANS."
KAHUNA, IF YOU CAN HEAR US, PLEASE CONJURE UP SOME CLOTHING AND A TENT FOR US.
POOF!
HE GAVE US CLOTHING.
BUT HE GAVE US ONLY ONE TENT.
AND ONE SLEEPING BAG.
THIS GOES TO OUR GRAVES.
WHO'S GOT THE COLD FEET?
GUYS, COME OUT HERE! YOU GOTTA SEE THIS STAR!
WOW. IT'S SO BRIGHT.
AND BIG.
GETTING BIGGER.
GETTING REALLY BIG.
GETTING ABDUCTED.
KEEP CALM, EVERYONE.

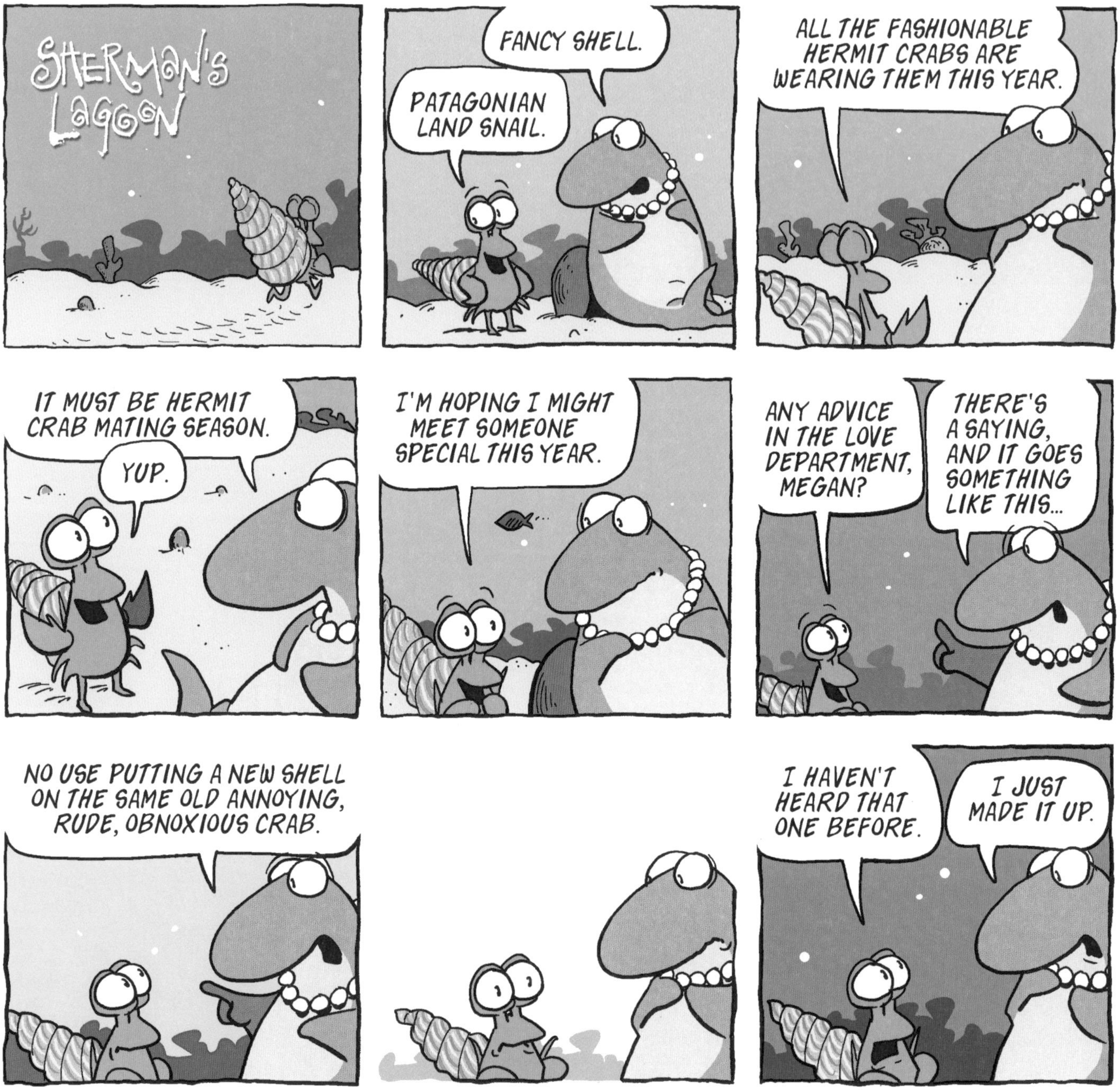
SHERMAN'S LAGOON
FANCY SHELL.
PATAGONIAN LAND SNAIL.
ALL THE FASHIONABLE HERMIT CRABS ARE WEARING THEM THIS YEAR.
IT MUST BE HERMIT CRAB MATING SEASON.
YUP.
I'M HOPING I MIGHT MEET SOMEONE SPECIAL THIS YEAR.
ANY ADVICE IN THE LOVE DEPARTMENT, MEGAN?
THERE'S A SAYING, AND IT GOES SOMETHING LIKE THIS...
NO USE PUTTING A NEW SHELL ON THE SAME OLD ANNOYING, RUDE, OBNOXIOUS CRAB.
I HAVEN'T HEARD THAT ONE BEFORE.
I JUST MADE IT UP.

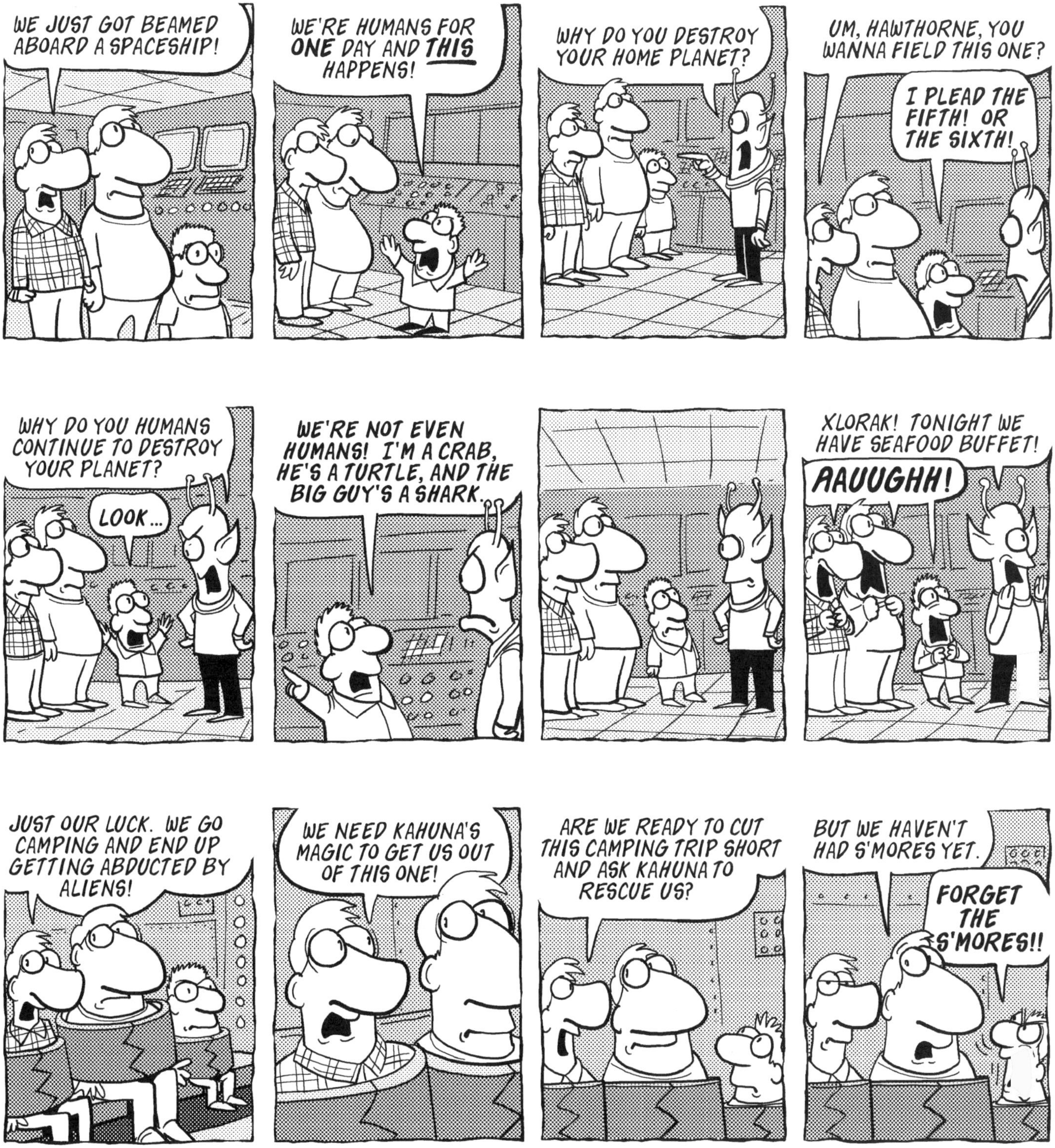
WE JUST GOT BEAMED ABOARD A SPACESHIP!
WE'RE HUMANS FOR ONE DAY AND THIS HAPPENS!
WHY DO YOU DESTROY YOUR HOME PLANET?
UM, HAWTHORNE, YOU WANNA FIELD THIS ONE?
I PLEAD THE FIFTH! OR THE SIXTH!
WHY DO YOU HUMANS CONTINUE TO DESTROY YOUR PLANET?
LOOK...
WE'RE NOT EVEN HUMANS! I'M A CRAB, HE'S A TURTLE, AND THE BIG GUY'S A SHARK.
XLORAK! TONIGHT WE HAVE SEAFOOD BUFFET!
AAUUGHH!
JUST OUR LUCK. WE GO CAMPING AND END UP GETTING ABDUCTED BY ALIENS!
WE NEED KAHUNA'S MAGIC TO GET US OUT OF THIS ONE!
ARE WE READY TO CUT THIS CAMPING TRIP SHORT AND ASK KAHUNA TO RESCUE US?
BUT WE HAVEN'T HAD S'MORES YET.
FORGET THE S'MORES!!

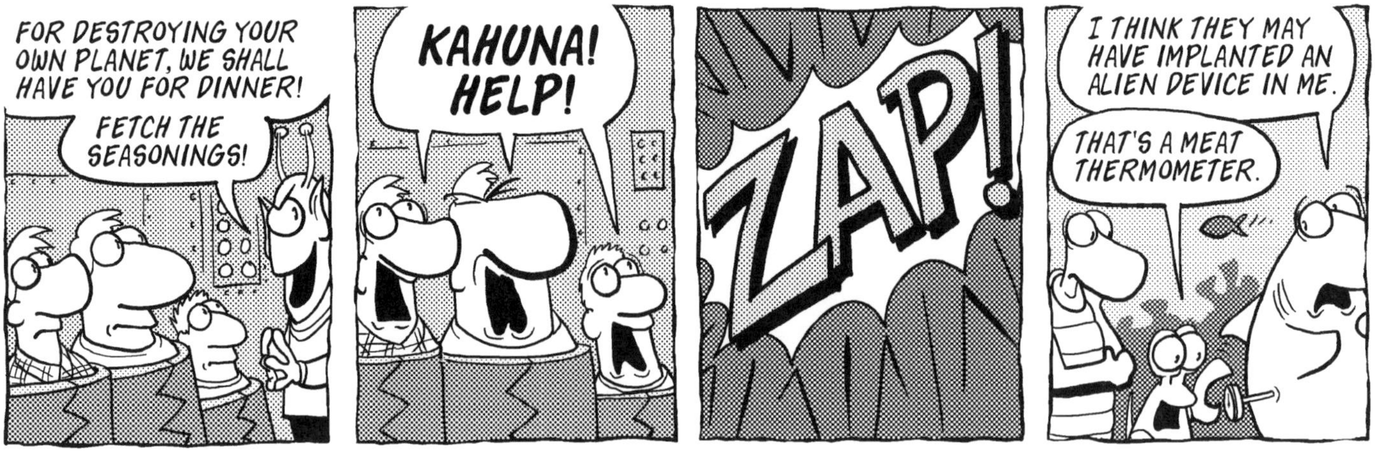
FOR DESTROYING YOUR OWN PLANET, WE SHALL HAVE YOU FOR DINNER!
FETCH THE SEASONINGS!
KAHUNA! HELP!
ZAP!
I THINK THEY MAY HAVE IMPLANTED AN ALIEN DEVICE IN ME.
THAT'S A MEAT THERMOMETER.

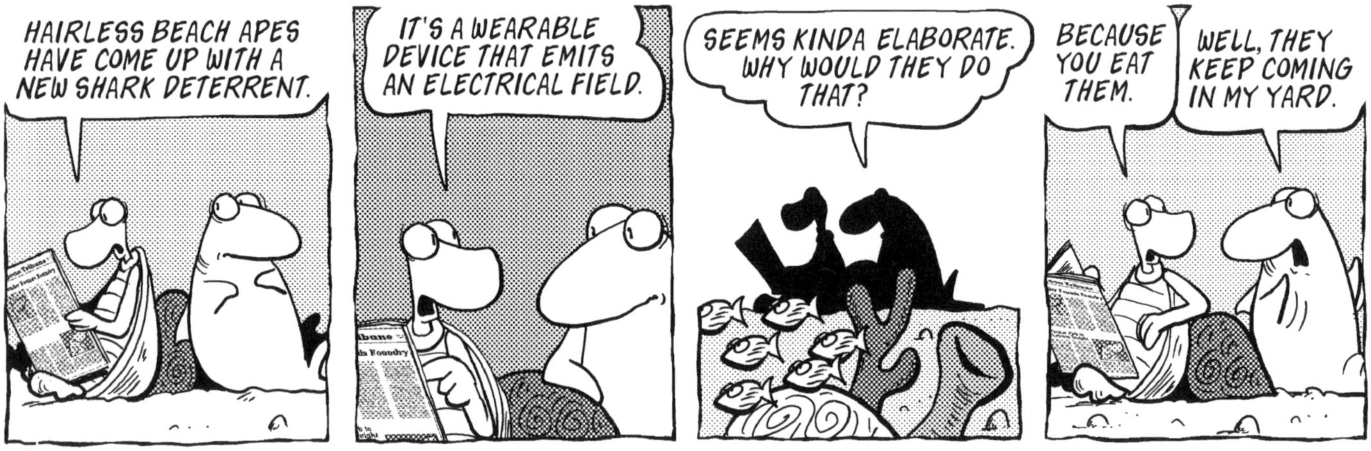
HAIRLESS BEACH APES HAVE COME UP WITH A NEW SHARK DETERRENT.
IT'S A WEARABLE DEVICE THAT EMITS AN ELECTRICAL FIELD.
SEEMS KINDA ELABORATE. WHY WOULD THEY DO THAT?
BECAUSE YOU EAT THEM.
WELL, THEY KEEP COMING IN MY YARD.

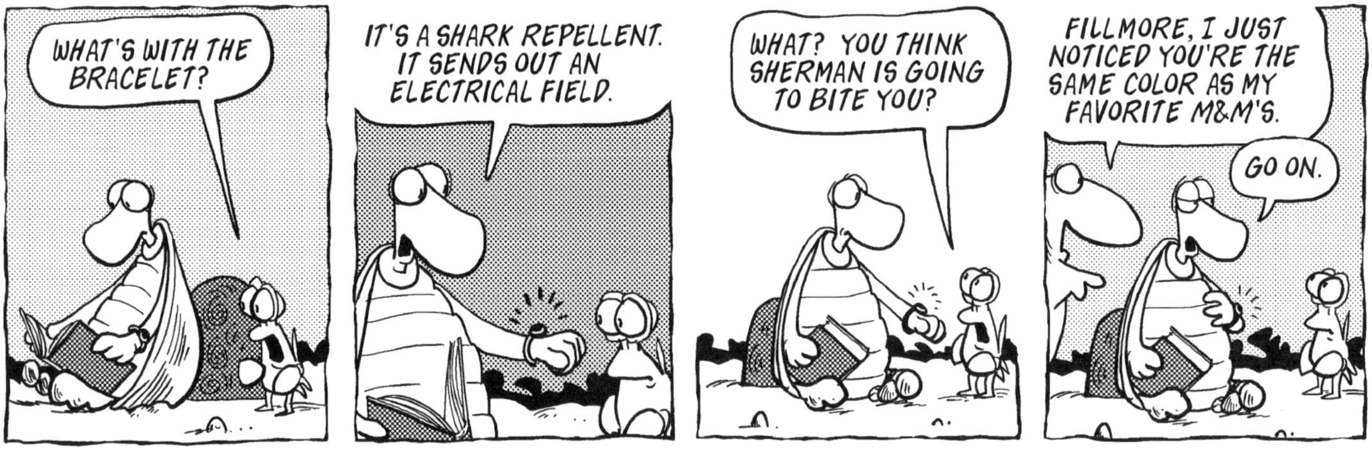
WHAT'S WITH THE BRACELET?
IT'S A SHARK REPELLENT. IT SENDS OUT AN ELECTRICAL FIELD.
WHAT? YOU THINK SHERMAN IS GOING TO BITE YOU?
FILLMORE, I JUST NOTICED YOU'RE THE SAME COLOR AS MY FAVORITE M&M'S.
GO ON.

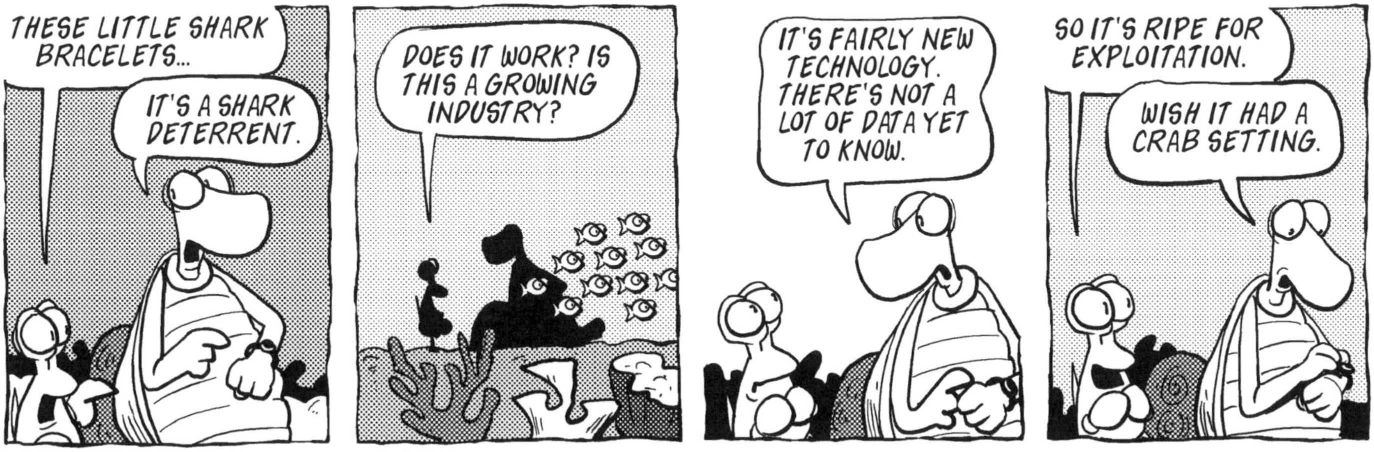
THESE LITTLE SHARK BRACELETS...
IT'S A SHARK DETERRENT.
DOES IT WORK? IS THIS A GROWING INDUSTRY?
IT'S FAIRLY NEW TECHNOLOGY. THERE'S NOT A LOT OF DATA YET TO KNOW.
SO IT'S RIPE FOR EXPLOITATION.
WISH IT HAD A CRAB SETTING.

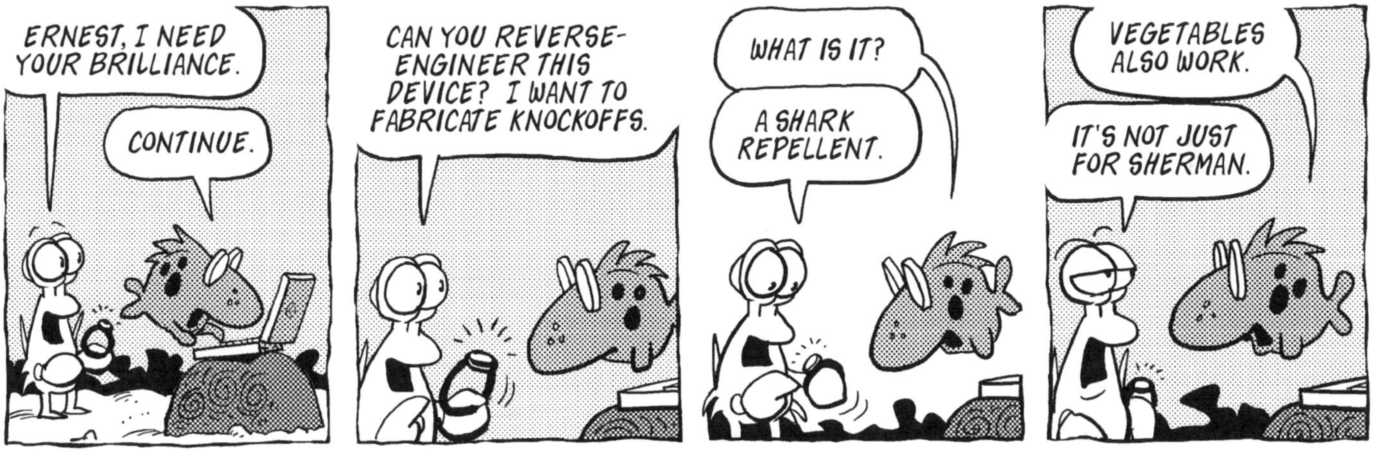
ERNEST, I NEED YOUR BRILLIANCE.
CONTINUE.
CAN YOU REVERSE-ENGINEER THIS DEVICE? I WANT TO FABRICATE KNOCKOFFS.
WHAT IS IT?
A SHARK REPELLENT.
VEGETABLES ALSO WORK.
IT'S NOT JUST FOR SHERMAN.

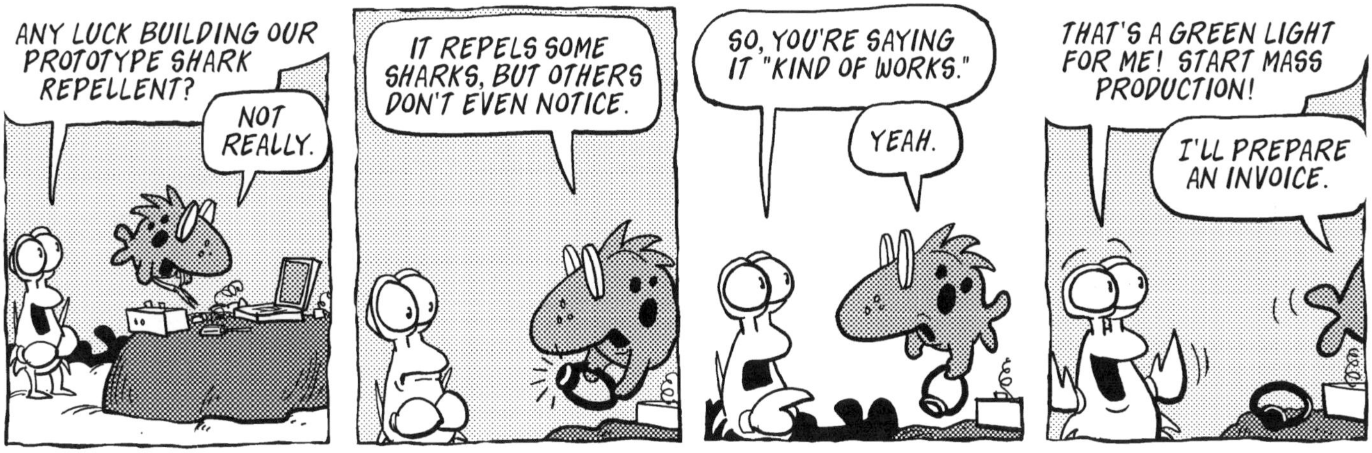
ANY LUCK BUILDING OUR PROTOTYPE SHARK REPELLENT?
NOT REALLY.
IT REPELS SOME SHARKS, BUT OTHERS DON'T EVEN NOTICE.
SO, YOU'RE SAYING IT "KIND OF WORKS."
YEAH.
THAT'S A GREEN LIGHT FOR ME! START MASS PRODUCTION!
I'LL PREPARE AN INVOICE.

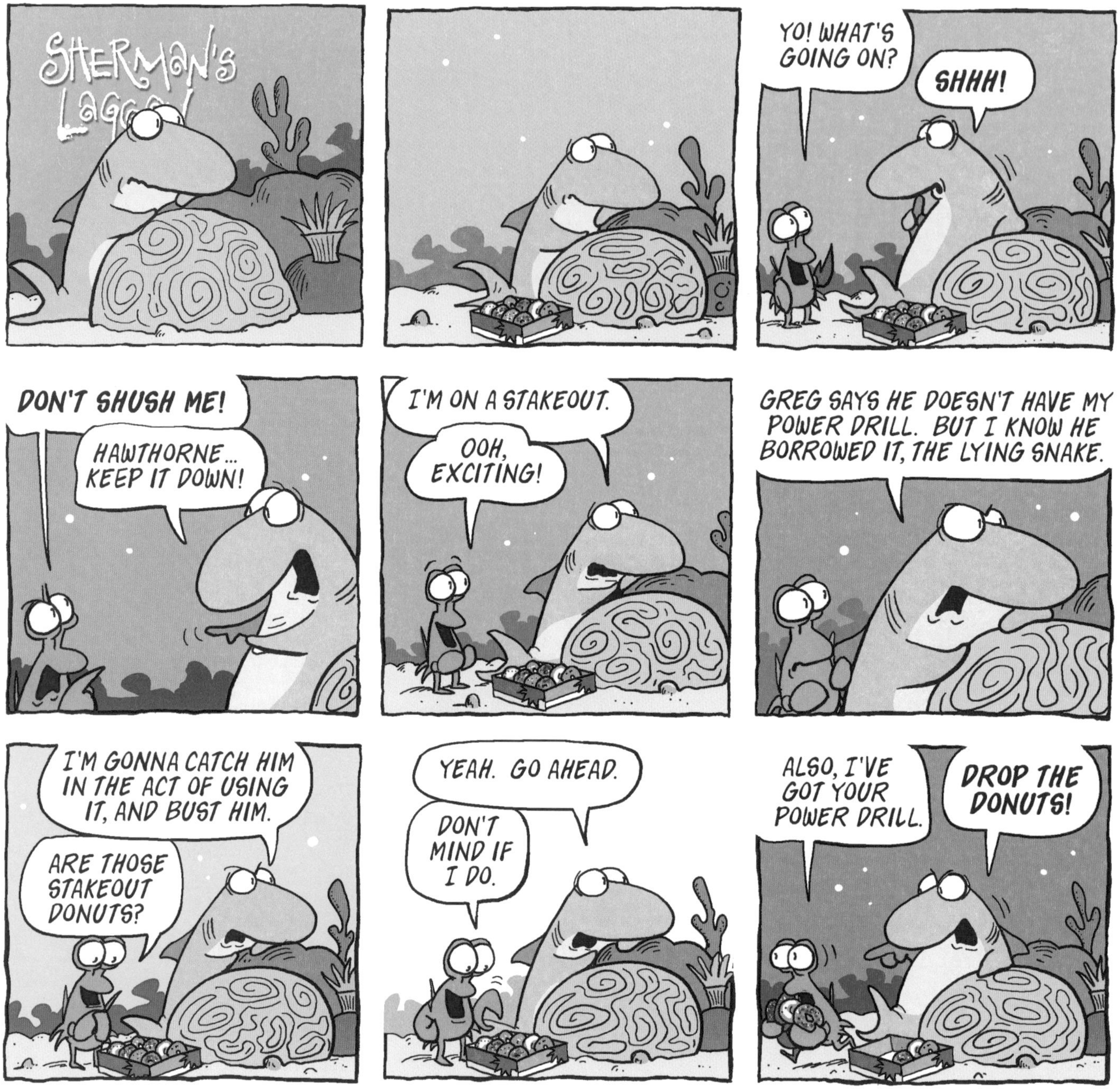
Sherman's Lagoon
YO! WHAT'S GOING ON?
SHHH!
DON'T SHUSH ME!
HAWTHORNE... KEEP IT DOWN!
I'M ON A STAKEOUT.
OOH, EXCITING!
GREG SAYS HE DOESN'T HAVE MY POWER DRILL. BUT I KNOW HE BORROWED IT, THE LYING SNAKE.
I'M GONNA CATCH HIM IN THE ACT OF USING IT, AND BUST HIM.
ARE THOSE STAKEOUT DONUTS?
YEAH. GO AHEAD.
DON'T MIND IF I DO.
ALSO, I'VE GOT YOUR POWER DRILL.
DROP THE DONUTS!

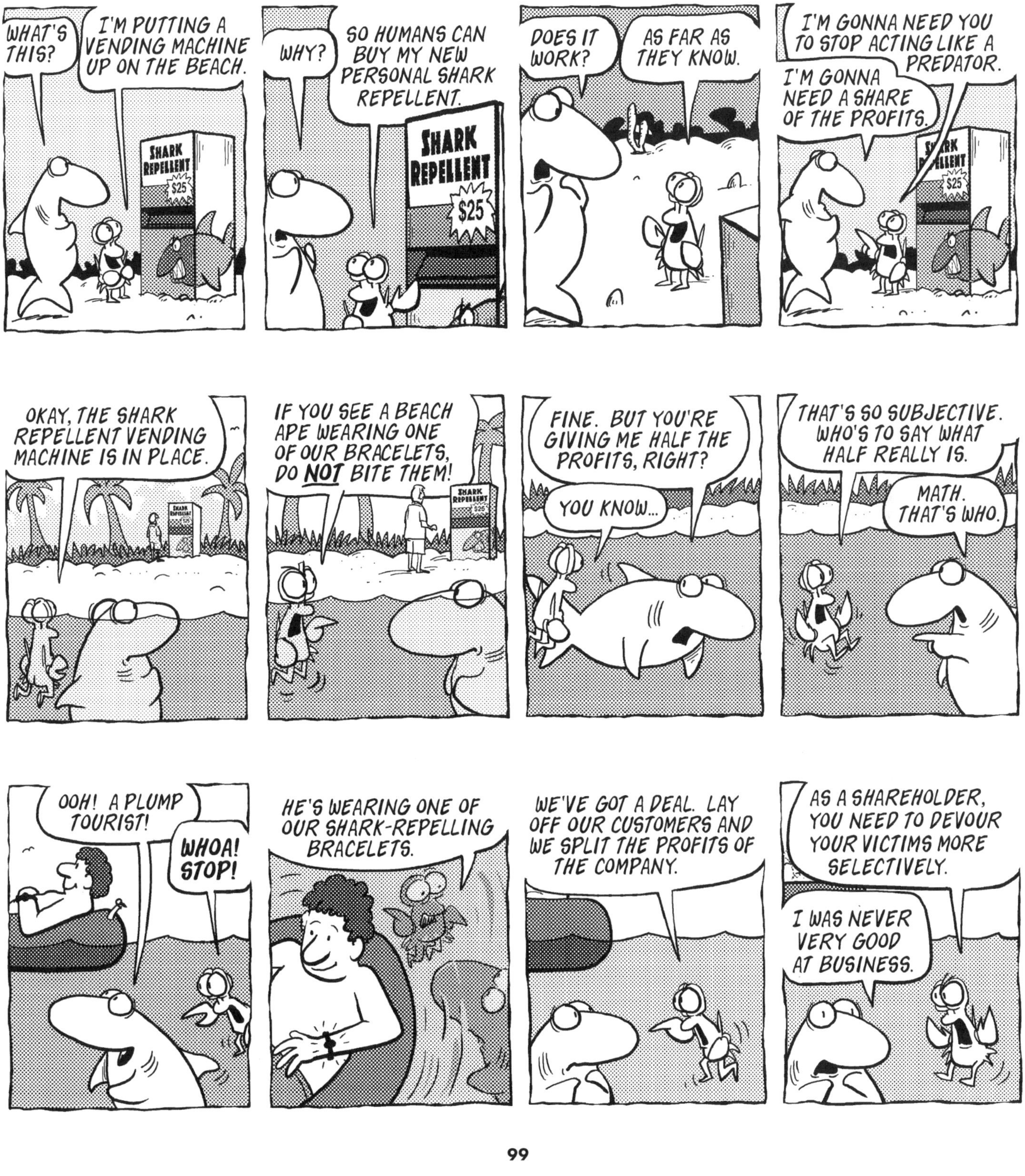
WHAT'S THIS?
I'M PUTTING A VENDING MACHINE UP ON THE BEACH.
SHARK REPELLENT
$25
WHY?
SO HUMANS CAN BUY MY NEW PERSONAL SHARK REPELLENT.
SHARK REPELLENT
$25
DOES IT WORK?
AS FAR AS THEY KNOW.
I'M GONNA NEED YOU TO STOP ACTING LIKE A PREDATOR.
I'M GONNA NEED A SHARE OF THE PROFITS.
$25
OKAY, THE SHARK REPELLENT VENDING MACHINE IS IN PLACE.
IF YOU SEE A BEACH APE WEARING ONE OF OUR BRACELETS, DO **NOT** BITE THEM!
SHARK REPELLENT
$25
FINE. BUT YOU'RE GIVING ME HALF THE PROFITS, RIGHT?
YOU KNOW...
THAT'S SO SUBJECTIVE. WHO'S TO SAY WHAT HALF REALLY IS.
MATH. THAT'S WHO.
OOH! A PLUMP TOURIST!
WHOA! STOP!
HE'S WEARING ONE OF OUR SHARK-REPELLING BRACELETS.
WE'VE GOT A DEAL. LAY OFF OUR CUSTOMERS AND WE SPLIT THE PROFITS OF THE COMPANY.
AS A SHAREHOLDER, YOU NEED TO DEVOUR YOUR VICTIMS MORE SELECTIVELY.
I WAS NEVER VERY GOOD AT BUSINESS.

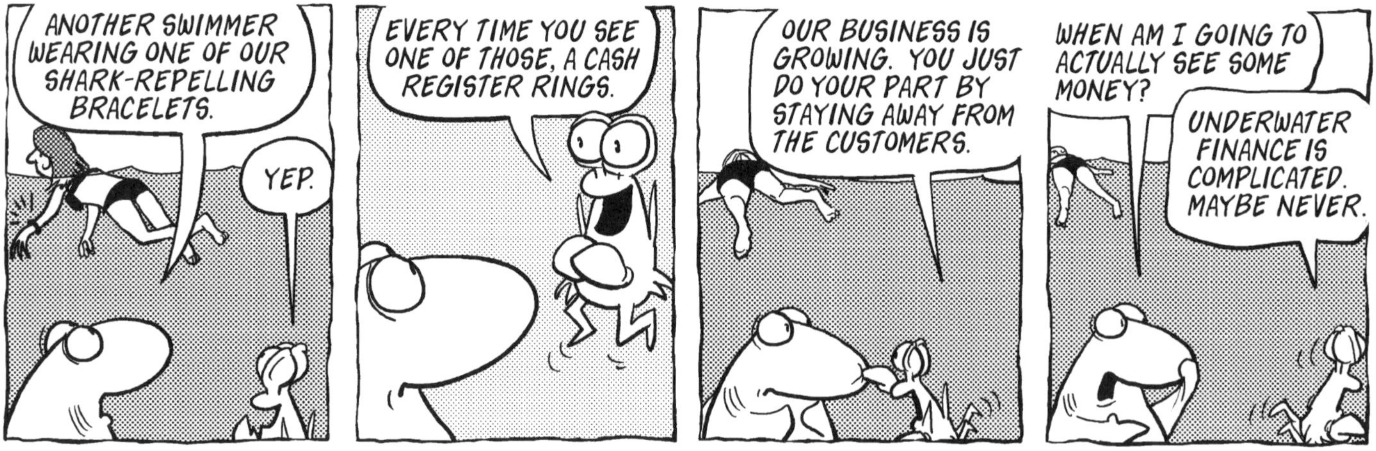
ANOTHER SWIMMER WEARING ONE OF OUR SHARK-REPELLING BRACELETS.
YEP.
EVERY TIME YOU SEE ONE OF THOSE, A CASH REGISTER RINGS.
OUR BUSINESS IS GROWING. YOU JUST DO YOUR PART BY STAYING AWAY FROM THE CUSTOMERS.
WHEN AM I GOING TO ACTUALLY SEE SOME MONEY?
UNDERWATER FINANCE IS COMPLICATED. MAYBE NEVER.

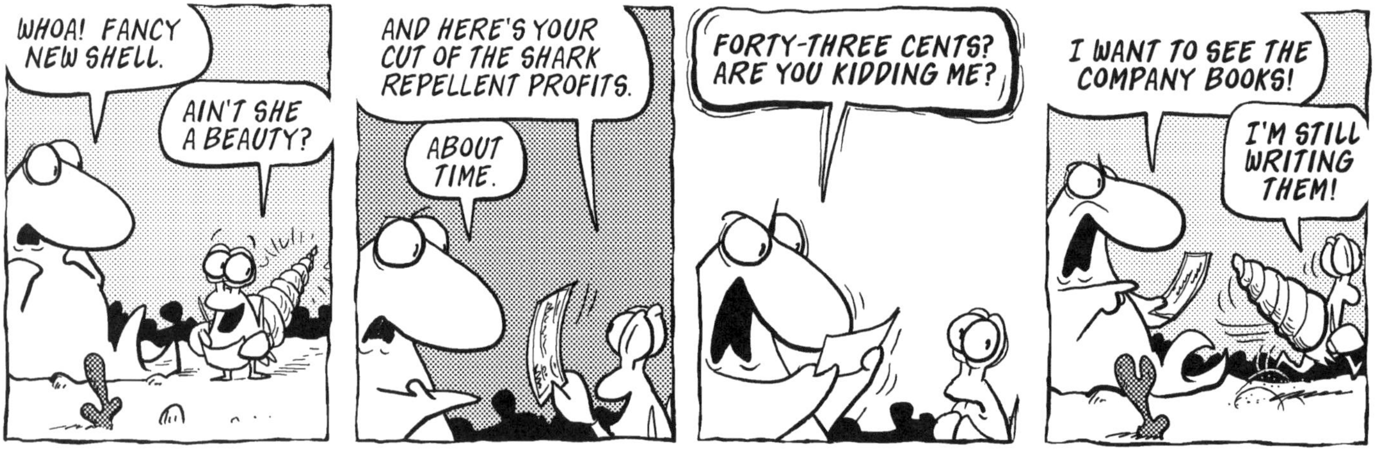
WHOA! FANCY NEW SHELL.
AIN'T SHE A BEAUTY?
AND HERE'S YOUR CUT OF THE SHARK REPELLENT PROFITS.
ABOUT TIME.
FORTY-THREE CENTS? ARE YOU KIDDING ME?
I WANT TO SEE THE COMPANY BOOKS!
I'M STILL WRITING THEM!

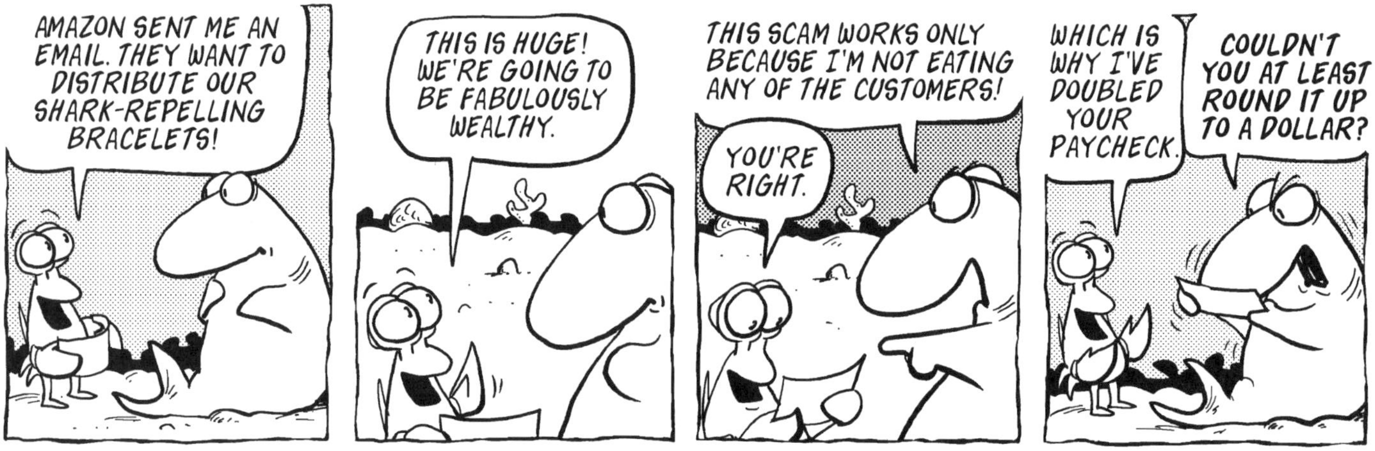
AMAZON SENT ME AN EMAIL. THEY WANT TO DISTRIBUTE OUR SHARK-REPELLING BRACELETS!
THIS IS HUGE! WE'RE GOING TO BE FABULOUSLY WEALTHY.
THIS SCAM WORKS ONLY BECAUSE I'M NOT EATING ANY OF THE CUSTOMERS!
YOU'RE RIGHT.
WHICH IS WHY I'VE DOUBLED YOUR PAYCHECK.
COULDN'T YOU AT LEAST ROUND IT UP TO A DOLLAR?

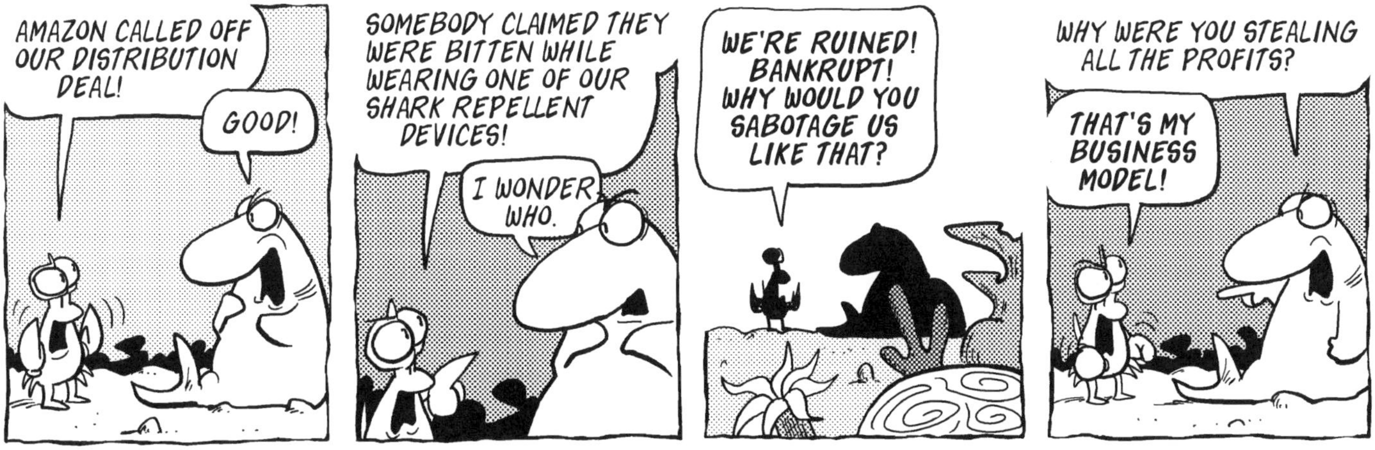
AMAZON CALLED OFF OUR DISTRIBUTION DEAL!
GOOD!
SOMEBODY CLAIMED THEY WERE BITTEN WHILE WEARING ONE OF OUR SHARK REPELLENT DEVICES!
I WONDER WHO.
WE'RE RUINED! BANKRUPT! WHY WOULD YOU SABOTAGE US LIKE THAT?
WHY WERE YOU STEALING ALL THE PROFITS?
THAT'S MY BUSINESS MODEL!

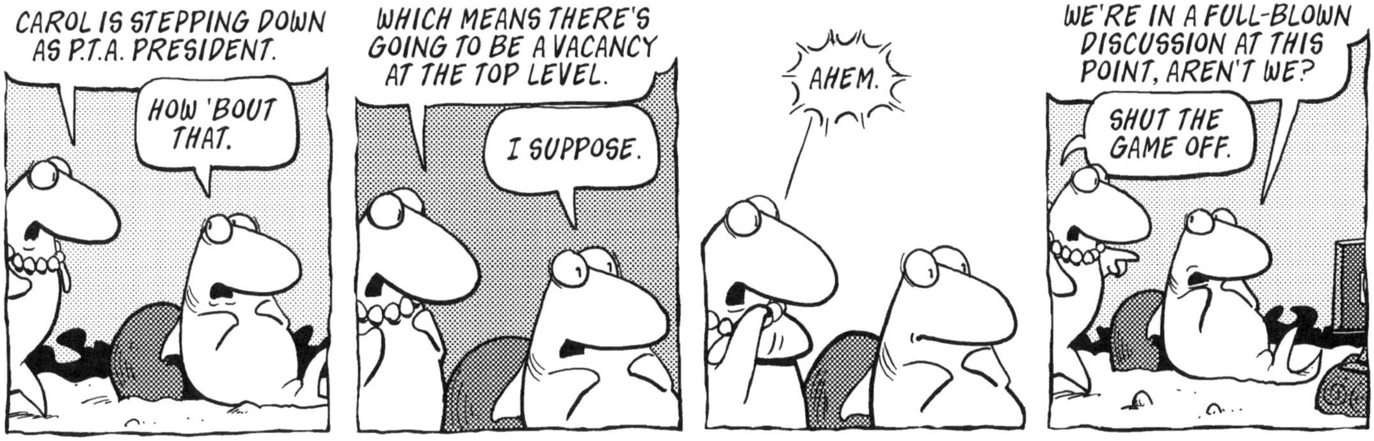
CAROL IS STEPPING DOWN AS P.T.A. PRESIDENT.
HOW 'BOUT THAT.
WHICH MEANS THERE'S GOING TO BE A VACANCY AT THE TOP LEVEL.
I SUPPOSE.
AHEM.
WE'RE IN A FULL-BLOWN DISCUSSION AT THIS POINT, AREN'T WE?
SHUT THE GAME OFF.

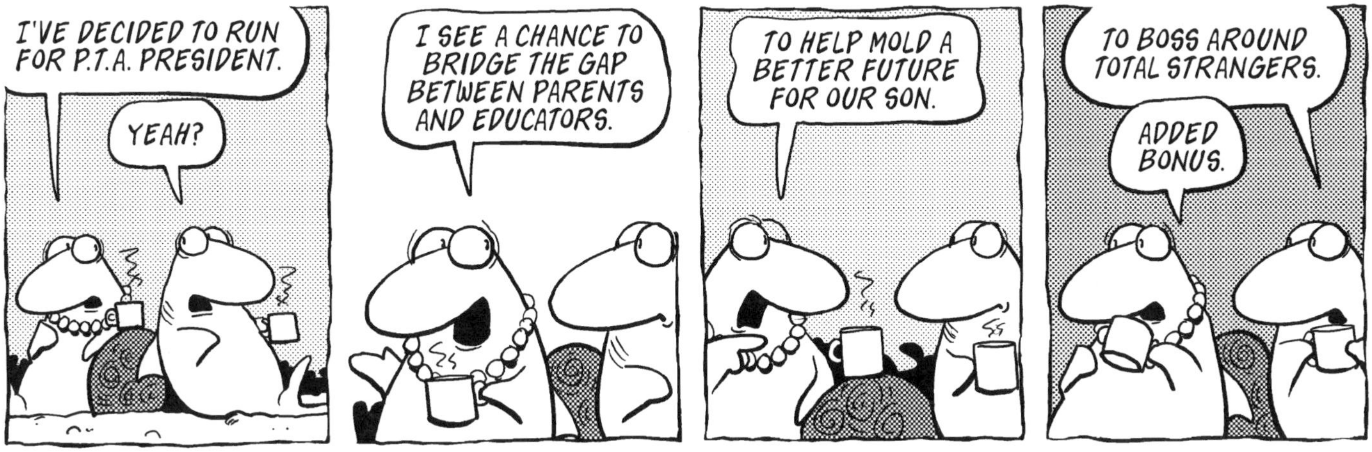
I'VE DECIDED TO RUN FOR P.T.A. PRESIDENT.
YEAH?
I SEE A CHANCE TO BRIDGE THE GAP BETWEEN PARENTS AND EDUCATORS.
TO HELP MOLD A BETTER FUTURE FOR OUR SON.
TO BOSS AROUND TOTAL STRANGERS.
ADDED BONUS.

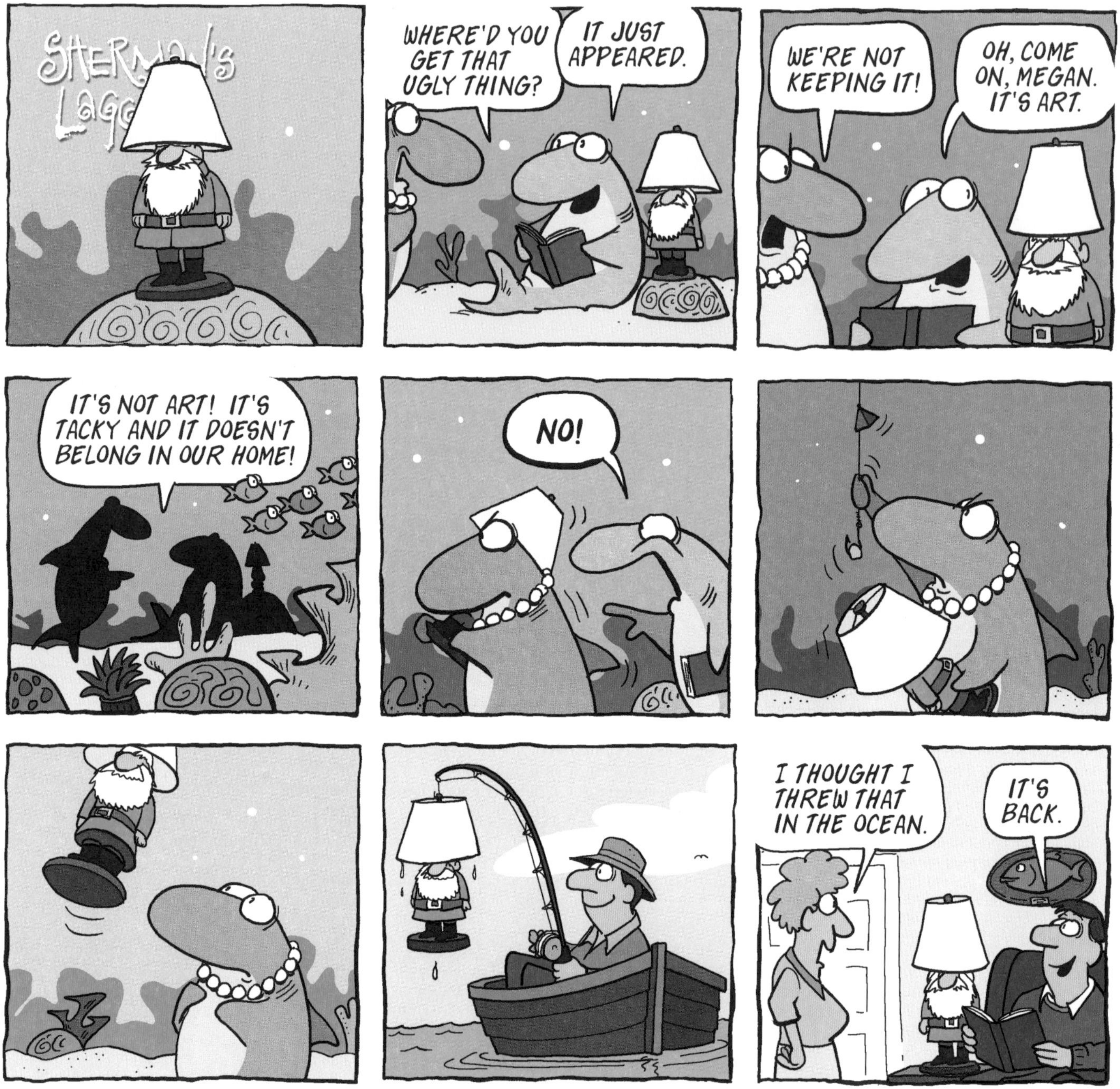
WHERE'D YOU GET THAT UGLY THING?
IT JUST APPEARED.
WE'RE NOT KEEPING IT!
OH, COME ON, MEGAN. IT'S ART.
IT'S NOT ART! IT'S TACKY AND IT DOESN'T BELONG IN OUR HOME!
NO!
I THOUGHT I THREW THAT IN THE OCEAN.
IT'S BACK.

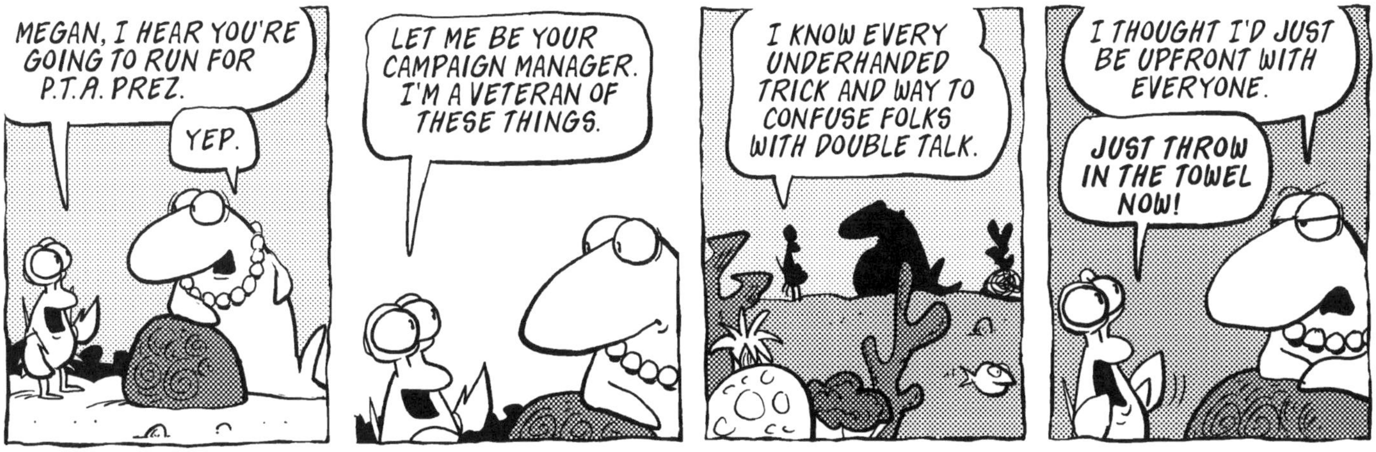
MEGAN, I HEAR YOU'RE GOING TO RUN FOR P.T.A. PREZ.
YEP.
LET ME BE YOUR CAMPAIGN MANAGER. I'M A VETERAN OF THESE THINGS.
I KNOW EVERY UNDERHANDED TRICK AND WAY TO CONFUSE FOLKS WITH DOUBLE TALK.
I THOUGHT I'D JUST BE UPFRONT WITH EVERYONE.
JUST THROW IN THE TOWEL NOW!

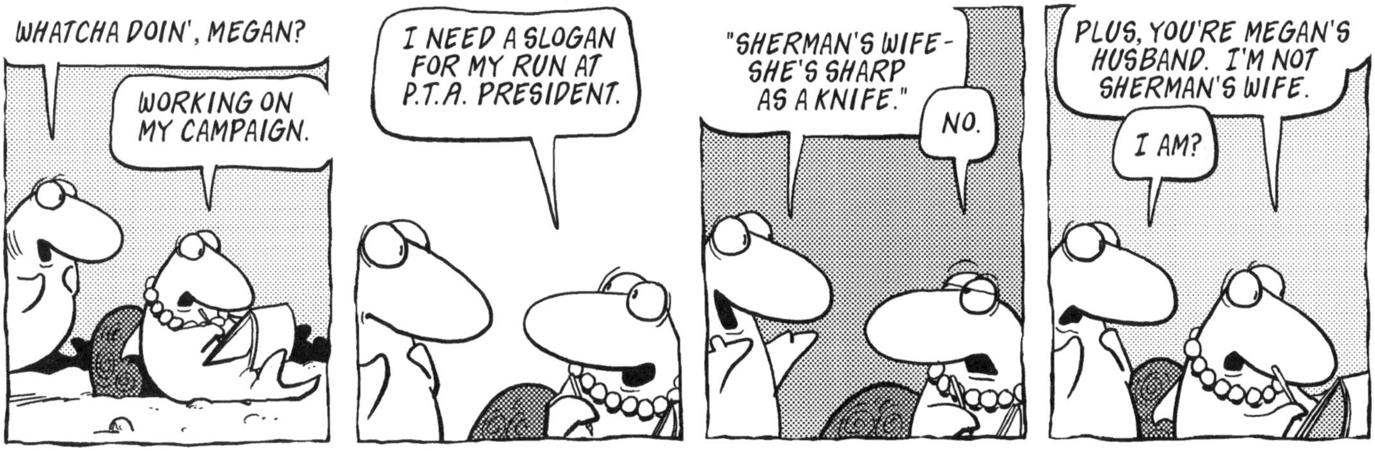
WHATCHA DOIN', MEGAN?
WORKING ON MY CAMPAIGN.
I NEED A SLOGAN FOR MY RUN AT P.T.A. PRESIDENT.
"SHERMAN'S WIFE - SHE'S SHARP AS A KNIFE."
NO.
PLUS, YOU'RE MEGAN'S HUSBAND. I'M NOT SHERMAN'S WIFE.
I AM?

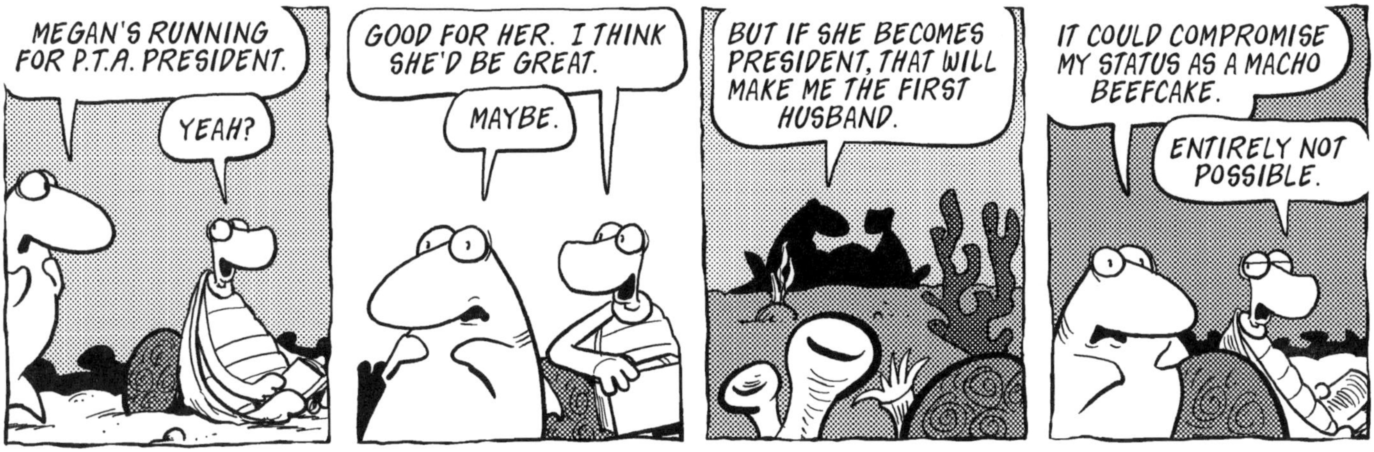
MEGAN'S RUNNING FOR P.T.A. PRESIDENT.
YEAH?
GOOD FOR HER. I THINK SHE'D BE GREAT.
MAYBE.
BUT IF SHE BECOMES PRESIDENT, THAT WILL MAKE ME THE FIRST HUSBAND.
IT COULD COMPROMISE MY STATUS AS A MACHO BEEFCAKE.
ENTIRELY NOT POSSIBLE.

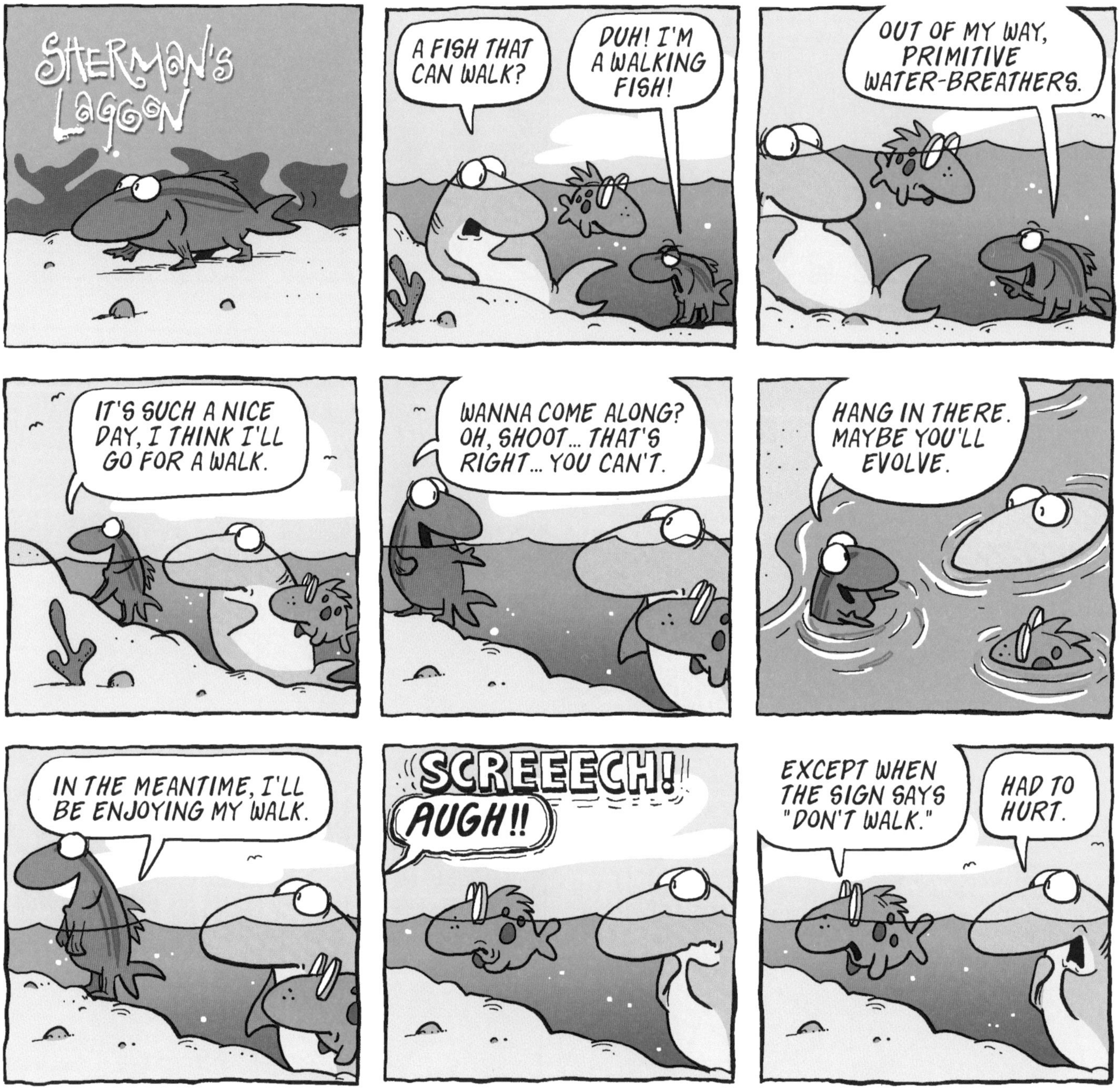
SHERMAN'S LAGOON
A FISH THAT CAN WALK?
DUH! I'M A WALKING FISH!
OUT OF MY WAY, PRIMITIVE WATER-BREATHERS.
IT'S SUCH A NICE DAY, I THINK I'LL GO FOR A WALK.
WANNA COME ALONG? OH, SHOOT... THAT'S RIGHT... YOU CAN'T.
HANG IN THERE. MAYBE YOU'LL EVOLVE.
IN THE MEANTIME, I'LL BE ENJOYING MY WALK.
SCREEECH!
AUGH!!
EXCEPT WHEN THE SIGN SAYS "DON'T WALK."
HAD TO HURT.

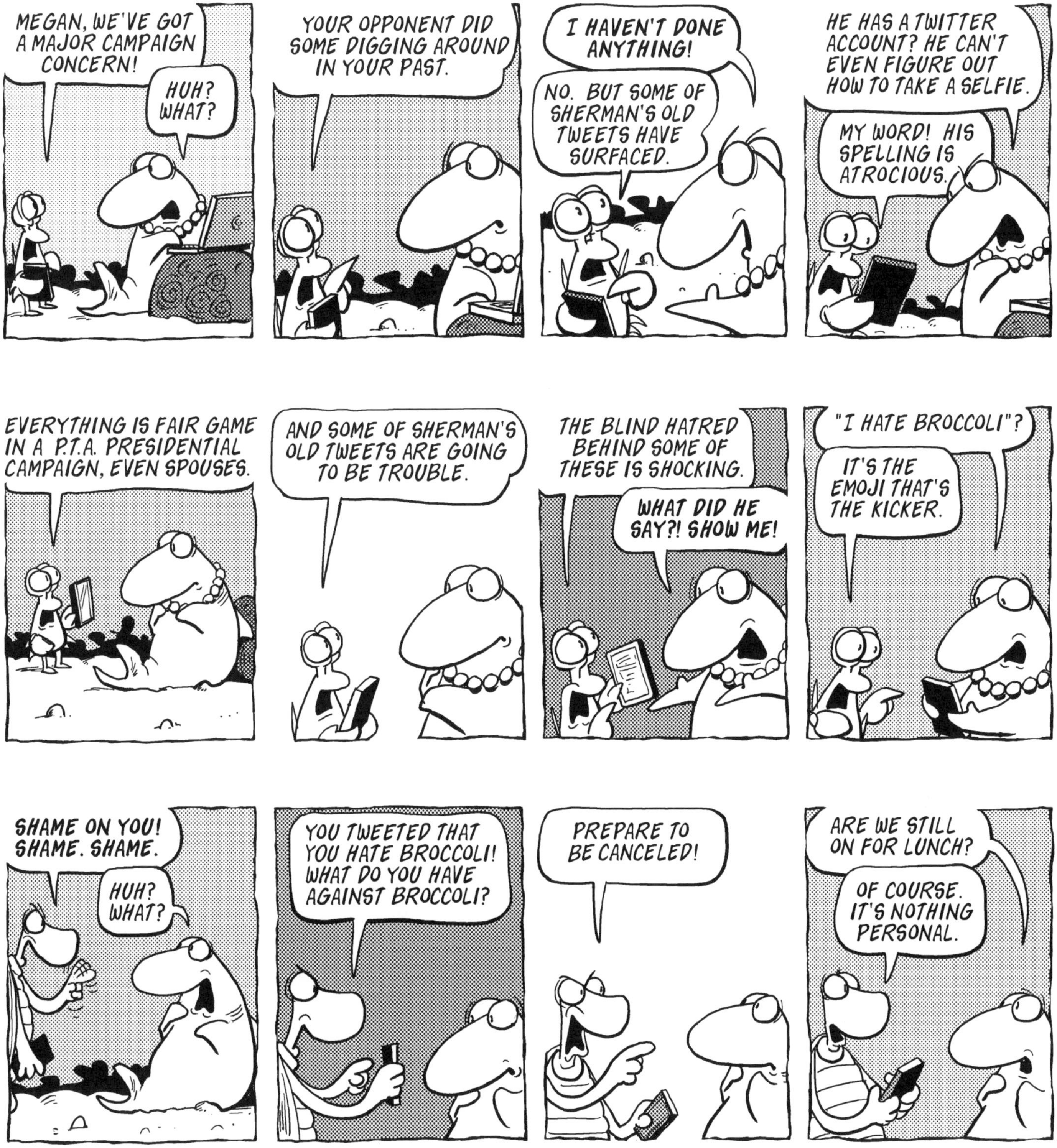
MEGAN, WE'VE GOT A MAJOR CAMPAIGN CONCERN!
HUH? WHAT?
YOUR OPPONENT DID SOME DIGGING AROUND IN YOUR PAST.
I HAVEN'T DONE ANYTHING!
NO. BUT SOME OF SHERMAN'S OLD TWEETS HAVE SURFACED.
HE HAS A TWITTER ACCOUNT? HE CAN'T EVEN FIGURE OUT HOW TO TAKE A SELFIE.
MY WORD! HIS SPELLING IS ATROCIOUS.
EVERYTHING IS FAIR GAME IN A P.T.A. PRESIDENTIAL CAMPAIGN, EVEN SPOUSES.
AND SOME OF SHERMAN'S OLD TWEETS ARE GOING TO BE TROUBLE.
THE BLIND HATRED BEHIND SOME OF THESE IS SHOCKING.
WHAT DID HE SAY?! SHOW ME!
"I HATE BROCCOLI"?
IT'S THE EMOJI THAT'S THE KICKER.
SHAME ON YOU! SHAME. SHAME.
HUH? WHAT?
YOU TWEETED THAT YOU HATE BROCCOLI! WHAT DO YOU HAVE AGAINST BROCCOLI?
PREPARE TO BE CANCELED!
ARE WE STILL ON FOR LUNCH?
OF COURSE. IT'S NOTHING PERSONAL.

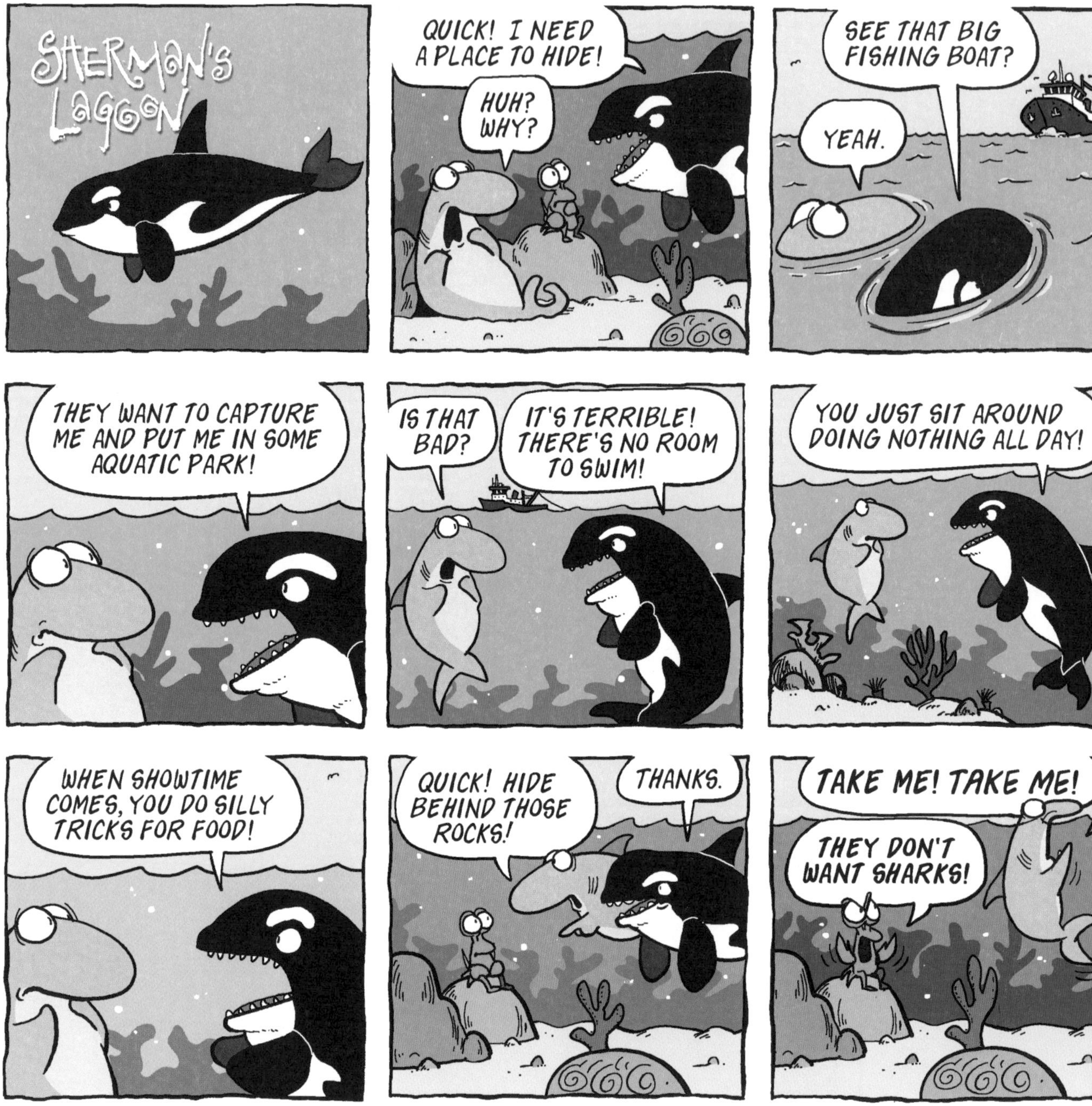
SHERMAN'S LAGOON
QUICK! I NEED A PLACE TO HIDE!
HUH? WHY?
SEE THAT BIG FISHING BOAT?
YEAH.
THEY WANT TO CAPTURE ME AND PUT ME IN SOME AQUATIC PARK!
IS THAT BAD?
IT'S TERRIBLE! THERE'S NO ROOM TO SWIM!
YOU JUST SIT AROUND DOING NOTHING ALL DAY!
WHEN SHOWTIME COMES, YOU DO SILLY TRICKS FOR FOOD!
QUICK! HIDE BEHIND THOSE ROCKS!
THANKS.
TAKE ME! TAKE ME!
THEY DON'T WANT SHARKS!

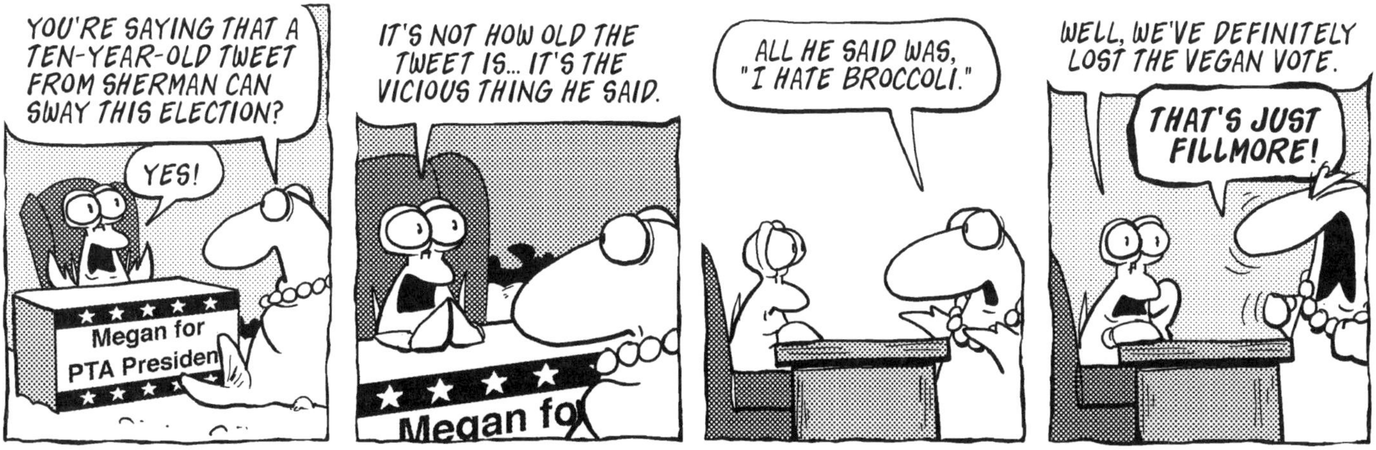
YOU'RE SAYING THAT A TEN-YEAR-OLD TWEET FROM SHERMAN CAN SWAY THIS ELECTION?
YES!
Megan for PTA Presiden
IT'S NOT HOW OLD THE TWEET IS... IT'S THE VICIOUS THING HE SAID.
Megan fo
ALL HE SAID WAS, "I HATE BROCCOLI."
WELL, WE'VE DEFINITELY LOST THE VEGAN VOTE.
THAT'S JUST FILLMORE!

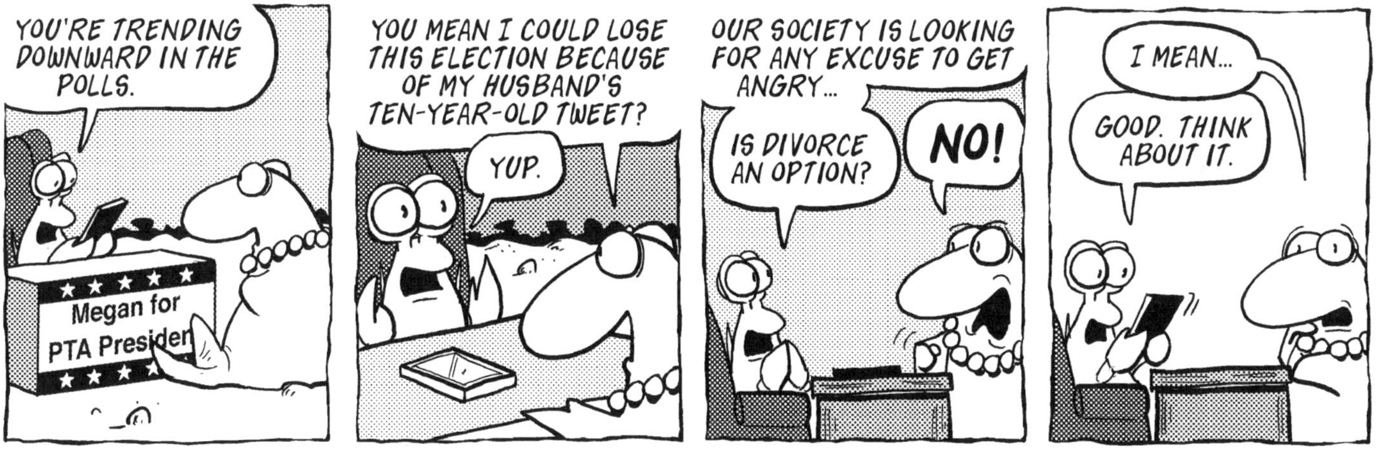
YOU'RE TRENDING DOWNWARD IN THE POLLS.
Megan for PTA Presiden
YOU MEAN I COULD LOSE THIS ELECTION BECAUSE OF MY HUSBAND'S TEN-YEAR-OLD TWEET?
YUP.
OUR SOCIETY IS LOOKING FOR ANY EXCUSE TO GET ANGRY...
IS DIVORCE AN OPTION?
NO!
I MEAN...
GOOD. THINK ABOUT IT.

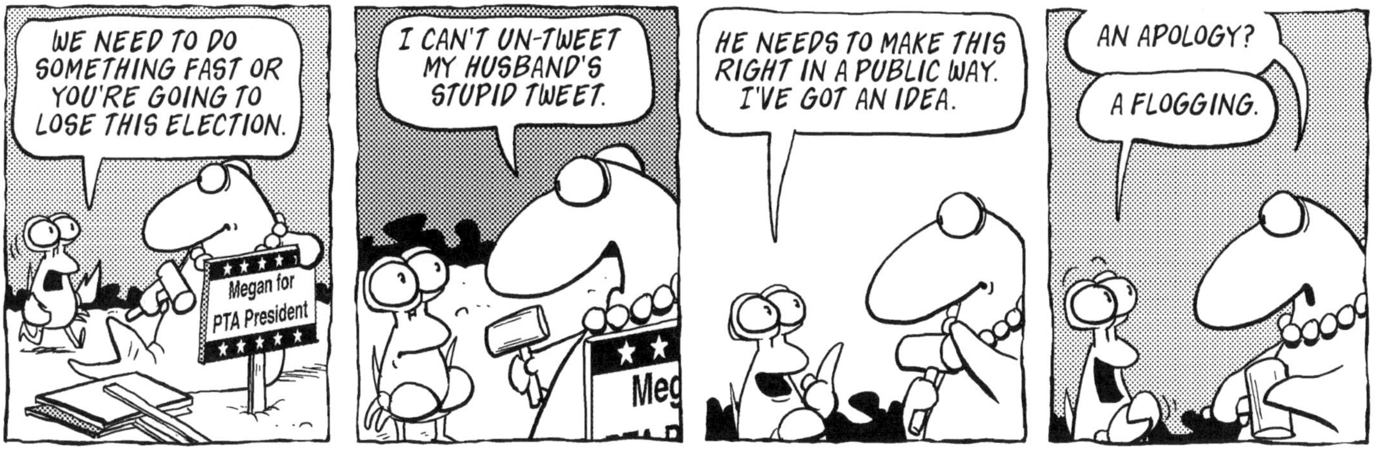
WE NEED TO DO SOMETHING FAST OR YOU'RE GOING TO LOSE THIS ELECTION.
Megan for PTA President
I CAN'T UN-TWEET MY HUSBAND'S STUPID TWEET.
Meg
HE NEEDS TO MAKE THIS RIGHT IN A PUBLIC WAY. I'VE GOT AN IDEA.
AN APOLOGY?
A FLOGGING.

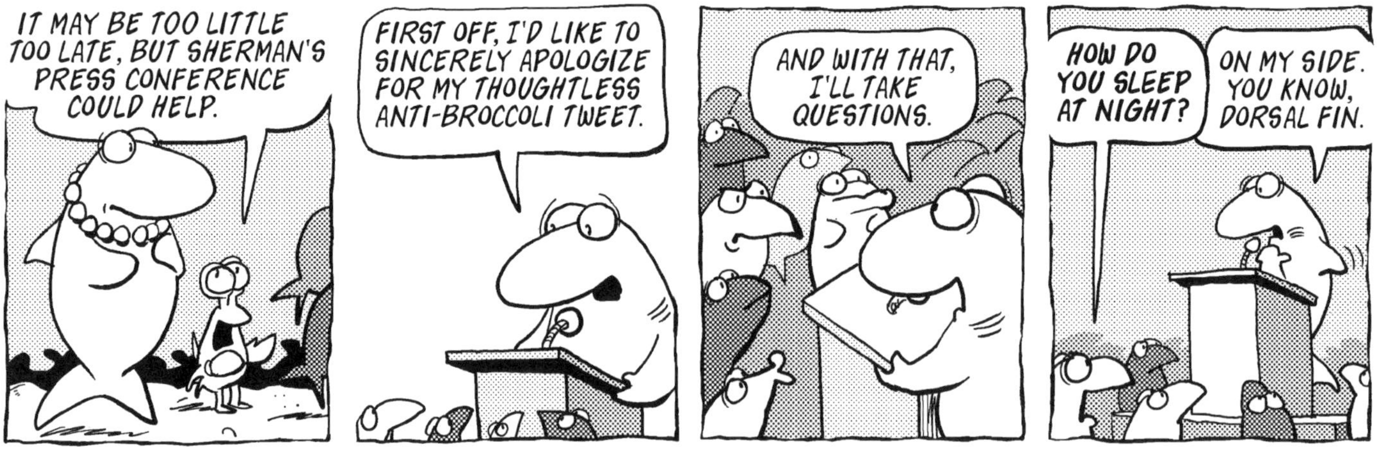
IT MAY BE TOO LITTLE TOO LATE, BUT SHERMAN'S PRESS CONFERENCE COULD HELP.
FIRST OFF, I'D LIKE TO SINCERELY APOLOGIZE FOR MY THOUGHTLESS ANTI-BROCCOLI TWEET.
AND WITH THAT, I'LL TAKE QUESTIONS.
HOW DO YOU SLEEP AT NIGHT?
ON MY SIDE. YOU KNOW, DORSAL FIN.

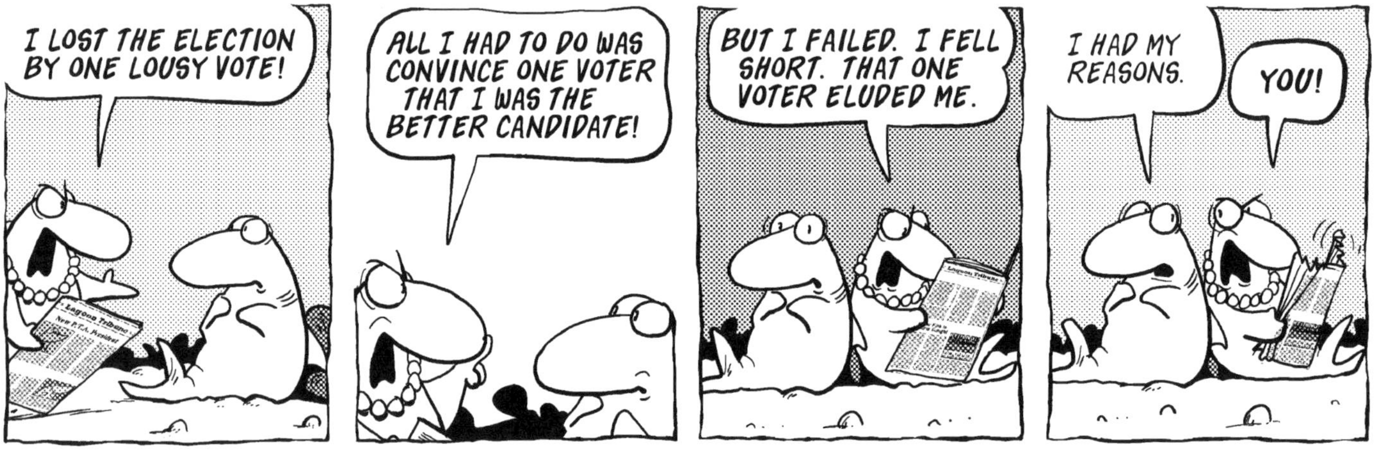
I LOST THE ELECTION BY ONE LOUSY VOTE!
ALL I HAD TO DO WAS CONVINCE ONE VOTER THAT I WAS THE BETTER CANDIDATE!
BUT I FAILED. I FELL SHORT. THAT ONE VOTER ELUDED ME.
I HAD MY REASONS.
YOU!

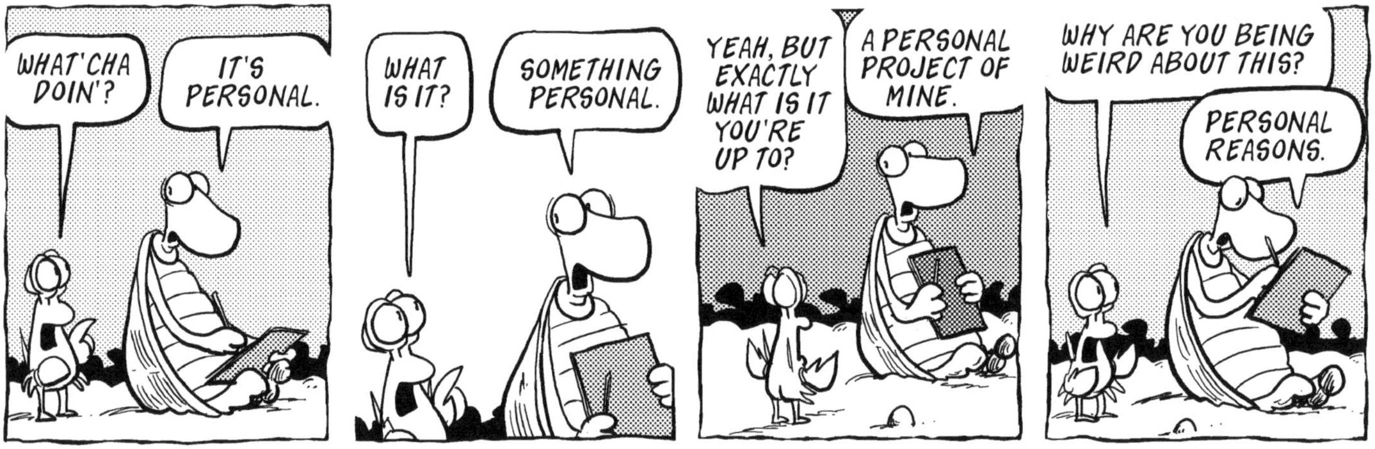
WHAT'CHA DOIN'?
IT'S PERSONAL.
WHAT IS IT?
SOMETHING PERSONAL.
YEAH, BUT EXACTLY WHAT IS IT YOU'RE UP TO?
A PERSONAL PROJECT OF MINE.
WHY ARE YOU BEING WEIRD ABOUT THIS?
PERSONAL REASONS.

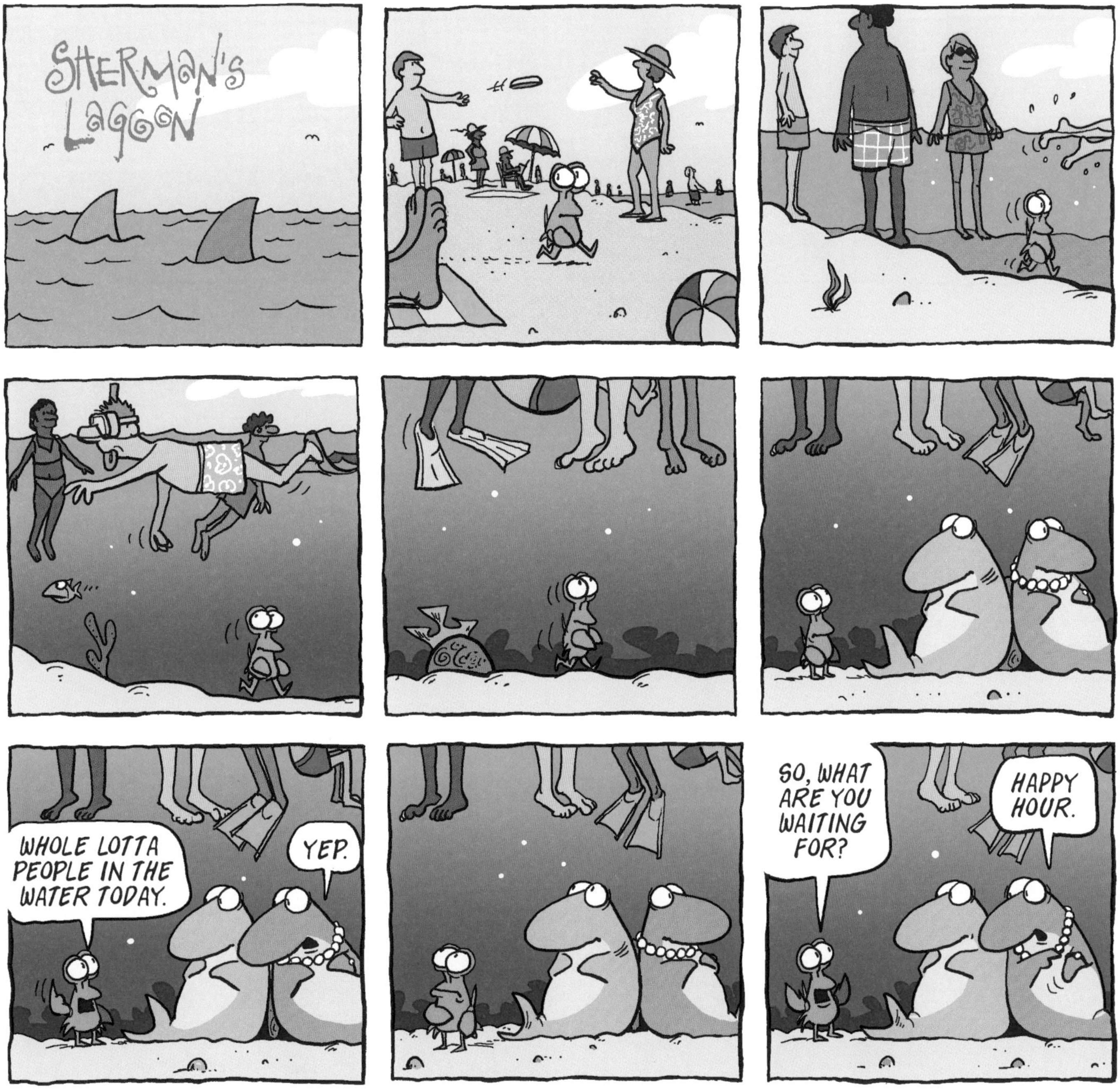
SHERMAN'S LAGOON
WHOLE LOTTA PEOPLE IN THE WATER TODAY.
YEP.
SO, WHAT ARE YOU WAITING FOR?
HAPPY HOUR.

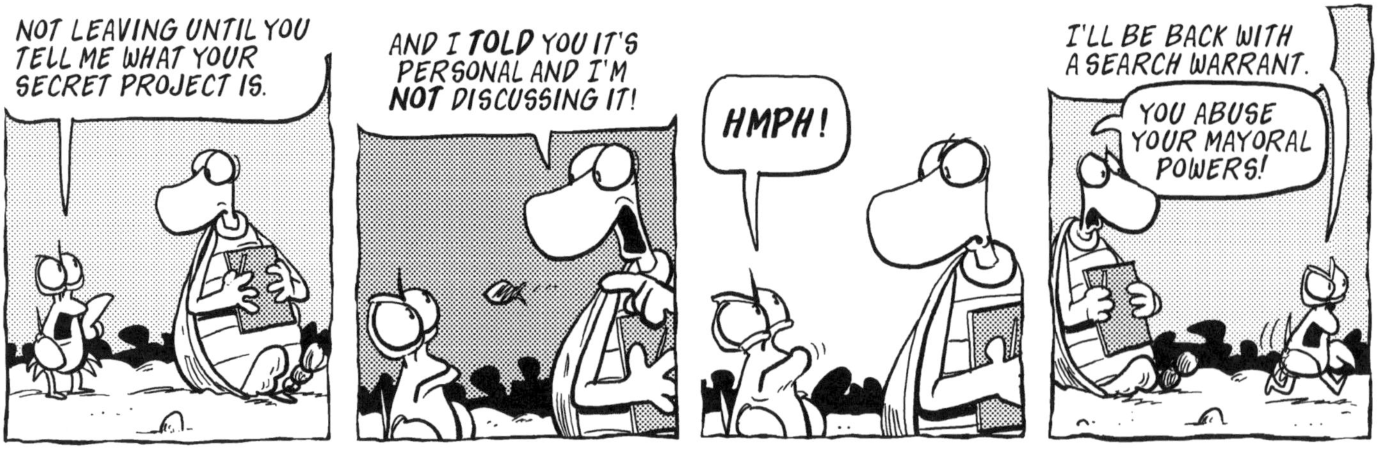
NOT LEAVING UNTIL YOU TELL ME WHAT YOUR SECRET PROJECT IS.
AND I **TOLD** YOU IT'S PERSONAL AND I'M **NOT** DISCUSSING IT!
HMPH!
I'LL BE BACK WITH A SEARCH WARRANT.
YOU ABUSE YOUR MAYORAL POWERS!

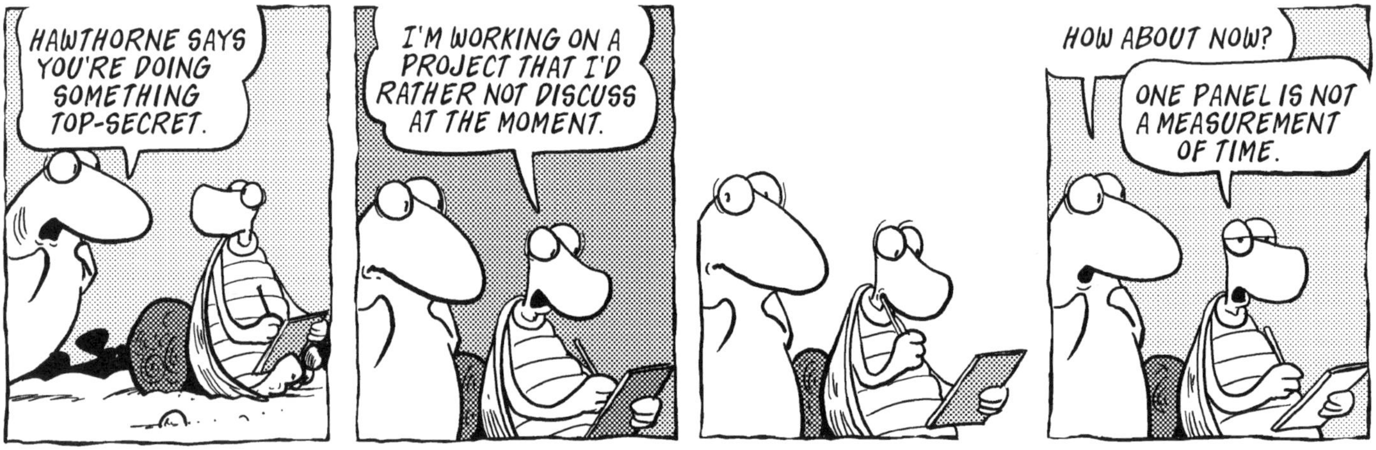
HAWTHORNE SAYS YOU'RE DOING SOMETHING TOP-SECRET.
I'M WORKING ON A PROJECT THAT I'D RATHER NOT DISCUSS AT THE MOMENT.
HOW ABOUT NOW?
ONE PANEL IS NOT A MEASUREMENT OF TIME.

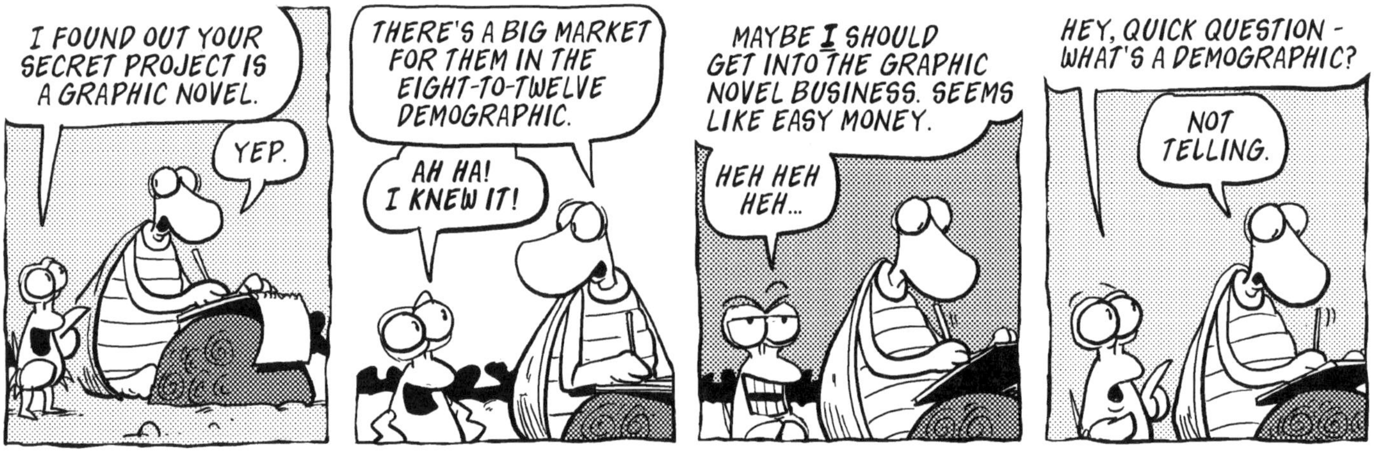
I FOUND OUT YOUR SECRET PROJECT IS A GRAPHIC NOVEL.
YEP.
THERE'S A BIG MARKET FOR THEM IN THE EIGHT-TO-TWELVE DEMOGRAPHIC.
AH HA! I KNEW IT!
MAYBE I SHOULD GET INTO THE GRAPHIC NOVEL BUSINESS. SEEMS LIKE EASY MONEY.
HEH HEH HEH...
HEY, QUICK QUESTION - WHAT'S A DEMOGRAPHIC?
NOT TELLING.

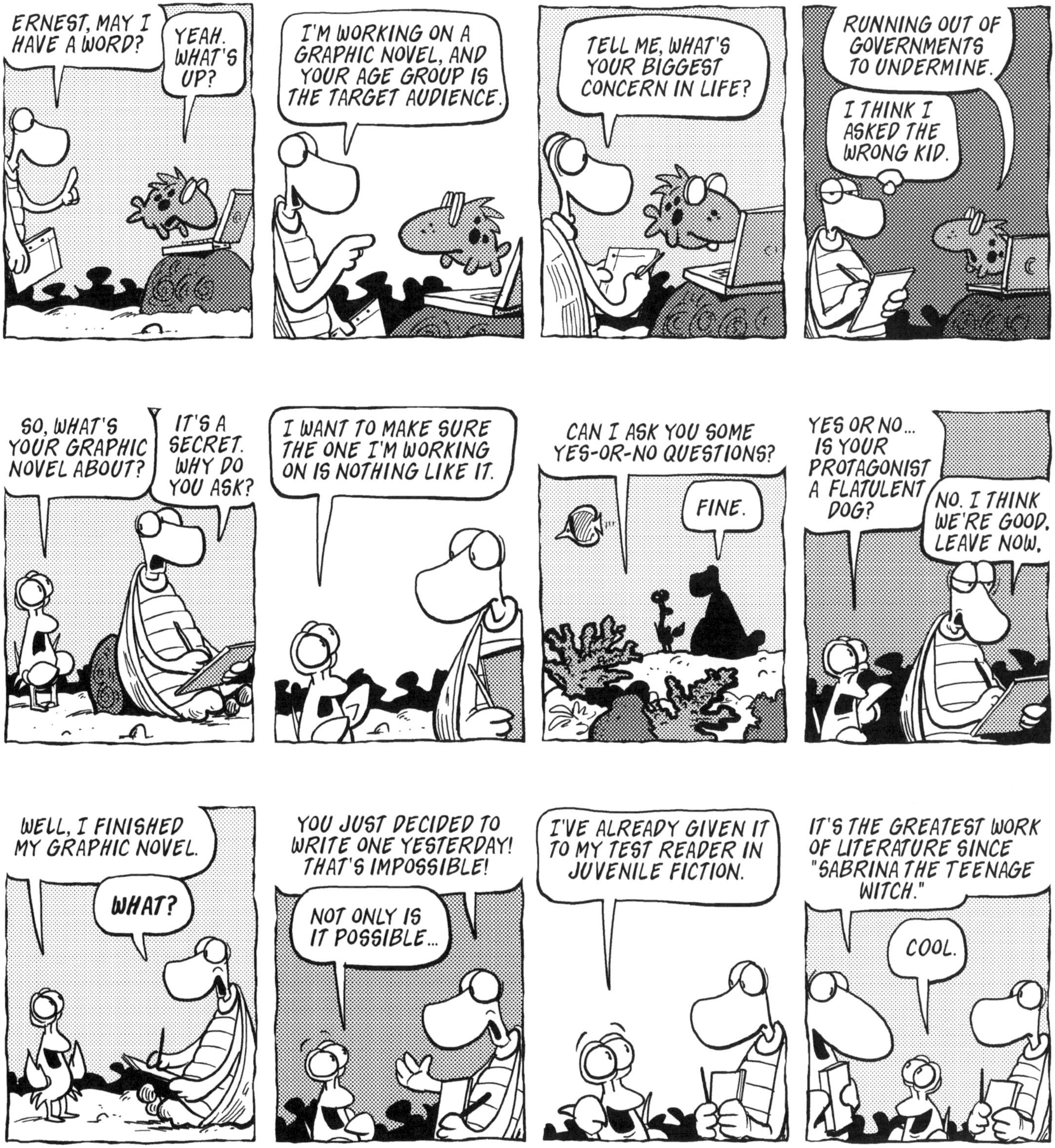
ERNEST, MAY I HAVE A WORD?
YEAH. WHAT'S UP?
I'M WORKING ON A GRAPHIC NOVEL, AND YOUR AGE GROUP IS THE TARGET AUDIENCE.
TELL ME, WHAT'S YOUR BIGGEST CONCERN IN LIFE?
RUNNING OUT OF GOVERNMENTS TO UNDERMINE.
I THINK I ASKED THE WRONG KID.
SO, WHAT'S YOUR GRAPHIC NOVEL ABOUT?
IT'S A SECRET. WHY DO YOU ASK?
I WANT TO MAKE SURE THE ONE I'M WORKING ON IS NOTHING LIKE IT.
CAN I ASK YOU SOME YES-OR-NO QUESTIONS?
FINE.
YES OR NO... IS YOUR PROTAGONIST A FLATULENT DOG?
NO. I THINK WE'RE GOOD. LEAVE NOW.
WELL, I FINISHED MY GRAPHIC NOVEL.
WHAT?
YOU JUST DECIDED TO WRITE ONE YESTERDAY! THAT'S IMPOSSIBLE!
NOT ONLY IS IT POSSIBLE...
I'VE ALREADY GIVEN IT TO MY TEST READER IN JUVENILE FICTION.
IT'S THE GREATEST WORK OF LITERATURE SINCE "SABRINA THE TEENAGE WITCH."
COOL.

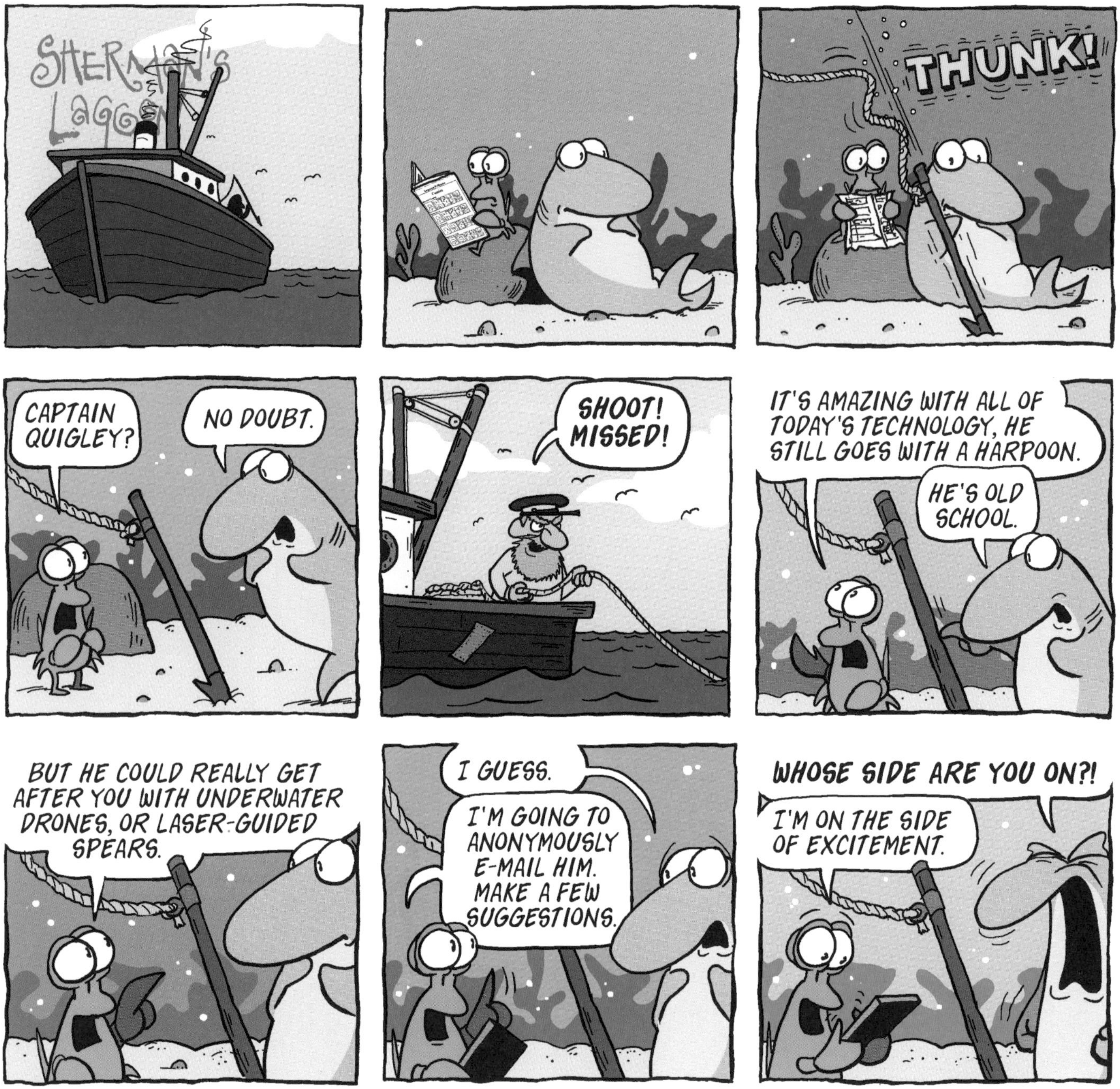
THUNK!
CAPTAIN QUIGLEY?
NO DOUBT.
SHOOT! MISSED!
IT'S AMAZING WITH ALL OF TODAY'S TECHNOLOGY, HE STILL GOES WITH A HARPOON.
HE'S OLD SCHOOL.
BUT HE COULD REALLY GET AFTER YOU WITH UNDERWATER DRONES, OR LASER-GUIDED SPEARS.
I GUESS.
I'M GOING TO ANONYMOUSLY E-MAIL HIM. MAKE A FEW SUGGESTIONS.
WHOSE SIDE ARE YOU ON?!
I'M ON THE SIDE OF EXCITEMENT.

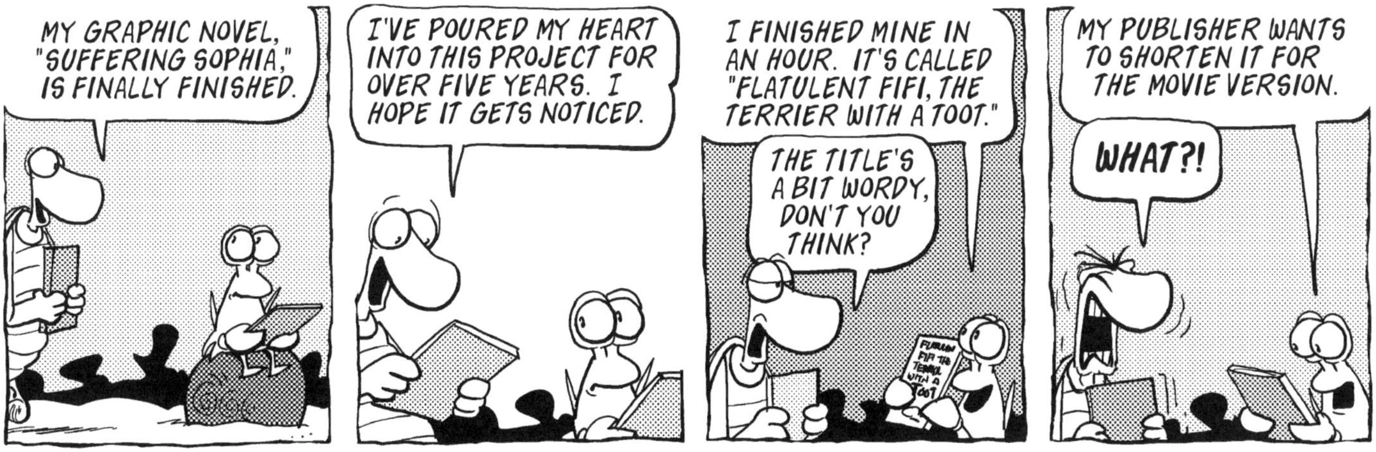
MY GRAPHIC NOVEL, "SUFFERING SOPHIA," IS FINALLY FINISHED.
I'VE POURED MY HEART INTO THIS PROJECT FOR OVER FIVE YEARS. I HOPE IT GETS NOTICED.
I FINISHED MINE IN AN HOUR. IT'S CALLED "FLATULENT FIFI, THE TERRIER WITH A TOOT."
THE TITLE'S A BIT WORDY, DON'T YOU THINK?
MY PUBLISHER WANTS TO SHORTEN IT FOR THE MOVIE VERSION.
WHAT?!

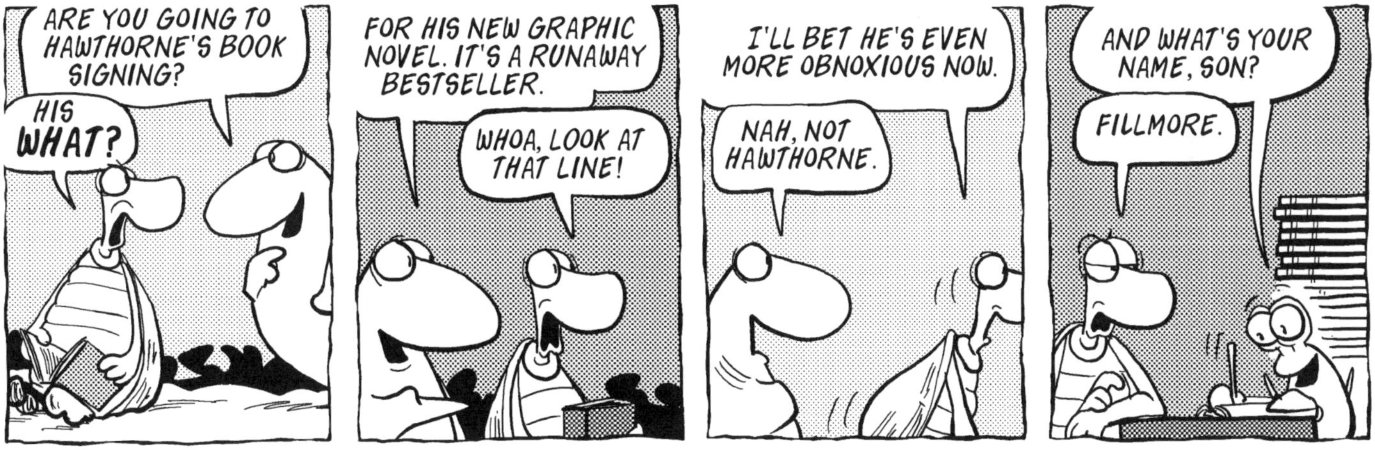
ARE YOU GOING TO HAWTHORNE'S BOOK SIGNING?
HIS WHAT?
FOR HIS NEW GRAPHIC NOVEL. IT'S A RUNAWAY BESTSELLER.
WHOA, LOOK AT THAT LINE!
I'LL BET HE'S EVEN MORE OBNOXIOUS NOW.
NAH, NOT HAWTHORNE.
AND WHAT'S YOUR NAME, SON?
FILLMORE.

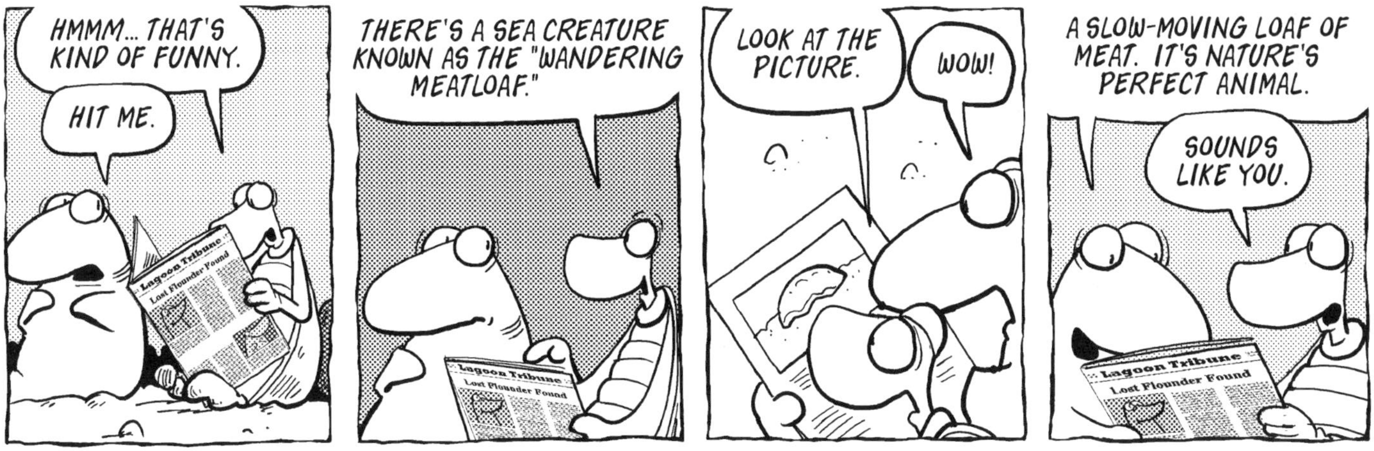
HMMM... THAT'S KIND OF FUNNY.
HIT ME.
Lagoon Tribune
Lost Flounder Found
THERE'S A SEA CREATURE KNOWN AS THE "WANDERING MEATLOAF."
Lagoon Tribune
Lost Flounder Found
LOOK AT THE PICTURE.
WOW!
A SLOW-MOVING LOAF OF MEAT. IT'S NATURE'S PERFECT ANIMAL.
SOUNDS LIKE YOU.
Lagoon Tribune
Lost Flounder Found

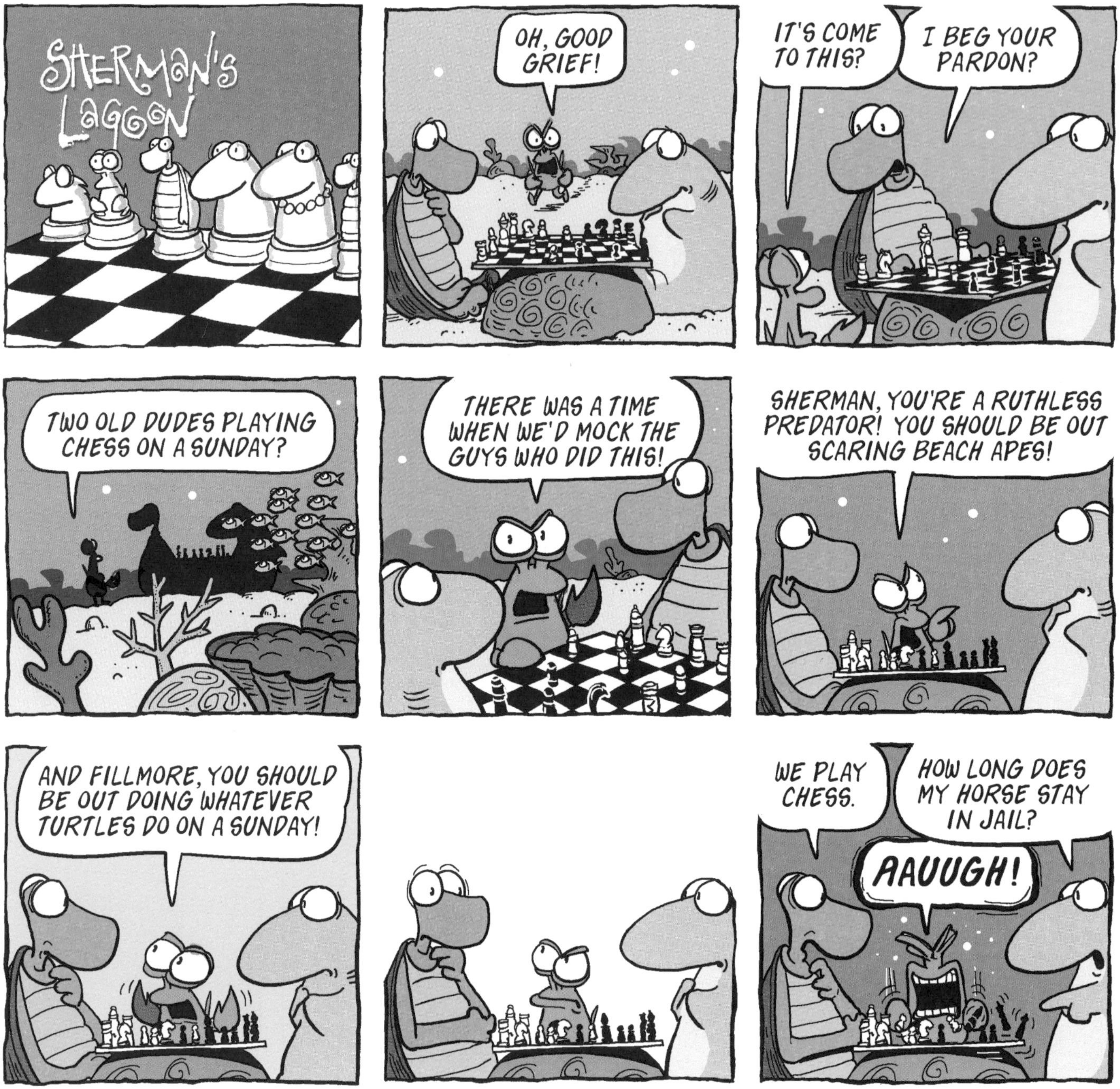
SHERMAN'S LAGOON
OH, GOOD GRIEF!
IT'S COME TO THIS?
I BEG YOUR PARDON?
TWO OLD DUDES PLAYING CHESS ON A SUNDAY?
THERE WAS A TIME WHEN WE'D MOCK THE GUYS WHO DID THIS!
SHERMAN, YOU'RE A RUTHLESS PREDATOR! YOU SHOULD BE OUT SCARING BEACH APES!
AND FILLMORE, YOU SHOULD BE OUT DOING WHATEVER TURTLES DO ON A SUNDAY!
WE PLAY CHESS.
HOW LONG DOES MY HORSE STAY IN JAIL?
AAUUGH!

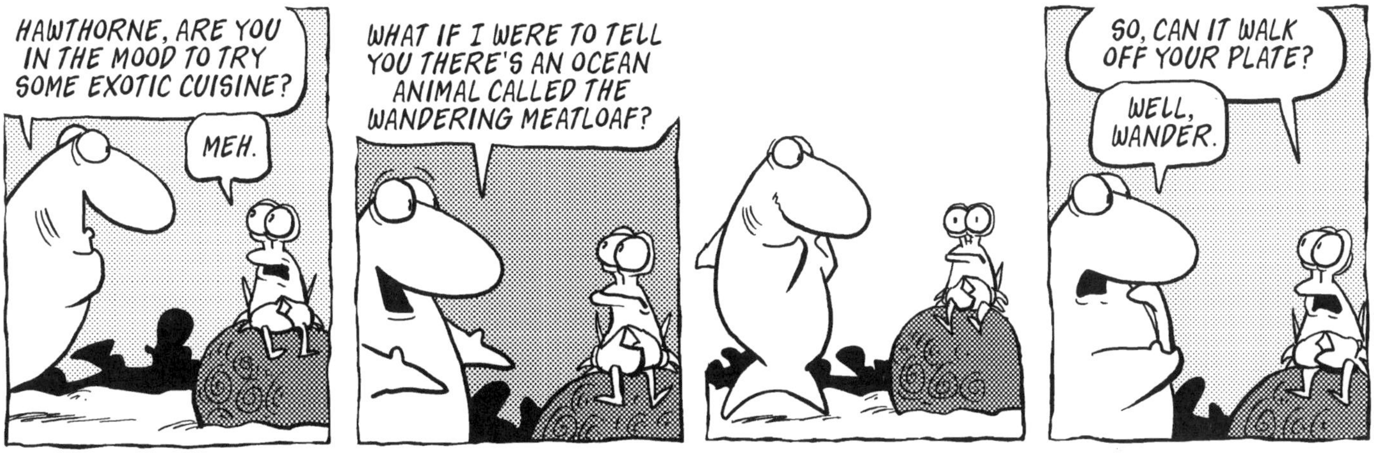
HAWTHORNE, ARE YOU IN THE MOOD TO TRY SOME EXOTIC CUISINE?
MEH.
WHAT IF I WERE TO TELL YOU THERE'S AN OCEAN ANIMAL CALLED THE WANDERING MEATLOAF?
SO, CAN IT WALK OFF YOUR PLATE?
WELL, WANDER.

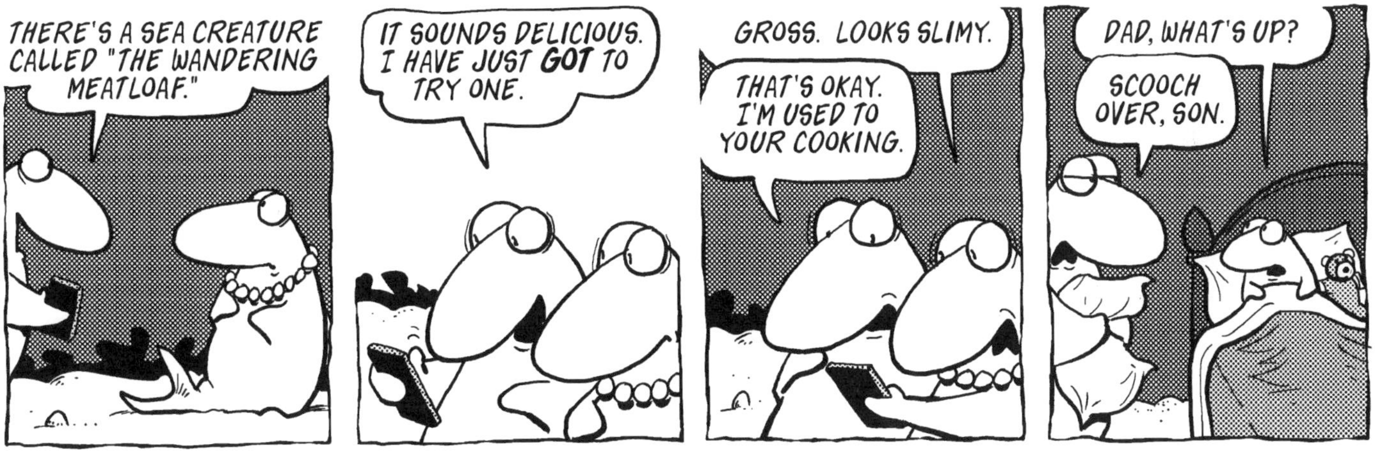
THERE'S A SEA CREATURE CALLED "THE WANDERING MEATLOAF."
IT SOUNDS DELICIOUS. I HAVE JUST GOT TO TRY ONE.
GROSS. LOOKS SLIMY.
THAT'S OKAY. I'M USED TO YOUR COOKING.
DAD, WHAT'S UP?
SCOOCH OVER, SON.

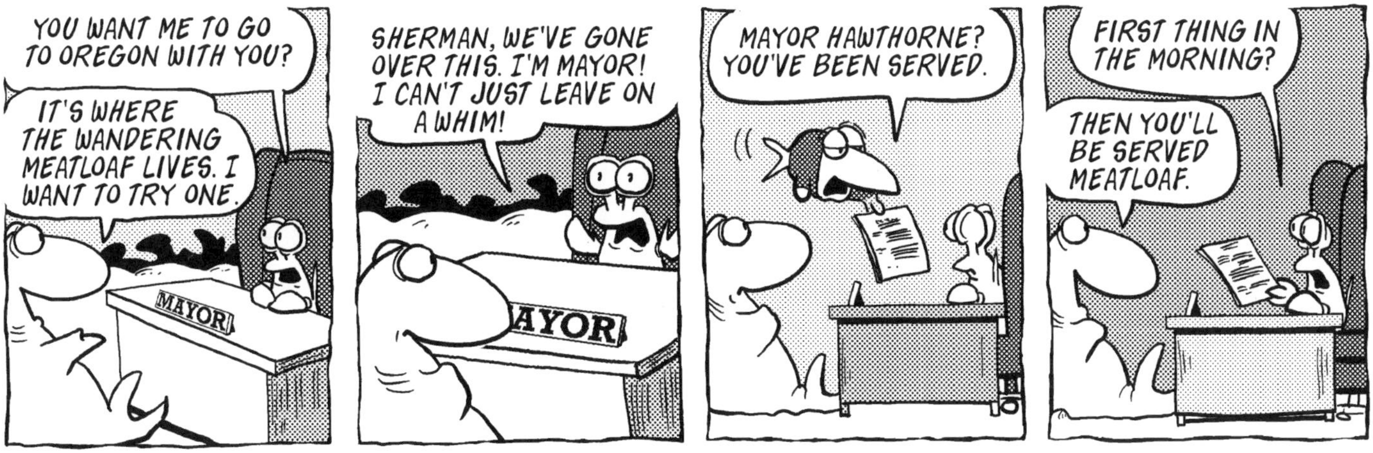
YOU WANT ME TO GO TO OREGON WITH YOU?
IT'S WHERE THE WANDERING MEATLOAF LIVES. I WANT TO TRY ONE.
MAYOR
SHERMAN, WE'VE GONE OVER THIS. I'M MAYOR! I CAN'T JUST LEAVE ON A WHIM!
MAYOR
MAYOR HAWTHORNE? YOU'VE BEEN SERVED.
FIRST THING IN THE MORNING?
THEN YOU'LL BE SERVED MEATLOAF.

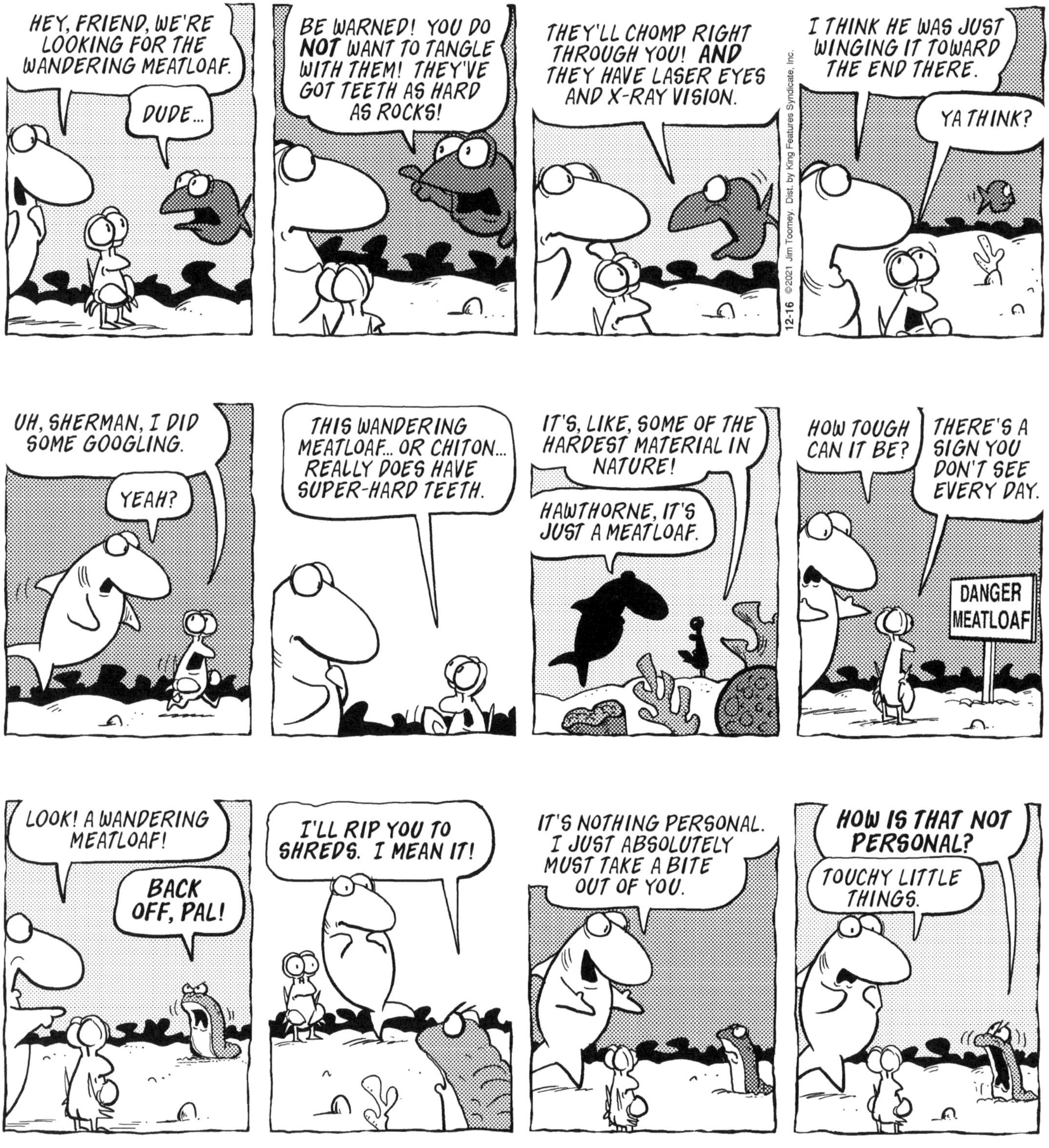
HEY, FRIEND, WE'RE LOOKING FOR THE WANDERING MEATLOAF.
DUDE...
BE WARNED! YOU DO **NOT** WANT TO TANGLE WITH THEM! THEY'VE GOT TEETH AS HARD AS ROCKS!
THEY'LL CHOMP RIGHT THROUGH YOU! **AND** THEY HAVE LASER EYES AND X-RAY VISION.
12-16 ©2021 Jim Toomey. Dist. by King Features Syndicate, Inc.
I THINK HE WAS JUST WINGING IT TOWARD THE END THERE.
YA THINK?
UH, SHERMAN, I DID SOME GOOGLING.
YEAH?
THIS WANDERING MEATLOAF... OR CHITON... REALLY DOES HAVE SUPER-HARD TEETH.
IT'S, LIKE, SOME OF THE HARDEST MATERIAL IN NATURE!
HAWTHORNE, IT'S JUST A MEATLOAF.
HOW TOUGH CAN IT BE?
THERE'S A SIGN YOU DON'T SEE EVERY DAY.
DANGER MEATLOAF
LOOK! A WANDERING MEATLOAF!
BACK OFF, PAL!
I'LL RIP YOU TO SHREDS. I MEAN IT!
IT'S NOTHING PERSONAL. I JUST ABSOLUTELY MUST TAKE A BITE OUT OF YOU.
HOW IS THAT NOT PERSONAL?
TOUCHY LITTLE THINGS.

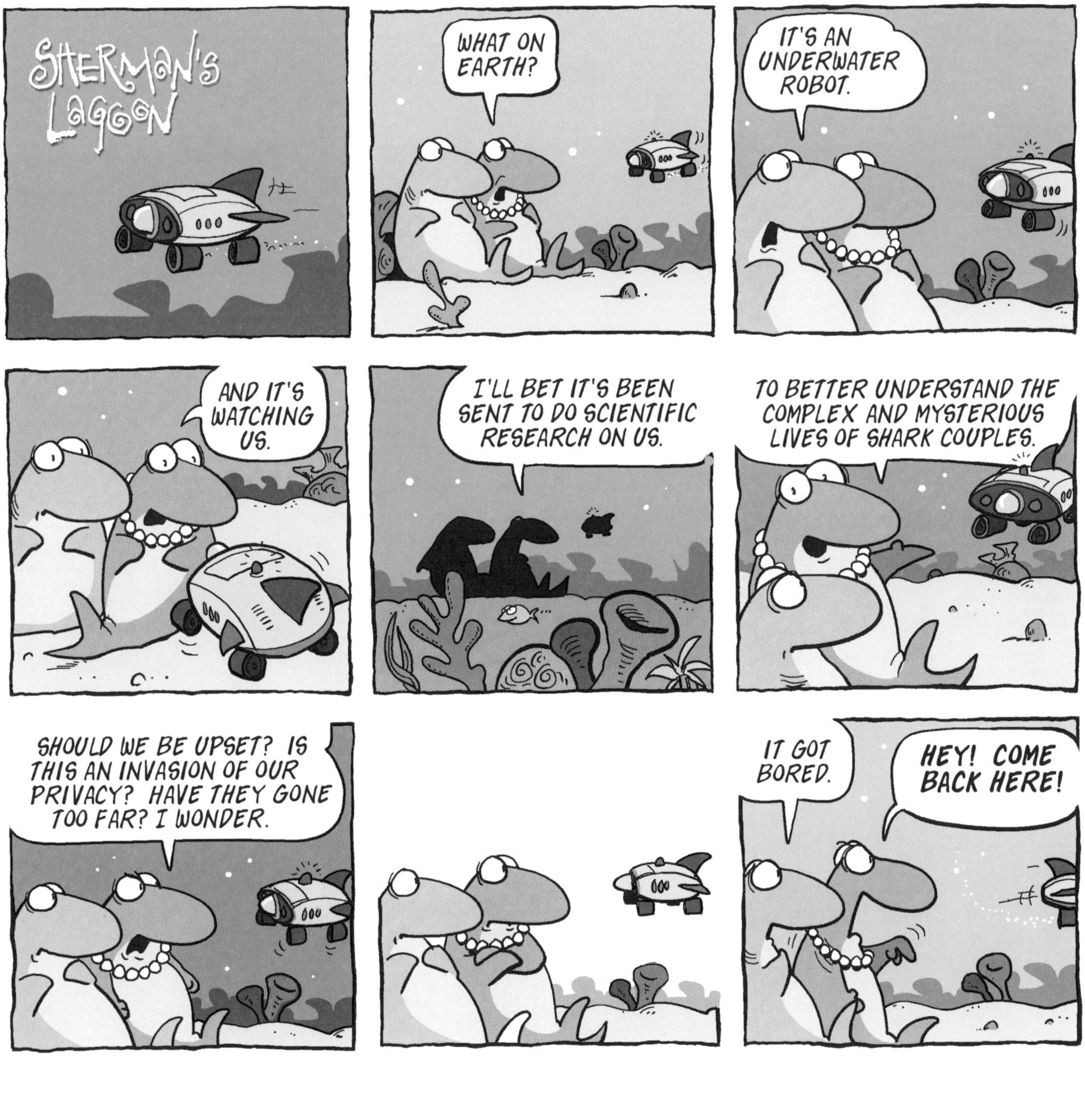
SHERMAN'S LAGOON
WHAT ON EARTH?
IT'S AN UNDERWATER ROBOT.
AND IT'S WATCHING US.
I'LL BET IT'S BEEN SENT TO DO SCIENTIFIC RESEARCH ON US.
TO BETTER UNDERSTAND THE COMPLEX AND MYSTERIOUS LIVES OF SHARK COUPLES.
SHOULD WE BE UPSET? IS THIS AN INVASION OF OUR PRIVACY? HAVE THEY GONE TOO FAR? I WONDER.
IT GOT BORED.
HEY! COME BACK HERE!

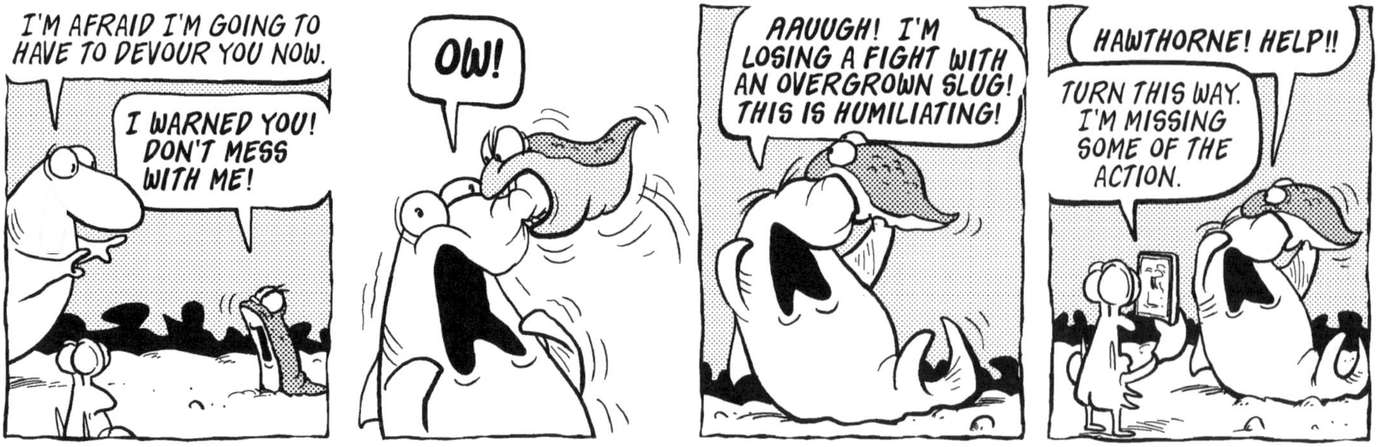
I'M AFRAID I'M GOING TO HAVE TO DEVOUR YOU NOW.
I WARNED YOU! DON'T MESS WITH ME!
OW!
AAUUGH! I'M LOSING A FIGHT WITH AN OVERGROWN SLUG! THIS IS HUMILIATING!
HAWTHORNE! HELP!!
TURN THIS WAY. I'M MISSING SOME OF THE ACTION.

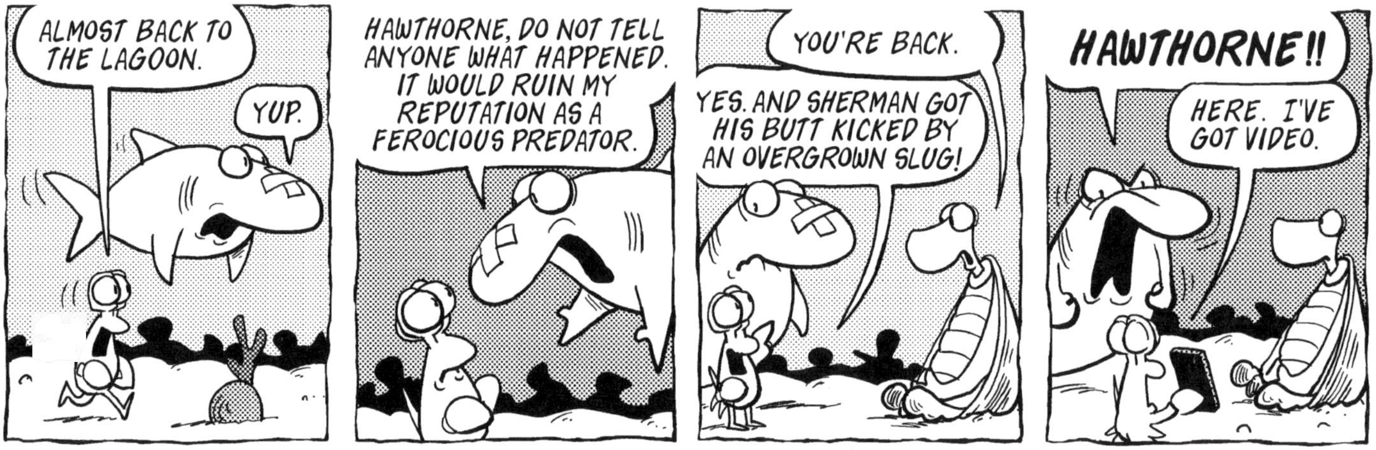
ALMOST BACK TO THE LAGOON.
YUP.
HAWTHORNE, DO NOT TELL ANYONE WHAT HAPPENED. IT WOULD RUIN MY REPUTATION AS A FEROCIOUS PREDATOR.
YOU'RE BACK.
YES. AND SHERMAN GOT HIS BUTT KICKED BY AN OVERGROWN SLUG!
HAWTHORNE!!
HERE. I'VE GOT VIDEO.

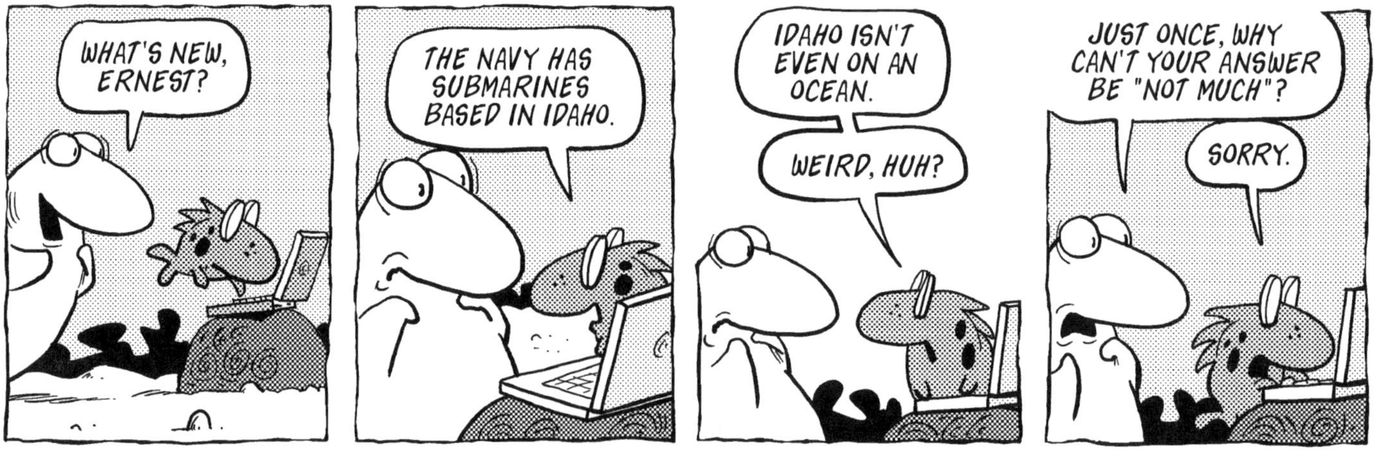
WHAT'S NEW, ERNEST?
THE NAVY HAS SUBMARINES BASED IN IDAHO.
IDAHO ISN'T EVEN ON AN OCEAN.
WEIRD, HUH?
JUST ONCE, WHY CAN'T YOUR ANSWER BE "NOT MUCH"?
SORRY.

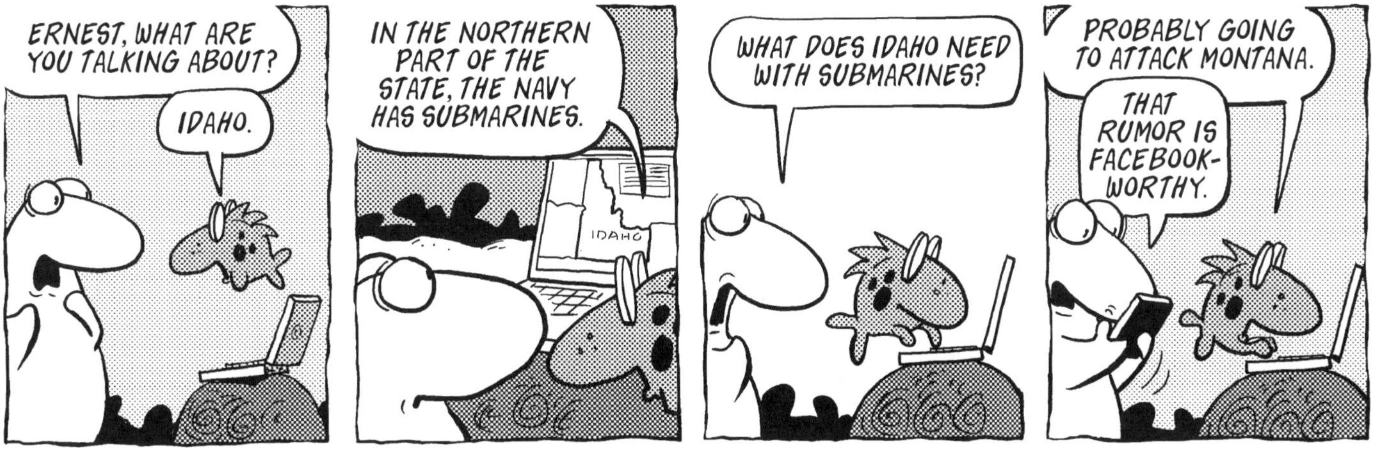
ERNEST, WHAT ARE YOU TALKING ABOUT?
IDAHO.
IN THE NORTHERN PART OF THE STATE, THE NAVY HAS SUBMARINES.
IDAHO
WHAT DOES IDAHO NEED WITH SUBMARINES?
PROBABLY GOING TO ATTACK MONTANA.
THAT RUMOR IS FACEBOOK-WORTHY.

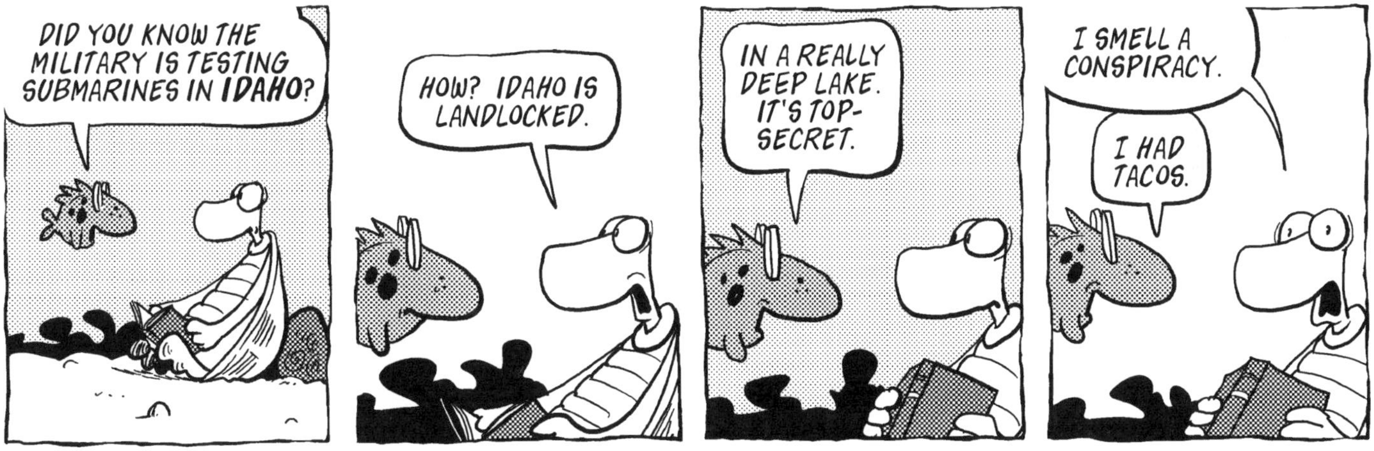
DID YOU KNOW THE MILITARY IS TESTING SUBMARINES IN IDAHO?
HOW? IDAHO IS LANDLOCKED.
IN A REALLY DEEP LAKE. IT'S TOP-SECRET.
I SMELL A CONSPIRACY.
I HAD TACOS.

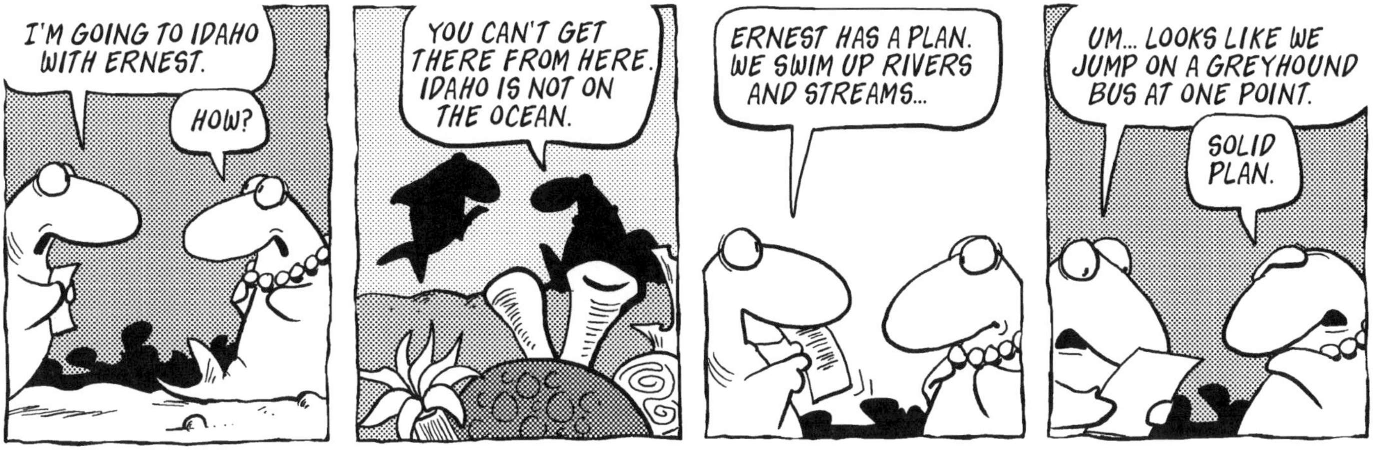
I'M GOING TO IDAHO WITH ERNEST.
HOW?
YOU CAN'T GET THERE FROM HERE. IDAHO IS NOT ON THE OCEAN.
ERNEST HAS A PLAN. WE SWIM UP RIVERS AND STREAMS...
UM... LOOKS LIKE WE JUMP ON A GREYHOUND BUS AT ONE POINT.
SOLID PLAN.

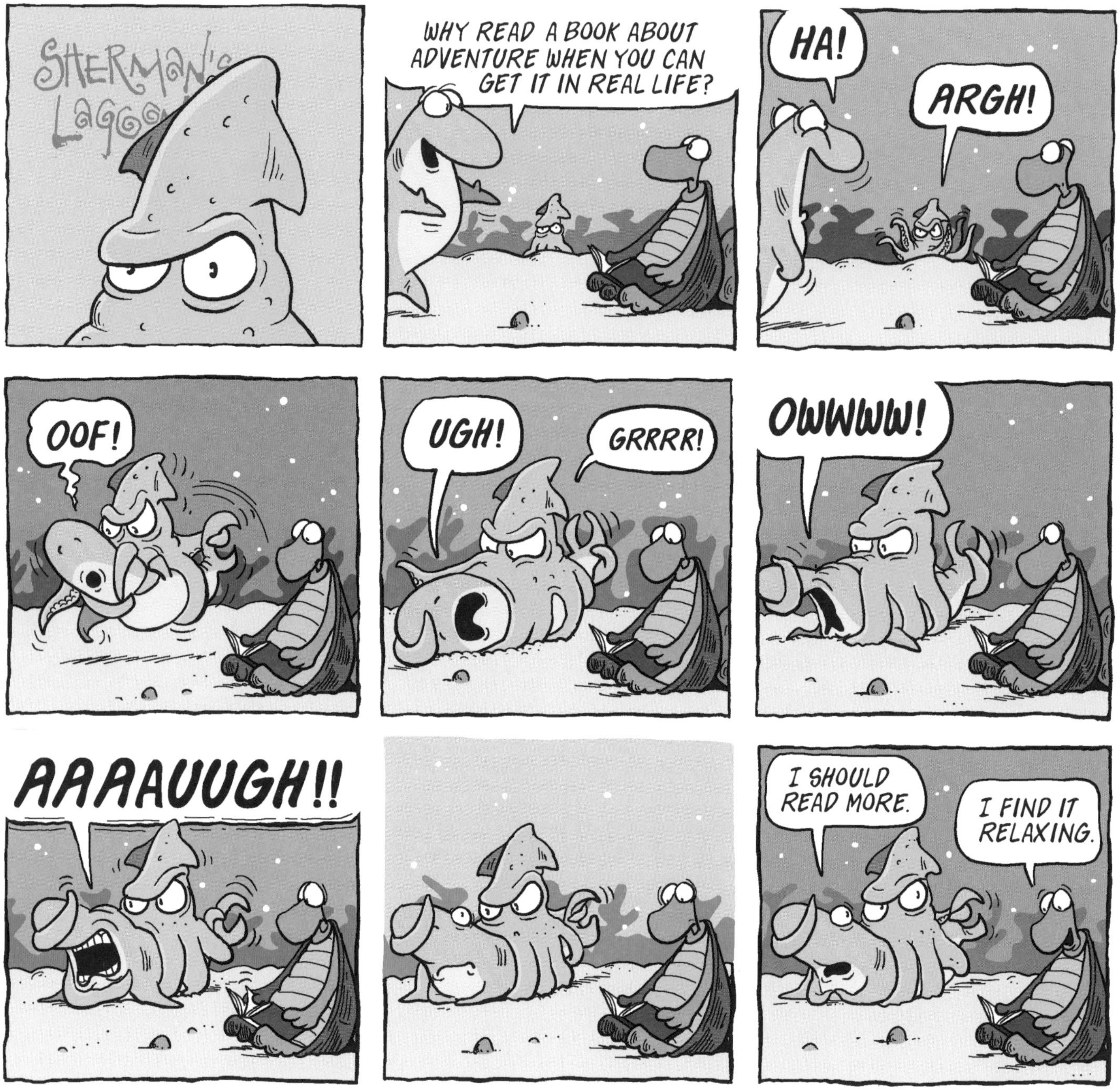
SHERMAN'S LAGOON
WHY READ A BOOK ABOUT ADVENTURE WHEN YOU CAN GET IT IN REAL LIFE?
HA!
ARGH!
OOF!
UGH!
GRRRR!
OWWWW!
AAAAUUGH!!
I SHOULD READ MORE.
I FIND IT RELAXING.